THE ECONOMICS OF 1992

THE ECONOMICS OF 1992

The E. C. Commission's Assessment of the Economic Effects of Completing the Internal Market

MICHAEL EMERSON
MICHEL AUJEAN
MICHEL CATINAT
PHILIPPE GOYBET
ALEXIS JACQUEMIN

OXFORD UNIVERSITY PRESS

Oxford University Press, Walton Street, Oxford OX2 6DP

Oxford New York Toronto
Delhi Bombay Calcutta Madras Karachi
Petaling Jaya Singapore Hong Kong Tokyo
Nairobi Dar es Salaam Cape Town
Melbourne Auckland

and associated companies in
Berlin Ibadan

Oxford is a trade mark of Oxford University Press

Published in the United States
by Oxford University Press, New York

First published 1988 in hardback and paperback
Paperback reprinted 1989

British Library Cataloguing in Publication Data
Emerson, Michael
The economics of 1992: the E.C.
Commission's assessment of the economic
effects of completing the internal market.
1. European Community countries.
Economic integration
I. Title
337.1'42
ISBN 0–19–828681–3
ISBN 0–19–877294–7 (Pbk.)

Library of Congress Cataloging-in-Publication Data
The Economics of 1992: the E.C. Commissions assessment of the
economic effects of completing the internal market / Michael Emerson
. . . [et al.]. p. cm. Bibliography: p. Includes index.
1. Europe—Economic integration. 2. European Economic Community.
I. Emerson, Michael. II. Commission of the European Communities.
HC241.E26 1988 337.1'42—dc 19 88-25032 CIP
ISBN 0–19–828681–3
ISBN 0–19–877294–7 (Pbk.)

Printed and bound
in Great Britain by Biddles Ltd
Guildford and King's Lynn

Steering Committee of the 'Costs of non-Europe' project

Chairman: Paolo Cecchini

External members:

Sergio Alessandrini
Jean-Michel Charpin
Wolfgang Gerstenberger
Jacques Pelkmans
Manfred Wegner

Paul Champsaur
Michel Deleau
Peter Holmes
Carlo Secchi

Commission of the European Communities:

Directorate-General for Economic and Financial Affairs

Michael Emerson
Michel Catinat
Alexis Jacquemin[1]

Michel Aujean
Philippe Goybet

Directorate-General for the Internal Market and Industrial Affairs

Michael Loy (coordinator)
Michel Ayral

Jean-François Marchipont

Also contributing to the present study from the Directorate-General for Economic and Financial Affairs were:

Pierre Buigues, Brendan Cardiff, Richard Cawley, Christian Dewaleyne, Michael Green, Fabienne Ilzkovitz, Alexander Italianer, Morten Jung-Olsen, Marianne Klingbeil, Gernot Nerb, Silvano Presa, Angelo Reati, Pedro Santos, Frank Schönborn and Marc Vanheukelen; Dirk Bol, Jim McKenna, Francine Preud'homme, Roland Van Thuyne and Christopher Smyth; Alison Molders, Cecilia Mulligan, Chantal Mathieu, Thérèse Delplace, Maria Peart, Gertrude Chakroun, Arlette Langlet and Brigitte Jung.

In addition to the consultants indicated in the list of studies, our appreciation is due to Michael Davenport, who was responsible for the microeconomic modelling methodology, and to Paul Geroski, Cliff Pratten, Pippo Ranci, Joachim Schwalbach, Alasdair Smith and Tony Venables for special studies; to John Whalley and Alan Winters for comments and advice; to Eric Donni and Pierre Valette and national teams responsible for econometric simulations conducted on the Hermes model, and to the OECD for permitting Alexander Italianer to undertake simulations, on the responsibility of the Commission, on the Interlink model; and to many colleagues in other services of the Commission who have collaborated on this project.

[1] Until September 1987, external member of the Steering Committee.

v

Foreword

This study contributes to a project initiated by the Commission, whose objective was to evaluate the potential economic impact of completing the internal market by 1992. The overall results of the project are made available in two complementary reports: a book addressed to a general readership (separate form the present one), issued under the responsibility of Paolo Cecchini, who directed the project as a whole, and the present study, issued under the responsibility of the Directorate-General for Economic and Financial Affairs, which contains a more detailed economic analysis.

The objective of the present study has been to assemble a comprehensive view of the possible impact of completing the internal market. This has meant necessarily a book of substantial length, because the subject-matter is one that is built upon the specific situation of many branches of the economy. Indeed, almost all sectors producing goods and services will be affected by one or other of the several hundred items of legislation set out in the Commission's White Paper of 1985.

As regards the methods of economic analysis and sources of empirical information, it has been necessary to approach the question from several different angles: for example by examining the situation of both producers and consumers, by using information derived from business surveys as well as quantitative methods of economic analysis, and finally in fitting the aggregation of much microeconomic information into a coherent picture at the macro-economic level. The latter point — the reconciliation of microeconomic and macroeconomic analyses — is perhaps the most original feature of the study.

Notwithstanding the precautions taken in drafting the report and, wherever possible, in cross-checking all estimates with different independent sources of information, two limits to the conclusions need to be underlined. First, the overall quantitative estimates should be considered potential and conditional, not inevitable, consequences of the internal market programme. Indeed, this report emphasizes the supporting role of macroeconomic policy in translating potential economic gains into a tangible improvement in Europe's growth. Second, the figures should be viewed as being only very approximative and illustrative. The essential question is whether the completion of the internal market should be viewed as a matter of marginal or substantial importance to the European economy. The study clearly concludes that it is of potentially substantial importance.

Finally, I should like to express my appreciation of the remarkable work of Michael Emerson and his team of economists in our Directorate for the Economic Evaluation of Community Policies.

Antonio Maria Costa
Director-General for Economic and Financial Affairs

Contents

ix

Contents

List of tables

List of Annex tables

List of figures

List of Annex figures

PART A

Summary and conclusions

1. *Purpose*. The objective of the present study is to contribute a deeper under-standing of the channels through which the removal of the Community's internal market barriers may result in economic gains. An attempt is made also to quantify the potential size of these gains. While quantification of such a complex process is indeed hazardous, the essential point is to ascertain not the exact but the broad orders of magnitude. The political effort required to complete the internal market will be very considerable. Will it be worth the trouble? The findings of this study are affirmative. A significant improvement in the Community's macroeconomic performance could indeed be made possible as a result of the numerous microeconomic measures proposed in the internal market programme. But a certain number of supporting conditions, beyond simply legislating the 300 items in the White Paper, are also required to secure the potential economic gains.

2. *The nature of the Community's internal market barriers*. Tariffs and quantitat-ive restrictions on trade have been largely eliminated in the Community. The remaining barriers essentially consist of:
(i)   differences in technical regulations between countries, which impose extra costs on intra-EC trade;
(ii) delays at frontiers for customs purposes, and related administrative bur-dens for companies and public administrations, which impose further costs on trade;
(iii) restrictions on competition for public purchases through excluding bids from other Community suppliers, which often result in excessively high costs of purchase;
(iv) restrictions on freedom to engage in certain service transactions, or to become established in certain service activities in other Community countries. This concerns particularly financial and transport services, where the costs of market-entry barriers also appear to be substantial.
   While quite a number of these individual barriers can be overcome at a moderate cost, when taken together with the oligopolistic structure of many markets, they add up to a considerable degree of non-competitive segmentation of the market. This is suggested by the substantial consumer price differences between countries. This discrepancy between the gains from eliminating the direct costs of barriers and those from achieving a full, competitive integration of the market is of capital importance for the conclusions of this study. It has clear implications for how competition policy is to be conducted, alongside the

1

removal of the technical, physical and fiscal frontiers proposed in the White Paper.

3. *The nature of the economic gains to be measured.* Since the economic concepts involved in this study are several and complex, it is important to be clear about the essentials at the outset.

The creation of a true European internal market will, on the one hand, suppress a series of constraints that today prevent enterprises from being as efficient as they could be and from employing their resources to the full, and, on the other hand, establish a more competitive environment which will incite them to exploit new opportunities. The removal of the constraints and the emergence of the new competitive incentives will lead to four principal types of effect:

(i) a significant reduction in costs due to a better exploitation of several kinds of economies of scale associated with the size of production units and enterprises;

(ii) an improved efficiency in enterprises, a rationalization of industrial structures and a setting of prices closer to costs of production, all resulting from more competitive markets;

(iii) adjustments between industries on the basis of a fuller play of comparative advantages in an integrated market;

(iv) a flow of innovations, new processes and new products, stimulated by the dynamics of the internal market.

These processes liberate resources for alternative productive uses, and when they are so used the total, sustainable level of consumption and investment in the economy will be increased. This is the fundamental criterion of economic gain.

These gains in economic welfare will also be reflected in macroeconomic indicators. It is implicit, in order to attain the highest sustainable level of consumption and investment, that productivity and employment be also of a high order. In particular, where rationalization efforts cause labour to be made redundant, this resource has to be successfully re-employed. Also implicit is a high rate of growth in the economy. The sustainability condition, moreover, requires that the major macroeconomic equilibrium constraints are respected, notably as regards price stability, balance of payments and budget balances. It further implies a positive performance in terms of world-wide competitivity. These different objectives can, however, be achieved in different mixes; it is for macroeconomic policy to determine how to dispose of the potential economic gains made available by the microeconomic measures taken in order to complete the internal market.

Costs and prices are the key elements in the attempt to quantify the economic gains mentioned. The percentage reduction in costs or prices resulting from the removal of the market barriers, or change in competitive conditions, is the essential starting point in the quantification process. A first approximation of the economic gain, in money terms, may be arrived at by multiplying these percentage costs or price changes against the initial value of the goods or services in question. While this measure has the great merit of simplicity, it ignores some important secondary effects. The most important of these are seen in continuing and cumulative impacts on the economy that may follow from a change in the competitive environment. These and other effects, including those which distinguish the position of consumers and producers, are built into the quantification methods used in this study.

4. *Empirical estimates*. Any estimates of the effects of a complex action like completing the internal market can only be regarded as very approximate. Apart from being subject to a number of policy conditions, such estimates are extremely difficult to make, especially as regards some of the more speculative and long-term effects. With these strong reservations to be kept in mind, some rough orders of magnitude may be suggested. For perspective, the Community's total gross domestic product in 1985 (the base year for most estimates in this study) was 3 300 billion ECU for the 12 Member States (or 2 900 billion ECU for the seven countries essentially covered by the empirical estimates that follow).

(i) The direct costs of frontier formalities, and associated administrative costs for the private and public sector, may be of the order of 1,8 % of the value of goods traded within the Community or around 9 billion ECU.

(ii) The total costs for industry of identifiable barriers in the internal market, including not only frontier formalities as above but also technical regulations and other barriers, have been estimated, in opinion surveys of industrialists, to average a little under 2 % of those companies' total costs. This represents about 40 billion ECU, or $3\frac{1}{2}$ % of industrial value-added.

(iii) Several industry studies corroborate these findings, with cost reductions of the order of 1 to 2 % estimated to result for the food and beverage industry, construction materials, pharmaceuticals, and textiles and clothing, and 5 % for automobiles. It is to be stressed that these relatively moderate figures typically reflect the cost of identifiable market barriers, and not the total gains that could be expected from a full, competitive integration of these product markets (see further below).

(iv) In particular, industries and service sector branches subject to market entry restrictions could experience considerably bigger potential cost and price reductions. Examples include branches of industry for which government procurement is important (energy generating, transport, office and defence equipment), financial services (banking, insurance and securities) and road and air transport. In these cases cost and price reductions often of the order of 10 to 20 %, and even more in some cases, could be expected. For public procurement alone the gains could amount to around 20 billion ECU. For financial services also a range around 20 billion ECU in potential savings has been proposed, although the margin of uncertainty here is particularly large.

(v) The relatively large percentage reductions for some categories of public procurement reflect the fact that these estimates include the broader effects of open competition in these sectors, including the realization of previously unexploited economies of scale (which are not reflected in the figures reported in paragraphs (i) to (iii)). A study of potential economies of scale in European industry shows that, in more than half of all branches of industry, 20 firms of efficient size can co-exist in the Community market whereas the largest national markets could only have four each. It is evident, therefore, that only the European internal market could combine the advantages of technical and economic efficiency, 20 firms being more likely to assure effective competition than 4 firms. Comparing the present industrial structure with a more rationalized but still less than optimal one, it is estimated that about one third of European industry could profit from varying cost reductions of between 1 to 7 %, yielding an aggregate cost-saving of the order of 60 billion ECU.

(vi) It becomes progressively more hazardous to suggest magnitudes for other types of gain resulting from enhanced competition, including the reduction of what has been termed 'X-inefficiency'. This covers a poor internal allocation of resources — human, physical and financial. Conditions of weak competition cause 'X-inefficiency', and also permit excess profit margins (monopoly profits, or economic rent). There are, in this area, some sources of information ranging from industry case-studies to theoretical models of corporate behaviour in different market environments. The costs of 'X-inefficiency' may often be as great as those resulting from unexploited economies of scale. The total effect of moving to a competitive, integrated market, with fuller achievement of potential economies of scale and reduction of 'X-inefficiency', may be twice to three times the direct cost of identified barriers in an environment where competition is less effective.

(vii) The totality of the foregoing effects could be reflected, in the new equilibrium situation in the economy after several years, in a downward convergence of presently disparate price levels. Detailed information exists on these price differences at the consumer level, with and without indirect taxes. This permits a number of purely illustrative hypotheses to be examined, as regards the magnitude of savings that would be obtained in the event of different degrees of downward price convergence depending upon the extent of existing internal market barriers and the degree of natural protection represented by transport costs and differences in tastes. Under one set of hypotheses, implying strong market integration but far from complete price convergence and with incomplete sectoral coverage, the gains amounted to about 140 billion ECU.

(viii) Overall these estimates offer a range, starting with around 70 billion ECU (2½ % of GDP) for a rather narrow conception of the benefits of removing the remaining internal market barriers, to around 125 to 190 billion ECU ($4\frac{1}{4}$ to $6\frac{1}{2}$ % of GDP) in the hypothesis of a much more competitive, integrated market. (As already indicated, the above amounts in ECU are scaled in relation to the 1985 GDP of seven Member States, acounting for 88 % of the EUR 12 total. The same percentages of GDP, for the 1988 GDP of EUR 12, give a range of around 175 to 255 billion ECU). Overall, it would seem possible to enhance the Community's annual potential growth rate, for both output and consumption, by around 1 percentage point for the period up to 1992. In addition, there would be good prospects that longer-run dynamic effects could sustain a buoyant growth rate further into the 1990s.

(ix) The common assumptions underlying the foregoing estimates (notably the cumulative totals) are that (a) it might take five or possibly more years for the larger part of the effects to be reached, and (b) in any event it is assumed that micro and macroeconomic policies would ensure that the resources released as costs are reduced, are effectively re-employed productively. This concerns labour in particular. These were simplifying assumptions since it is not possible to project the evolution of complex economic structures in many dimensions at the same time (for example, by industry branch, over time, and for many economic variables). In order to make good some of these limitations, a number of macroeconomic simulation exercises have been conducted, injecting some of the foregoing estimates into macro-dynamic models. For this purpose, the effects of the internal market programme have been grouped under four major headings, each having a different type of macroeconomic impact: (a) the removal of customs delays and costs, (b) the opening of public markets to competition, (c) the liberalization and integration of financial markets, and (d) more general supply-side effects, reflecting changes in the strategic behaviour of enterprises in a new competitive environment. The simulated macroeconomic results are presented, first, under the assumption of a passive macroeconomic policy, and, secondly, under the assumption that improved room for manoeuvre is actively exploited.

(x) *With a passive macroeconomic policy.* The overall impact of the measures is manifest most strongly in the initial years in the downward pressure on prices and costs, but this is followed with only a modest time-lag by increases in output. The major impacts, however, appear in the medium-run, after about five to six years, by which time a cumulative impact of $+4\frac{1}{2}$ % in terms of GDP and -6 % in terms of the price level might be expected from a full implementation of the internal market programme. These macroeconomic simulations thus tend to converge with the results of the aggregated microeconomic calculations. The total impact on employment is initially slightly negative, but in the medium-term it increases by about 2 million jobs (nearly 2 % of the initial employment level). The budget balance is improved markedly, and the current account of the balance of payments is improved significantly. Each of the simulated measures or changes in economic behaviour contributes to the positive results, cutting costs and prices, stimulating gains in productivity and investment, increasing real incomes and expenditure.

(xi) *With a more active macroeconomic policy*. Since all the main indicators of monetary and financial equilibrium would be thus improved, it would be legitimate to consider adjusting medium-term macroeconomic strategy onto a somewhat more expansionary trajectory. The extent of this adjustment would depend upon which constraint (inflation, budget or balance of payments deficits) was considered binding. A number of variants are illustrated in the text. In the middle of the range, for example, lies a case in which the GDP level after a medium-term period might be $2\frac{1}{2}$ % higher, in addition to the $4\frac{1}{2}$ % gain suggested under the passive macroeconomic policy, thus totalling 7 %. In this case, inflation would still have been held well below the course initially projected in the absence of the internal market programme, the budget balance would also be improved, while the balance of payments might be worsened by a moderate but sustainable amount.

(xii) *The microeconomic and macroeconomic synthesis*. The foregoing paragraphs have set out quantitative estimates on matters that are extremely difficult to evaluate at all precisely. There should be no misunderstanding about the nature of such figures. They are the product of many sources of very approximate information, combined with economic assumptions and judgments that are defendable but also only approximate. The important conclusions are basically the following. The estimates have been assembled in an eclectic manner, using various techniques of microeconomic and macroeconomic analysis. These different approaches suggest consistent results. The potential gains from a full, competitive integration of the internal market are not trivial in macroeconomic terms. They could be about large enough to make the difference between a disappointing and very satisfactory economic performance for the Community economy as a whole.

(xiii) Notwithstanding these qualifications, the largest benefits suggested above are unlikely to be overestimates of the potential benefit of fully integrating the Community's market. This is because the figures exclude some important categories of dynamic impact on economic performance. Three examples may be mentioned. Firstly, there is increasing evidence that the trend rate of technological innovation in the economy depends upon the presence of competition; only an integrated market can offer the benefits both of scale of operation and competition. Secondly, there is evidence in fast-growing high technology industries of dynamic or learning economies of scale, whereby costs decline as the total accumulated production of certain goods and services increase; market segmentation gravely limits the scope for these benefits and damages performance in key high-growth industries of the future. Thirdly, the business strategies of European enterprises are likely to be greatly affected in the event of a rapid and extensive implementation of the internal market programme; a full integration of the internal market will foster the emergence of truly European companies, with structures and strategies that are better suited to securing a strong place in world market competition.

5. *From the removal of technical barriers to full market integration.* The range of quantitative estimates just presented draws attention to the major difference between:
(a) a narrow, technical, and short-term view of the costs of 'tangibly' identifiable frontier barriers, such as customs delays and various regulations; and
(b) a broader, strategic and long-term view of the benefits from having a fully integrated, competitive and rationalized internal market.
Since the magnitudes involved under the second concept are at least twice as big as under the first one, it is important to be clear about the conditions required to achieve the larger results.
(i) The most fundamental condition is the credibility of the operation: that within a medium-term period the European market environment is to be transformed in a way that will oblige all enterprises producing or marketing tradeable goods and services to adopt European business strategies. Businesses have in effect to make up their minds over two questions: (a) whether the market is going to be much more competitive or not, and (b) in the affirmative case, whether this will be combined with a more dynamic macroeconomic environment. This implies, in turn, being clear about the microeconomic and macroeconomic policies associated with the internal market policy.
(ii) As regards microeconomic policies, the first condition for the credibility of the programme is that economic agents should easily be able to engage in arbitrage between national markets to profit from price differences, and so impose more nearly common and competitive price levels. This means that the frontiers must be truly open: drive-through at the geographic frontiers, open also for individuals to engage in cross-frontier shopping to add to competition for producers and distributors, and free of administrative complications within Member States. Thus all the essential barriers have to be removed, otherwise the last remaining barriers may on their own be sufficient to restrain competition.
The second condition, which concerns competition policy as regards public subsidies, is that enterprises contemplating European market strategies must be assured that if they advance in their penetration of other countries' markets, they will not find themselves confronted by defensive subsidies in those countries. For the medium-term planning of enterprises, what is most important is the degree of certainty surrounding their planning assumptions. Thus the barrier of uncertainty must be removed. Does the enterprise have to compete just with known commercial rivals, or will it have also to compete with governments standing behind these rivals? Only the public authorities can assure this condition. In the first place the

Commission itself already has powers to restrain State subsidies, indeed forbid them where appropriate. But this needs to be reinforced by the demonstrable willingness of Member States to accept these 'rules of the game', rather than conduct long political and procedural struggles over illegal subsidy regimes.

The third condition concerns competition policy addressed to private enterprises. Here it is necessary for the business world to understand clearly that commercial practices which tend to segment markets, or lead to the abuse of dominant positions, will be vigourously countered. At the present time, price discrimination between national markets is widespread and substantial, to the considerable cost of consumers. Competition policy must, for the market to be fully integrated, make it clearly understood, for example, that parallel imports are to be welcomed wherever undue price differences are seen to exist.

(iii) As regards macroeconomic policies, the issue is essentially whether demand policy will accommodate the increased potential for non-inflationary growth, and indeed be perceived as determined to do so over a medium-term period. This point has been illustrated by the simulations reported above. It is sure that implementation of the internal market programme will put downward pressure on costs and prices, and create the potential for greater non-inflationary growth. It is not sure, however, how far this potential will materialize. From the standpoint of macroeconomic analysis there are a range of possibilities: the benefits from the more competitive market pressures may be taken mainly in the form of less price inflation, or mainly in the form of more output with unchanged inflation (i.e. activity is expanded to the point that the initial disinflationary impulse is completely offset by higher demand pressure), or by a more even mix of disinflation and output gains.

Business opinion was relatively optimistic that increased sales and output would result, when surveyed for the present study, in the late summer of 1987. On average, industrialists expect the internal market programme to lead to a lifting of total sales by about 5 % over a period of years. This is entirely consistent with the other calculations reported above on the potential gains from market integration. It is necessary, however, that the credibility of these favourable expectations be supported by a well coordinated, growth-oriented macroeconomic policy. If this is not done, the market liberalization process risks generating defensive and negative reactions, in which case the viability of the programme could be threatened.

While the approach adopted in this study is a structural one, and therefore does not discuss current issues of the world and European business cycle, the implementation of the internal market programme cannot, to be successful in practice, ignore current macroeconomic realities. Early 1988 sees a weakening of the world and European business cycle, and a much higher level of European exchange rates against the US dollar and other currencies linked to it. Some international competitors are going to be well placed to make strategic gains in their share of a weakening European market. These trends hold out obvious dangers. While Europe must, of course, make its contribution to the rebalancing of the world economy, it must also take steps to safeguard the successful implementation of the internal market programme. These safeguards can be summarized under two headings: (a) support for the European business cycle, sufficient to counter its weakening in the short run, and favour the acceleration of growth thereafter, (b) endeavours to assure that international exchange rate adjustments are adequate but not excessive.

6. *Adjustment costs and the distribution of gains*. Accelerated market integration certainly means that more people will have to change their jobs more frequently. However, the counterpart to this should be rising employment and rising real incomes in the aggregate, as the foregoing estimates and simulations have suggested. Experience suggests that the costs of market adjustments become very serious above all where necessary sectoral adjustments are delayed (see agriculture and steel).

Difficult as it is to estimate the aggregate gains from market integration, this task is relatively manageable compared to that of forecasting its distribution by country or region. While the latter task has not been attempted, it is worth noting that neither economic theory nor relevant economic history can point to any clear-cut pattern of likely distributional advantage or disadvantage. Theories of vicious circles of divergence of regional fortunes resulting from market integration exist, but so do alternative theses that point to more balanced or indeterminate outcomes; the latter theses including important recent developments in the analysis of trade between industrialized countries. Smaller countries, in particular those having recently joined the Community with relatively protected economic structures, have proportionately the biggest opportunities for gain from market integration. In any case, policy instruments exist to provide an insurance policy to help initial losers recover (e.g. the Community's structural Funds, whose substantial expansion has recently been agreed).

7. *Final remarks*. The study supports the following essential conclusions:
(i) In the present condition of the European economy the segmentation and weak competitiveness of many markets means that there is large potential for the rationalization of production and distribution structures, leading to improvements in productivity, and reductions in many costs and prices.
(ii) The completion of the internal market could, if strongly reinforced by the competition policies of both the Community and Member States, have a deep and extensive impact on economic structures and performance. The size of this impact, in terms of the potential for increased non-inflationary growth, could be sufficient to transform the Community's macroeconomic performance from a mediocre to a very satisfactory one.

(iii) In order to achieve a prize of this magnitude, all the main features of the internal market programme would need to be implemented with sufficient speed and conviction, such that the credibility of the total operation is not just safeguarded, but reinforced. Implementation of half of the actions proposed in the White Paper will deliver much less than half of the total potential benefits.

(iv) In fact, more than full implementation of the White Paper is required in order to achieve the full potential benefits of an integrated European market. There must be a strong competition policy, which was discussed only in very summary terms in the White Paper. Macroeconomic policy has to be set on a coherent, growth-oriented strategy. The White Paper represents a policy aimed at making the supply potential of the Community economy more flexible and competitive. The counterpart in terms of the demand side needs to be clearly agreed among policy-makers and credibly communicated to business and public opinion. In normal cyclical conditions it would be appropriate, as soon as sufficient market actions are beginning to be implemented, for macroeconomic policy to ratify these measures by ensuring that the economy climbs onto the higher growth trajectory. But in the actual business climate of early 1988, such steps should not be delayed.

PART B

The European market, its barriers and methods of evaluation

1. Dimensions and structure of the internal market

1.1. Size and performance

In terms of population, the European Community, with 323 million inhabitants in 1987, constitutes the largest market in the industrialized world (244 million in the United States and 122 million in Japan). But it remains a fragmented market. Calculated in ECU, the GDP of the Community of Twelve was 3 669 billion ECU in 1987, compared with 3 869 billion ECU for the United States and 2 058 billion ECU for Japan (see Table 1.1.1). Yet this aggregation of GDP is really meaningful only if the internal market is completed and all non-tariff barriers have been removed. Taken separately, each of the Member States carries relatively little weight compared with the two major trading blocs.

A closer examination of the economic structures and relative sizes of the three main industrial areas (see Table 1.1.1) shows that, for a certain number of activities, the Community's value-added is larger than that of the United States: financial services in the tertiary sector and food products, beverages, tobacco, textiles, leather, clothing, metalliferous ores and steel products in the industrial sector. These latter examples are industrial activities for which there is weak growth in demand (see Table 1.1.2) and which are, in some cases, sensitive to business recessions. The European chemical, transport equipment and industrial machinery industries also bear comparison with their counterparts in the United States and Japan.

By contrast, the Community lags well behind the United States and is at a comparable level to Japan in respect of other industrial activities. This is particularly true for the data-processing, office-automation and precision instruments industries but also for electrical goods (electrical appliances, heavy equipment) and electronics (industrial and consumer electronics, telecommunications equipment). In these industries, demand growth is very strong (see Table 1.1.2) in the industrialized countries (over 5 % per year in volume terms since the first oil shock) and the technological content high: these are leading sectors in terms of R&D (OECD, 1984). The fragmentation of Community industry constitutes a serious handicap on these industrial markets. In these high-tech sectors, the critical mass for R&D is considerable and requires the active cooperation if not the integration of European firms if the Community is to match the level and effectiveness of expenditure in this area by American

Table 1.1.1.

1985: Value-added in the EC, the United States and Japan by sector (1985, current prices)

Branch	EUR %	EUR 12 billion ECU	Japan billion ECU	USA billion ECU
1. *Agricultural, forestry and fishery products*	*2,9*	*92*	*55*	*134*
2. *Fuel and power products*	*6,8*	*215*	*70*	*281*
3. *Manufactured products*	*26,1*	*825*	*505*	*1 024*
5. Ores and metals	1,1	35	24	30
6. Non-metallic minerals and mineral products	1,3	41	24	40
7. Chemical products	2,4	76	44	103
8. Metal products (except machinery and transport equipment)	2,3	73	68	84
9. Agricultural and industrial machinery	2,5	79	40	88
10. Office and data-processing machines, precision and optical instruments	0,8	25	20	80
11. Electrical goods	2,6	82	79	92
12. Transport equipment	2,9	92	49	145
13. Food, beverages, tobacco	4,1	129	56	108
14. Textiles and clothing, leather and footwear	2,1	66	40	53
15. Paper and printing products	1,8	57	14	113
16. Rubber and plastic goods	1,0	32	21	38
17. Other manufactured products	1,2	38	26	51
19. *Building and construction*	*5,7*	*180*	*128*	*245*
20. *Market services*	*44,0*	*1 391*	*880*	*2 694*
22. Wholesale and retail trade services, repair services	11,8	373	252	780
23. Lodging and catering services	2,0	63	99	163
24. Inland transport services	2,3	73	31	124
25. Maritime and air transport services	0,5	16	29	41
26. Auxiliary transport services	1,1	35	27	38
27. Communication services	2,0	63	22	142
28. Services of credit and insurance institutions	8,0	253	69	163
29. Other market services	16,3	515	351	1 244
33. *Non-market services*	*14,5*	*459*	*180*	*869*
37. *Total value-added*	*100,0*	*3 162*	*1 817*	*5 246*
Gross domestic product 1985				
(in billion ECU — current exchange rates)		3 314	1 754	5 172
(in billion ECU — EUR 12 = 100)		100	53	156
(in purchasing power standards — EUR 12 = 100)		100	42	117
Gross domestic product 1987				
(in billion ECU — current exchange rates)		3 669	2 058	3 869
(in purchasing power standards — EUR 12 = 100)		100	43	118

Source: Commission services (sectoral data bank-VISA).

Table 1.1.2.

Evolution of volume of domestic demand by industrial branch in the EC, the United States and Japan (1973-85, average annual rate of growth)

%

	EUR	USA	Japan
Strong demand sectors	*5,0*	*5,2*	*14,3*
Office and data-processing machines	9,0	6,5	7,2
Electrical and electronic goods	3,5	7,2	20,7
Chemical and pharmaceutical products	5,3	2,3	9,9
Moderate demand sectors	*1,2*	*2,8*	*3,1*
Rubber and plastic products	2,8	5,4	2,0
Transport equipment	1,7	2,7	5,2
Food, beverages, tobacco	1,2	0,4	0,0
Paper and printing products	1,6	2,9	2,7
Industrial and agricultural machinery	− 0,1	5,6	5,6
Weak demand sectors	*− 0,3*	*0,5*	*2,4*
Metal products	− 0,5	− 0,4	3,4
Miscellaneous manufactured products	− 0,6	2,1	1,9
Ferrous and non-ferrous ores and metals	0,6	− 1,8	2,0
Textiles, leather, clothing	− 0,2	2,0	2,2
Non-metallic minerals (construction materials)	0,1	1,7	1,1

NB: The sectors are divided into those in which demand in OECD countries between 1979 and 1985 increased by more than 5% (strong demand), by around 3% (moderate demand), and by less than 2% (weak demand).

Source: Volimex, Commission services.

and Japanese multinational companies. Furthermore, economies of scale play a vital role in these industries and call for production units which can without difficulty serve a unified market which is perfectly integrated as regards standards and marketing requirements.

These findings broadly coincide with the conclusions of other studies carried out for the European Commission (Buigues, Goybet, 1985; EC Commission, 1986). The Community's industrial base devoted to the production of goods with a high technological content remains relatively narrow. The sectors in which demand is growing strongly account for 22,4 % of the value-added of the whole of Community industry, as compared with nearly 27 % in the United States and more than 28 % in Japan. Between 1979 and 1985, the proportion of industry accounted for by sectors in which world demand is growing sharply increased by 3 % a year in the Community, compared with 3,7 % in the United States and 17,1 % in Japan.

The Community's relative weakness in these dynamic sectors is also partly reflected in the fact that Community industrial output is lagging behind that

13

of the United States and Japan, although there are additional factors which play an important role in explaining this less rapid growth (wage costs, productivity). In 1986, the index of European industrial output stood at 105, as against 115 for the United States and 121 for Japan (1980 = 100). The discrepancy in growth between the Community, the United States and Japan is therefore substantial. Although the Community average conceals fairly marked national differences, none of the six most industrialized countries in the Community (B, D, F, I, NL and UK) shows a rate of growth comparable to that of the United States over the period 1980-86.

This performance is very much in line with labour productivity in industry. A country-by-country comparison of industrial productivity based on value-added per person employed converted into a common currency applying a nominal exchange rate poses very serious problems because of the variability of those rates. Thanks to the work carried out by Roy (1982), Guinchard (1984) and, more recently, Mathis and Mazier (1987) based on the use of purchasing power parities, a consistent method of comparing productivity levels between different economic areas is now available (see Table 1.1.3). In 1950, the productivity of European industry was two and a half times lower than that of the

Table 1.1.3.

Level of productivity in the United Kingdom, France, Germany, the United States and Japan (value-added per employee in specific purchasing power parities) — 1985 (USA = 100)

	UK	F	D	USA	Japan
Strong demand sectors					
Electrical and electronic goods	28	47	43	100	236
Office and data-processing machines	37	43	45	100	94
Chemical and pharmaceutical products	54	79	75	100	119
Moderate demand sectors					
Transport equipment	23	54	60	100	95
Food, beverages, tobacco	56	73	47	100	37
Paper and printing products	43	67	76	100	89
Industrial and agricultural machinery	20	49	46	100	103
Weak demand sectors					
Metal products	38	60	54	100	143
Ferrous and non-ferrous ores and metals (steel)	66	72	92	100	149
Textiles, leather, clothing	59	62	71	100	53
Non-metallic minerals (construction materials)	40	64	71	100	43
Total	42	65	65	100	100

Sources: CEPII, Commission services.

United States, while that of Japanese industry was six times lower than that of the United States. By 1985, the situation had changed appreciably. The best European performances were about 65 % of the level in the United States, while the average Japanese performance was equal to that of the United States.

The relatively low level of productivity achieved by European countries in the high-tech industries goes a long way towards explaining weak performance in international trade and on their own domestic markets in such products as electrical goods and electronics, office machinery and information technology. These results are consistent with the theory of comparative advantage, which highlights the importance of these productivity differences as an essential basis for trade.

The best productivity performances of the major Community countries are achieved in industries which have a national market large enough to compensate for the effect of non-tariff barriers: food products, beverages, tobacco, textiles, leather, clothing, non-metalliferous ores and building materials.

The Japanese results also suggest that there is no threshold beyond which productivity gains tend to diminish. In many branches, Japanese industry has now exceeded the United States level, even reaching twice that level in the electrical goods and electronics branches; in other branches, however, it still lags well behind. Overall, Japanese industry in 1985 achieved a level of productivity comparable to that of United States industry and enjoys a comparative advantage in certain branches (electrical goods and electronics, chemicals and pharmaceuticals) and in metalworking (steel, metal products, machinery). These branches are generally the main foundations of Japanese competitiveness, since they now enjoy a substantial absolute productivity advantage.

The internal market should have a favourable impact on productivity, particularly in industries with heavy trade flows and strong potential for economies of scale. Through the combined effect of improved intra-Community specialization, economies of scale and greater competitive pressure, the large internal market should lead to greater efficiency and thus to improved productivity in European firms.

1.2. Market shares

Taking manufactured products as a whole, the Community lost 1,4 percentage points of market share on external markets between 1979 and 1985, as against gains of 0,7 of a percentage point for the United States and 5,4 percentage points for Japan. None the less, this contraction in the Community's share occurred at the beginning of the 1980s. Since 1984, there has been a slight improvement (+0,4 of a percentage point between 1984 and 1985), although that did not continue in 1986 since Community exports to non-member countries marked time that year.

The picture becomes clearer on detailed analysis by sector (see Table 1.2.1). On external markets, the Community is rapidly losing ground in the case of

Table 1.2.1.

Gains (+) and losses (−) of market share by the Community in third countries over the period 1979-85[1] (in descending order)

Branch	Loss	Branch	Gain
Electrical goods	−4,39	Leather and footwear	+5,45
Motor vehicles	−4,25	Timber, furniture	+4,86
Rubber and plastic products	−2,53	Textiles and clothing	+3,87
Industrial and agricultural machinery	−2,49	Non-metallic minerals and mineral products	+2,47
Other transport equipment	−2,27	Food, beverages, tobacco	+2,03
Office and data-processing machines, precision and optical instruments	−2,23	Paper and printing products	+1,25
Other manufactured products	−0,84	Ferrous and non-ferrous ores and metals, other than radioactive	+1,23
Metal products, except machinery and transport equipment	−0,65	Chemical products	+0,51

[1] Market share is defined as the exports of the USA, Japan or EUR 10 to the rest of the world compared with exports of OECD countries to the rest of the world.
Source: Volimex, Commission services.

electrical and electronic equipment, cars and other means of transport, office machinery, information technology and industrial machinery (i.e. products for which demand is growing strongly or which are linked to the growth in investment). By contrast, the Community has increased its market shares in such sectors as leather and footwear, timber and furniture, textiles and clothing, i.e. product sectors in which competition from the newly industrializing countries is strongest, except in the case of chemicals and pharmaceuticals, where Community industry maintains a powerful position.

However, in some of these sectors in which the Community is gaining market share, imported and exported products are frequently of a different quality. Many European countries tend in fact to export top-of-the-range articles and to import low or medium-quality articles. In the case of France, a recent article (Debonneuil and Delattre, 1987), clearly illustrates this tendency. In the leather goods sector, for example, the average price of articles exported is almost twice that of articles imported. These price differences depend, however, on trading areas. Thus, while the unit export price for articles of clothing is five times higher than the unit import price in trade between France and the newly industrializing countries, import and export prices are very similar in trade with other European countries: a difference of less than 2 % in trade between France and the Netherlands, Germany or the United Kingdom.

In the case of these top-of-the-range products (in terms of quality, design or fashion), world demand for which is growing, the Community's trading position is sound, although these markets are relatively narrow and sensitive to changes in the purchasing power of well-off households.

Japan and the United States are, for their part, continually pushing further ahead with specialization in the high-tech industries: between 1979 and 1985, Japan increased its market share by 11,7 percentage points for electrical and electronic equipment, by 9,4 percentage points for cars and by 5,5 percentage points in the information technology and office automation fields. The United States is in turn reinforcing its position in respect of office machinery and information technology (a gain of 3,3 percentage points in six years).

Shares of the Community market. Generally speaking, Community manufacturing firms have put up better resistance on the Community market than on external markets. In 1985, the Community countries' share of their own market stood at 69,6 %, i.e. 3 percentage points less than in 1979. On external markets (excluding the European Community), their market share was 39,7 % in 1985, which meant a fall of 6,2 percentage points compared with 1979 (see Table 1.2.1). In the case of electrical and electronic equipment, the Community countries lost more of their share of external markets in the six years between 1979 and 1985 than their share of the Community market. The pattern is the same for cars and for office machinery.

This situation is particularly evident in the case of Germany. In 1979, Germany's aggregate exports to Community countries were equivalent to 21,4 % of the exports of the other OECD countries to that market.

By 1985, that market share had even increased slightly to 21,7 %. By contrast, Germany's exports outside the Community stood, in 1979, at 15,8 % of the total exports of OECD countries to those non-Community markets, compared with 13,7 % in 1985, giving a loss of 2,1 percentage points in six years.

Share of national markets. The share of each Community country's domestic demand met from its own industrial production has steadily declined in favour of intra-Community trade and imports from outside the Community and by roughly equal proportions for the two components. Thus, while the proportion of domestic demand for manufactured products imports met from within the Community increased by 4,8 percentage points in 12 years to reach 17,6 % in 1985, that of imports from outside the Community increased by 4,4 percentage points to 13,1 % in 1985.

However, the overall increase in the penetration rate conceals widely differing situations according to sector (see Table 1.2.2). The Community is showing an increasing propensity to import high-tech products. Imports from outside the Community are growing appreciably more quickly than intra-Community trade in such branches as office machinery and information technology, electrical and electronic equipment, machinery and transport equipment. The pattern is reversed in branches in which there is weak or moderate growth in demand (food processing, paper, metal products) or in the chemical and pharmaceutical sector, where Community competitiveness remains strong.

Table 1.2.2.

Relative evolution of intra- and extra-Community trade (1979-85)

Branches in which intra-Community imports have increased more rapidly than extra-Community imports		Branches in which intra-Community imports have increased less rapidly than extra-Community imports	
Food, beverages, tobacco	+2,6	Office and data-processing machines	−7,0
Chemical and pharmaceutical products	+0,3	Electrical equipment and electronics	−6,0
Paper	+0,3	Industrial machinery	−3,1
Steel	+0,1	Motor vehicles, aerospace and other transport equipment	−2,2
Metal products	0,0	Textiles, leather, clothing	−1,2
		Rubber and plastic products	−0,3

The figures are the difference between the intra-Community penetration rates and the extra-Community penetration rates between 1979 and 1985.
Source: Volimex, Commission services.

FIGURE 1.1: **Shares of world market of EC exports of industrial goods EUR 10 (indices 1963 = 100)**

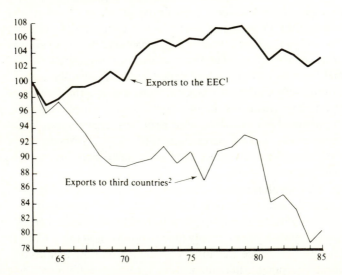

[1] Indices of the market share of intra-EC (EUR 10) exports with respect to exports of OECD countries towards the EC (EUR 10).
[2] Indices of the market share of EC (EUR 10) exports towards third countries with respect to the exports of OECD countries to those same countries.
Source: Commission services, Volimex data bank.

The study made by Jacquemin and Sapir (1987) has identified a set of variables which tend to give a significant boost to intra-Community imports as opposed to imports from the rest of the world. The growth in the share of intra-Community imports in total imports is described to be particularly apparent in such capital and skilled labour-intensive industries as steel, chemicals and paper pulp. Other variables, such as the common agricultural policy, have also promoted intra-Community trade in food products. According to that study, however, preference is given to buying on markets outside the Community in branches with much public purchasing (telecommunications, aerospace, electronics).

Trade in services. External trade has so far been analysed purely in terms of manufactured products. Trade in services is more difficult to study, since statistical information is more limited in that area. In 1984, exports of services by Community countries were equivalent to some 3,9 % of Community GDP,

Table 1.2.3.

The Community's external trade in services — EUR 10 (1984) [1]

	Absolute values of extra-Community exports of services (in billion ECU)	Structure of extra-Community exports of services (as %)	Cover rate EUR 10 extra-Community trade (exports as % of imports)	Share of intra-Community trade in overall trade (1982-84) (as %)
Goods	*356,4*	—	*99,7*	*49,9*
Services	*111,8*	*100*	*108,4*	*37,9*
Transport	37,4	33,4	99,0	36,1
• Sea freight	13,8	12,3	84,8	33,4
• Passenger transport by sea	1,1	1,0	272,1	n.a.
• Air freight	1,8	1,6	183,6	21,3
• Passenger transport by air	7,5	6,7	134,2	21,1
• Other	13,2	11,8	90,9	44,8
Insurance on transport	1,3	1,1	78,6	n.a.
Travel	23,4	20,9	97,1	45,3
Other services	49,8	44,5	125,3	35,2
• Income from property	3,6	3,2	67,7	24,1
• Banking	2,7	2,4	179,6	n.a.
• Non-merchandise insurance	3,1	2,8	128,3	n.a.
• Construction, engineering	11,9	10,6	253,4	n.a.
• Cinema, television	0,6	0,5	99,0	26,0
• Other	27,9	24,9	110,6	41,4

[1] If the results were extended from EUR 10 to EUR 12, there would be marked differences; the item 'travel' would then show a very considerable surplus, and so a cover rate greater than 100.
n.a. = not available.
Source: SOEC.

compared with approximately 11 % for exports of goods (Eurostat, 1984). As the rate of growth of trade in services is comparable to that for goods, the proportion of the Community's overall trade accounted for by services remains stable at around 20 % — a higher level than in the United States or Japan (approximately 17 %).

The Community's balance of trade in services is in substantial surplus for banking transactions, air transport (including freight), civil engineering, maritime transport and tourism. By contrast, the Community has so far had a structural deficit on income from property (see Table 1.2.3). Competitiveness in the service sector plays either a direct role in the case of internationally traded services or an indirect role in the case of services contributing to the competitiveness of manufacturing industry. Such is the case with information services (computer software, project study and development), banking and financial services which are anintegral part of trade in high-tech products (Office ofTechnology Assessment, 1987).

Trade in services is primarily extra-Community trade (62,1 % of total trade in services). More generally, trade in services is between developed countries: the Community's main trading partner remains the United States, which accounts for between 25 and 30 % of the Community's trade in services with the rest of the world. However, international and intra-Community trade in services is subject to many quantitative restrictions. Faced with these non-tariff barriers, many companies providing services have decided to set up subsidiaries abroad. This partly explains the low relative share of intra-Community trade in services.

2. Typology of market barriers and methods of evaluation

2.1. Typology of market barriers

The European Community's objective of completing the internal market by 1992 implies eliminating all barriers to the free flow of goods, services, capital and labour. These barriers are identified in the Commission's 1985 White Paper in terms of three categories:

(i)   physical frontiers, notably stoppages at intra-EC customs posts at geographical frontiers;

(ii) technical frontiers which include restrictions that operate within national territories, for example the need to respect different technical regulations and norms for goods and services, or discrimination against foreign bids for public purchases, or foreign companies' requests to establish subsidiaries;

(iii) fiscal frontiers, notably the need to levy value-added tax or excises on goods imported from other EC countries.

For the purposes of economic analysis, a regrouping in terms of the following five categories is more significant:

(i)   tariffs;

(ii) quantitative restrictions (quotas);

(iii) cost-increasing barriers;

(iv) market-entry restrictions;

(v)   market-distorting subsidies and practices.

The list starts with traditional types of trade barriers such as tariffs and quantitative restrictions, which the Community has in principle eliminated, although not completely so in practice. It goes on to cover those categories of barrier that are the main target of the measures proposed in the White Paper. It concludes with various market-distorting measures which are the subject of competition policy rules.

Tariffs have, in general, long been eliminated in the Community. However, the agricultural monetary compensatory amounts have reintroduced border taxes (and subsidies) for this sector. The new Member States will eliminate their remaining tariffs towards the rest of the Community by 1992.

Quantitative restrictions have also in general been eliminated for intra-Community trade. However, production quotas have been introduced, in principle temporarily, for steel and some agricultural products and their effects have similarities to trade quotas. In some service sectors (road and air transport) licensing and regulatory regimes effectively impose quotas on intra-Community trade. Also some of the Community's external trade policies (concerning textiles and cars notably) involve national quotas, which require intra-Community frontiers for their enforcement.

Cost-increasing barriers are the target of many of the specific measures identified in the White Paper. Delays at customs posts are of this category, be it for value-added tax or excise tax assessment, the collection of statistics, or the verification of technical regulations. In addition, the cost of respecting different technical regulations in production, packaging or marketing have analogous economic effects, as also the overhead costs within the enterprise, of respecting any of the above requirements.

Market-entry restrictions are also the target of many measures specified in the White Paper. These include government procurement restrictions, the right of establishment for various service industries and professions, restrictions in some services sectors that prevent or limit direct trading across frontiers (e.g. insurance, electricity), and restrictions upon entry into some regulated markets (e.g. civil aviation). In some instances the distinction between cost-increasing barriers and market entry restrictions may be not so clear, for example technical regulations that are virtually impossible for foreign suppliers to meet. However, the distinction is none the less fundamental, since the former type of barriers still allows competition to work, whereas the latter type excludes it.

Market-distorting subsidies and practices are already the subject of Community powers of competition policy, both as regards aids by public authorities and collusion and the abusive use of dominant positions by private enterprises. While some new powers in this area are proposed (for example concerning mergers), the White Paper principally argues in favour of the strong, complementary exercise of existing powers. Price controls and specific taxes may also distort some markets in ways relevant to the internal market programme.

2.2. Economic impact of barriers of different types

The economic impact of market barriers may be analysed in terms of the cost of their presence (their 'opportunity cost'), or the benefit of their removal. However, there is no real difference, only a change of sign from minus to plus, between these two expressions. Thus the 'cost of non-Europe', a term often used to denote the costs of internal market barriers, are the same analytically as the benefits of completing the internal market. The box inset defines more precisely the nature of the economic gains to be obtained from removing market barriers and distortions. The different types of barrier tend to have the following types of economic impact:

Tariffs impose a cost on consumers both by increasing the cost of imports and by allowing a degree of inefficiency or extra profits for domestic producers. However, tariff revenue for the budget offsets the consumers' loss in part.

Quantitative restrictions (quotas) by contrast, give rise to no tariff revenue (except when they are auctioned to importers, which does not occur in the Community). The exporter will normally gain instead through higher profits. The application of quantitative restrictions means there is no fixed ceiling on the cost of the protection afforded to domestic producers. Consumers can therefore be particularly adversely affected. Production quotas at the enterprise level have analogous effects, except that they also limit competition within countries and so risk leading to even greater inefficiency.

Cost-increasing barriers are similar to tariffs in that they impose an extra cost on consumers, and allow a corresponding margin of inefficiency and/or extra profits for domestic producers. However, the foreign supplier has, in this case, to bear the extra costs, and there is no tariff revenue offsetting the unfavourable impact on the consumer.

Market-entry restrictions may be similar in effect either to quantitative restrictions or cost-increasing barriers. Where the entry barrier is absolute, the effect is equivalent to a zero quota. In other cases, such as some exchange controls on capital movements and the case of establishment in certain sectors, the restriction may be overcome, but with a certain cost or delay for the entrants.

Market-distorting subsidies may be similar to tariffs as a competitive disadvantage for foreign suppliers, and as a protection of inefficiency for domestic suppliers. However, the consumer pays through taxes, rather than higher prices.

What kinds of economic gains are to be measured?

It is familiar from macroeconomic analysis that several types of objective may be pursued by economic policy, for example increasing real output, or real incomes, and, possibly, reducing the rate of inflation.

The removal of market barriers and distortions is likely to give positive results under each of these three headings. However, to be more precise and rigorous in measuring these effects of microeconomic policy changes, the methods of microeconomic analysis use a particular concept of economic gain, called the 'net welfare gain' (see Dixit and Norman 1980, Corden 1984 and Baldwin 1984 for basic texts). This may approximately be thought of in terms of gains in real incomes, i.e. the net gain of consumers and producers together. More precisely the net welfare gains consist of the sum of:

(i) the consumer's gain resulting from a decline in price, but taking into account not only the lower cost of his initial consumption, but also his expanded consumption possibilities;

(ii) plus or minus the producer's gain or loss as a result of the decline in price. The outcome for the producer is subject to different influences. Monopoly profits, if they exist, may be eliminated. However, the reduction of inefficiency will not affect profit, and a greater volume of normal profits may be earned on a larger volume of sales.

These consumer and producer gains are illustrated in a little more detail in Figures 3.1 and 3.2, and their associated commentaries.

Measures of 'net welfare gain' can be expected to exceed by some margin the simplest, 'common sense' notion of the 'cost' of a barrier that may come to mind. Such a cost measure may be thought of as consisting of a percentage cost or price reduction, multiplied against the initial value of production or consumption. This cost measure is a convenient first approximation of economic gain and is used in several studies summarized in Part B, but it does not allow for various effects that are mentioned in Section 2.3 and analysed in some detail in Part C.

Other market-distorting practices may include discriminatory pricing by enterprises, price controls imposed by governments, and specific taxes that discriminate between different products. In principle all such market distortions will reduce net economic welfare in the aggregate, even where the average price is not affected.

In general terms the benefits from removing these various types of market barriers and distortions arise in two kinds of situation, firstly those resulting from the creation of the traditional 'comparative advantage' type of trade (this is illustrated in Figure 2.1), and, secondly, those following from an increase in competition for products for which the countries in question have no differences in comparative advantage (this is illustrated in Figure 2.2).

2.3. Methods of evaluation

In making an empirical evaluation of these costs and benefits, several methods of analysis are needed. The easiest methods may have the advantage of being more readily understood and more rapidly implemented. However, such methods will be less complete in their coverage of some of the important impacts and this requires that more complex economic methodologies will be used. The approaches used or referred to in this study are, accordingly, several in number as follows:

Business economics. Enterprises were invited to give judgmental opinions in response to questionnaires about the 'costs' of given barriers, and their likely response to their removal. The results of a comprehensive survey of industrialists' opinions are given at various places in this study (Sections 3.1, 8.1, and a separate study by G. Nerb).

Microeconomic studies. Industry case-studies were made of the cost structure of enterprises and of the market barriers that they face, including attempts to estimate the possible impact of restructuring of the industry branch in response to increased competitive pressures. A considerable number of sectoral studies of this type was commissioned by consultants, and the results are reported in Chapters 3 to 5.

Partial equilibrium microeconomics. This approach inserts information obtained from microeconomic studies and other sources into a more complete framework distinguishing the ultimate ('equilibrium') impacts on consumers, producers and government, all of which add up to the impact in terms of net economic welfare (Figures 2.1 and 2.2 illustrate graphically). 'Partial' in the present context means analysing the impact on individual product markets one at a time. In aggregating the results of partial equilibrium findings for the impact on all individual branches of the economy, a first idea can be obtained about the total macroeconomic impact of the policy changes such as implementation of the whole internal market programme. The methodology used for the present study is set out in Annex A, and the main results presented in Section 10.1. This broad approach can also incorporate the results of more specialized

FIGURE 2.1: **Effects of eliminating market barriers and distortions for a given commodity (the case in which comparative advantage can be exploited by trade)**

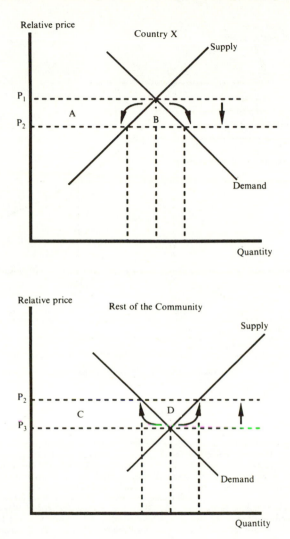

Comments on Figure 2.1

As a result of removing certain market barriers or distortions, the relative price of a given commodity is equalized throughout the economy, at P_2, compared to the higher protected price P_1 in country X, and the lower price P_3 elsewhere, that prevailed earlier. These differences in supply conditions between country X and the rest of the Community reflect the existence of a comparative disadvantage for country X.

In country X, consumers gain to the extent of the areas $A + B$, while producers lose to the extent of area A. In the rest of the Community, producers gain to the extent of areas $C + D$, while consumers lose to the extent of area C. Overall, the Community economy makes an aggregate net welfare gain to the extent of areas $B + D$, and both consumer and producer groups make net gains too in the economy as a whole.

Analogous reasoning can be used to show how net gains are made when price distortions between two products within a single economy (due for example to subsidies for one product, financed by taxes on another) are removed.

FIGURE 2.2: **Effects of eliminating cost-increasing trade barriers (the case of enhanced competition where there are no comparative advantages between countries)**

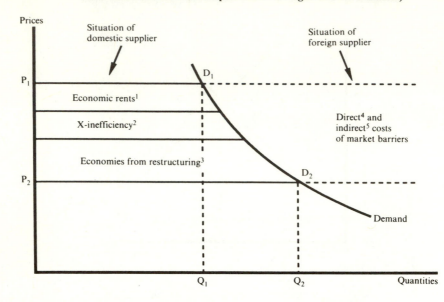

[1] Economic rents consist of the margin of excess profits or wage rates that result from market protection.
[2] X-inefficiency consists of, for example, the costs of overmanning, excess overhead costs and excess inventories (i.e. inefficiencies not related to the production technology of the firm's investments).
[3] Economies from restructuring include, for example, the greater economies of scale or scope obtained when inefficient production capacity is eliminated and new investments made.
[4] Direct costs are those, such as delays at frontiers and the cost of differing technical regulations, that would immediately fall if the market barriers were eliminated.
[5] Indirect costs are those that would fall as foreign suppliers adjust to the more competitive situation with more efficient production and marketing.

Comments on Figure 2.2

As barriers are eliminated, importers are able to reduce their prices down from P_1, initially in line with the direct costs of these barriers. Domestic suppliers of the same product respond in order to defend their market, and in the first instance they reduce excess profits or wages, or eliminate inefficiency of different kinds (overhead costs, excess manning and inventories, etc.). As prices decline, demand also increases from Q_1 and this is partly responsible for triggering investment in new productive capacity, and this results in improved economies of scale and further price reductions. Further, the more competitive market environment leads enterprises to reconsider their business strategies in a more fundamental way. As a result, a process of restructuring ensues over a period of years (mergers and liquidations as well as new investments), which leads to a still fuller exploitation of technically available economies of scale. The price eventually falls to the lower equilibrium level of P_2 with total demand increasing to Q_2.

Consumers gain as a result of these price reductions, both with respect to their initial level of purchases and the increased purchases induced by the fall in price. This gain is indicated in the figure by area $P_1 - D_1 - D_2 - P_2$.

Producers are largely able to offset the price reductions by cost reductions, although there will be some losses of 'economic rents' (excess profits or wages in the previously protected enterprises, represented by the rectangle under P_1-D_1). On the other hand, producers have become more efficient, and so may gain world market shares, thereby increasing production and profits. To some extent this may be offset by increased home market penetration by suppliers from third countries, since the reduction in barriers may benefit not only other Community suppliers, but also those from third countries (these third country effects are not shown in the figure).

The total welfare gain for the economy, in this simplified case, amounts to the consumer gain, less the loss of protected profits. This assumes that all the resources released in the reduction of costs are re-employed productively in the economy, although there may be some time-lag before this happens completely.

microeconomic analyses such as of various economies of scale phenomena, and the impact of different types of competitive or uncompetitive behaviour of enterprises (see Part C).

General equilibrium microeconomics. The results for individual product markets will often affect the supply and demand conditions for other branches of the economy. These secondary effects may have the result that the aggregate result for the economy ends up being different, and possibly bigger, than the total of the partial equilibrium results. The purpose of the general equilibrium method is to bring these secondary effects into account. A comment on the likely importance of these effects is given in Chapter 10.

Macroeconomic developments. While these microeconomic methods usually describe the final ('equilibrium') situation after all effects have worked through, this ignores what happens in the adjustment period, and the conditions affecting this adjustment process. It only describes the destination, not the journey. Macroeconomic analysis and models can help compensate for some of these shortcomings, by showing how the evolution of costs, prices, income and other macroeconomic variables, including macroeconomic policy, interact in response to changes in market policies. Of particular importance at present for the European economy is how quickly employees, made redundant in one branch of industry as a result of restructuring, may be re-employed elsewhere in the economy. Macrosectoral models also have a capacity to estimate the evolution by sector of a considerable number of variables, such as employment, investment and trade, as well as prices and output. The macroeconomic and macrosectoral models used for simulation purposes are briefly described in Annex B, and the main results given in Section 10.2.

Dynamic effects. It has long been recognized that changes in the market and trading environment can have an important impact on the continuing, 'dynamic' evolution of the economy, this contrasting with the 'comparative static' approach that underlies the larger part of microeconomic studies and partial or general equilibrium analysis. Unfortunately, these dynamic features are extremely difficult to explain with scientific rigour, or to quantify. This in turn means that it is equally difficult to incorporate such effects into the analytical or modelling methods so far mentioned. There are none the less some studies of how market conditions appear to influence the trend rate of technological progress and innovation in enterprises and these are reported in Sections 6.1 and 7.2. In addition, and more broadly, there is the question of how businessmen are influenced by perceptions of how public policy may be changing the market environment and how they can strategically react. This is necessarily a speculative matter, but one that is none the less highly relevant to the Community's internal market programme. This subject is discussed in Chapter 8.

2.4. The important economic concepts for the internal market programme

In view of this complex set of economic concepts, it is natural to ask where the heart of the matter lies. Which of the concepts is likely to account for the most important part of the total expected impact of the internal market programme?

In general it can be expected that for the Community's internal market programme, the direct effects of the market opening measures (e.g. the resource costs of overcoming certain barriers) may be less big than the indirect effects on efficiency and costs as a result of enhanced competition, and that the medium to long-run and dynamic effects may be relatively large compared to the short-term static effects.

One way of appreciating the great importance in the case of the Community's internal market programme of the longer-run and indirect effects, is in contrasting the impact on trade prices with that on the prices for domestically produced consumption. The direct and short-run effects of reducing market barriers will principally affect the price of traded goods. The longer-run and indirect effects will to a larger degree be reflected in the prices and costs of domestically consumed production, as well as trade. Clearly the total money amount of the impact is likely to be much higher when the larger domestic part of the economy is also affected.

This point has been illustrated empirically in the study of Owen (1983) on the effects of the formation of the common market of the EC up to the end of the 1970s. Owen based his estimates on detailed case-studies of some major manufacturing industries. Taking into account how increased competition resulted in a restructuring of these industries and a widespread lowering of costs and prices of total production, he estimated that the welfare gains from the opening of markets amounted to as much as 50 to 100% of the total value of the additional trade created, or 3 to 6% of the total gross domestic product of the Community. For the internal market programme also, it is necessary to assess how the costs and prices of domestically produced consumption is affected, not just trade. The impact on domestic production costs will be particularly high when in the initial situation many countries are producers of the same goods, each in a weakly competitive home market situation. Such is typically the case for sectors presently protected by the internal market barriers of the Community. This argument also underlines the importance of competition policy in complementing the removal of barriers, if the maximum economic benefits from the Community internal market are to be harvested.

These relatively large economic effects from market integration contrast with the much smaller estimates made of the effects of the main GATT trade liberalization rounds, for example welfare gains only of the order of 0,1% of GDP each in the case of the tariff and non-tariff barrier reductions in the Tokyo Round (see Baldwin, 1984, for a survey).

A second point, further reinforcing the importance of the long-term versus short-term impacts, is the issue of adjustment of the labour market. Where jobs

FIGURE 2.3: Illustration of the static and dynamic impacts of completing the internal market on the growth path of the European economy

I — Comparative static impact on level of economic welfare

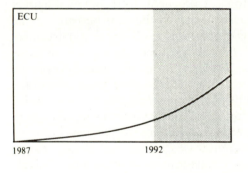

Static impact. The effects quantified below (in Chapter 10) may be called 'comparative static' in the sense that they represent a once and for all increase in the level of economic welfare. These effects are, of course, only achieved over a period of years. It is possible that a rapid completion of the internal market could see a large part of the gains achieved by around 1992, although actual knowledge about such time-paths is quite limited.

II — Dynamic impact

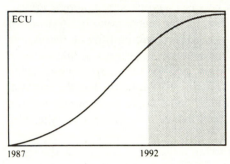

Dynamic impact. In Chapter 7 attention is drawn to the likely positive impact of increased competition and market size on innovation and technological progress; such effects are 'dynamic' in the sense that they raise the permanent, potential growth rate of the economy. Such effects are likely to build up only very gradually, but, once established, yield continuing and cumulative economic gains.

III — Total impact (I + II)

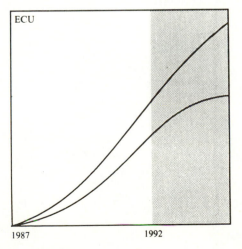

Total impact. These static and dynamic effects would both be developing at the same time in the years ahead. The static effects would be more important to begin with, but as these become exhausted the dynamic effects would take over and sustain a continuing, buoyant growth performance.

are lost in a restructuring of a previously inefficient industry, it may take time to re-employ the redundant workers. Until the redundant workers are productively re-employed there are unemployment costs to be counted against the benefits.

A third point concerns the distinction between 'static' and 'dynamic' effects. As is indicated in Figure 2.3 in more detail, the microeconomic (partial or general) equilibrium approach involves assessing a once-and-for-all increase in the level of economic welfare, due to changes in market policies. It takes several years, however, to move to this new situation, and the time-path may in reality be influenced by cyclical macroeconomic conditions. None the less the essential distinction is between this once-and-for-all 'static' increase in economic welfare, versus continuing 'dynamic' effects that may induce a permanently higher rate of economic growth.

As is suggested in Figure 2.3, and argued in more detail in Part D, the static effects are likely to be more important in the first few years, but gradually the dynamic effects will take on an increasing importance.

The full impact of the internal market programme has therefore to be assessed with a wide-ranging set of analytical tools. The benefits of the internal market programme are likely to be progressively bigger as the time-horizon for the analysis is extended, and the analytical approach made more sophisticated. However, the technical difficulty of the analysis and the margin of error surrounding quantitative estimates also increase. This may appear unfortunate, but should not be considered surprising when one reflects on the nature of the internal market programme: around 300 microeconomic measures are proposed with the objective of changing the competitive environment in the European economy sufficiently radically to trigger a change in macroeconomic performance. If the analysis were to stop at the most easily observable (direct, short-term) effects, it would give a serious understatement of the programme's likely effects.

PART C

The effects of market barriers

A double approach is adopted for evaluating the impact of market barriers: first a horizontal one that reviews the main types of barrier that affect many different industries, and secondly a vertical one that reviews the situation of specific branches of the goods and services sectors. Neither the list of barriers or of branches is exhaustive, but between them they give a fair view of the important barriers and the variety of situations that arise.

The goods-producing branches are typically affected by three types of barriers — customs procedures, technical regulations and norms, and fiscal frontiers. Several industrial branches are also seriously affected by government procurement restrictions. The service branches are usually affected relatively little by these types of barriers, but rather more by specific policies of market regulation. While some features of regulatory regimes for services (prudential or safety rules for example) are equivalent to technical regulations and norms for goods, it is often the case that service branch regulations also restrict market entry in more fundamental ways.

As pointed out in the preceding chapter, there tends to be a large difference in economic impact between those barriers that impose some limited costs on trade between countries compared to domestic supplies, and those which limit market access or control production or quantities traded. The economic effects of cost-increasing barriers often turn out, as the following case studies will illustrate, to be of moderate size. On the other hand, barriers that limit market entry, or control production or quantities traded, can result in relatively large economic costs. This is because market-entry restrictions can have a far more drastic impact in dampening competition, even to the point of excluding it where national monopoly situations are protected.

3. Principal types of barriers

3.1. Industrialists' perceptions of the main barriers

The perceptions of industrialists of the importance of the different barriers to trade within the Community have been ascertained in a special survey undertaken with an identical questionnaire in all 12 Member States, involving in all about 20 000 enterprises (see the study by G. Nerb for a detailed presentation). The questionnaire was concerned with how enterprises evaluated given barriers in the Community market as a whole, not just in the respondent's home country.

On average, the seriousness of the different categories of barriers were rank-ordered as follows:

1. Technical standards and regulations ⎫
2. Administrative barriers ⎬ approx. equal
3. Frontiers formalities ⎭
4. Freight transport regulations
5. Value-added tax differences ⎫
6. Capital markets control ⎪
7. Government procurement restrictions ⎬ approx. equal
8. Implementation of Community law ⎭

Most of these categories of barrier will be analysed in some detail in the following sections and chapters. These average survey results cover a wide range of different situations by branch of industry or country (see Figures 3.1, 3.2 and 3.3), as well as by size of enterprise. The strongest general impression to be retained is that the entire set of market barriers is of great multiplicity and variety. This suggests that a comprehensive programme of actions, implying many detailed measures, may indeed be necessary to convince industrialists to base their business strategies on the assumption of an integrated European market.

Some highlights from the survey illustrate important points of detail. The problem of disparate technical standards and regulations was found to be especially severe in engineering industries. Government procurement restrictions, while of minor importance in several branches, were reported to be an important barrier for certain categories of transport equipment, office equipment and electrical engineering.

Large firms are more seriously concerned by government procurement restrictions than small firms. However, the reverse is true of frontier costs, which small and medium-sized firms find more onerous than large firms.

As between countries, the new Member States, Portugal, Spain and Greece, report the most onerous barriers, in particular administrative barriers, frontier delays and in some cases capital controls. Of the original Member States, Italy and Belgium report the most severe barriers, especially of the administrative category. The countries whose enterprises experience the least severe obstacles are Germany, France, the United Kingdom, Denmark and the Netherlands.

Further use of this survey will be made later on in this report, notably concerning estimates of the cost savings that the removal of barriers would allow, and the possible impact on sales and business strategies.

3.2. Customs procedures

Intra-EC trade in goods, much of which has to cross several, not just one frontier, amounts to some 500 billion ECU, or 14 % of Community GDP and a little over half of the Community's total trade.

Customs procedures, involving frontier stops either at internal Community borders or inland, and related administrative costs borne inland by companies and the public authorities, are at present maintained within the Community for the following reasons:

(i)   differences in value-added tax rates and excise duties, which are currently applied in accordance with the 'destination principle', and thus necessitate border tax adjustments in the Member State of destination;

(ii)   application of monetary compensatory amounts to trade in certain agricultural products in accordance with the common agricultural policy;

(iii) differences in national public health standards involve veterinary and plant health checks;

(iv)   checks to control road transport licenses, and the compliance of vehicles with national regulations including safety rules for the transport of dangerous products;

(v)   formalities carried out for statistical purposes;

(vi)   the enforcement of certain bilateral trade quota regimes that Member States maintain with third countries, for example textile quotas under the multi-fibre agreement of the GATT and other miscellaneous national measures authorized under Article 115 of the Treaty of Rome.

Since the White Paper proposes eliminating frontier controls and checks in their entirety, all of the above procedures will have to be either eliminated or reformed in ways that do not require frontier formalities.

Economic costs. The direct costs associated with existing formalities and controls in intra-Community trade fall under the following headings:

(i)   internal administrative costs borne by exporting and importing firms, including the staff, computing and overhead costs of paperwork and the corresponding costs to consumers of higher prices;

FIGURE 3.1: **Importance of barriers by country**

□ Standards, technical regulations

✷ Public purchase of goods

■ Administrative barriers (customs)

✗ Frontier delays and costs

○ Differences in VAT, excise taxes

△ Transport market regulations

● Capital market restrictions

▲ Implementation of EC law

− Other barriers

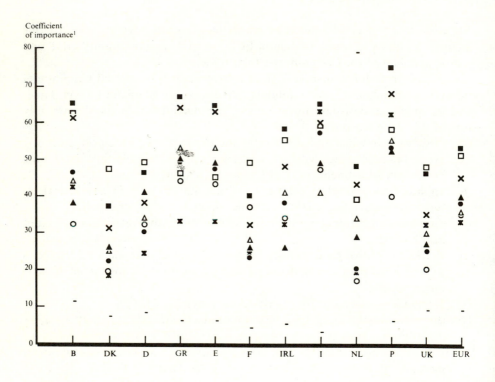

[1] All barriers are classified as: (a) very important; (b) important; (c) not so important. The coefficient is 100 when all firms consider the particular barrier to be very important.

Source: EC Commission survey (Nerb, 1987).

FIGURE 3.2: **Importance of barriers by industry**

□ Standards, technical regulations

✖ Public purchase of goods

■ Administrative barriers (customs)

✗ Frontier delays and costs

○ Differences in VAT, excise taxes

△ Transport market regulations

● Capital market restrictions

▲ Implementation of EC law

– Other barriers

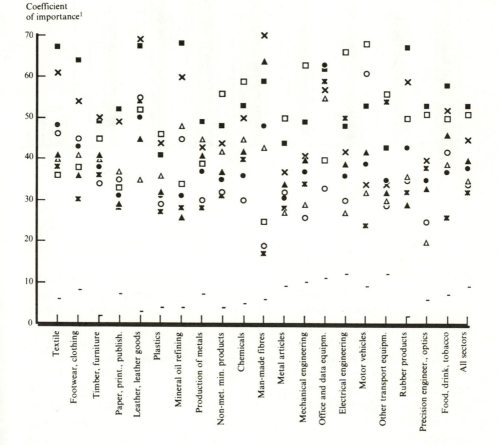

Note: See Figure 3.1.
Source: EC Commission survey (Nerb, 1987).

FIGURE 3.3 : **Importance of barriers by firm size**

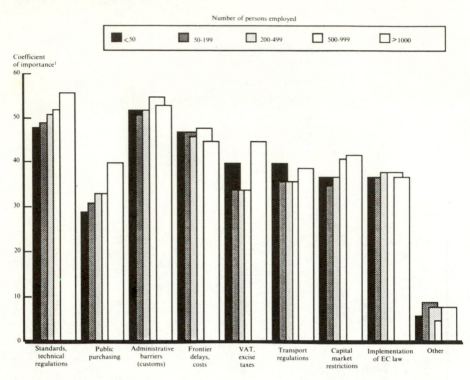

Note: See Figure 3.1.
Source: EC Commission survey (Nerb, 1987).

(ii)   external costs borne by exporting or importing firms through services directly associated with customs clearance, such as customs agents, advice and support services at the frontier points;

(iii) costs to exporting and importing firms through delays imposed by customs procedures, which amount to an increase in both inventory and transport costs, as goods are immobilized in containers, trucks, trains or ships at customs points;

(iv)   the costs to public authorities in terms of material and human resources in maintaining customs posts and associated administrative services.

The indirect costs of customs procedures are those arising from the lesser pressure of competition on the domestic economy from foreign suppliers. The combination of direct customs costs and the lack of transparency, for reasons of indirect taxation and other distribution costs, in price comparisons between markets, means that the possibilities for merchants to engage in arbitrage trade between countries are considerably hampered. Thus the market sanctions against non-competitive production and distribution systems are much weaker than they could be in a completely integrated Community market. Customs procedures represent the most explicit and symbolic of barriers supporting non-competitive business practices, but the full indirect effects of customs barriers cannot be separated from the many other factors that determine the competitiveness of markets. While later chapters evaluate these wider concepts of market fragmentation, the present section principally evaluates the direct costs of customs procedures.

To this end, a study was undertaken by Ernst and Whinney. The study of administrative costs to firms involved questionnaires and interviews with 467 industrial firms in Belgium, France, Germany, Italy, the Netherlands and the United Kingdom, engaged in intra-Community trade. Details of internal costings and trade values were obtained from 267 firms for imports and 224 for exports. This sample accounts for 0,8 % of intra-EC trade and covers a wide range of firm sizes and industries. Evaluation of the cost of delays at customs posts involved a similar method and country coverage, with a sample of 85 road transport operators. Calculation of budgetary cost to the public authorities was based initially on publicly available data, which was then discussed with the officials in the agencies concerned.

The largest item was found to be the administrative costs to firms including agents' fees, totalling 7,5 billion ECU, corresponding to 1,5 % of the value of total internal Community trade. This total is based on estimated average administration costs per consignment in the sample study of some 86 ECU on the export side, plus 67 ECU on the import side, corresponding to 0,7 and 0,8 % of value of imports and exports, respectively.

Significant differences exist between countries and between export and import costs (see Table 3.2.2). Costs, in terms of ECU per consignment, are found by the study to be below average in the Benelux, which indicates that the existence of simplified documentation procedures within these countries have contributed to a lowering of the customs clearance costs. For Italy however, the cost per consignment was found to be outstandingly high, which is fully in accordance with anecdotal information from industry sources, including traffic congestion at the land frontier posts on Italy's northern border.

The cost burden was found also to be markedly higher for smaller firms. Cost per consignment was 30 to 45 % higher for firms with fewer than 250 employees than for larger firms. The larger firms account for over 65 % of trade and their lower costs are therefore the more important influence on the average for firms as a whole. Large firms are sometimes able to arrange special customs procedures, such as periodic recapitulative declarations, as well as checks made by customs and other officials in the firm, thus dispensing with the need to present goods at customs offices (inland or at the border). Thus the deterrent effect of physical barriers and the associated compliance costs is of special concern to the small and medium-sized enterprises.

The cost of external services borne by exporters and importers was estimated to amount to 1,6 billion ECU. These costs consist largely of the activities of customs clearing agents, which involve around 40 000 full-time jobs. Customs advice and support services account for only a small part of the total (60 million ECU).

The cost of delays of road haulage transport was estimated at between 0,4 and 0,8 billion ECU. The upper limit corresponds to the total costs of delay. Delay time is not necessarily effective time lost as legitimate and compulsory rest periods may be timed to coincide with delays at customs points. The lower limit is based on the assumption that only a 50 % saving can be achieved.

Table 3.2.1.

Direct cost of customs formalities borne on intra-Community trade in goods (billion ECU)

Administrative costs to firms:	
Internal	5,9
External	1,6
Total	7,5
Costs of frontier delays to firms	0,4-0,8
Total costs to firms[1]	7,9-8,3
Administrative costs to public authorities	0,5-1,0
Total costs of customs formalities	8,4-9,3

[1]   1,6-1,7% of total intra-Community trade.
Source: Ernst and Whinney.

Table 3.2.2.

Administrative costs to firms per consignment (ECU)

	Imports	Exports
Belgium	26	34
Germany	42	79
France	92	87
Italy	130	205
The Netherlands	46	50
United Kingdom	75	49
Average	67	86

Source: Ernst and Whinney.

Illustrating the extent of frontier delays, the example is reported of two 750-mile truck trips. The first within the United Kingdom took 36 hours. The second involved travelling from London to Milan. This trip, excluding the time lost in crossing the Channel, took 58 hours. This example suggests that frontier delays between the UK and Italy amount to increasing transport costs between these two markets by over a half. Furthermore, the cost of delays does not take account of the costs associated with the unpredictability of delays in relation to delivery deadlines. Presumably this adds a further margin to the costs of holding inventories and managing transport systems.

The budgetary cost to the public authorities was estimated to be of the order of 0,5 to 1,0 billion ECU. The lower figure represents the customs services' own view of the possible administrative savings, and the upper limit represents an independent estimate. These estimates include the staff costs of some 15 000 to 30 000 customs officials.

The costs of customs procedures may have been reduced over the last 10 years due to improved procedures and efficiency in the handling of customs formalities. However, total customs-related costs of between 8 to 9 billion ECU per year, corresponding to 1,7 to 1,9 % of the value of total intra-Community trade are still economically significant, in particular in relation to profit margins for trade.

Beyond these direct cost estimates, a simple and very partial attempt was made in the Ernst and Whinney study to evaluate the possible extent to which companies might expand trading activities in the event that customs formalities were abolished. This involved conducting opinion surveys among exporting and importing companies.

According to this survey, importers estimated that they would increase trade volumes by 1,0 %, whereas exporters would expect larger increases averaging 3,2 %. The results suggest that exporters are more optimistic about increased opportunities than importers. It is in particular among the smaller firms that the trade expansion would be significant. Both on the export and the import side the expected increases by small firms were more than double those expected by the large firms. However, these results take no account of possible increases in trade by firms which are not engaged in trade at present, or the increase in trade between border regions by small traders or individuals.

3.3. Technical regulations

Rated by industrialists as the most important single category of trade barrier, technical regulations are as a subject enormously detailed and complex. It was once estimated that there exist over 100 000 different technical regulations and standards in the Community. Moreover, the field is continuously growing, as a result of technological developments and increasing concern for health, safety and consumer protection issues.

For these reasons a quantification of the cost of these barriers, separately from other barriers to trade and competition, has only proved possible for a few examples — insufficient to justify an aggregate estimate. On the other hand, it is possible to give a reasonably ordered account of the nature and qualitative importance of these barriers by industrial branch. Moreover, the Community's policy approach to removing these barriers has been evolving in important ways in recent years, and there could be quite rapid and widespread progress in the legislative actions of the Community. This is of strategic importance to the Community's industrial sector, since very often the technical barriers are greatest in high-tech sectors where market fragmentation in Europe is a major competitive disadvantage *vis-à-vis* producers in the United States and Japan.

Industry standards, which are of growing importance as an indicator of the quality of products, often represent an effective barrier, in spite of their voluntary character for several reasons. They may be used as a point of reference in court actions, insurers similarly often require conformity with national standards, and government procurement practices may also make analogous demands.

The legal character of technical regulations is what distinguishes them from standards (written by national standardization bodies like DIN, BSI, Afnor). The latter are voluntarily agreed codifications regarding products and production methods. Standards are not legally binding and arise from the self-interests of the producers and consumers involved, for example, to improve information in commercial transactions and ensure compatibility between products.

Policy instruments for removing technical barriers. The Community now has a considerable arsenal of weapons for combating the market-segmenting effect of technical barriers:

(i)   by application of the mutual recognition principle towards national regulations, such that products lawfully produced or marketed in one Member State can have access to all Member States. This was the main message of the ruling of the European Court of Justice in 1978 in the *Cassis de Dijon* case, subsequently followed by a whole line of further judgments. In a recent case the Court required Germany to allow beer from other Member States — not brewed in accordance with German purity laws — to be freely imported. While the mutual recognition principle reduces the need for harmonization, this does not solve the whole problem. In the absence of specific Community legislation, Member States may still invoke certain provisions in the Treaty (notably Article 36) to restrict the free movement of goods on grounds of certain public policies or interests, and thus other policy instruments are also required.

(ii) by harmonization of national technical regulations, whereby Community directives indicate mandatory requirements for national regulations. Since 1985, a so-called 'new approach' to harmonization has been adopted. This dispenses with the earlier type of exhaustively detailed directives, which were difficult to agree and quick to become obsolete. The new type of directive only indicates essential requirements and leaves greater freedom to manufacturers as to how to satisfy these requirements. However, a privileged means of proving conformity is through following European standards worked out by European standardization bodies on mandates deriving from the directives. The 'new approach' should permit much faster progress in eliminating technical barriers, also because the new directives cover a much broader range of products. In 1987 the first directive along these lines was adopted by the Council for pressure vessels. Also in 1987 the Commission submitted new proposals for toys, construction products and industrial machinery. In 1988 further proposals will concern wood-working equipment, earth-moving equipment, electro-medical equipment, gas appliances, lifting appliances and personal protection equipment.

(iii) by the better functioning of European standardization bodies (CEN and Cenelec) which the Commission is promoting not only through the 'new approach' to harmonization. The European bodies are also to help provide technical specifications needed by public authorities, and for new industrial technologies where the weight of older national standards is less or absent. This is particularly important for telecommunications and informatics. The work of CEN and Cenelec is also attentive to wider international aspects of standardization; EFTA countries are in fact members of these bodies.

(iv) by means of the mutual information directive as regards new regulations and standards. Since its adoption in 1983, Member States are obliged to notify new regulations and standards. The Commission has the power to freeze the introduction of new national regulations for up to a year, if it decides that a Community action is necessary. This power has been used 30 times (in response to 450 notifications, which implies a widespread acceptance of regulatory diversity, as long as this does not cause new barriers to trade). The directive effectively restrains the creation of new trade barriers, and aims to encourage the reconciliation of national demands for new standards at an early stage.

Economic costs. The costs of technical barriers may in principle be analysed in terms of the methodology outlined earlier (Chapter 3). The profusion of different regulations causes:

(a) for companies:
  (i) duplication in costs of research and development;
  (ii) loss of manufacturing efficiency as production runs have to be adapted to different needs, although new computerized flexible manufacturing technologies may be attenuating this problem;
  (iii) increased inventory and distribution costs;
  (iv) competition weaknesses on world markets as a result of the small national market base;

(b) for public authorities: duplication in costs of testing and certification;

(c) for consumers and taxpayers:
   (i)   direct costs, borne initially by producers and governments as above, that translate into high prices and taxes;
   (ii) indirect losses, often perhaps larger in size, due to less competition and rationalization in production and marketing structures at the European level.

While it has not been possible to estimate the costs of all technical barriers separately from other barriers, the implicit cost is included in several estimates exploited elsewhere in this study. The business survey includes estimates of the direct cost of all barriers; various sectoral studies contain such estimates also and the analyses of the effects of market integration (Part D) implicitly do so as well.

The importance of technical barriers, by industry.[1] In the business survey undertaken for this study, managers were asked how important they considered the removal of technical trade barriers to be for their company. The results have been compared with the judgments of Commission experts responsible for policy actions to overcome these trade barriers. The business survey results have been converted into a numerical score and are presented in Table 3.3.1.

Thus, trade in investment goods, especially electrical and mechanical engineering products, public and commercial transport goods and precision and office equipment, appears to suffer relatively most from technical barriers. This is often because of differing safety regulations concerning the use of investment goods.

This is clearly the case for the mechanical engineering sector. In this area, the Commission has recently submitted a comprehensive proposal following the 'new approach' of specifying the essential requirements that products must meet. This directive, when fully implemented, should remove technical barriers for a variety of investment goods covering about half the engineering machinery market (worth 200 billion ECU per annum).

The electrical engineering sector suffers from differences in standards in telecommunications equipment (see Section 4.6 below). These are often set by national PTTs, with problems of product incompatibility. Consumer electrical appliances, however, no longer experience significant technical trade barriers as a result of the low-voltage directive of 1973.

The business survey suggests that trade in transport goods is strongly affected by technical obstacles, with motor vehicles heading the table and other transport equipment (trains, aircraft, ships) also figuring relatively high on the list. This is probably due to a few remaining technical disparities which are very difficult to harmonize, such as the left-hand drive in the United Kingdom and Ireland, and temporary disparities in national anti-pollution regulations which have

---

[1]   The business survey only covered industry. However, many technical barriers concern agricultural and horticultural produce, and the situation in this sector is outlined in Section 4.7.1.

received much attention. However, technical harmonization for cars is in fact well advanced, with 41 directives adopted and only 3 more missing for the entire programme to be completed. The missing elements mean, none the less, that Community-wide type approval is not yet possible, and manufacturers can choose between individual Community directives which are optional, or varying national specifications.

Manufacturers of precision and medical equipment rate technical barriers as being of medium severity. However, this industry embraces a number of subsectors for which different national regulations on health and safety aspects constitute prohibitive export hurdles. This applies notably to medical and surgical equipment for which, as a result, the market is still overwhelmingly

Table 3.3.1.

Importance of technical barriers, by industry

| | | Judgment of expert services of the Commission | | |
| Rank order from the business survey | | Degree of importance | | |
		Great	Medium	Less
1. Motor vehicles	68		X	
2. Electrical engineering	66	X		
3. Mechanical engineering	63	X		
4. Chemicals, of which:	60			
— pharmaceuticals		X		
— other				X
5. Non-metallic mineral products	56		X	
6. Other transport equipment	55			X
7. Food and tobacco	52	X		
8. Leather	51			X
9. Precision and medical equipment	50	X		
10. Metal articles	50		X	
11. Rubber products	50		X	
12. Plastics	47			X
13. Wood and furniture	44			X
14. Metals	41			X
15. Office and data-processing machinery	41		X	
16. Textiles	38			X
17. Footwear and clothing	37			X
18. Mineral oil refining	37			X
19. Paper and printing	35			X
20. Artificial fibres	31			X

A regrouping of these industrial sectors into broader product categories yields the following result:

I. Investment goods	59			
II. Consumer goods	52			
III. Intermediate goods	45			

national. As a result, European manufacturers often find themselves in a weak competitive position *vis-à-vis* US enterprises who can produce at lower costs given the scale of their own domestic market. The Commission is therefore preparing a 'new approach' directive to harmonize electro-medical equipment regulations, for proposal in the course of 1988.

For chemicals technical trade barriers also impinge unevenly on different product categories. As is the case with many intermediate goods, like artificial fibres, textiles, oil and metals, trade in bulk and petrochemicals does not suffer appreciably from technical regulations. As regards pharmaceuticals serious problems persist at the certification and registration stages, often resulting in costly time delays. Trade in fertilizers still faces difficulties due to differences in national labelling and packaging requirements. Lack of uniformity between Member States on issues of consumer and environmental protection is also still giving rise to technical obstacles to trade in chemical preparations, like household detergents. Here also progress is expected with the likely adoption by the Council of a 'new approach' directive on the classification, packaging and labelling of dangerous preparations.

Consumer and environmental protection tend to motivate different technical regulations governing the foodstuffs and tobacco industry, especially concerning the ingredients, packaging and labelling, and the use of generic descriptions (see further in Section 4.1).

While the business survey suggests that trade in intermediate goods is least hindered by technical barriers, a notable exception to this general finding is the building materials sector. Construction itself, as well as the use of materials therein, has in most Member States been heavily regulated for the sake of public health, safety and, increasingly, the environment. It is therefore not surprising to observe that technical barriers to trade in building materials still loom large, as a result of differences both in legally binding technical specifications and testing and certification prescriptions. The greater part of these barriers is expected to be eliminated once a 'new approach' harmonizing directive on construction products, for which the Commission submitted a proposal in 1986, will have been passed. A further problem still, though, is that architects and contractors often insist, for example to reduce their liability risks, that products conform to the national standard.

A sectoral subdivision of planned national technical regulations that have to be notified to the Commission since April 1984 in conformity with the mutual information directive is given in Table 3.3.2 which is presented in accordance with the rank order from the business survey.[1]

This list broadly accords with the rank order from the business survey, and the judgment of the Commission's expert services. Thus the electrical and mechanical engineering, construction materials, chemicals, transport and precision and medical equipment sectors not only suffer relatively most from

---

[1] Regulations regarding foodstuffs, pharmaceuticals and cosmetics were exempted from the notification obligations, which explains the absence of these relative sectors in the table

current technical barriers to trade, they also tend to be subject to most new national regulations. Accordingly, it is these sectors that are the first targets of harmonization directives of the 'new approach'.

Table 3.3.2.

Notification of planned national technical regulations since April 1984

Transport (motor vehicles and other transport equipment)	81
Electrical engineering (including data processing)	125
Mechanical engineering	103
Chemicals (exclusive of pharmaceuticals)	38
Construction products and other non-metallic mineral products	57
Precision and medical equipment	40
Metal products	5
Total:	449

Source: Commission Services.

Some examples. Because the cost of technical barriers varies so much by product, it has not been possible to estimate an aggregate for this type of barrier. However, a number of examples can show how these costs can be high. They have been selected in such a way as to illustrate the three forms, or combination thereof, that technical trade barriers can take, as is shown in Table 3.3.3.

Table 3.3.3.

Technical barriers: a sectoral illustration

Barrier	Type		
	Standard	Regulation	Certification
Pasta purity law		X	
Registration process of pharmaceuticals			X
Type approval of automobiles		X	X
Electrical wood-cutting tools		X	X
Building tiles	X		X
PABX standards	X		X

Source: Group Mac.

Pasta purity laws exist in France, Greece and Italy, but the one in Italy has the most significant economic incidence on account of the large volume of pasta consumed in that country. In 1967, a law was passed in Italy stipulating that the generic product name 'pasta' can only be used for products consisting exclusively of durum wheat, and not for products that are made partly on the basis of soft wheat, which is 10 to 15 % less expensive. This case is elaborated in Chapter 4.1. We limit ourselves here to stating that according to the study by MAC, the repeal of this law would lead to a 10 to 20 % market share for the cheaper 'mixed' pasta, which could mean direct cost savings for Italian consumers of the order of 20 to 60 million ECU per annum and a rise of imports from nil to up to 5 % of the domestic market.

If a pharmaceutical product is to be admitted to a particular national market within the EC, it must first be approved by the national registration authority. In spite of the harmonization of approval criteria laid down in Community legislation, national authorities still impose specific requirements. Adjusting to such country- specific certification procedures causes extra administrative costs and time delays that can go up to three years, shortening the effective lifetime of patents. As is explained in Chapter 4.2, the costs associated with the need to go through multiple certification procedures has been calculated to lie between 160 and 260 million ECU in 1985, or between 0,5 and 0,8 % of total industry costs.

Also, car imports still need to be subjected to national technical controls as regulations on only 41 out of 44 essential car parts have been harmonized at EC level. Although the resulting costs are rather negligible for manufacturers, European consumers suffer more from the ensuing market fragmentation. The need to conform to divergent technical regulations discourages parallel imports to take advantage of the sizeable price differences between car markets. In addition, national technical certification procedures are kept in place to facilitate the control of the compliance with the national quantitative restraints that Italy, Spain, France and the United Kingdom apply to Japanese automobiles (see Chapter 4.3).

Another example concerns the electrical wood-working machines sector. Regulations on the marketing of single-spindle machines, for which the market in the four largest EC countries amounted to about 2 billion ECU in 1985, differ significantly in France as compared to Germany, Italy and the United Kingdom. In France additional safety devices are required and machines must be approved by the Ministry of Labour. According to a consultant's study, conforming to the specific French rules, along with the approval procedure, which can take up to one year, puts firms exporting to France at a cost disadvantage relative to domestic competitors of about 1 500 ECU per piece, increasing the cost of imported machines by 7 to 15 % of the machines' value. Further indirect cost reductions, due to economies-of-scale effects of trade expansion and rationalization among producers could range from 3,5 to about 10 % of production costs. This type of barrier will be the subject of a new directive on wood-working machinery due to be adopted by the Commission in 1988.

The last two instances illustrate how industry standards, in conjunction with conformity test procedures can seriously hinder imports.

In France, domestic tile manufactures working through the national standardization body Afnor have created particularly stringent standards for tiles. As the Afnor specifications are not legally binding, non-standard tiles can still be sold in France but they cannot be used in public construction works (about 40 % of the market) and architects and engineers will be reluctant to employ them for insurance reasons. The standard is linked to a conformity marking process, which reportedly can take up to one year's delay. These technical barriers have effectively curbed imports from traditional tile manufacturing countries like Italy and Spain. Spanish tiles are reckoned to be on average more than 25 % cheaper than French ones. According to a study by MAC, if these standard-induced restrictions prevent the Spanish producers from gaining an incremental 10 % of the market, they are costing French consumers about 3 % of the value of their domestic expenditures on tiles. Indirect costs could be more pronounced as tile manufacturing lends itself to significant scale economies. The technical barriers in question may be removed when Afnor replaces its standard by the prospective European one to be elaborated following the adoption of a recently proposed directive on construction products.

Despite earlier efforts to harmonize standards for private automatic branch exchanges (PABX), used in telecommunications systems, important differences still exist accross major EC Member States. As a result, highly costly and complex tests need to be repeated in each export market. The objectivity of type approval procedures, which take at least three months but often absorb an entire year, is not always guaranteed as the controlling bodies, the national PTT's, are themselves suppliers of PABX and formal appeal procedures are unavailable, except in the United Kingdom. This contrasts with the situation in the USA where delays typically do not exceed 10 weeks and applicants can go to appeal. Harmonizing PABX standards and eliminating the national type approval procedure could bring important cost savings. PABX manufactured prices are for example over twice as high in Germany as those in France, yet exports from France to Germany are almost non-existent. MAC estimated that a direct cost reduction of up to 6 % (some 7 million ECU) of total German expenditure on PABX could be realized if French manufacturers could capture a 10 % market share.

3.4. Public procurement

Public procurement, which accounts for a substantial proportion of economic activity, continues to be subject to discriminatory practices. By systematically favouring domestic suppliers over foreign suppliers, public sector purchasing bodies are depriving themselves of the advantages offered by wider competition.

Public purchasing as a whole includes all purchases of goods and services by government (central government, national government agencies, and regional and local government) and by public enterprises, i.e. enterprises that benefit from a monopoly, franchise or special status in the provision of public services (energy supply, posts and telecommunications, railways, etc.). In 1986, such purchases represented approximately 530 billion ECU in the Community of Twelve (15 % of GDP).

Only part of public purchasing is put out to tender or is the subject of formal contracts. Minor current expenditure, rents, heating and electricity expenses, insurance costs and telephone and postal charges are incurred without using such procedures. The contractual part of public purchasing, frequently called public (or government) procurement, was worth between 240 and 340 billion ECU in the Community in 1986 (between 6,8 and 9,8 % of GDP), with significant variations between Member States (see Table 3.4.1).

In the short term, the opening-up of public purchasing to EC-wide competition will only affect the part covered by formal contracts (i.e. public procurement). For historical reasons, however, major differences exist in the structure of the public sector and in public purchasing practices between the various Community countries: centralization in purchasing in the United Kingdom (with 700 purchasing entities), decentralization in Italy and Germany (over 20 000 purchasing entities). Also, the procedures for awarding contracts vary from one country and one purchasing body to another. In the majority of cases, public authorities prefer restricted tenders or negotiation with individual suppliers to open tenders, which adds to the general lack of transparency in public procurement. In the long term, the major part of public purchasing of goods and services should be thrown open to foreign suppliers (80 % of the total or 12 % of GDP) apart from current expenditure which is incurred locally and is estimated at around 20 % of total public purchasing.

Public purchases are concentrated in certain industries. Over 85 % of the total is made from less than 20 of the 60 broad industry groups distinguished in this analysis (see Table 3.4.2). This is especially true of capital expenditure: 85 % is concentrated in two sectors, namely transport equipment other than motor vehicles, and construction and civil engineering.

The significance of non-tariff barriers in public procurement

At the present time the huge market represented by public-sector construction and public purchasing of goods and services is virtually closed to intra-Community competition. Only 2 % of public supply contracts and 2 % of public construction contracts have so far been awarded to firms from other Member States. These figures do not, however, allow for the import content of the goods purchased under public contracts. The first Community directives in this regard sought to introduce common rules in the technical field, to harmonize award procedures, and to lay down common rules for the advertising of contracts. But the Commission has found that the Community rules are frequently broken. Typical infringements include failure to advertise tenders in the *Official Journal of the European Communities*, abuse of the exceptions from the normal tendering and award rules, illegal exclusion of bidders from other Member States, discrimi-

Table 3.4.1.

Economic dimensions of public procurement (billion ECU), 1984

	B	D	F	I	UK	Total for the five countries
Total purchasing by general government	6,3	58,5	53,7	43,6	64,7	226,8
Total purchasing by public enterprises	10,6	34,4	34,2	24,8	54,2	158,2
Total public purchasing (as % of GDP)	16,9 (17,5)	92,9 (11,8)	87,9 (14,1)	68,4 (13,1)	118,9 (21,8)	385,0 (15,0)
Total public procurement[1] (as % of GDP)	7,7-11,0 (8,0-11,4)	42,5-62,6 (5,4-8,0)	39,3-58,2 (6,3-9,3)	31,1-43,4 (6,0-8,3)	54,2-76,2 (10,0-14,1)	174,8-251,4 (6,8-9,8)

[1] Public procurement: that part of public purchasing which is the subject of contracts, estimated by Atkins at between 45 and 65% of total public purchasing.

Source: Eurostat, Atkins.

nation in scrutinizing bidders' technical capacity and financial standing, and discrimination in the awarding of contracts.

In 1986 the Commission presented proposals designed to tighten up significantly enforcement of the current legislation to ensure that firms from other Member States have an equal chance and to increase the general transparency of public procurement.

Table 3.4.2.

Breakdown of public purchasing of goods and services by product[1] in 1984
Extrapolation of figures for five countries (B, D, F, I, UK) to EUR 12

NACE-CLIO Group	billion ECU		% of total public purchasing
01 *Agriculture, forestry and fishery products*	*2,7*		*0,6*
06 *Energy products*	*73,2*		*16,3*
of which: 031 Coal and coal briquettes		15,6	3,5
073 Refined petroleum products		36,0	8,0
097 Electrical power		9,9	2,2
30 *Manufactured goods*	*147,2*		*32,7*
of which: 170 Chemical goods		14,5	3,2
190 Metal goods		9,8	2,2
210 Agricultural and industrial machinery		12,2	2,7
230 Office equipment, etc.		8,6	1,9
250 Electrical goods		19,9	4,4
270 Motor vehicles		8,2	1,8
290 Other transport equipment		37,5	8,3
473 Paper and printing products		10,5	2,3
53 *Construction*			
530 Building and construction	*129,1*		*28,6*
68 *Market services*	*98,3*		*21,8*
of which: 570 Wholesale and retail distribution		11,0	2,4
590 Hotels and catering		6,0	1,3
611 Road transport		5,4	1,2
670 Communications		8,0	1,8
690 Banking and insurance		8,4	1,9
710 Business services		20,7	4,6
730 Letting of buildings		6,2	1,4
790 Market services n.e.s.		12,1	2,7
Total	*450,5* [2]		*100*

---

[1] Within each sector, only product groups accounting for over 1% of total public purchasing are listed.
[2] In 1984 the total of public purchasing at 450,5 billion ECU for EUR 12 was equivalent to 15% of GDP. The figure for 1986, assuming an unchanged proportion of GDP, is 530 billion ECU.
Source: Atkins, using input-output tables.

Proposals are also being prepared to extend the directives to the sectors so far excluded from the Community rules, namely the four very important sectors of energy, water, transport and telecommunications. Finally, it is planned to open up public procurement of services other than public building and works to EC-wide competition to a greater extent than is provided for in the present legislation.

Evaluation of the economic implications of liberalizing public procurement

The opening-up of public procurement will not have the same effect across all industries and products. In some industries (housing construction, for example) trade is slight. In other cases, government procurement relates to prototype products made to order under the customer's control (e.g. military hardware).

The purchasing of manufactured products accounts for one third of all public purchasing. A study made by Atkins for five Member States (B, D, F, I, UK), taking 1984 as the reference year, evaluated the potential benefits that could be anticipated from liberalization of public procurement, distinguishing from the generality of products those for which the public sector was a major purchaser. For standard products the direct effects of current purchasing practices were analysed by means of surveys of actual prices in the Member States. About 40 of the products most purchased by government and public enterprises were selected. On the basis of the average prices of these products in each Member State, the potential saving gains were estimated after subtracting from the price differentials between Member States the extra costs associated with intra-Community trade. These costs include the cost of transport, marketing, insurance and exchange risk cover. Different assumptions on the magnitude of these extra costs can be made. The estimated benefits were thus the potential savings achievable if the public purchasing body selected the most competitive supplier. It should be noted that surveys of public purchasing agencies show that the number of suppliers competing for projects is usually small. According to Atkins 30 % of contracts are arranged with a single supplier. This shows that the gains to be expected from a single European market in terms of increased competition could be considerable.

The savings achievable for these representative products were then extrapolated to the level of the industries producing them, assuming that the degree of import penetration from other Community countries in the public sector would reach a similar level to that observed in the private sector. Multiplying total public purchasing less current expenditure in these industries by the existing potential gain due to price differences, and by the increase in import penetration, gives an estimate of the direct economic effects for each sector (see Table 3.4.3). For 1984, the total direct effects were estimated at around 3 billion ECU.

The direct effects on purchase price are amplified by indirect effects. These indirect effects due to rationalization of production structures will occur in industries where the public sector is the dominant purchaser (see Table 3.4.4).

Table 3.4.3.

Reductions in costs and prices associated with liberalization of public procurement[1] (billion ECU), 1984

	Direct static effect[2]	Competition effect[3]	Restructuring effect[3]	Total
Agriculture	—	—	—	—
Energy[4]	—	—	—	—
Manufactured goods	2,7	2,0	6,0	10,7
Plant and machinery	1,7	2,0	6,0	9,7
Current consumption goods	0,2	—	—	0,2
Intermediate goods	0,8	—	—	0,8
Building and construction[5]	0,8	—	—	0,8
Market services[5]	0,2	—	—	0,2
Total	3,7	2,0	6,0	11,7

[1] Calculated for five Member States (B, D, F, I, UK).
[2] Assuming that, in the public sector, the rate of import penetration from other EC countries rises to the level now found in the private sector, for 80 % of public purchasing.
[3] Atkins only estimated the effects of competition and restructuring in sectors where public purchasing is so significant as to be liable to influence producers' behaviour. This is only the case in the plant and machinery sector.
[4] Energy is dealt with in Chapter 4.7.3.
[5] In both these sectors a 10 % rise in import penetration and a 10 % fall in prices are assumed for 80 % of public purchasing.
Source: Atkins.

Table 3.4.4.

Breakdown of the economic effects of liberalization of public procurement by country (billion ECU), 1984

	B	D	F	I	UK	EUR 5	EUR 12[1]
Static effect	0,4	1,0	0,3	1,0	1,0	3,7	4,4
Competition effect	0,2	0,8	0,3	0,4	0,3	2,0	2,3
Restructuring effect	0,5	1,0	1,4	1,0	2,1	6,0	7,2
Total 1984	1,1	2,8	2,0	2,4	3,4	11,7	13,9
(as % of GDP)	(1,1)	(0,4)	(0,3)	(0,4)	(0,6)	(0,5)	(0,5)
Additional savings in defence sector						3,7	4,0
Total (including defence)						15,14	17,9

[1] The extrapolation of the figures to EUR 12 is based on the effects remaining constant as a % of GDP.
Source: Atkins, Commission departments.

In the short term, a competition effect due to the lifting of barriers will predominate. The increased competition will induce an alignment of domestic suppliers' prices to those of the most competitive foreign suppliers. The competition effect assumes that the fall in prices is fully reflected in costs, for instance by the elimination of 'X-inefficiency'. This is a 'best-case' assumption, which if it is not fulfilled, will make the gain smaller. This lowering of prices should lead to savings of the order of 2 billion ECU for the five Member States studied.

In the medium term, a reduction in the number of producers should first significantly raise capacity utilization rates, which are currently very low in some of the industries: 20 % in boilermaking for the electricity industry, 50 % in locomotives, 60-70 % in turbine generators and telephone exchanges. Later on, mergers and reorganization, the rationalization of Community production on a smaller number of sites, falls in development costs due to a reduction in the range of products to offer, and coordination of R&D will favour cost reductions (see box on case-studies and Table 3.4.5). These restructuring effects, which will occur over a relatively long period and in a small number of industries, are estimated at 6 billion ECU for the five countries. Clearly, however, not all the dynamic long-term effects can be quantified.

Construction and public works account for 29 % of total public purchasing, or some 150 billion ECU in 1986 for the Community of Twelve. The creation of a single market by 1992 should have a twofold impact on this sector: first, through the opening of public construction markets, and secondly by the undertaking of major European infrastructure projects. At present, other European markets are marginal for the construction industry. According to a 1987 report by the French Commissariat du Plan, the share of Community countries in all public works contracts awarded by Member States to foreign firms is only 2,9 % for Germany, 3,2 % for France, nil for Italy, 1,8 % for the United Kingdom and 1,5 % for Spain. Thus, in construction we find the paradoxical situation that in 1986 US construction firms won 6 billion ECU worth of contracts in European countries, whereas the value of those won by European firms in European countries other than their own came to only 0,6 billion ECU.

While it is true that the construction sector has some specific characteristics, notably that small and medium-sized firms predominate in the industry (95 % of firms are SMEs with fewer than 50 employees), firms that are close to borders or highly specialized, and large firms, could find opportunities opened up to them in an integrated market. Finally, major infrastructure investments are required in Europe: the Rhine-Rhone link, the European high-speed train network, the Channel tunnel, the Splügen tunnel to improve communications between northern Italy and Germany, the Messina bridge, the road link between Central Europe and the Atlantic coast, the Rhine, Main Danube link and tunnels under the Pyrenees. Such projects could involve consortia of firms from different Community countries and receive European financial backing. Assuming that 10 % of domestic demand for construction works was supplied by imports in the various European countries, and that a potential saving of 10 % was obtainable on imported construction services, then the minimum saving in the five Member States studied would be around 1 billion ECU for 1984. These effects will nevertheless be quite small and the increased intra-Community competition that might result should only exert modest pressure for restructuring of the industry.

Purchases of market services by government are considerable (21,8 % of total public purchasing), but do not loom large in the general business of the supplying industries. Business services, insurance and banking will benefit from the liberalization of services taking place under the internal market programme. Government and public enterprises will benefit from this liberalization just as will other economic agents. If the same assumptions are made as for the construction sector, a minimum saving of 0,2 billion ECU is obtained (see Table 3.4.3) for the five countries. The indirect effects of the change in public procurement practices would be negligible.

Defence procurement. The Atkins study did not cover defence. But a report on this subject by a working party chaired by H. Vredeling was published in 1987 by NATO (Independent European Programme Group). Defence procurement includes products manufactured for civilian uses discussed above as well as weapon and missile systems, but the latter account for a major proportion of the total. In 1985, expenditure on weapons and missiles represented between

Table 3.4.5.

Cases of industrial restructuring linked to the liberalization of public procurement

	Community market (billion ECU[1])	Current capacity utilization	Intra-EC trade	Number of EC producers	Number of US producers	Economies of scale[1]
Boilermaking	2	20%	very little	12	6	20%
Turbine generators	2	60%	very little	10	2	12%
Locomotives	0,1	50-80%	very little	16	2	20%
Mainframe computers	10	80%	30-100%[2]	5	9	5%
Telephone exchanges	7	70%	15-45%[2]	11	4	20%
Telephone handsets	5	90%	very little	12	17	—
Lasers	0,5	50%	substantial	over 1 000	over 1 000	n.a.

[1] Scale economies resulting from a doubling of output.
[2] Percentages of total demand.
Source: Atkins.

15 and 25 % of European countries' defence budgets, at some 29 billion ECU for the countries of the Community. The fragmentation of the armaments industries, however, means considerable extra costs (see Table 3.4.6).

Expenditure on R&D before projects reach the production stage accounts for up to 25 % of arms expenditure. For certain sophisticated weapons systems (radar, military aircraft), the proportion can rise to 40 %. The extra costs of research and product development undertaken on a strictly national basis are thus considerable. On the assumption that the potential savings in this sector are comparable to those calculated for transport equipment other than motor vehicles, the total saving for the Community of Twelve would come to 6,2 billion ECU (see Table 3.4.6). Over two-thirds of this gain would come from the restructuring of production.

This 6,2 billion cannot, however, be directly added to the savings achieved elsewhere. Part will already have been counted in the savings achievable in the 'other transport equipment' sector. It is estimated that approximately 4 billion ECU are additional savings (see Table 3.4.4).

Thus, the total savings associated with the liberalization of public procurement are potentially considerable: including savings on defence equipment, they come to around 18 billion ECU for 1984 which is 0,6 % of Community GDP (see Table 3.4.4). A corresponding figure of 21,5 billion ECU of savings is estimated for 1987. The main impact of the liberalization will, however, only be seen in the medium to long term, after restructuring (by mergers, reorganization, etc.) in the industries largely dependent on public purchasing.

Table 3.4.6.

Public procurement of weapons and missile systems in 1985 (billion ECU)

	B	D	F[1]	I	NL	UK	EUR 6	EUR 12
Defence budget	3,4	28,1	28,3	15,0	5,3	31,5	111,6	132,6
(as % of GDP)	(3,3)	(3,4)	(4,2)	(2,7)	(3,2)	(5,3)	(4,0)	(4,0)
Expenditure on weapons and missile systems	0,4	3,9	7,6	2,8	1,2	8,5	24,4	29,3
Potential savings[2]								6,2

[1] French expenditure on weapons and missile systems is assumed to be the same proportion of the defence budget as in the United Kingdom.
[2] Assuming that the potential savings on this type of defence procurement are comparable to those estimated in the Atkins study for transport equipment other than motor vehicles.
Source: NATO, Commission departments.

Case-studies on the impact of liberalizing public procurement

(*Source*: Atkins)

The case-studies related to seven manufacturing industries mainly supplying the public sector. Atkins interviewed 60 companies operating in the seven industries in the five countries studied.

(i)   The manufacture of industrial boilers is a traditional industry undergoing technological change. The small number of producers remaining in Europe (about 12) have considerable excess capacity. There are no significant price differences between Community countries and intra-Community trade is marginal. Restructuring of the industry requires a reduction in the number of European producers to about four (the US now has only two). The fall in production costs could amount to 20 %. In the long run this industry could be subject to competition from low-wage countries.

(ii) The turbine generator industry has similar structural characteristics to the boilermaking industry. Here too there is little intra-Community competition and capacity utilization rates are relatively low. Price differences are evident between Community countries. Power plant builders in Italy and the UK could be sensitive to competition from German and French producers. The eventual restructuring of the industry should be achieved without major closures of production facilities but through mergers, acquisition and rationalization. The fall in production costs could come to about 12 %.

(iii) The electric locomotives industry is oligopolistic. The current technological development (such as the French TGV) is taking place in a traditional industry. While collaborative link-ups between firms are beginning to appear, the opening-up of public procurement will be slow because present-day locomotives were developed under agreements between the national railway companies and domestic suppliers and to technical specifications peculiar to each national network. The large number of European manufacturers (16, compared with only two in the US) is a major handicap. A one-third reduction in the number of suppliers by mergers or rationalization would raise present capacity utilization rates by 50 %. In the long term, harmonization of railway systems and a reduction in the number of locomotive types available would yield substantial reductions in development costs and economies of scale (20 % reduction in unit costs). An integrated European locomotives industry could eventually be reduced to four large groups.

(iv) The mainframe computer industry is a highly competitive industry. In each of the large Member States a domestic manufacturer competes with the local IBM subsidiary. There is little difference in prices between countries but rationalization of the industry would help reduce R&D and marketing costs.

(v)   The telephone exchange industry is notable for the scale of public funding of its R&D costs. There are seven different digital technologies in the European countries, five of them developed under protected public purchasing arrangements. The price per line in Europe is said to be significantly (2,5 to 5 times) higher than in the US. Major reorganization (mergers, cooperation arrangements) is currently taking place in the industry. This should eventually leave only two domestic European producers.

(vi) The telephone handset industry is an industry producing volume products at low unit cost. The price differences between countries are partly explicable by different quality standards and differences in regulations. However, free competition between producing countries would yield cost reductions of 30 to 40 % in Belgium, France and Germany, following a rationalization and reorganization of production facilities.

(vii) The laser industry is a very competitive, young industry with a predominance of small firms. Public procurement is more open than in other sectors. Substantial falls in prices and major restructuring are likely but these will not be a consequence of liberalization of public procurement.

Defence procurement

(*Source*: NATO Independent European Programme Group, Report of a group of experts presided by H. Vredeling, 1987)

(i) Armoured vehicles: Europe has a solid technological base but the desire of many countries to make their own tanks means short production runs and high unit costs.

(ii) Conventional munitions: The US benefits from large-scale production and low unit costs, although the level of technological sophistication of US products is similar to that in Europe.

(iii) Guided missiles: Europe's position is weakened by the technology gap in electronics and the fragmentation of markets, which extends from development to production.

(iv) Aircraft and helicopters: The excellent performance of the European industry make it vital to develop collaborative programmes covering the full range of military aircraft.

3.5. Fiscal frontiers

The examination of the results of the enquiry carried out with European industrialists (see Nerb, 1987) shows that physical barriers (customs delays and other frontier costs) have been classified as third in order of importance just after technical rules and standards and administrative formalities. In addition, we find differences in the rate and structure of indirect taxes (VAT and excises) regarded as a further, significant obstacle. While rate differences are not perceived to be among the severest barriers, it has to be remembered that they are intimately linked to two of the other categories of barriers. It is primarily because of the current rate differences and the current practice of detaxing goods for intra-Community 'export' and re-taxing them on 'import' that the administrative barriers and frontier-related controls exist. This was pointed out in Section 3.2 above where the reasons for maintaining customs procedures and frontier barriers between Member States are listed. Most of this list concerns issues which, while important in themselves, are either not trade-related (for example, checks on road transport licences, veterinary and plant health checks) or relate to certain specialized sectors or trade regimes (for example, textile quotas and agricultural monetary compensatory amounts). Another reason for frontier controls is the collection of trade statistics. However, the statistical procedures are linked to frontier formalities largely as a matter of convenience profiting from the fact that customs administrations have established frontier control systems for their own purposes and they could be reorganized in other ways.

The only element in this list which unavoidably requires the present frontier barriers is the wide difference in the rates and coverage of indirect taxes among Member States.

These wide differences in indirect tax rates, combined with the consequential need to detax intra-Community trade upon 'export' and tax it upon 'import', in effect divide the Community up into 12 self-contained fiscal compartments.

The elimination of fiscal frontiers can only be achieved if the system of detaxation at 'export' and taxation at 'import' for intra-Community trade is abolished, so that goods and services throughout the single market are treated the same way as goods and services within a Member State. This objective was clearly described in the First Council Directive of 11 April 1967 on the harmonization of legislation of Member States concerning turnover taxes and was subsequently incorporated into the Sixth VAT Directive. However, the removal of tax frontiers presupposes the approximation of laws so that distortions of competition and potential fraud are avoided. At present, the disparities in VAT are still wide, not only because of the gaps between the rates applied (see Table 3.5.1) but also because of the differences in tax structure (tax base, number of rates, exemptions, etc.). Table 3.5.2 shows some of the significant differences between Member States, focusing on VAT. As regards the main excises, there has been little progress in either approximating rates or harmonizing the tax base (see Table 3.5.3.)

In accordance with the programme set out in the White Paper, the Commission has drawn up proposals (see box, page 65), on the approximation of the rates and harmonization of the structures of VAT and on the harmonization of excise duties. These are not intended as an actual tax reform, still less are they aimed at achieving an optimum tax system for the Community. They merely seek, taking the present differences between Member States in the structures and rates of indirect taxes, to secure that measure of tax approximation which will make it possible to abolish the frontiers.

VAT proposals. With regard to VAT, harmonization of structures is based on the Sixth Council Directive of 17 May 1977, which provides for a basis of assessment determined in a uniform manner and in accordance with Community rules.

At present, the great majority of Member States apply more than one rate of VAT (see Table 3.5.1). A common feature of these systems is that basic necessities are taxed at a reduced rate. To simplify the operation of the VAT system while maintaining this special feature, it is proposed that a two-tier system be adopted: a reduced rate to apply to goods regarded as basic necessities (see Table 3.5.1), and a standard rate to all other products. The prior approximation of rates — essential if tax frontiers are to be abolished — was studied, on the basis of existing rates (see Table 3.5.1), to find an arrangement that would allow the maximum number of Member States to choose rates involving a minimum of change compared with the situation obtaining now. The idea thus is that the standard rate of VAT should be between 14 and 20 %, and the reduced rate between 4 and 9 %.

Table 3.5.1.

VAT rates in the Community (Rates applicable at 1 April 1987)

%

	Reduced rate	Standard rate	Higher rate
Belgium[2]	1 and 6	19	25 and 25 + 8
Denmark	—	22	—
France	2,1 and 4 5,5 and 7	18,6	$33\frac{1}{3}$
Germany	7	14	—
Greece	6	18	36
Ireland[3]	2,4 and 10	25	—
Italy	2 and 9	18	38
Luxembourg	3 and 6	12	—
Netherlands	6	20	—
Portugal[3]	8	16	30
Spain	6	12	33
United Kingdom[3]	—	15	—
Commission proposal	4 to 9[1]	14 to 20	abolished

[1] Taking account of the division by products and services existing at the present time in the majority of Member States, the Commission proposes that the reduced rate should be applied to the following categories of goods or services:
  (i) foodstuffs (except alcoholic beverages);
  (ii) energy products for heating and lighting;
  (iii) water supplies;
  (iv) pharmaceutical products;
  (v) books, newspapers and periodicals;
  (vi) passenger transport.
  Altogether, these goods and services represent about one third of the common tax base.
[2] An intermediate rate of 17% is also applied.
[3] These countries also refund tax paid at the previous stage on certain domestic transactions (i.e. they apply a zero rate).
  (*NB:* All Member States' zero-rate exports and similar transactions).

The Commission's proposals are based on the principle, already incorporated in the Sixth VAT Directive, that products will be taxed in the country where the sale takes place. Consequently, cross-border sales and purchases will be treated in the same way as sales and purchases within the frontiers of the Member States: for all sales, VAT will be charged to the purchaser at that rate applicable in the country of sale, whether he is a national or from another Member State. If the purchaser is the final consumer, he will therefore pay VAT in the country of purchase. If he is subject to turnover tax, he will be able to deduct the VAT already paid in another Member State and, when the goods are resold, will have to charge the VAT of his own country to the customer. The principle of the neutrality of impact of VAT on taxable persons is thereby maintained. For the Member State of consumption really to receive the tax

Table 3.5.2.

Disparities in the rates and structure of VAT

Products	Example of rates applied[1] in certain countries (%)		
	Reduced rate	Standard rate	Higher rate
Records, cassettes, tapes	9 (I)	14* (D)	25 (B)
Gas	6* (NL)	17 (B)	
Wine, spirits, etc.	9 (I)	14* (D)	25 (B) 38[2] (I)
Cameras and cine cameras, hi-fi and TV sets, etc.		12* (L)	33⅓ (F)
Pharmaceutical products	10* (IRL)	20 (NL)	
Property transactions	10 (IRL)	20* (NL)	
Hotel trade	6 (NL)	14* (D)	
Passenger transport	7* (D)	22 (DK)	
Motor vehicles		12* (L)	38[3] (I)
Jewellery and precious stones		15* (UK)	33⅓ (F)

[1] The examples given apply to certain countries only. Listed here are cases where, because of the differences in tax structure, certain products are taxed at the reduced or higher rate, while elsewhere they are generally taxed at the standard rate; or where, conversely, products taxed in some countries at the standard rate, while they are generally taxed at the reduced rate. The type of rate generally applied is marked with an asterisk. This is also the rate chosen in the Commission's proposals.
[2] Sparkling wines fermenting naturally in the bottle.
[3] With an engine capacity in excess of 2 000 cc.

levied, a clearing mechanism is envisaged which will make it possible to refund to the country of consumption the tax collected by the exporting country.

Proposals on excise duties. When, in 1972, the Commission presented its proposal on the harmonization of excise structures, it opted for the maintenance and harmonization at Community level of the excise duties on manufactured tobaccos, mineral oils, alcohol, wine and beer. In the final stage of the programme, the conditions were to be established for the abolition of tax frontiers. This objective can of course be attained only if common excise duty rates are applied to a structure that has been harmonized throughout the Community. In this regard, the proposals on the harmonization of the structure of excise duties are still under discussion.

There are, at present, wide disparities between the rates of the five excise duties which are to be harmonized (see Table 3.5.3). However, since VAT is calculated on a product's price inclusive of excise duty, any flexibility in the rates of excise duty would result in differences in VAT greater than the bands adopted for that tax. The Commission has thought it preferable, therefore, to propose that excise duty rates be fully harmonized. Table 3.5.3 gives the rates the Commission has in mind.

Table 3.5.3.

Excise duty rates: current situation (1 April 1987); proposals for harmonization

	Pure alcohol (ECU per hl)	Wine (ECU per hl)	Beer (ECU per hl)	Cigarettes[1]		Petrol (ECU per 1 000 l)
				(ECU per 1 000)	(ad valorem %)	
B	1 252	33	10	2,5	66,4	261
DK	3 499	157	56	77,5	39,3	473
D	1 174	20	7	27,3	43,8	256
GR	48	0	10	0,6	60,4	349
E	309	0	3	0,7	51,9	254
F	1 149	3	3	1,3	71,1	369
IRL	2 722	279	82	48,9	33,6	362
I	230	0	17	1,8	68,6	557
L	842	13	5	1,7	63,6	209
NL	1 298	33	20	26,0	35,7	340
P	248	0	9	2,2	64,8	352
UK	2 483	154	49	42,8	34,0	271
Rates proposed	1 271	17	17	19,5	52-54	340

[1] The taxes on cigarettes comprise a specific excise duty, the rate of which is given here for 1 000 cigarettes, an *ad valorem* duty and VAT, the rate being shown here as a percentage of the retail price. The proposals of the Commission, referred to above, also comprise a specific as well as an *ad valorem* element (the sum of the *ad valorem* duty and of the VAT). The latter could be between 52 and 54% of the retail price according to the level retained in each country for the normal rate of VAT taken from the range 14 to 20%.

General economic consequences. It should be remembered that the approach adopted by the Commission is designed to limit as far as possible, given the differences in the initial situation, the budgetary consequences of its proposals for the maximum number of Member States. Accordingly, subject to the rate which Member States choose within the ranges proposed for VAT, the net budgetary effect could be broadly neutral in the large majority of countries. Exact quantitative estimates would have to take account of the effects of changes in demand which tax and price changes may generate (operation of price elasticities), the effects on frontier trade, the effects specific to certain sectors more immediately concerned (notably those whose products are subject to excise duty) and, lastly, the macroeconomic stabilization mechanisms (where a net budgetary effect is produced which has not been offset by other measures). Taking such effects into account would in general reduce the initial impacts. However, since Member States are free to decide how to make the necessary tax adjustments between now and 31 December 1992, it is impossible, at this stage, to evaluate all the economic consequences of these proposals.

Subject to these qualifications, it seems probable that three Member States (Belgium, Italy and the Netherlands) would manage to keep the same level of indirect tax revenue. One Member State (France) would suffer a slight loss, whereas three Member States (Germany, Greece and the United Kingdom) would see their revenue go up slightly. In two Member States (Denmark and Ireland) there would be a considerable loss of revenue, and in the three others (Spain, Luxembourg and Portugal) there would be a significant increase. Overall, therefore, the budgetary consequences of these proposals will be very limited in seven Member States. In certain cases, however, it might be appropriate to introduce certain complementary measures, for instance to avoid appreciable distributional effects. Also, the Commission has always acknowledged that the difficulties which some Member States could face might justify the granting of certain temporary derogations to avoid jeopardizing the fundamental objective of creating a single European market.

As regards sectoral consequences, it should be noted that in some cases — especially where products are subject to excise duty — specific policies are being pursued (energy, health and environment). These were taken into account in the Commission's proposals as far as possible through the choice of the tax level. Nevertheless, a harmonized tax system should not stand in the way of the coordinated adjustment of such policies.

The benefits of removing tax frontiers. The benefits are, first, the immediate cost savings to enterprises as customs formalities and related administrative costs are eliminated; second, the subsequent price and cost reductions that will result from increased competition.

As regards customs formalities, estimates of their direct costs have already been given (in Section 3.2 above). These estimates do not distinguish between fiscal and other reasons for customs formalities. However, as already remarked, differences in indirect taxation is the most pervasive reason for the maintenance of frontiers.

As regards the competition effect, this does not arise directly for companies or persons who are assessed for VAT. The levying of VAT is already neutral as between domestic and external supplies, just as it will also be under the Commission's proposals for the future. A competition effect will, however, arise directly in the case of 'non-taxable persons' (e.g. cross-frontier shopping by individuals). This will put pressure on non-competitive price levels, especially in heavily-populated frontier regions. It will also be more easily possible for enterprises to conduct arbitrage trade, and so profit from price discrimination practised by suppliers and distributors between countries. The elimination of other types of non-tariff barriers, as well as fiscal frontiers, are of course also important in order to eliminate the non-competitive segmentation of national markets in this way. It is, for this reason, again impossible to distinguish quantitatively between the potential contribution of the different non-tariff barriers in securing the desired change in corporate behaviour into more competitive modes. However, as the extensive analysis (in Part D) of the effects of market integration shows, these competition effects are potentially of very large orders of magnitude.

Thus the major benefit from suppressing fiscal frontiers is not so much, for example, the relatively small resource savings from changing accounting procedures in firms and cutting out frontier delays, but rather the contribution that the complete suppression of frontier halts and formalities could have, together with other factors, in integrating the Community market and thereby forcing all industries into competitive behaviour. The psychological impact alone, of it becoming possible for both enterprises and individuals to drive across frontiers with absolutely no hindrance, can hardly be underestimated.

A third type of benefit would arise from the convergence (within the proposed VAT bands) or the harmonization (in the case of excise duties) of indirect taxes which could, in most countries, tend to reduce the distortions introduced into the relative prices of goods and services by widely different rates of tax. The measures proposed by the Commission are far from the theoretical optimum where all expenditure would be subject to a single rate. They are, however, a step in that direction, and this implies welfare gains for consumers (such gains could in principle be quantified, but to do this one would have to know which rate within the VAT bands Member States consider to be the best). In practice, of course, governments should discourage excessive consumption of certain products — e.g. ones that are harmful to health — through taxation. Part of such taxation is warranted in economic terms by the negative external effects on a country (cost of accidents, care, illness, etc.). In other cases the State may consider, however, that households may not be sufficiently aware of the advantages of consuming certain goods or services (education, health, housing, etc.). It may then choose to encourage such consumption by acting on prices through taxation (e.g. VAT at a reduced rate). Yet when the differentiations introduced into prices by taxation start to multiply they become less justifiable, much less transparent and less effective. Such practices may also foster forms of secondary protectionism (encouraging or discouraging certain types of consumption, depending on whether or not the goods consumed are produced in the country) which clearly involves a loss of consumer welfare.

Fourthly, the removal of tax barriers may produce a greater credibility and predictability of indirect taxation policy for firms and individuals. Investment choices and competition in the various Community markets will be less affected by uncertainty as to the evolution of the main indirect taxes. While Member States lose a degree of autonomy they had in setting tax rates, there is some counterpart for each country through elimination of the risk that other countries manipulate such taxes for defensive or quasi-protectionist purposes.

Overall, the benefits of removing tax frontiers are, essentially, inseparable from those resulting from the removal of all the other barriers to the large market. The various barriers reinforce each other, especially where they are a shelter for market segmentation practices, as can be seen from the large price differences between Member States. As the price surveys show (see Section 7.1) indirect taxation (VAT plus excise duties) accounts for only about a quarter of the average dispersion of consumer prices among Member States. At all events, the removal of tax frontiers will contribute significantly, through greater competition and more transparent conditions, to attaining the objective of reducing prices in the Community to competitive levels.

Direct taxation of businesses. The Commission's proposals focus on the removal of barriers to the free movement of goods and services and do not cover the taxation of businesses. This taxation will be dealt with in a communication which the Commission intends to publish soon and which will seek to fit the various proposals still pending before the Council into a modern taxation framework that will encourage economic efficiency and facilitate investment and innovation. This approach is the necessary complement to achieving an economic allocation of resources and activities within the large market. It is all the more necessary because completion of the internal market implies that capital markets will be completely opened. In this respect, the harmonization of capital taxation will become much more important, since the elasticity of capital movements in relation to differences in taxation will increase very significantly as those movements are liberalized.

Commission (1987): Proposals concerning the approximation of rates and the harmonization of the structure of indirect taxes

A. Completion of the internal market: approximation of indirect tax rates and harmonization of indirect tax structure. Global communication from the Commission (COM(87) 320 final of 4 August 1987).

B. VAT

1. Proposal for a Council Directive supplementing the common system of value-added tax and amending Directive 77/388/EEC (COM(87) 321 final).
2. Proposal for a Council Directive completing and amending Directive 77/388/EEC — Removal of fiscal frontiers (COM(87) 322 final).
3. Draft proposal on the introduction of a VAT clearing mechanism for intra-Community sales (COM(87) 323 final).
4. Proposal for a Council Directive instituting a process of convergence of rates of value-added tax and excise duties (COM(87) 324 final).

C. Excise duties

1. Proposal for a Council Directive on the approximation of taxes on cigarettes (COM(87) 325 final).
2. Proposal for a Council Directive on the approximation of taxes on manufactured tobacco other than cigarettes (COM(87) 326 final).
3. Proposal for a Council Directive on the approximation of the rates of excise duty on mineral oils (COM(87) 327 final).
4. Proposal for a Council Directive on the approximation of the rates of excise duty on alcoholic beverages and on the alcohol contained in other products (COM(87) 328).

4. Industry case-studies

The short case-studies in this chapter cover mainly six branches of industry: foodstuffs, pharmaceuticals, automobiles, textiles and clothing, building materials and telecommunications equipment. This sample is already of considerable size, amounting to 43 % of total industrial output and 13 % of the economy's total value-added. The industries were, however, specially selected as representing a wide range of situations according to variables that are most relevant in assessing the likely impact of the internal market programme, notably where:

(i)   barriers to internal trade are slight (textiles and or important (telecommunications equipment);

(ii) transport costs are slight (pharmaceuticals) or important (building materials);

(iii) economies of scale at the European level are slight (clothing) or important (automobiles);

(iv) technology is 'low' (clothing) or 'high' (telecommunications equipment);

(v)   tastes are relatively homogeneous (automobiles) or heterogeneous (foodstuffs);

(vi) the internal market policy is linked with external trade policy hardly at all (building materials) or to an important degree (clothing);

(vii) government procurement is slight (foodstuffs) or important (pharmaceuticals and telecommunications equipment).

A feature common to five out of six of the industries is the importance of differences in technical regulations in hindering market integration. The findings thus confirm the pervasiveness of this type of barrier. In several cases, these problems appear to be relatively benign in imposing limited extra costs (clothing, pharmaceuticals, building materials). However in other branches, notably telecommunications equipment, policies on norms are a matter of strategic importance to the industry's future in world-wide competition.

It is also confirmed that the government procurement issue is of very major importance to selected industries (pharmaceuticals and telecommunications equipment) but a minor matter in other industries covered here.

Several cases point to the importance of policies that are often viewed as being at the edge rather than the core of the 1992 internal market objective. This concerns competition policy with respect to discriminatory marketing practices (pharmaceuticals and automobiles), and certain external trade policies that rely upon national frontier controls for their implementation (clothing and automobiles).

A further widespread finding concerns implications for the strategic organization and world-wide competitivity of European enterprises. In several cases it is clear that European enterprises are not so strongly positioned and rationalized with respect to the European market itself, compared to multinational firms from the United States, Japan and some EFTA countries (as in foodstuffs, pharmaceuticals, and telecommunications equipment). European firms would need therefore to adapt their business strategies very fast in the next few years, in order to avoid losing shares in an integrated internal market.

A widespread finding is that the size of the potential economic gains from achieving a more competitive integrated market — are usually much larger than a narrow, technical measure of the costs of identifiable barriers.

The chapter concludes with a brief consideration of the agricultural, steel and energy sectors. While these cases have not been the subject of special studies, the particuliarity and importance of their market regimes is such that they should not be ignored. Together they account for about 11 % of the economy's total value-added. In the case of agriculture, in particular, there is now available a considerable number of economic analyses of types that are consistent with the methodologies being used elsewhere in this study.

4.1. Food-processing industry

In 1985, the food-processing industry accounted for 4 % of the value-added of the economy (3 % for agriculture). Food products, beverages and tobacco are the leading manufacturing sectors in the Community in terms of employment and value-added. The products covered by the MAC study represent some 18 % of European households' total consumption of agricultural and food products (i.e. 67 billion ECU out of a total of 377 billion ECU in 1985): biscuits, ice-cream, chocolate, beer, mineral water, pasta, soup, baby-food, non-alcoholic beverages and spirits.[1]

The principal barriers to trade. There are a number of different barriers in the food-processing sector (see Table 4.1.1):

(i)   restrictions on the use of specific ingredients (for example, the ban on aspartame in non-alcoholic beverages in France). Products containing such ingredients cannot be consumed in the country concerned;

(ii) regulations relating to content and its description (for example, the purity law on pasta in Italy). Products affected by such regulations may be imported and sold but may not use the generic term describing them;

(iii) packaging and labelling; for example, compulsory use of recyclable containers for non-alcoholic beverages in Denmark;

(iv) tax discrimination; for example, specific taxes on beer in the United Kingdom and Italy. In the United Kingdom, the method of calculating the wort excise duty on beer favours national producers at the expense of importers;

(v)   specific import restrictions; for example, health regulations in the United Kingdom, or in Spain.

---

[1]   In order to avoid any confusion due to the Community's enlargement, it should be noted that these figures relate to EUR 7 (Belgium, Denmark, Germany, France, Italy, the Netherlands and the United Kingdom).

Table 4.1.1.

Non-tariff barriers in food processing

	Number of barriers recorded	As % of total
Specific import restrictions	64	29,4
Labelling, packaging	68	31,2
Ban on specific ingredients	33	15,1
Rules governing product descriptions and their contents	39	17,9
Tax discrimination	14	6,4
Total	218	100

Source: MAC.

In recent years, a number of new non-tariff barriers have been introduced. For example, Spain brought in legislation relating to registration on health grounds when it joined the Community. In Italy, 150 municipalities now prohibit the use of plastic containers for mineral water and non-alcoholic beverages, thereby penalizing importers because of the transport costs involved and favouring local producers, who use glass containers. However, the 1979 'Cassis de Dijon' judgment put a first stop to the introduction of new non-tariff barriers. At that time, the Court of Justice introduced the concept of 'mutual recognition and equivalence' and the Commission is now watching over the applications of this principle more actively than in the past.

The impact of removing non-tariff barriers (see Table 4.1.2). The direct economic effects of removing non-tariff barriers are an immediate reduction in costs. The scale of the effect has been estimated by MAC, which made an assessment of the size of the market by 1992 and the reduction in production costs associated with the removal of barriers. Overall, the net direct benefit from the elimination of non-tariff barriers has been put at between 500 million ECU and 1 billion ECU per year. This is between 1 % and 2 % of the turnover of the food-processing industry or between 2 % and 3 % of the sector's total value-added.

The direct benefits come from three different sources:

(i) The use of less expensive ingredients. In Italy, for example, the consumption of pasta produced with common wheat has been prohibited since the 1960s. Yet pasta made with a combination of durum and common wheat costs between 10 % and 15 % less to produce than that made exclusively with durum wheat. Experts believe that the removal of this non-tariff

Table 4.1.2.

Economic effects of the removal of non-tariff barriers in food processing

Barriers	Countries concerned	Direct benefit (million ECU per year)	Indirect benefit		Increased trade	Total benefit (million ECU per year)
			Increased competition	Restructuring (million ECU per year)		
1. Purity law on beer	D, GR	15 to 20	M	L (90 to 215)	+5%	105-235
2. Purity law on pasta	I, F, GR	35-100	M	M	M	35-100
3. Aspartame	F, B, E	0-10	S	S	S	0-10
4. Vegetable fat — chocolate	all except UK, DK, IRL	190-235	M	S	S	190-235
5. Vegetable fat — ice cream	D, F, GR, L	75-100	M	M	S	75-100
6. Recycling of containers	DK	<1	L	M	+5%	<1
7. 'Wort' tax on beer	UK, B, IRL, NL, L	<1	M	S	+0,1%	<1
8. Health regulations	E	<1	S	S	S	<1
9. Bulk transport	all except UK, NL	<1	S	S	M	<1
10. Saccharine	I, E, GR	20-45	M	S	M	20-45
11. Chlorine	UK, IRL	<1	M	S	M	<1
12. Labelling	E	<5	S	S	S	<5
13. 'German' water	D	<1	M	M	L (+2 to 3%)	<1
14. Plastic containers	I	15-50	M	M	+5%	15-50
15. Double inspection	E	<1	M	L	S	<1
Other (200 barriers)	all countries	0 to 200	S	S	S/M	0 to 200
Total		350-775	M	S/M	M	440 to 975

L = large.
M = moderate.
S = slight.
Source: MAC.

barrier would permit penetration of the Italian mixed pasta market amounting to between 10 % and 20 % of total pasta consumption in Italy, giving a saving of between 20 million and 60 million ECU by 1992. If the calculation of these benefits is extended to other countries in which the situation is comparable to that in Italy, we arrive at an aggregate benefit for the Community as a whole of between 35 million and 100 million ECU per year.

(ii) The reduction in packaging and labelling costs. These costs are generally relatively slight but may be significant in some special cases; for example, the ban on the use of plastic containers in Italy for mineral water and non-alcoholic beverages represents an overall cost of 115 million ECU.

(iii) The removal of bureaucratic obstacles to imports. In Spain, for example, imported spirits are subject to double inspection on importation; the cost of these checks is equivalent to 1 % of the value of spirits imported into Spain.

The direct benefits are very heavily concentrated on 10 products. Some 80 % of the total benefit to be derived from removing non-tariff barriers is thus concentrated on six barriers (see Table 4.1.2).

The indirect economic effects stem from the increase in competition which restructuring will ultimately entail. For example, the repeal of the purity standards for beer in Germany should bring about a reorganization of production in this sector, in which 75 % of all European breweries are operating at present. The opening up of the German market will encourage amalgamations and mergers between German producers and will also promote imports from other Community countries. The likely growth in the average size of breweries in Germany should lead to an appreciable fall in production costs, amounting to between 3 and 7 % of the German beer industry's value-added. Finally, once balance has been achieved, intra-Community trade could well grow appreciably. There could then be an increase of beer into Germany and of pasta into Italy amounting to between 3 and 5 % of domestic consumption, compared with the current negligible level of such imports. Consumers will at all events have a wider choice of products.

However, MAC has not been able to put figures on the likely effects of the restructuring of the food industry and the creation of truly European-scale industrial groups for all food products: economies of scale, specialization, improved learning curve. The removal of non-tariff barriers should lead to appreciable changes in the strategies pursued by food-processing companies.

Strategic aspects of a changing food-processing industry. Over the last 10 years, nearly 100 major acquisitions and mergers have occurred in the food-processing industry (involving assets in excess of USD 50 million). The world's food-processing industry is currently in a phase of consolidation and groups operating on a worldwide scale are in the process of being created.

American companies occupy an important position in this sector: the 10 largest food-processing groups (with the exception of Unilever and Nestlé) are American companies. These companies have pursued a twofold strategy over the last five years: on the one hand, they have specialized in products for which they have the largest market share and on which they therefore earn the best return; on the other, they have achieved economies of scale by obtaining the highest possible volume of production through geographical diversification.

By contrast, European companies generally operate on a much more limited geographical scale. Of the 46 largest European companies in the food-processing sector, 44 % operate in only one Community country in addition to their country of origin. Only 10 % of these major companies operate in at least four of the largest Community countries. The major European groups are therefore very largely oriented towards their national markets alone.

The removal of non-tariff barriers should trigger a major reorganization process which will promote increased specialization in product areas in which the large European groups are leaders and a wider geographical spread of their activities in Europe.

4.2. Pharmaceuticals industry

The importance of the pharmaceuticals industry for this study lies less in its size, accounting as it does for under 1 % of GDP, than in the fact that governments intervene decisively to influence price levels and conditions governing market access.

The market is characterized by a relatively small group of large multinational companies heavily involved in research (some 60 or so, of which half are of Community origin) and by around 2 000 smaller companies specializing in generic products or exploiting local markets with well-established standardized products (see Table 4.2.1). The industry, therefore, is highly concentrated, with the large companies controlling 70 to 80 % of the market in France, Germany, Italy and the United Kingdom.

While the manufacture of active ingredients is confined to a limited number of sites, their conversion into dosage form is highly decentralized.

On average, national markets are supplied to the tune of:
(i)   43 % by locally based companies (subsidiary of a multinational or purely national company);
(ii) 23 % by imports from other Member States;
(iii) 34 % by imports from third countries, especially the United States and Switzerland.

Basic research is highly centralized and is normally carried out in the multinational's country of origin whereas clinical research is more often than not undertaken in a number of countries.

Consumption patterns for pharmaceuticals differ a great deal from one Member State to another. This is true not only for the level of per capita consumption (see Table 4.2.2), but also for the types of product consumed.

Table 4.2.1.

Production of pharmaceuticals in the EC in 1984

	Number of companies	R&D costs		Total employment (1 000)
		million ECU	as % of sales	
Belgium	80	125	10	10
Denmark	39	65	7	8
Germany	308	1 430	14	87
Greece	90	—	—	3
Spain	370	40	2	32
France	331	1 090	13	66
Ireland	153	15	5	4
Italy	365	380	6	64
Netherlands	47	110	11	10
Portugal	96	—	—	3
United Kingdom	333	910	14	66
EUR 11	2 212	4 165	10	353

Source: Study by the Economists Advisory Group (EAG).

Table 4.2.2.

Consumption and prices of pharmaceuticals in the EC in 1984

	Sales as % of GDP	Sales as % of spending on health[1]	Prices in 1985 EUR 9 = 100	
			inclusive of taxes	exclusive of taxes
Belgium	0,81	8,6	83	85
Denmark	0,50	7,0	140	123
Germany	0,89	11,0	157	148
Greece	0,95	20,2	—	—
Spain	0,81	12,1	—	—
France	0,81	8,8	66	66
Ireland	0,67	8,8	116	124
Italy	0,91	12,4	69	68
Luxembourg	—	—	84	85
Netherlands	0,38	4,1	136	139
Portugal	1,08	18,9	—	—
United Kingdom	0,59	9,6	91	97
EUR 12	0,78	9,5		

[1] Data refer to 1983
Source: EAG study
for prices: Eurostat.

Price differentials are also very marked. For example, the average price level (inclusive of taxes) in Germany in 1985 was 2,4 times higher than in France (Table 4.2.2). A study by Adriaenssens and Sermeus (1987) revealed that, for some products, prices actually differed by a factor of 10. For example, unit prices ranged from 5 ECU in Spain to 47 ECU in Ireland for Zyloric, from 2 ECU in Italy to 18 ECU in the Netherlands for Dogmatil, and from 4 ECU in Portugal to 35 ECU in Ireland for Stugeron. In fact, the countries with the lowest prices are also those with a high level of per capita consumption of pharmaceuticals. These disparities cannot easily be explained since the demand for pharmaceuticals is often price-insensitive, at least directly.

The main barriers to market entry exist in the shape of a registration requirement in each Member State and price controls. In principle, national registration procedures are similar, notably as a result of action taken by the Commission to harmonize legislation. For instance:
(i)   technical requirements differ very little from one Member State to another;
(ii) all Member States accept evidence obtained abroad;
(iii) all Member States have introduced a simplified procedure for registering products containing known ingredients; they have all agreed to a maximum 120-day limit for deciding on registration applications.

In actual fact, appreciable differences in judgment still exist between Member States, with multinationals being obliged to adapt to the specific requirements imposed by each national authority. In addition, there are considerable delays in the registration process (up to two years in Germany and the United Kingdom, and up to three years or even more in Italy and Spain).

Freedom to set prices exists only in Germany, and, to a lesser extent, in the Netherlands and Denmark. In the United Kingdom, the profitability of pharmaceutical companies is controlled. In Ireland, prices are actually tied to those charged in the United Kingdom. In France and Belgium, companies are, in principle, free to set prices, but for a pharmaceutical to qualify for the national reimbursement system its price must be approved by the administration. Greece, Italy, Portugal and Spain control the prices of individual pharmaceuticals by the use of cost-plus methods. This system of setting prices, which benefits both consumers and public finances in those countries, has drawbacks for the companies. It also produces discriminatory effects; it is used on occasions to favour local companies and may lead to unnecessary decentralization of particular functions, with resulting losses in economies of scale. Lastly, price differentials between countries may distort markets in ways that are difficult to rectify through parallel imports.

Impact of removing barriers: the direct costs associated with multiple registration are small. According to an estimate contained in a study by the Economists Advisory Group (EAG) with 1984 as the reference year, the extra staff needed cost between 40 and 55 million ECU. Against this, the negative effects of delays in the registration process are more important: first, assuming a rate of discount of 8 or 10 %, the opportunity cost of money tied up in the development of new therapeutic substances amounts to 20 million ECU or 28 million ECU respectively for EUR 12; second, registration delays reduce the effective duration of patents, resulting in a loss of revenue. It is estimated that, in this industry, a patent — which is normally granted for a period of 20 years — has an effective life of nine years, with the resulting shortfall in sales being put at 100 to 175 million ECU. Overall, the cost of multiple registration amounts, therefore, to 160 to 260 million ECU, or 0,5 to 0,8 % of costs in 1984 for EUR 12.

As regards registration, two solutions are possible: automatic recognition by all Member States of the marketing authorization issued by another Member State, or establishment of a single European registration agency. Mutual recognition comes up against the problem of the differences that exist between the registration requirements imposed by agencies in northern Europe and those imposed by their counterparts in southern Europe. By contrast, a single European agency would offer guarantees of impartiality and uniformity of approach, although steps would have to be taken to ensure that it was not more costly than the present system. The EAG study cites the case of the US Food and Drug Administration, which, with a staff of some 1 500, has an administrative cost of 150 million ECU a year, whereas the corresponding figure for the different agencies in Europe, which employ the same number of staff, is between 55 and 70 million ECU.

While the proposed registration system will reduce delays, research will also benefit. In the case of non-patented products, where competition on price is relatively more intense, lower registration costs may stimulate competition.

The existing fragmentation of the market does not seem to have any drawbacks as regards research, which is normally concentrated in the multinational's country of origin. As for production, however, cost reductions can be obtained at the stage when the active ingredients are converted into dosage form. This is because the large multinationals would be able to concentrate the whole of this stage of production for the Community market at a very limited number of sites and to close down their existing plants in the other Member States. This concentration of production would make for a higher rate of capacity utilization, which, in some cases is fairly low at the moment (between one third and a half, according to some US multinationals). Quantifying this aspect is particularly difficult since there is no guarantee that the multinationals will actually close down a number of their plants as this may be politically unacceptable and commercially damaging. The EAG has estimated the effects of possible restructuring of this kind on the basis of two scenarios: in the first, companies close down only a limited number of plants while, in the second, they achieve maximum concentration. At the level of EUR 12, in 1984 the resulting savings in terms of total unit cost were 0,13 to 0,19 %, or 44 to 65 million ECU in the first scenario, and 0,32 to 0,81 %, or 109 to 273 million ECU in the second.

As regards prices, no harmonization is expected in the Community in the immediate future since this will depend on two factors: (i) the way in which national social security systems are administered, and (ii) an equalization of income levels. The Commission has opted for a more progressive approach, in the shape of a proposal for a Directive (COM(86) 765 of 23 December 1986) relating to the transparency of measures regulating the pricing of medical products for human use and their inclusion within the scope of the national health insurance system. Knowledge of the criteria applied by a Member State in authorizing or rejecting an application to raise prices should foster some convergence of price levels.

However, it is evident that one of the main economic effects of market fragmentation in the pharmaceuticals industry is the wide variations in prices between Member States. Even though this can be put down in part to the diversity of arrangements for controlling prices, the magnitude of price variations for a certain number of pharmaceuticals is a strong indication of the weak competition that exists between national markets in many pharmaceuticals. Under such circumstances, it is difficult to identify in advance the average level towards which prices will converge if the present fragmented national markets are effectively integrated. Normally, on an integrated and competitive market, there should be convergence towards an average price level lower than that in a group of fragmented markets. In the EAG study, this aspect was quantified on the assumption that prices in Member States are aligned on the present Community average. With a price elasticity of demand of 0,5, this gives, for the Community as a whole, a fall in consumer or social security spending of 720 million ECU, equivalent to some 3 % of total expenditure. This figure significantly exceeds the costs associated with the trade barriers that exist in the industry.

Integration of pharmaceutical markets in the Community will probably have far-reaching implications for European pharmaceutical companies. A large proportion of the best-placed companies on the world markets are US or Swiss companies. In the Community, the leading German and United Kingdom companies have markets that extend beyond national frontiers; in the other Member States the activities of many companies are at the moment very much geared to their national market.

4.3. Automobile industry

With 6 % of value-added and 7 % of employment in manufacturing, the car industry in the Community plays a major role in the economy. In 1985, the total value of car production in the Community was 72 billion ECU, of which almost half was accounted for by Germany. Community manufacturers export 27 % of their production, with close on 90 % of that figure going to other Community countries. The Community car market is dominated by 10 or so manufacturers. Competition in terms of product differentiation and price is intense. In 1986, seven groups offering full product ranges shared 77 % of the market in Western Europe (Community plus EFTA) (see Table 4.3.1).

By contrast, the components industry is much more fragmented, although a process of concentration is under way. The value of components produced in

Table 4.3.1.

Structure of the European automobile market in 1986

	Sales in Western Europe			Exports to non-Community countries	
	× 1 000	on the national market (%)	Share of Community market	× 1 000	as % of sales in the Community
Volkswagen/Audi/Seat	1 687	53	14,6	378	22,4
Fiat/Alfa	1 625	67	14,1	16	1,0
Ford	1 352	33[1]	11,7	35[1]	2,6
PSA	1 318	49	11,4	146	11,1
GM	1 260	45[2]	10,9	22[2]	1,7
Renault	1 225	57	10,6	110	9,0
Austin-Rover	408	73	3,5	11	2,7

[1] Ford Werke only.
[2] Opel only.
Source: Commission departments.

the Community is equivalent to 61 % of the value of car production and is highest in Germany and France, which account for 42 % and 22 % respectively of Community production.

Car manufacturing processes are becoming increasingly characterized by the use of 'platforms', which combine certain features of a production line and a flexible workshop, permitting both mass production and the production of differentiated products. With only minor modifications to the platform, cars can be produced for different segments of the market. A platform can even be operated with independent manufacturers. This technique can lead to substantial economies of scale.

Main market barriers. The first type of barrier results from the fact that technical requirements for the initial placing into service of vehicles have not yet been fully harmonized in the Community. As a result, manufacturers have to seek type-approval in each Member State and to adapt vehicles to local requirements (e.g. 'dim-dip' headlights in the United Kingdom). A second type of barrier takes the form of delays at customs posts and the administrative cost of processing customs documents. A third type of barrier has to do with differing VAT rates, which are regarded as a major obstacle to trade by Italian, French and United Kingdom manufacturers.

In addition one must consider the so-called selective distribution system, which the Commission authorized in 1985 for a period of 10 years. This is a network of exclusive-dealing contracts concluded by all manufacturers in the Community which, while allowing customers to purchase vehicles in other Member States (where prices are lower), contributes in fact to a reinforcement of the segmentation of markets which follows from the abovementioned factors, as well as from policies regarding imports from third countries.

The segmentation of national markets which results from these factors leads to a high degree of price discrimination. This aspect has been empirically verified by Mertens and Ginsburgh (1985) (see Table 4.3.2) and by Gual (1987). For instance, the same type of car of the same quality was sold in the United Kingdom in 1983 for a pre-tax price 42 % higher than the price charged in Belgium while the average disparity in Italy was, in most cases, close to 30 %. Price disparities between countries have narrowed considerably since then.

Lastly, protective measures have been taken against Japanese competitors in France, Italy, the United Kingdom and Spain. At present, Japanese imports account for less than 1 % of the Italian and Spanish markets, for 3 % of the French market and for 11 % of the United Kingdom market.[1]

Outlook. Completion of the internal market is expected to speed up the present processes of restructuring and technical change, which are affecting car and component production alike.

In the car industry, significant economies of scale can be achieved from the widespread introduction of 'platforms', from their joint use by different manufacturers and from greater specialization in specific types of car. This aspect has been quantified in the Ludvigsen study, which assumed a reduction in the number of 'platforms' from 30 to 21, with an accompanying increase in production per 'platform' (see Table 4.3.3.). This will result, among other things, in increased demand for components, the unit price of which, according to the findings of a survey of the prices of 90 components, could fall as a function of the quantity purchased. The resulting savings in terms of the variable unit cost are as follows:

Type of car:	
Utility	− 3,4 %
Small	− 2,7 %
Lower medium	− 2,9 %
Upper medium	− 1,2 %
Large	− 2,9 %

Assuming that total production remains at its present level but that its composition changes, savings in terms of the total unit cost for the Community as a whole would amount to 5 %, or 2,6 billion ECU. In France and Italy, these cost reductions would be more pronounced (around − 5,5 %) while a figure of − 4,3 % would be recorded in Germany and the United Kingdom. The point must be made, however, that these figures overstate the 'internal market' effect since they are calculated without regard to the technical changes that would have occurred anyway. Even so, as mentioned above, completion of the internal market would be the catalyst for this restructuring process.

---

[1] The effects of import quotas have been estimated by Greenaway and Hindley (1985) in the case of the United Kingdom, and by de Laussel *et al.* (1987) for both France and the United Kingdom.

Table 4.3.2.

**Price discrimination in the automobile industry in 1983
(Price indices: Japanese sales in Belgium = 100[1])**

Country of origin	Country of destination				
	Belgium	France	Germany	Italy	United Kingdom
France	106	122	124	137	151
Germany	111	128	130	143	158
Italy	107	123	125	138	153
United Kingdom	107	123	125	138	153
Japan	100	115	117	129	143
Other	79	91	92	102	113

[1] These indices were obtained on the basis of prices, excluding tax, expressed in a common currency for a sample of 100 makes of car. The authors separated by econometric techniques the gaps observed in two components, one concerning the differentiation of the product, and the other relating to price discrimination, which are not justified by differences in quality. The figures set out in the table concern the 'discrimination' aspect. For example, a German car sold in the United Kingdom is twice as expensive (index 158) as a similar Soviet car ('other') sold in Belgium (index 79).

Source: Mertens and Ginsburgh (1985), p. 163.

Table 4.3.3.

Changes in production structure in the automobile industry

Type of car	1985			1992		
	Number of 'platforms'	Unit production × 1 000	Total production × 1 000	Number of 'platforms'	Unit production × 1 000	Total production × 1 000
Utility	3	110	330	2	160	320
Small	6	440	2 640	4	650	2 600
Lower medium	6	525	3 150	4	800	3 200
Upper medium	6	315	1 890	5	380	1 900
Large:						
model a	6	140	840	4	220	880
model b	3	70	210	2	80	360
Total	30		9 060	21		9 060

Source: Ludvigsen study.

Economies of scale will have dynamic effects: the competitiveness of Community industry will be boosted and more cars will be sold as the lower costs mentioned above work through into prices. In turn, this higher level of production will make for additional economies of scale and will provide a further stimulus to demand. Competition within the Community will probably be keener, and this may lead to mergers and production agreements between groups within the Community and even outside the Community.

As for the components industry, several trends are already discernible: a reduction in the number of suppliers,[1] the elimination by car manufacturers of stocks of components, which, as a result, are being produced to order ('just-in-time' delivery), and close collaboration between car manufacturers and component manufacturers, with the latter assuming greater responsibility for component design. These are trends that will also be conducive to establishment of the internal market.

To sum up, the formal barriers to intra-Community trade in the car industry turn out to have a relatively marginal impact.

Even so, the trading practices of the leading manufacturers have led to significant market segmentation, as evidenced by the price differential for one and the same model on the different national markets. Furthermore, State subsidies have, in recent years, been granted on a very large scale to loss-making manufacturers, notably in the United Kingdom, France, Italy and Spain. Even though subsidies are now less generous or have actually been discontinued, the likelihood is that they represented a genuine constraint on the competitive behaviour of the leading manufacturers.

Furthermore, the effects of maintaining the present system of 'exclusive dealing' beyond its 1995 expiry deadline may be questioned, taking account of the price discrimination observed, together with divergences in the level of purchase tax and restrictions on imports from third countries.

4.4. Textiles and clothing

More so than in several other sectors covered in the present study, a good deal of integration between Member States has already taken place in textiles and clothing. Remaining internal barriers are of relatively small importance to Community producers. However, the internal frontiers that are needed to implement the Community quotas distributed among Member States *vis-à-vis* third countries have the effect that for both Community trade and the consumer the market is far from fully integrated, which may also contribute to the important price differences for the clothing sector in particular.

---

[1] For example, PSA had 2 000 suppliers in 1981 and 1 229 suppliers in 1986 and plans to have 950 by the end of 1988. Renault had 1 415 suppliers in 1985, compared with 900 at the moment. Austin-Rover reduced the number of its suppliers from 1 200 to 700 while, over the last five years, Ford reduced the number of its suppliers from 2 500 to 900.

Over the last two decades a considerable restructuring process has taken place in the textile and clothing sector world-wide. The main causes have been the rapidly increasing exports from developing countries, a slowdown in consumption in the industrialized countries and sustained technological change in the production process, especially in textile production. As a result of the first two factors mentioned, the Community's production of textiles and clothing stopped rising in the mid 1970s. In 10 years (1975-85) employment fell by 38 % in textiles and 40 % in clothing, with a loss of one million jobs. In 1985 the value-added of the textile and clothing industry in the Community (EUR 12) was about 54 billion ECU, and the number of people employed was 2,5 million (EUR 10), that is about 6 % and 10 % of total manufacturing, respectively.

As far as trade is concerned, a distinction must be made between the two major sub-sectors: textiles and clothing. In 1985 intra-Community imports in textile products met about one quarter of EC apparent consumption. Over the period 1978-85 that proportion rose from 19,2 % to 24,2 %. The clothing sub-sector appears to be less integrated, with the import ratio about half the value found for textiles. Incidentally, it is worth mentioning that man-made fibres, normally classified under the industrial branch 'chemicals', show a very high degree of integration: in 1985 almost half the EC consumption was met by intra-Community imports. Intra-Community trade (exports plus imports) accounted for about two thirds of the Community total trade in textiles (and man-made fibres), but less than 50 % in clothing.

Within the Community, Italian producers have substantially improved their relative position at almost all levels of the textile and clothing sector. In textiles, capacity was reduced primarily in France and the United Kingdom, whereas the largest capacity reduction in the clothing industry took place in Germany. In terms of intra-EC export specialization, the leading position is held by Italy in the clothing sector and by Germany in textiles.

Trade barriers. Most of the producers interviewed, in the course of a study undertaken by IFO and Prometeia, reported no complaint about the existence of significant obstacles to intra-Community trade. For dynamic companies it does not make much difference to sell on the domestic market or abroad. An Italian firm even said that there are more difficulties in selling in southern Italy than in Germany or France. The prevailing picture, from the producer's point of view, is that the integrated Community market is not far from being achieved, even though some barriers to trade can still be pointed out. Some companies complained about administrative barriers, time losses at the border, labelling requirements, difficulties in interpreting requirements of the 'country of origin', and different VAT rates.

Costs of barriers. The removal of the remaining trade barriers is therefore likely to have only marginal effects on the industry exports within the EC. In the IFO/Prometeia study, it was estimated that direct unit cost reductions could amount to between 0,1 and 0,3 % for the four large Member States. The indirect cost reductions are also likely to be rather limited: a fall of some 0,3 to 0,6 % in the unit costs of production, with the higher cost savings to be expected in France and the United Kingdom. In the core areas of the European textile industry, (spinning and weaving), considerable specialization has already taken place, and not much progress appears to be left in terms of economies of scale. In the clothing sector, increasing returns to scale cannot be realized to the same extent as in the textile industry. This is primarily due to the fact that the production of clothing does not lend itself easily to mechanization and automation. In part the manufacture of large production runs has been shifted to low-wage developing countries, whereas the European producers have specialized increasingly in the manufacture of high-quality and fashionable products. This requires producers to be highly flexible, to cope with rapid changes in consumer tastes. In the textile market too, the ability to react rapidly to changing market demand has become increasingly important. Thus strategies based on mass production and concentration have become less advantageous. In recent years, the main strategy of the European textile and clothing industries has been, precisely, to raise flexibility and to find profitable market niches.

Although the scope for potential economies of scale at the production level looks rather limited, some gains are to be expected at the marketing stage. There seems to be a tendency now towards more concentrated distribution systems, where, for example, advertising costs can be spread over a larger amount of retail outlets. The removal of the still existing trade barriers will help accelerate this process.

The more competitive environment induced by the completion of the internal market is also likely to favour an increased recourse to direct investment and contracted processing work in low-wage countries outside the Community. France is likely to be affected most by this development, which should result in a reduction of the wage bill corresponding to a decrease in unit labour costs of about 1 %. The effect on German labour costs will be more moderate (0,2 to 0,5 %), and in Italy and the United Kingdom this effect should be negligible.

Market structure and consumer prices. The major sub-sectors covered by the study must be treated rather differently. On the one hand, textiles and even more, man-made fibres, are sectors where products sold on the market are quite homogeneous, economies of scale have been largely exploited, and price competition is relatively fierce. Therefore, any measure which tends to eliminate existing barriers, even if small, is likely to be reflected in final prices. On the other hand, clothing is a sector where many companies aim to capture segments of the market where price is not necessarily the main factor affecting consumers' behaviour (according to the IFO-Prometeia study, some businessmen said that they set prices in the EC within a discretionary range of about 10 % around the net final price). In this case it is not so likely that potential reductions in production costs will be translated automatically into production prices.

The effects on consumer prices of a rationalization at the marketing stage are not clear-cut either. If, on the one hand, the concentration process is based on a sales network relying mainly on large shops, supermarkets, mail order systems, where price competition plays an effective role (in this regard the United Kingdom and Germany are better placed than Italy and France), then consumer price reductions are likely to take place. On the other hand, where systems such as franchising predominate, and the marketing objective is to reinforce the brand image, and therefore the market power of the producer, it is more likely that the gains accruing from the economies of scale will result in higher profits. It is not even certain that reductions in production prices of clothing products will not be absorbed by the retail system, where mark-ups often account for more than half the final consumer price. To that must be added the fact that demand tends to be rather inelastic to price changes.

Internal market and rest of the world. The main barriers to intra-Community trade at present result from the EC quotas that are distributed among Member States, and from those that can be introduced for individual regions of the Community. In 1986 some 70 % of the Community imports of textiles and clothing from third countries were covered by bilateral textile agreements within the Multifibre Arrangement (MFA) of the GATT, or other arrangements. Under this system imports into EC countries are often limited by bilateral quantitative restrictions.

If, on the one hand, the existing commercial policy has created the conditions for a more gradual adjustment of the Community textile and clothing industry, on the other it might have had the effect of keeping consumer prices at a relatively higher level. Differences in the degree of import restrictions in individual Member States are likely to be partly responsible for the large price differentials observed across the Community, since they make commodity arbitrage particularly difficult. Moreover, the enforcement of quotas *vis-à-vis* third countries and sometimes different interpretations by individual Member States of the 'country of origin' rule make border controls necessary for all products, whether they come from a Member State or from the rest of the world. This system of quotas, which imposes an extra cost on intra-Community trade, suffered by European producers and consumers, will thus be incompatible with the abolition of all intra-Community frontiers by 1992.

4.5. Building products

Although the construction sector is often regarded as an example of non-tradeable activity, there are several sub-sectors for which this does not hold true, notably building products, engineering expertise, and large cross-frontier infrastructure works. The completion of the internal market is therefore of some consequence for the construction sector as a whole, whose value-added in 1985 accounted for about 189 billion ECU in the Community.

In 1985 the value of the market for building products alone in the Community amounted to about 110 billion ECU. The largest share (some 42 %) is represented by non-metallic minerals, i.e. cement, lime, plaster, glass, ceramic, bricks and other similar products (see Table 4.5.1). It is therefore apparent that a significant share of the sector consists of goods that to a certain extent exhibit a low value per unit of weight or volume. As a consequence, transport costs can assume particular importance. There are several examples of products used for construction whose price doubles because of transport costs for every 150 km of delivery distance.

Cultural, traditional and climatic factors also affect the way construction works are conceived and constructed. The methods used to build can vary not only across countries, but also at a regional level. These differences are by far the most important in explaining the difficulties met by the European exporters in penetrating the Community market.

Although it is possible that increased trade across Member States is going to reduce those differences, changes are going to be rather slow and their effects are going to be felt well beyond the 1992 horizon. None the less, intra-Community trade is already significant. For the four larger Member States the average import penetration rate ranges between 15 % in Italy and 50 % in the United Kingdom.

Trade barriers. Among the barriers pointed out by the firms interviewed in the course of the study undertaken by BIPE, technical certification is the most important. Seventy per cent of the products covered by the study face some difficulties in order to comply with foreign technical regulations, and in general about 60 % do not meet those regulations. That is primarily due to the great number and to the complexity of technical regulations in the field of construction. The difficulties linked to the need for obtaining technical certification mainly impose administrative costs and delays. As an example, it took about five years for a French producer of girders to obtain the technical certification necessary to sell its products on the German market.

Table 4.5.1.

Breakdown of the branches that supply building products to the construction sector

%

Code	Branches	EUR 6 production
130	Ferrous and non-ferrous metals	9,1
150	Non-metallic minerals	42,4
170	Chemical products	4,5
190	Metal products	13,2
250	Electrical goods	7,0
410	Textiles, clothing	0,9
450	Timber and wooden products	14,5
470	Paper and printing	1,6
490	Rubber and plastic	6,5
510	Other manufactures	0,2
		100,0

Source: Input-output tables 1980, Eurostat.

Germany and France are the countries where the difficulties linked to technical certification are felt more strongly by foreign suppliers. The two countries are mentioned by 85 % of the companies interviewed. In these countries the number of technical regulations is higher, and their influence on the choices of engineers, architects and buyers of building products is larger. Exporters underline that in Germany great attention is paid by construction firms, foremen and consumers to these regulations, such that it is almost impossible to sell products circumventing them. The other countries where barriers linked to technical regulations are found are essentially in the north of Europe, namely the United Kingdom and the Benelux. Southern countries, where fewer regulations exist, often accept foreign technical standards and regulations.

Some of the more discriminating technical regulations and norms stem from the particular environment where the building materials and products are used, and this can vary from one country to the other. This is the case of some electrical appliances, sanitary ware and other products for building interiors. Constraints such as the mains voltage, plug size, water pressure, etc., represent a serious obstacle to the use of such products in an identical form throughout the Community. The removal of these constraints is not just a matter of mutual recognition of technical regulations. It would imply wide-ranging changes in the infrastructure systems of the Member States, which cannot fully be expected by 1992. Standardization through the establishment of technical regulations at the Community level can only be conceived in a long-term perspective, since their acceptance also implies a modification of professional habits and the technical expertise of those involved in the building activity.

The cost of barriers. The direct effect of the removal of the existing trade barriers will be a reduction in the cost borne by European exporters. The harmonization of technical regulations will reduce the costs of obtaining the certifications, and to a lesser extent, cost reductions will result from the removal of customs controls. Reductions in transport costs would also affect trade positively. In the BIPE study, the resulting cost reduction has been estimated at 0,7 % of the sector's total production value for the four large Member States (820 million ECU for the Community as a whole). The effects of these cost reductions should be more noticeable for Italian firms, only moderate in France, and weaker in Germany and the United Kingdom. The indirect effects of the removal of barriers are estimated at 1,7 billion ECU for the five large Member States, or 1,7 % of the value of production in 1985. The detailed results for the five countries covered by the study are shown in Table 4.5.2.

The completion of the internal market will require a change in the attitude of many European enterprises in this sector. With reinforced competitive pressure, the more dynamic and adaptable companies will strengthen their international strategies, through an increase in their size and a rationalization of marketing policies. Shifts in the location of production between Member States will play a less important role, because over the medium term most companies will tend to privilege the penetration of foreign markets through the establishment of subsidiaries. Companies will face two broad strategic choices:

Table 4.5.2.

Building products: indirect effects on prices of the removal of barriers

	D	F	I	UK	E	Total
1. Change in price level	− 1%	− 4%	− 2%	0	− 2%	− 1,7%
2. Production in 1985 (billion ECU)	36,8	16,9	22,6	14,0	11,2	101,5
3. 'Gains' in billion ECU (1 × 2)	− 0,37	− 0,68	− 0,45	0	− 0,22	− 1,72

Source: BIPE.

one characterized by a supply of products with an advanced technological content and with relatively high unit prices, and the other where production is concentrated on medium or low technology products, favoured by relatively undemanding technical regulations. The mutual recognition of regulations in respect of basic requirements, partly neglecting the burdensome technicalities of the northern countries, would favour companies from the less stringently regulated regions.

4.6. Telecommunications equipment

The value of the Community telecommunications equipment market in 1986 is estimated at almost 17,5 billion ECU, or almost 0,5 % of Community GDP. The three main segments of this market are: (i) that for switching, or central office equipment, which switches traffic along the network and which account for some 47 % of the market; (ii) transmission equipment, including cables, microwave transmitters, antennas and satellites (13 %); and customer premises equipment, handphones, telexes, private exchanges (24 %). Other equipment, including mobile radios, accounts for 15 %.

The sector is not only growing rapidly but changing rapidly. As a consequence of the introduction of the new digital systems of sending traffic along the networks, the sector is now converging with that of data processing and stimulating a wide range of new customer premises equipment which exploits the new medium. As a result the level of non-voice traffic is growing about three times faster than that for voice telephony. These new digital systems are known as integrated services digital networks, or ISDNs.

Historically, telecommunications networks were considered to be a prime example of a natural monopoly in which the enormous fixed cost of investment in the network contrasted with the low marginal cost of use of the network.

So national telecommunications authorities became the norm; these maintained monopoly control of access to the network, operating as monopsony purchasers of equipment whose technical standards they determined and procured from designated national suppliers. As a result of this a unique system of barriers to trade in telecommunications equipment has been maintained within the Community, so that intra-Community trade is only a fraction of extra-Community trade, economies of scale are low compared with major competitors and traditional comparative advantage is falling rapidly. Among the main barriers to intra-Community trade are: those of different technical standards, especially for switching equipment; selective procurement policies, usually involving a limited number of domestic suppliers; strict control by certification of products, including those which customers are authorized to attach to the network; and, input specificity whereby new equipment must conform technically to the standards of existing capital equipment and which acts as a barrier to entry and exit from the market.

The result has been a continued fragmentation of the internal market. While one quarter of total Community product is exported only a third of such exports are destined for other member countries. Whereas Community exports amounted to almost 4 billion ECU in 1986, with a surplus of 1,2 billion ECU, this surplus had fallen from 1,5 billion ECU in 1984, while a large and growing sectoral deficit was recorded with the US and Japan.

Fragmentation of the internal market is particularly evident in the market for central office switching equipment, where development costs of each system are now estimated at about 1 billion ECU, almost 80 % of which may account for software development. Different technical standards have resulted in such software costs being replicated over five times by Community equipment producers. Economies of scale are also affected by low levels of output compared to the USA and Japan, as national procurement agencies order from fragmented domestic production units. Even the largest equipment markets in the Community account for less than 5 % of the world total, compared to 38 % in the USA and almost 9 % in Japan. A typical European plant for switching equipment produces 1 million lines annually: this compares to an American plant which produces 7 million lines.

Economies of scale for transmission and customer premises equipment are lower than for switching, but are both significant and increasing due to a greater degree of international specialization and recent technological advance. Convergence of the services sector with computers further increases the potential advantages of a greater degree of integration and risks penalizing further the smaller, fragmented Community producers of telecommunications and EDP equipment.

Community proposals. One of the main objectives of the Community Green Paper (EC Commission, 1987) is that for completion of the internal market for telecommunications equipment. This involves a range of policy recommendations, including the opening-up of public procurement to other Community suppliers. The paper requests an almost complete opening up for customer premises equipment and a far greater degree of openness in the supply of core equipment. As a result of Community-wide publication of tendering, certification of terminal equipment on a Europe-wide basis, full mutual recognition of type approval, allied to the creation of a European Telecommunications Standards Institute, it is hoped to achieve a minimum 40 % opening of the Community equipment procurement market by 1992.

The introduction of such measures should result in a number of static and dynamic benefits. Economies of scale should increase considerably as a result of standardization and the stimulation of greater competitiveness in open procurement markets. The falling specialization of the Community on international markets could be halted. Investment in a broad range of terminal equipment based on the new technologies and a greater degree of competitiveness could be stimulated. A more competitive market structure should extend outwards the demand schedule for this 'learning industry' (see Section 6.1). Inefficiencies resulting from protected national procurement policies should be reduced.

Estimated costs of non-Europe in telecommunications equipment. The benefits from completing the internal market has been estimated by J. Müller. He has estimated the cost on the equipment side for two main scenarios: firstly, a status quo scenario where current trends continue; and, secondly, based on the Green Paper, a comparative scenario allowing for the effects of standardization and with two levels of procurement liberalization, one at 40 %, the other at 100 %. A summary of the results is shown in Table 4.6.1.

Table 4.6.1

Possible gains in the telecommunications equipment sector from actions under the Green Paper scenario

billion ECU

Product	Effects of standardization		Supplementary effects from procurement liberalization			
			40%		100%	
	Static	Dynamic	Static	Dynamic	Static	Dynamic
Central office switching	0,25/0,5	0,2	0,8	:	1,3	0,5
Transmission	:	0,2	0,4	:	0,5	:
Customer premises equipment	:	0,1	0,4	:	0,7	0,3[1]
Other	:	0,1	0,4	:	0,7	0,2[1]
Total	0,25/0,5	0,6	2,0	0,2[1]	3,2	0,5[1]

[1] Market expansion effects.

Source: J. Müller; and W.S. Atkins (public procurement study).

Thus, the gains from standardization (because of better exploitation of economies of scale) are estimated at 0,85 billion ECU to 1,1 billion ECU. The additional gains from competitive procurement are estimated at 2,2 billion ECU under the 40 % scenario and 3,7 billion ECU under the 100 % scenario. So, totalling all effects, these can vary between 3 billion ECU and 4,8 billion ECU, depending on the degree of openness of the procurement market.

Due to a sharp increase in international competition in the sector and rapid developments based on a fundamental change in technology the diseconomies of maintaining a fragmented Community market are increasing, as the potential benefits of completing the internal market are also increasing.

4.7. Particular market regimes: agriculture, steel and energy

4.7.1. Agriculture

The White Paper calls for two types of action in the field of agricultural policy in order to permit the suppression of frontier controls: the harmonization of veterinary and phytosanitary rules, and the elimination of monetary compensatory amounts in order to re-establish common support price levels. The latter raises, however, the broader issue as to the level at which the present different prices should converge.

The harmonization of animal and plant health requirements is necessary both to eliminate obstacles to trade and to strengthen the system for controlling diseases of live animals and plants. Of the 300 measures envisaged in the White Paper, no less than 74 concern veterinary or phytosanitary regulations. By end December 1987 the Commission had submitted 34 proposals to the Council of which 17 have been adopted. It is proposed that before 1992, as a first step, all controls concerning intra-Community trade be transferred inland. Controls of the products shall be limited to the place of departure, whereas the verification of certificates will be made at the place of destination.

The most important actions concern live animals and fresh meat. Harmonized rules on the use of hormones and antibiotics take effect from 1989. Common requirements for slaughterhouses and the storage and transportation of fresh meat exist, but need to be extended in their application. Common actions are being stepped up to eliminate diseases such as swine fever, tuberculosis, brucellosis and leukosis. Common regulations for live poultry will be proposed in 1988, and common health rules for heat-treated milk will take effect in 1989. For cereals, Community legislation on pesticide residues adopted in 1986 means that major restrictions on trade are being eliminated in this sector.

Common agricultural support prices are established in ECU[1] for the Community as a whole. However, these are largely theoretical prices, since they are

---

[1] The value of the ECU used in the CAP ('Green ECU') is 13,7 % higher than the value of the real ECU.

converted into national currencies used by intervention agencies at the so-called 'green' rates of exchange which differ from 'green' central rates. Hence national support prices, when converted into ECU at central exchange rates, can differ significantly by country and by product. As of end December 1987, the highest support price levels, on average[1] for all products, prevailed in Germany and the Netherlands (7 % above the Community's effective average) and the lowest prices prevailed in the United Kingdom and Greece (12 % and 38 % respectively below the Community's average). Prices in France and Ireland are closest to the Community's effective average being 0,4 % above. Inter-country price differentials for individual products are even more striking. In the representative case of cereals, for instance, support prices in Germany are 8 % higher than in France and Ireland, 26 % higher than in the United Kingdom and 64 % above Greek prices.

In order to sustain these different price levels, a system of border taxes and subsidies, called monetary compensatory amounts, operates.

These taxes and subsidies, as shown in Table 4.7.1 by product and country, approximate in amount the support price difference mentioned above.[2] At present, only three countries (Belgium, Luxembourg and Denmark) have green rates at levels which do not require such border taxes or subsidies to be levied on agricultural trade. This system will be clearly incompatible with the suppression of internal market frontiers, and it is therefore relevant to note the economic effects of eliminating monetary compensatory amounts.

These border taxes and subsidies are receipts or expenditures of the Community budget. In 1987 the net cost of these transactions in respect of intra-EC trade was relatively small: 207 million ECU. This does not reflect, however, the full economic impact of these measures.

The economic effects of price differences maintained by monetary compensatory amounts may be analysed in terms of familiar trade policy concepts, notably their denial of the principles of comparative advantage and avoiding an optimal allocation of production resources. Producers in high-price countries gain at the expense of producers in low-price countries, and there is a net loss of welfare for the economy as a whole. (Graphically, this was illustrated in Figure 2.1.)

However, the larger question affecting any such considerations concerns the price level at which common support prices should converge if monetary compensatory amounts would be eliminated. This question cannot be simply answered. On the one hand certain rules, adopted by the Council and concerning the gradual elimination of monetary compensatory amounts, point to a conver-

---

[1] Weighted by 1986 production values.
[2] In principle, monetary compensatory amounts are equivalent to the differences between actual prices and the theoretical common price, reduced by a franchise of 1 % for the Netherlands and 1,5 % for all other countries.

Table 4.7.1.

Agricultural monetary compensatory amounts for countries and products, in %, applicable from 28 December 1987

	Beef	Milk	Pork	Sugar	Cereals	Eggs/poultry	Wine	Olive oil	Average by country[1]
D	0,0	1,4	0,0	0,0	1,0	0,0	0,0	0,0	0,5
NL	0,0	1,4	0,0	0,0	1,0	0,0	0,0	0,0	0,5
BLEU	0,0	0,0	0,0	0,0	0,0	0,0	0,0	0,0	0,0
DK	0,0	0,0	0,0	0,0	0,0	0,0	0,0	0,0	0,0
F	− 1,0	− 3,5	0,0	− 3,5	− 3,5	0,0	− 1,0	0,0	− 2,3
IRL	− 2,0	− 3,5	− 2,1	− 3,6	− 3,6	0,0	0,0	0,0	− 2,7
I	− 4,2	− 4,2	− 1,6	− 4,2	− 5,3	− 1,8	− 1,4	0,0	− 3,3
UK	− 8,4	− 15,8	− 10,9	− 17,5	− 17,5	− 14,0	0,0	− 9,0	− 14,4
GR	− 45,9	− 45,9	− 37,5	− 35,6	− 35,6	− 32,1	− 32,1	− 26,2	− 37,1
Community average[1]	− 2,5	− 3,9	− 1,8	− 4,0	− 6,7	− 3,5	− 1,4	− 9,9	− 3,7

[1] Average weighted by 1986 production values.

Note: Prices in Denmark, Belgium and Luxembourg are sufficiently close to the theoretical common prices that no monetary compensatory amounts are applied. Portugal and Spain are excluded from the table because transitional arrangements relating to their accession result in further temporary differences from the theoretical consumer price level.

Source: Commission of the EC.

gence of prices at the high end of the existing range. On the other hand, the Community's broader policy strategy, and most clearly that proposed by the Commission, is to move common prices progressively closer to underlying world market prices, and to lower prices (or adopt other analogous measures) where production or budgetary expenditure exceeds target levels.

Given this range of possibilities for the medium-term evolution of common prices, it is relevant at least to note the sensitivity of the economic gains or losses of producers, consumers and tax-payers to hypothetical changes in support prices. Estimates for a standard 10 % price reduction, available from simulations conducted on a model of the common agricultural policy by K. Thomson of Aberdeen University, are reproduced in Table 4.7.2. A net gain to the economy of 6,8 billion ECU (0,2 % of GDP) is indicated, with the important and divergent consequences for the consumers and taxpayers, who would gain by a larger amount, and producers who would experience substantial losses. The size of these redistributive effects is, of course, an important reason why it is difficult to secure agreement on significant price changes.

Agricultural policy has probably been the subject of more economic analysis recently than any other sector. International comparisons have been made by the OECD (1987) which evaluate the total impact of policy intervention in the Community for the period 1979-81 at a 43 % producer subsidy equivalent

(PSE) on average for all products, or between -4 to -24 % consumer subsidy equivalents (CSE) for major products. In this study, the PSE has been defined as the payment that would be required to compensate farmers for loss of income resulting from removal of a given policy. The CSE is related to the value of consumption and corresponds to an implicit tax on consumption resulting from a given policy. A review of different studies of the economic costs of agricultural policy in the industrialized countries by Winters (1987) offers several estimates in terms of consumer and taxpayer losses, producer gains and net impacts on economic welfare. The typical result for the Community stresses the large transfer effect from consumers and taxpayers to producers of the order of 3 % of GDP, and a smaller but significant loss to economic welfare as a whole of less than 1 % of GDP, due to the fact that not all the full amount of the costs paid by consumers and taxpayers results in extra income for producers. These studies of the total impact of agricultural policy, as opposed to the sensitivity analysis cited earlier, relate to an extreme and politically implausible 'anti-monde' hypothesis of eliminating all public price or income support in this sector. As such, they should be viewed only as points of reference that offer some parameters for scaling the possible effects of policy reforms of different amplitudes.

For the purpose of the calculations assembled in Part E, and in the light of the considerations indicated above, alternative assumptions, both conservative ones, have been made as regards the medium-term adjustment of prices. In the minimalist case no change in prices is assumed; in the other case there is 5 % price reduction.

4.7.2. Steel industry

The structural crisis in this sector, which has given rise in particular to a great deal of spare capacity, has required a policy of restructuring which has now been pursued for some 10 years. The Community has opted for an orderly run-down of obsolete and unprofitable production capacity, together with a modernization policy and a policy for monitoring the installation of new capacity. Where necessary, this policy was supported by State aids, whose allocation was strictly controlled within the framework of procedures established, for the purpose, in the form of an aids code.

In order to make it possible for firms to continue their restructuring in a suitable commercial climate, two series of complementary measures were implemented:
(i)   internal measures, in the form of production quotas (Article 58 ECSC) and, in certain cases, the setting of minimum prices (Article 61 ECSC);
(ii) external measures involving the search for bilateral agreements with the principal trading partners (while respecting the GATT regulations) for the voluntary limitation of imports and for the maintenance of import prices at the same level as those effective internally.

Table 4.7.2.

Changes in economic welfare resulting from a 10% average agricultural support price reduction in EUR 10, 1986 (billion ECU)

	Producers[1]	Consumers[2]	Taxpayers[3]	Overall[4]
Cereals	− 2,5	+ 0,8	+ 1,3	− 0,4
Milk	− 3,3	+ 3,7	+ 2,4	+ 2,8
Meat and eggs	− 3,5	+ 4,3	+ 1,3	+ 2,1
Sugar	− 0,7	+ 0,5	+ 0,2	0
Total[5]	− 10,7	+ 9,6	+ 7,9	+ 6,8

[1] Taking account of lower feed costs for livestock product producers.
[2] Excluding EC agricultural consumers of cereals amounting to two thirds of total domestic consumption.
[3] Reduction in price-guarantee expenditure net of import and producer levy revenue.
[4] Sum of producer, consumer and taxpayer effects plus losses assumed for non-modelled products.
[5] Including all products.
Source: Estimates made by K.J. Thomson, Aberdeen. For a description of the model used, see K.J. Thomson: 'A model of the common agricultural policy' *Journal of Agricultural Economics,* May 1985.

The aids code, in its original form, expired at the end of 1985, and the only authorized aids that remain are those relating to the closure of an undertaking. The quota system, the coverage of which in terms of products has been progressively reduced between 1986 and 1988, continues to be applicable for a certain range of sensitive products so as to allow the firms concerned to pursue their restructuring and rationalization efforts within an orderly commercial climate. Agreements relating to imports with certain third countries have also been maintained.

This restructuring policy has already made its mark on labour productivity, technical competitiveness and profitability. The reduction in production capacity has been large (31 million tonnes between 1981 and 1986) which has permitted the achievement of a capacity utilization rate of some 70 %, a distinct improvement on the situation in 1980, and during the years 1982-83, when capacity utilization rates averaged 50 %. However, the capacity problem has not yet been resolved since, in the Commission's opinion, there are still some 30 million tonnes of spare capacity.

The approach taken and the social back-up measures have mitigated the social repercussions of iron and steel plant closures, which would otherwise have been even more dramatic.

One direct effect of the restrictions on Community output and imports into the Community has been the maintenance of a price level higher than the equilibrium price under the conditions of unfettered competition, and, in any case, higher than the 'world price'. It should, however, be noted that world market prices for specific purchases do not necessarily always reflect the cost to the producer and that they are normally lower than the internal prices effective within the Community, in Japan or in the USA. Internal prices within the Community are, on the other hand, traditionally the lowest of the prices to be found in these three large iron and steel-using zones. In fact, if the EC price index is set at 100, prices in Japan equalled 125 in 1985 and 120 in 1986, while those in the USA equalled 136 and 102 respectively, a situation which clearly favours the competitiveness of the European metal- working industries *vis-à-vis* its largest industrial competitors.

It is, obviously, very difficult to predict the equilibrium price in the medium term for steel products when the present Community market regime is completely or partially reserved, given that international prices do not necessarily constitute an adequate reference point. The sensitivity of costs for certain steel-user branches of the economy is shown, on an illustrative basis, in Table 4.7.3 which is based on the assumption of a reduction in the price of steel that reduces the differential between internal prices and international prices to 10 %. Although this calculation does not take account of all the indirect effects of such an assumption, the impact observed is relatively weak. In the metal products industry, which is the largest user of steel, the impact on prices is of the order of 1,5 to 2 %.

For the purposes of the senstivity analysis calculated in Part E, two hypotheses regarding the medium-term price of steel were retained, both assuming a progressive elimination of production quotas. In one scenario it was assumed that there were no price changes; in the other, the reduction in prices was put at 5 %.

4.7.3. Energy

In 1985 fuel and power products as defined in the national accounts (coal, coke, oil and oil products, natural gas, nuclear fuels, electricity) accounted for about 8 % (509 billion ECU) of Community total production. It is therefore a major sector, which raises important issues of internal market policy. Consumption patterns in terms of energy sources differ considerably between countries. For example, in 1986 nuclear energy accounted for 21,7 % and 32,8 % of total gross energy consumption in Belgium and France respectively, whereas it was only at 1,8 % in Italy and the Netherlands.

From the point of view of the internal market a rough distinction can be made between energy distributed via networks (electricity, natural gas) and energy, or more precisely, fuels, which are more or less freely traded on the market place (oil, solid fuels). Whereas the first category is characterized by the existence of monopoly suppliers, in the second case the economic environment is usually more competitive.

There are, none the less, examples of obstacles to competitive trade even in the latter case. In the case of oil for instance, some countries still operate national marketing monopolies, although on a diminishing scale, and others

Table 4.7.3.

Direct effects (as %) on the main steel-using branches of a variation of 10% in the price of steel[1]

	D[2]	F	I	UK
Cars	0,5	0,5	0,4	0,5
Metal products	1,8	0,9	2,0	1,5
Construction	0,2	0,1	0,4	0,1
Electrical equipment	0,5	0,1	0,3	0,2
Agricultural and industrial machinery	0,5	0,5	0,8	0,5

Source for basic data: Input-output tables 1980, Eurostat.

[1] The calculation involved multiplying the price differential (10%) by the share of the inputs of steel products in the branch in question with respect to its output.
Headings 135 (iron and ECSC products) and 136 (non-ECSC steel products) in the input-output tables were used in determining the steel industry's share of the output of the user branch concerned.

[2] Data not comparable with data in other countries since inputs of steel products are classified together with inputs of non-ferrous metals.

retain price controls or import licensing systems. Different national specifications for oil products, concerning sulphur and lead content, or other technical characteristics such as the viscosity and density of the products, are also an element of extra cost for refiners which could be reduced with the adoption of common standards at the Community level.

The coal sector is subject to Community (ECSC) rules governing State aids to the coal industry. These rules aim to limit such aids strictly in terms of volume, purpose and duration. The coal policy guidelines, set out in a recent Commission Decision,[1] allow State aid to the coal industry when it contributes to the following aims: (a) improvement of competitivity of the coal industry, contributing to assuring a better security of supply; (b) creating new capacities provided that they are economically viable; and (c) solving the social and regional problems related to developments in the coal industry. Thus, the current principles for national aids to the coal sector recognize the need to take account of the major adjustment problems of the industry, and the social and regional consequences of that adjustment, but are also based on the view that the need for aids should be progressively reduced by taking steps to restore the industry to a state of economic viability. In fact, the financial situation of the coal industry has steadily deteriorated in the last 10 years. Losses and the aid required have risen appreciably. In 1985 the aid granted totalled 3 billion ECU, and in 1986 it amounted to 3,3 billion ECU. In recent years the falls in oil

[1] Commission Decision No 2064/86/ECSC of 30 June 1986 establishing rules for State aid to the coal industry, OJ L 177, 1.7.1986.

prices, the world market price for coal, and the exchange rate of the dollar have been major factors behind these trends.

The problems are of a different nature in the sub-sectors relying on distribution networks, that is the electricity and gas industries. There is a wide variety of organizational structures for the electricity supply industries in the Member States. These vary from very large, publicly-owned undertakings, which account for all or most of the electricity supplied, to systems which rely on a number of large and small public, semi-public or privately-owned companies. In their geographic areas, these enterprises usually enjoy a monopoly of supply. The purpose of such monopolies is, generally, to provide to customers the most economic conditions of supply. The relative lack of trade between regional networks, both within countries and across frontiers, does, however, hinder achievement of that goal. Electricity costs can vary widely between one Member State and another for equivalent categories of consumers. In addition, the choice of fuels for power stations can be affected by national policies, for instance embargoes on nuclear power, or measures to favour the use of nationally-produced coal in the electricity sector. There is, therefore, scope for offsetting these problems, at least in part, by greater recourse to drawing supplies from neighbouring undertakings, including those across borders, and such possibilities should be considered as a serious option alongside indigenous production. This is, of course, only feasible if supplies from other countries can offer the same degree of security as domestic production. This can be achieved by contractual arrangements, established in a climate of confidence between trading partners along the lines of recognized Community principles.

Cross-frontier transfers of electricity already take place between Member States, although a substantial part of it consists of equal quantities exported and imported at differing times (see Table 4.7.4). Net imports or exports are important in the case of some Member States (France, Italy, Luxembourg, Portugal).

An efficient allocation of resources requires that electricity prices reflect true costs in supplying each category of users and avoid discrimination between different types of consumers — an agreed Community pricing principle.[1] In practice pricing policies are such that the distribution of costs between households and industrial consumers differs widely between individual Member States. Some countries tend to favour industry with respect to the household consumer, whereas the reverse appears to be the case for other Member States. The further integration of the electricity industry in the Community requires both increased price transparency and more consistent pricing policies, as well as increased trade through grid interconnections. In the case of natural gas, modifications of the monopoly rights of companies which transport and distribute gas could encourage a certain degree of dissociation between their area of

---

[1] Council Recommendation of 27 October 1981 on electricity tariff structures in the Community (OJ L 337, 24.11.1981).

operation and national frontiers. The resulting increase in price competition could benefit consumers, especially in neighbouring regions, while gas utilities would also benefit from larger markets for their investment planning. As a consequence, energy-consuming industries in certain Member States would cease to be penalized in terms of competitiveness *vis-a-vis* their foreign competitors who can rely on cheaper energy inputs.

An accurate estimate of the economic gains that could be obtained by the removal of the existing trade barriers in the energy sector is a difficult task given the issues at stake. A detailed study on this question has not been undertaken, but would be warranted. The following indications should therefore be viewed as an initial rough impression of the orders of magnitude involved. For oil products the adoption of common specifications at the Community level would reduce refineries production costs. Refiners are at present forced to supply different ranges of products, varying from one Member State to another. The potential cost reductions might be around 500 million ECU. For coal, direct State aids to coal production totalled 3,3 billion ECU in 1986 (EUR 12). This figure only reflects direct costs for taxpayers, and does not take into account the cost of other forms of protection. These may, however, be viewed as implicitly included in some degree in the possible benefits from more extensive linkages between electricity grids and gas networks, beyond national boundaries. The latter would favour a growth in trade of electricity and gas, and an improved use of production equipment. Although such a development would affect only parts of the market, it would none the less create an increased, competitive price discipline, including among the sources of finance for power-generating utilities. Resulting cost reductions might amount to around 8 billion ECU for electricity and gas supplies. To give another perspective on these figures, if electricity prices in countries presently experiencing above Community average prices (see Table 4.7.5) were to be reduced to that average price, savings would total about 6 billion ECU, that is about 5 % of the value of total Community production.

Table 4.7.4.

Cross-frontier transfers of electricity (including trade with some European non-EC countries)

	B	DK	D	GR	E	F	IRL	I	L	NL	P	UK	EUR 12
(1) Balanced exchanges (TWh)[1]	5,3	0,7	14,5	0,3	2,9	7,6	—	1,8	0,4	0,0	1,0	—	61,6
(2) Net import (+)/export (−) (TWh)	−0,2	+1,4	+4,6	+1,2	+1,2	−25,5	—	+22,1	+3,5	+2,3	+1,9	+4,2	+14,2
(3) Electricity demand (TWh)	53,9	28,8	383,7	27,3	119,7	316,8	11,3	199,9	3,8	66,9	21,2	282,8	1 516,3
(4) (2) as % of (3)	0,3	4,5	1,1	4,0	0,9	7,6	—	10,3	78,0	3,3	8,6	1,4	0,8

TWh = kWh × 10^9.
[1] Balanced interchanges consist of equal quantities exported and imported at differing times. The one-way quantities of these exchanges are given in (1) above. The additional net import or export quantities are given in (2) above.

Source: Commission services.

Table 4.7.5.

Ratio of electricity prices to the unweighted average price (EUR 12 = 1) for the 12 capital cities of the Member States[1] for typical domestic and industrial consumers (January 1985) (including taxes, except VAT where deductible)

Consumer sector	B	DK	D	GR	E	F	IRL	I	L	NL	P	UK
Domestic[2]	1,13	1,02	1,05	0,87	0,79	1,03	0,88	1,64	0,81	1,08	0,89	0,81
Industrial[2]	0,94	1,12	0,97	1,16	0,89	0,77	1,13	1,24	0,84	1,10	0,98	0,86

[1] Prices were collected in Dusseldorf, Milan and Rotterdam for Germany, Italy and the Netherlands respectively.
[2] Domestic consumer with annual consumption of 3 500 kWh of which 1 300 kWh at night. Industrial consumer with annual consumption of 10 GWh, maximum demand of 2 500 kW and a load factor of 4 000 hours.

Source: Eurostat.

5. Services case-studies

The service branches covered in this chapter are financial services (including banking, securities markets and insurance), business services (including a variety of professions), surface and air transport and telecommunications services. These branches account for 15 % of the economy's total value-added, over half of all market services, and well over half of those witnessing a large amount of international business.

A common feature of the financial, transport and telecommunications service branches is that the regulatory functions of government, while aiming primarily at prudential or safety objectives, also often tend to limit entry into the market as a side-effect. These restrictions on market access can severely dampen competitive pressures and allow high-price, inefficient suppliers to go unchallenged. The general objective of European market integration in these branches is, therefore, to separate out far more clearly the setting and supervision of prudential and safety standards from the issue of market entry; indeed to assure simultaneously, on the one hand, adequate prudential and safety standards, and on the other hand, high levels of market openness.

The internal market programme is, in effect, an important means for securing this double objective. The starting position in Community countries is, broadly, that adequate prudential and safety standards are assured, but that market openness, competition and low-cost efficiency is often definitely not so. The size of the potential gains from opening these markets, consistent with retaining adequate standards, appear to be quite large.

5.1. Financial services

The financial services sector is of growing importance to the Community economy in terms of output produced (6$\frac{1}{2}$ % of total value-added) and numbers employed (3 % of total employment). The integration of financial markets across Community borders is uniquely important, however, in the sense that it will not only have important effects on the efficiency of the sector itself but also on the efficiency of resource allocation of sectors using financial markets. It will also profoundly influence the conduct of macroeconomic policy, especially when taken with exchange rate commitments as in the European Monetary System.

For the EC as a whole, rather more than half of the total output of credit and insurance institutions serves for intermediate purchases by other industries and only a lesser proportion is accounted for by the final uses by households (20 %). Credit and insurance services accounted in total for about 6 % of intermediate inputs into industry (this figure excludes, of course, interest payments or capital raised). Details by country of these and other measures of the economic dimensions of financial services are given in Tables 5.1.1 and 5.1.2.

Table 5.1.1.

Economic dimensions of the financial services sector (1985) [1]

	Gross value-added as a % of GDP[2]	Employment as a % of total employment[3]	Compensation of employees as a % of total for the economy
B	5,7	3,8	6,3
D	5,4	3,0	4,4
E	6,4	2,8	6,7
F	4,3	2,8	3,8
I	4,9	1,8	5,6
L[4]	14,9	5,7	12,2
NL	5,2	3,7	4,9
UK	11,8	3,7	8,5
EUR 8[5]	6,4	2,9	6,2

[1] Defined in the narrow sense as credit and insurance institutions.
[2] Including net interest payments.
[3] Employees in employment plus the self-employed.
[4] 1982.
[5] This aggregate accounted for 95 % of total Community GDP in 1985.

Source: Eurostat as quoted by Price Waterhouse.

Table 5.1.2.

Economic dimensions of the main financial services branches: insurance premiums, bank loans outstanding and stock market capitalization, as % of GDP

	Insurance premiums[1]	Bank loans[2]	Stock market capitalization[3]
B	3,9	142[4]	90
D	6,6	139	87
E	2,5	99	69
F	4,3	93[4]	52
I	2,2	96	63
L	3,1	6 916	11 980
NL	6,1	130	94
UK	8,1	208	147
EUR 8[5]	5,2	142	104

[1] Average 1978-84.
[2] 1984.
[3] End 1985.
[4] 1982.
[5] Weighted average.

Source: Price Waterhouse.

The present regulatory barriers. In each Community country there is freedom of establishment for foreign banks. However, the conditions under which this may be done differ markedly from country to country. As establishment costs vary substantially across the Community it may be difficult for foreign banks to compete successfully, in many countries, with an existing domestic retail banking network. These difficulties are aggravated in certain countries (for example Italy, and Spain), where there are restrictions on foreign acquisitions or participations in indigenous banks.

While wholesale banking activities are largely unfettered, cross-frontier banking services, at least in certain Member States, would still be hampered, even after exchange controls are removed, by some national banking regulations. For example, certain rules prevent the active soliciting of deposits on a cross-frontier basis. In some Member States there are also limitations which prevent banks from engaging in certain types of financial transaction (notably in securities business), which are permitted elsewhere.

What is needed is for such freedoms as are already enjoyed, sometimes on a rather tenuous basis, to be secured, and for the full scope of freedom to provide services to be made generally available, so that the competitive marketing of these services can take place. The Commission aims to achieve this with the proposed second Council Directive on credit institutions which is the centre-piece of the banking proposals and which was communicated to the Council in February (COM(88)751C). This Directive will be supported by four technical directives and together with them will establish a single banking licence valid for both establishment and freedom of services throughout the Community by no later than the end of 1992. This will be done by harmonizing, to the extent which Member States will have agreed as being necessary, the rules on such matters as capital (starting and continuing), qualifications of managers, control rules, solvency ratios, deposit guarantees and other matters commonly accepted as the precondition for mutual recognition of banking licences. This would effectively create a coherent body of European banking law, at any rate for institutional, as opposed to private, matters.

With regard to insurance there is also freedom to establish throughout the Community although national regulations differ substantially from country to country. With regard to cross-border trade in insurance services, a majority of Member States do not permit foreign insurers to solicit business directly, especially as regarding compulsory insurance. Instead it is required that all insurance contracts be provided by established or authorized insurers. Member States that apply such restrictions to cross-border trade seek to justify them on the grounds of consumer protection.

With regard to the re-insurance market (i.e. where the supplier and the user are both insurers), trade is already almost entirely liberalized.

To complete the opening of insurance to intra-Community competition, the Commission has proposed the second Council Directive on insurance services which has been awaiting adoption for almost 10 years. Given the lack of progress the Commission, in the early 1980s, opened proceedings in the European Court against various countries deemed to be violating the Treaty with regard to the provision of insurance services. The Court's judgment in 1986 stated that the insurance of certain types of risks required the protection of the consumer to be assured, and countries were justified in requiring that such insurers should be authorized. With regard to other risks no such requirements were justified. The Commission was, by implication, required to determine where the frontier between these two types of risk should lie. At the same time for those risks where consumer protection is a major consideration, the Commission was also required to determine to what extent establishment rules should be harmonized and at which point mutual recognition should become effective. Agreement on these points was reached in the Council in February 1988, and this should enable the second Council Directive to be adopted in the near future.

Concerning stock markets and securities a number of directives have already been adopted which coordinate investor's protection, improve market transparency, and facilitate simultaneous listing on the stock exchange of different Member States based on the principle of mutual recognition. In addition, a Directive concerning unit trusts (already adopted, and due to be progressively implemented from 1989) will enable unit trusts established in a Member State and covered by the Directive to market their units throughout the Community. In order to remove the remaining obstacles for brokers, dealers and portfolio managers, resulting from uncoordinated prudential regulations of Member States, the Commission is preparing a proposal for a Directive in the field of investment services. It is intended that this Directive should be adopted in 1989.

Completing the internal market in financial services is also dependent upon the removal of all exchange controls between Community countries. Already the free movement of capital is assured for residents of the United Kingdom, Germany and the Netherlands. However, Belgium and Luxembourg have a two-tier exchange rate system which separates capital from current transactions, and reporting and authorization procedures remain in force for certain transactions. France and Italy are in the process of liberalizing exchange controls, whilst Spain, Greece and Portugal still retain them on an extensive basis.

With the internal market programme in mind, the Commission has pursued a two-stage process for the liberalization of all exchange controls by 1992. The first stage of this process came into effect at the end of February 1987 when liberalization measures were agreed covering the countries mentioned above except Spain, Greece, Portugal and Ireland which were allowed more time to comply with these arrangements. These measures finally liberalized cross-border transactions in unlisted securities, unit trusts, national securities issued on foreign stock exchanges, longer-term trade credits, and allowed for the admission of foreign securities to domestic markets if quoted on a stock exchange. With regard to the second stage, the Commission has now sent to the Council a proposed Directive, the purpose of which is to remove all remaining exchange controls between member countries by 1992. However the Directive will still permit Member States to resort to exchange controls in the case of acute balance of payments difficulties, providing that the prior agreement of the other Member States has been obtained.

Table 5.1.3.

List of standard financial services or products surveyed

Name of standard service	Description of standard service
Banking services	
1. Consumer credit	Annual cost of consumer loan of 500 ECU. Excess interest rate over money market rates
2. Credit cards	Annual cost assuming 500 ECU debit. Excess interest rate over money market rates
3. Mortgages	Annual cost of home loan of 25 000 ECU. Excess interest rate over money market rates
4. Letters of credit	Cost of letter of credit of 50 000 ECU for three months
5. Foreign exchange drafts	Cost to a large commercial client of purchasing a commercial draft for 30 000 ECU
6. Travellers cheques	Cost for a private consumer of purchasing 500 ECU worth of travellers cheques
7. Commercial loans	Annual cost (including commissions and charges) to a medium-sized firm of a commercial loan of 250 000 ECU
Insurance services	
1. Life insurance	Average annual cost of term (life) insurance
2. Home insurance	Annual cost of fire and theft cover for house valued at 70 000 ECU with 28 000 ECU contents
3. Motor insurance	Annual cost of comprehensive insurance, 1,6 litre car, driver 10 years experience, no claims bonus
4. Commercial fire and theft	Annual cover for premises valued at 387 240 ECU and stock at 232 344 ECU
5. Public liability cover	Annual premium for engineering company with 20 employees and annual turnover of 1,29 million ECU
Brokerage services	
1. Private equity transactions	Commission costs of cash bargain of 1 440 ECU
2. Private gilt transactions	Commission costs of cash bargain of 14 000 ECU
3. Institutional equity transactions	Commission costs of cash bargain of 288 000 ECU
4. Institutional gilt transactions	Commission costs of cash bargain of 7,2 million ECU

Source: Price Waterhouse.

Possible reductions in the cost of financial services. Among the several types of economic effects to be expected in theory, as a result of the integration of financial markets, that which is perhaps the most amenable to quantitative illustration is the possible reduction in costs of intermediation by banks, or of providing insurance and other financial services. Such an approach is equivalent to that adopted for other sectors reviewed in Part C. Other types of microeconomic and macroeconomic effects are reviewed, without attempting quantification, at the end of this section.

With this aim in mind, the study undertaken by Price Waterhouse has been based on estimates of the prices of a set of representative financial products, before and after the removal of the regulatory barriers, including the abolition of exchange controls. This approach is clearly different from that adopted in an earlier OECD study on the costs and margins in banking (Revell 1980) where estimates of the latter were largely based on data from the operating accounts of banks. However, given the time scale involved and the original objectives of the Price Waterhouse study, the direct price estimation method was considered more appropriate for present purposes. None the less it must be stressed that this exercise in quantification is extremely difficult to undertake for several reasons. The representativity of any given set of financial products will vary from country to country. It is also difficult to ensure that the prices quoted for a given financial product, in different countries, are strictly comparable.

More fundamentally, when considering the prospects for price reductions, it is hardly possible to separate the likely influence of Community actions to liberalize financial markets from other influences, both domestic and international, that may also be pushing in the same direction (see Baltensperger and Dermine, 1987 for a broad review of these issues). In practice it is best to view all these influences as being mutually supporting, with the Community action representing an important catalyst in the wider process. Such an approach is broadly consistent with the general approach set out later in this study, namely to recognize an important distinction between the direct effects of removing intra-Community barriers on the one hand, and the much larger effects of achieving fully competitive behaviour by enterprises in a large, integrated market. This latter concept embraces national and Community competition policy, as well as the actions provided for under the White Paper.

These important reserves mean that the following quantification exercise can only be regarded as illustrative and hypothetical. However, the resulting figures may be used to help appreciate (a) whether financial integration is likely to have trivial or important consequences for the economy; the latter view is in fact supported; (b) whether there are important differences between countries; this is also supported; (c) whether these inter-country differences can be broadly correlated with known features of economic structure and regulatory policies; there is also evidence of this.

The study by Price Waterhouse was based on the prices for 16 financial products or services: seven banking services, five insurance services and four

Possible impacts on the prices of financial products through completion of the internal market

%

	Theoretical, potential price reductions	Indicative reductions	
		Range	Centre of range
1. Spain	34	16-26	21
2. Italy	29	9-19	14
3. France	24	7-17	12
4. Belgium	23	6-16	11
5. Germany	25	5-15	10
6. Luxembourg	17	3-13	8
7. United Kingdom	13	2-12	7
8. Netherlands	9	0-9	4
EUR 8	21	5-15	10

brokering or securities services. These 16 products are listed and defined in Table 5.1.3. For each of these products current prices were estimated on the basis of surveying a sample of market participants which, when converted into ECU, enabled inter-country comparisons to be made. The average of the four lowest prices was taken to represent a low, competitive price standard for the countries studied. The extent to which financial product prices, in each country, exceed this level is given by the figures in the first part of Table 5.1.4.

These differences are taken to represent a theoretical margin for potential price falls in countries with relatively high prices. Average potential price falls for each financial services sub-sector, namely banking, insurance and securities services, were calculated by weighting together the price data for the individual financial products. These averages for each sub-sector in turn yield a weighted average potential price fall per country for the sector as a whole. From these potential price falls, a substantial margin was subtracted to take account of the high probability that even with the fullest implementation of the White Paper and national and Community competition policies, the resulting market will always fall substantially short of being perfectly competitive and integrated. Thus the law of one price will not be established except for those financial products which are subject to the easiest and least costly conditions of arbitrage (foreign exchange transactions for example). For many products there are inevitable differences in market conditions in terms of risk and custom by country or even region, as well as the likelihood of some remaining degree of imperfect competition. In practice it is impossible to estimate the margin by which the fully integrated Community financial market of the future will fall short of the conditions that would establish the law of one price. A simple hypothesis was therefore adopted, in which the potential margin for price falls

Table 5.1.4.

Estimate of potential falls in financial product prices as a result of completing the internal market

%

	B	D	E	F	I	L	NL	UK
1. Percentage differences in prices of financial products[1] compared with the average of the four lowest observations[2]								
Banking								
Consumer credit	−41	136	39	105	:[4]	−26	31	121
Credit cards	79	60	26	−30	89	−12	43	16
Mortgages	31	57	118	78	−4	:[4]	−6	−20
Letters of credit	22	−10	59	−7	9	27	17	8
Foreign exchange	6	31	196	56	23	33	−46	16
Travellers cheques	35	−7	30	39	22	−7	33	−7
Commercial loans	−5	6	19	−7	9	6	43	46
Insurance								
Life	78	5	37	33	83	66	−9	−30
Home	−16	3	−4	39	81	57	17	90
Motor	30	15	100	9	148	77	−7	−17
Commercial fire, theft	−9	43	24	153	245	−15	−1	27
Public liability	13	47	60	117	77	9	−16	−7
Securities								
Private equity	36	7	65	−13	−3	7	114	123
Private gilts	14	90	217	21	−63	27	161	36
Institutional equity	26	69	153	−5	47	68	26	−47
Institutional gilts	284	−4	60	57	92	−36	21	:[4]
2. Theoretical, potential price reductions[2]								
Banking	15	33	34	25	18	16	10	18
Insurance	31	10	32	24	51	37	1	4
Securities	52	11	44	23	33	9	18	12
Total	23	25	34	24	29	17	9	13
3. Indicative price reductions[3]								
All financial services								
Range	6-16	5-15	16-26	7-17	9-19	3-13	0-9	2-12
Centre of range	11	10	21	12	14	8	4	7

[1] See Table 5.1.3 for definitions of the financial products.
[2] The figures in part 1 of the table show the extent to which financial product prices, in each country, are above a low reference level. Each of these price differences implies a theoretical potential price fall from existing price levels to the low reference level. Part 2 sets down the weighted averages of the theoretical potential falls for each sub-sector.
[3] Indicative price falls are based upon a scaling down of the theoretical potential price reductions, taking into account roughly the extent to which perfectly competitive and integrated conditions will not be attained, plus other information for each financial services sub-sector, such as gross margins and administrative costs as a proportion of total costs.
[4] Observations for consumer credit in Italy and mortgages in Luxembourg were not obtained, and have been represented by mechanical estimates in the calculations of the larger aggregates. The data for institutional gilts transactions in the UK were not available on a comparable basis, and so the figures for institutional equity transactions were used in the calculations.
Source: Price Waterhouse.

was on average reduced by one-half, with some variations, however, for cases of countries where particular circumstances suggested a higher or lower relative magnitude. The resulting indicative price reductions were then surrounded by a margin of plus/minus 5 percentage points, thus offering a range which symbolizes the undoubted margin of error in the calculations.

This scaling down from the theoretical potential price falls also allows for the possibility that when high individual product prices are driven down by competition, there may be some compensatory increase in other product prices (i.e. cross-subsidization between products is reduced).

The summary results for all financial services together, with countries ranked by the magnitude of the indicative price reductions, are as follows:

To give an overall quantitative perspective, the central indicative price reduction for the EC as a whole (8 countries) of 10 % amounts to 21 billion ECU in terms of a static reduction in the cost of financial services to the economy, or 0,7 % of GDP (see Table 5.1.5).

As between countries, Spain can be expected to experience the largest price falls: in an intermediate category lie Italy, France, Belgium and Germany: the lowest price falls would be expected in Luxembourg, the United Kingdom and the Netherlands.

Details of the potential price falls and the indicative price reductions, for each of the three sub-sectors of financial services are given in Table 5.1.4. These estimates suggest that the falls of financial services prices to be expected, on

---

Table 5.1.5.

Estimated gains resulting from the indicative price reductions for financial services

	Average indicative price reduction (%)	Direct impact on value-added for financial services (million ECU and as % of GDP)		Gain in consumer surplus as a result of average indicative price reduction[1] (million ECU and as %of GDP)	
B	11	656	0,6	685	0,7
D	10	4 442	0,5	4 619	0,6
E	21	2 925	1,4	3 189	1,5
F	12	3 513	0,5	3 683	0,5
I	14	3 780	0,7	3 996	0,7
L	8	43	1,2	44	1,2
NL	4	341	0,2	347	0,2
UK	7	4 917	0,8	5 051	0,8
EUR 8	10	20 617	0,7	21 614	0,7

[1] Based on the assumption that the elasticity of demand for financial services is 0,75.
Source: Price Waterhouse.

completing the internal market, differ significantly not only from country to country, but also from sub-sector to sub-sector within an individual country.

In the banking sector, an important distinction may be made between certain retail and personal banking services (such as consumer credit and mortgages), which are naturally least exposed to international competition, and other banking services which are used more by the corporate sector (such as commercial loans and foreign exchange drafts) and which are more easily susceptible to international competition. It may not be surprising, therefore, to observe on the whole a wider range of price differences in the former group of products than in the second.

Some particularly wide price differences are observed for consumer credit, with high apparent prices in Germany and France and the United Kingdom. In Germany this particular product market has not been favoured by the major banks, and the market as a result is rather weakly developed. In France the consumer credit market is highly concentrated and was until recently also subject to credit rationing regulations. In the United Kingdom the cost of consumer credit is also relatively high. The low price indicated for credit cards reflects the fact that there are no fixed annual charges on such accounts and small amounts can often be borrowed, for a short time, with modest interest charges. However, if substantial amounts are borrowed over a longer time then the interest charges become very high and this has recently been the subject of much comment in consumer protection circles.

For the banking products of most importance to commercial clients, particularly low prices are observed in Germany (it is recalled that 'prices' throughout are related to the costs of intermediation, and so do not reflect, for example, the low level of nominal interest rates in Germany). Most other countries find themselves grouped together relatively closely in an intermediate category as regards these product prices. Spain, however, is the major exception. In this case prices are particularly high — indeed, this is so for most financial products. This reflects the heavily regulated and weakly competitive situation which prevailed in Spanish banking for many years, and results, for example, in over-expanded branch networks and high overhead costs. Liberalization measures have now been initiated, but it will doubtless take time for the effects of new competitive pressures to mature into cost reductions. In Italy some banking services appear rather costly, for example, foreign exchange transactions which bear heavy administrative costs, and credit cards for which the market is not yet well developed.

Comparison of prices for insurance is particularly hazardous in view of objective differences that may exist in certain risks (e.g. of theft, mortality) between countries. None the less the broad impression resulting from price differences can be related to features of market structure, regulation and competition. The lowest prices were on average found in the Netherlands and the United Kingdom, which accords with the known depth, dimension and international competitivity of the market in those countries. The highest prices were observed in Belgium, Luxembourg, France, Spain and Italy. Various explanations may be of differing importance for these countries. For Belgium and Luxembourg the insurance markets are highly concentrated and have been substantially protected from external competition. In the case of Luxembourg, the insurance sector thus contrasts with this country's highly internationalized banking sector. In Belgium there is supporting evidence of relatively high overhead costs and profits in insurance. In France it is argued that the cost of public regulatory policies and taxation is relatively onerous, (however, indirect taxes on insurance have been excluded in the price comparisons) and also that the retail distribution system is not so modernized. In Italy the relatively high cost of life insurance is explained by the market for this product being somewhat smaller and less well developed than in other countries. It is also the case that, within Italy, the prices for home and commercial fire and theft insurance vary markedly from region to region and so there may be substantial variations of premiums about the single point estimates given.

In the securities branch, the lowest prices are observed in Luxembourg, Germany and the United Kingdom. In the United Kingdom, costs for large transactions in equities or bonds are particularly low, which accords with the known impact of the 'big bang' regulatory reform, which resulted in increased price differences as between large and small transactions. The large volume of international securities trading in London appears to have resulted in considerable economies of scale. At the other extreme, the prices for large transactions in government bonds are particularly high in Italy and Belgium, both of whose securities markets are characterized by very high volumes of public debt (stocks and new issues) and exchange controls (or, more precisely, in Belgium, the double exchange market) that have dampened the diversification of the portfolios of resident investors. The marketing of public debt is thus subject in these cases to particular economic or regulatory conditions. In Belgium, for example, the banks that market government securities form a syndicate for negotiating the terms with the government. In Italy the market for public bonds has been recently the subject of a decree aimed at making this more efficient and competitive, given the likely pressures that the liberalization of capital movements will bring to bear. In Spain, transaction prices for securities are very high, and this appears to reflect the thin and weakly developed quality of the market to date.

Wider implications of financial integration. The completion of the Community's financial integration is a uniquely important part of the internal market programme because of the extent of other effects on the economy, even if their magnitude cannot easily be estimated.

In a larger, integrated financial market investors will have access to a wider range of markets and financial instruments, and will be able to diversify their portfolios accordingly. In particular the investor will be able to obtain a given return on financial investments for a lower risk, or if a certain risk is acceptable, to obtain a higher return. Similar benefits will be available to the borrower. Given that the borrower must pay a premium to the lender to cover the risk involved, this premium will be reduced to the extent that the borrower can diversify the source of borrowed funds across a number of lenders. Relevant to the importance of this factor, the actual level of financial integration in Europe has been examined in a recent study which analysed the correlation between returns from different investments in various countries (Cho, Eun and Senbet, 1986). The low correlation of the various stock returns observed for the Community countries included in the study points, indeed, to a marked lack of capital market integration as between Member States. Other recent studies (Levy and Sarnat, 1970 and Grauer and Hakansson, 1987) also point to the gains to be made from portfolio diversification and suggest that the returns on a portfolio could increase quite substantially, once internal regulatory barriers and exchange controls are removed.

The completion of the internal market, and in particular the abolition of the remaining exchange controls, will also result in net gains, by ensuring that investment will take place for those projects which have the highest returns, irrespective of the country in which they are located. The capital flows generated by this pursuit of the highest returns should generate forces tending to equalize real interest rates, real rates of return, and so the marginal efficiency of capital throughout the Community. These movements will also increase the output and income of the Community as a whole. The outcome is illustrated, in a simple two-country case, in Figure 5.1.

FIGURE 5.1: **Impact of capital market integration on the level of production and income**

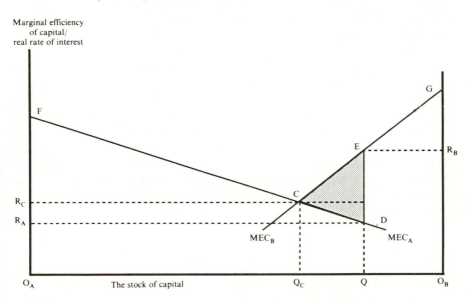

Note: In country A (left-hand axis) investment will proceed until the marginal efficiency of capital (MEC$_A$) equals the real interest R$_A$, at point D. For country B (right-hand axis) equilibrium is at point E. Before trade in capital takes place the national product of country A is given by O$_A$FDQ; the return to capital by O$_A$R$_A$DQ and the total of income from employment by the triangle R$_A$FD. For country B the relevant areas are O$_B$GEQ, O$_B$R$_B$EQ and the triangle R$_B$GE. After trade an equilibrium real interest rate R$_C$ is established and country A exports Q – Q$_C$ of capital to country B where the returns are higher. The national product of the two countries taken together increases by area CDE.

In the context of a fixed (or semi-fixed) exchange rate system, the integration of financial markets, and notably the elimination of controls on capital flows between countries, intensifies the need for a high degree of convergence and coordination in monetary and exchange control policy. As has been argued in detail elsewhere (Padoa-Schioppa *et al.*, 1987), this means in practice that the European Monetary System will need to be progressively reinforced as financial markets are integrated, and capital controls dismantled. A step in this direction was already taken by the Finance Ministers of the Community at their meeting in Nyborg in September 1987.

This linkage to macroeconomic and monetary policy in turn raises the question whether, or how, an intensified coordination, or integration of these policies may deliver gains to the economy. An extensive body of economic analysis has developed in recent years on this issue (see Bryant and Portes, 1987). While the amplitude of the gains from coordination are still debated, there is considerable theoretical and empirical evidence that the effects are likely, where the degree of economic interdependence is very high as in Europe, to be both positive and substantial. In the absence of coordination, macro-economic policy is likely to exhibit a deflationary bias, especially as trade and financial integration intensifies. An insufficiency of macroeconomic policy coordination may even tend to undo the potential gains from the microeconomic integration of financial markets (this is argued specifically by Krugman, 1987). The need for coherence between microeconomic and macroeconomic strategies is argued more fully elsewhere (Section 10.2 and the conclusions in Part A).

A full monetary union, i.e. creation of a common currency, offers further economic gains of a directly financial nature, such as the elimination of exchange rate transaction costs, and economies in the need for external reserves, or gaining possibilities for seigniorage through acceptance of the currency as a revenue by third countries. This topic must, however, lie beyond the scope of the present study.

In general, this short review of the wider implications of financial integration suggests two conclusions: (i) these implications are numerous, complex and important and (ii) on condition in some cases that they are paralleled by improved macroeconomic coordination or monetary integration, the additional effects are likely to add further economic gains, perhaps of substantial orders of magnitude, to the benefits through lower prices of financial services described in the earlier part of this section.

5.2. Business services

The business services sector makes an important contribution to the Community economy, with its value-added accounting for perhaps 5 % of Community GDP, and its output between 5 and 10 % of all intermediate inputs into the productive branches of the economy.

The turnover of business service activities (i.e. excluding local, operational services, functions such as catering, cleaning and security, etc.) has been estimated in the study on business services undertaken by Peat Marwick McLintock (PMM), for Germany, Italy, France, the United Kingdom, and the Netherlands taken together, to be as follows:

Turnover, 1986, billion ECU

Engineering and related services	8
Management consultancy	4
Commercial communications (incl. advertising)	59
Computing services	13
Accountancy, audit services etc.	13
Legal services	13
Research and development	15
Total	125

For many years the business services sector in the Community has witnessed a long-term trend towards the externalization of many such services by companies. This trend, which can be expected to continue, warrants giving particular attention to the market conditions for these services. Results from the PMM study reveal that 40 % of the companies studied had largely externalized these services, and about 70 % had partially done so. Also in 53 % of cases the use of external services had increased over the past five years. The study also showed that small firms (less than 50 employees) show a high degree of internalization. For medium-sized firms, up to 500 employees, the degree of externalization increases. For larger firms the relative importance of externalization appears to decrease again.

Thus externally purchased services appear to play an important role at a particular stage in the life of a company, but they may become less important once firms reach a certain size. It can therefore be argued that efficient, Community-wide networks of business services are of particular importance to those companies that will be seeking to develop their business strategies at a European level, once the internal market is completed. In addition, there are signs that European business service companies display a considerable comparative advantage in world markets (due to technical know-how regarding multinational business environments, linguistic skills etc.) and completing the internal market will further strengthen the sector, so enabling it to perform better in both domestic and overseas markets.

Present regulatory barriers. The PMM study examines the question of regulatory barriers in business services both from the demand (or user) side and from the supplier side.

Users do not, in general, feel that the supply of business services is limited by barriers to cross-border trade. Where such barriers are identified, the following are cited: differences in legal systems and technical regulations, the recognition of professional qualifications, and the effect of exchange controls and other administrative barriers involving a substantial amount of paper work. Financial and administrative barriers were normally regarded as being marginally more onerous than the others.

However, suppliers of business services clearly felt that, for certain activities, trade barriers are of importance. The situation is summarized in Table 5.2.1. The rank-ordering of the individual business services reflects the importance of trade barriers as perceived from the supply side. For engineering and related services there are significant barriers to trade between Community countries. These include problems of technical regulations, recognition of professional qualifications and restrictive government procurement. For four groups of services, commercial communications, computing, research and development, and legal services, barriers are also recognized, for example in government procurement practices and laws governing the media and satellite communications, and these are considered to have a moderate impact on trade.

For certain business service activities, including accounting and management consultancy, trade is conducted to a high degree through international networks or partnerships, formed from different firms in different countries. In these cases trade barriers and differences in regulations are considered to be of virtually no importance. For operational services (catering, security, cleaning, etc.) the issue of trade barriers appears, for practical reasons, to be of no significance.

Table 5.2.1.

Importance of barriers to professional business service activities in the EC market

Business service activity	Nature of the most important barriers	Significance[1]
1. Engineering and related services	Technical standards Recognition of qualifications Government procurement	3
2. Commercial communications	Satellite broadcasting barriers Differences in advertising law and allocation of media time Recognition of qualifications	2
3. Computing services	Government and PTT procurement	2
4. Research and development	Government procurement	2
5. Legal services	Licensing of professionals	2
6. Accountancy, audit etc.	None	1
7. Management consultancy	None	1
8. Operational services	None	1

[1] The numbers have the following meanings:
   3: Barriers considered significant obstacles to intra-Community trade.
   2: Barriers not considered very significant obstacles.
   1: No significant barriers to trade.
Source: Survey conducted by Peat Marwick McLintock.

In addition to the specific barriers listed, more general difficulties such as the high cost of the European telecommunications and air-transport networks are also cited as factors limiting the level of international trade in business services within the Community.

Possible benefits from market integration. The study by PMM offers some tentative estimates of cost savings that could arise as a result of a more competitive market environment for business services. Sources for the estimates include information on the cost structure of certain business service branches, and interviews conducted with a sample of enterprises. The most likely figure was judged to be a 3 % average cost reduction, albeit surrounded by a wide margin of uncertainty. This central estimate would imply savings of the order of 3,5 billion ECU for the Community economy as a whole.

There would also be secondary effects, in the direction of increased demand for business services as a result of these lower costs and prices, and a higher level of economic activity in the Community economy. These secondary magnitudes are even more difficult to estimate. In general the price elasticity of demand for business services is probably relatively low (0,2 %) because of the importance of non-price factors for the users of such services. However the elasticity of demand with respect to income and economic growth is estimated to be much higher (1,4 %).

5.3. Road transport

The total volume of international surface transport in the Community is estimated to be 730 million tonnes. In terms of tonnage the shares of the different modes of transport were in 1986 32 % for sea, 31 % for road haulage, 28 % for inland waterways and 9 % for rail.

In the road transport sector the movement and operation of vehicles throughout the Community is partly restricted, and competition is considerably distorted by different national regulations on capacity and access to the road haulage industry and tariff control. A system of licenses requires hauliers to apply for a limited number of permits in order to move goods between given Member States. In addition there is a general prohibition of 'cabotage', that is the possibility for non-resident hauliers to collect and deliver loads within the boundaries of another Member State.

There is a variety of regimes regulating road haulage within Member States. All countries apply qualitative controls (safety regulations etc.). A survey of six Community countries indicates that some countries also apply quantitative restrictions on market entry, through the restrictive issuance of permits. This is the case in Germany, the Netherlands, France and Italy. The United Kingdom and Belgium do not apply such restrictions. Tariff (price) controls also exist in some countries, notably France, Italy and the Netherlands. However France plans to eliminate tariff regulations by 1991, and in Italy it is considered that there is considerable illegal undercutting of minimum prices, as well as illegal 'cabotage'.

Following the judgment by the European Court of Justice of 22 May 1985 on the common transport policy, the Council has committed itself, by decisions in November 1985 and June 1986, to suppress all quantitative restrictions by 1992 at the latest and in the meantime, to increase the total number of Community-wide permits by 40 % each year and suppress gradually the remaining distortions of competition. The Commission has made appropriate proposals to this effect, however, the decision by the Council is still pending. A proposal on liberalization of 'cabotage' was discussed but not adopted by the Council in December 1987.

A liberalized regime for international road haulage in the Community, including permission for 'cabotage', would also imply pressure in favour of regulatory reform in the more heavily restricted national markets. As the United States example quoted below suggests, this might well lead to very substantial reductions in transport costs for industry and commerce, going well beyond cost savings for international traffic.

By contrast, restrictions on inland waterway transport in the Community are of less overall importance given the fact that Rhine navigation, which accounts for 80 % of the goods carried between Member States, has been liberalized. However, 'cabotage' still has to be fully liberalized in this sector. Sea transport services are subject to certain restrictions on marine 'cabotage'. For both modes of water transport, the Commission has put forward proposals to establish free competition by 1992.

The special nature of the rail transport system largely precludes competition or free market access in international rail transport services. Tariffs on international routes are negotiated bilaterally and the revenue from international rail traffic is shared between the participating national rail companies. The White Paper does not propose measures of liberalization for rail transport.

Costs of road transport regulations. The restrictions in the road transport sector inhibit competition and are likely to prevent an efficient use of transport equipment. As a result, transport costs are undoubtedly higher than would be the case in an unrestricted market, and there are possibilities for monopolistic profits for the holders of limited licences. While comprehensive information on the likely magnitude of these costs is not available, some quantitative indications are available from a number of sources.

The present permit system and prohibition of 'cabotage' is reflected among other things in the costs of empty moves. A study by Ernst and Whinney has estimated, at the Community level, the cost of empty moves at some 1,2 billion ECU, of which some 20 % may be related to regulatory restrictions. A study by DRI Europe (1986) has suggested that the potential market for consecutive 'cabotage' ('cabotage' on the return leg of an international journey) could be about 1,5 % of present domestic traffic.

The shortage of international road transport licences is suggested by the existence of a black market for permits in some countries and the complaints made by road transport organizations. The shortages are particularly marked for multilateral EC permits. One study by Cooper *et al.* (1987) found that in the United Kingdom the black market price of an annual multilateral EC permit was 17 000 ECU, which corresponds to 23 % of a truck's typical annual costs.

The experience of the United States in deregulating the trucking sector in 1980 provides an interesting point of reference. The prior licensing system there was analogous to that still prevailing in the Community. A number of studies provide evidence of increased capacity utilization, lower rates and better service. In a study by Delaney (1987), the savings from improved transportation efficiency have been estimated to amount to the very substantial sum of USD 26 billion in 1985, compared with transport costs of some USD 260 billion. Further cost savings are estimated to result from reduced inventories made possible by increased efficiency in the trucking industry.

For the calculations assembled in Part D, it is assumed, bearing in mind the foregoing information, that road haulage prices fall by 5 %.

5.4. Air transport

Civil aviation is a major and fast-growing industry. In Western Europe, the revenue of 17 major scheduled airlines amounted in 1985 to 31,3 billion ECU, of which 42 % was intra-European traffic (see Economic Intelligence Unit, 1986). In the context of the internal market, the provision of efficient and low-cost air services is important both to the consumer for his direct uses, and for businesses engaged in the European market as a whole. The economic interests of the geographically peripheral regions of the Community are particularly concerned, since uncompetitive air transport aggravates their locational disadvantages, and competition from other modes of transport is less intense.

The regulatory regime. Since the 1946 Bermuda Agreement on international air transport, with the exception of deregulation in the USA in the late 1970s, the economic model of international air services has been mainly one of licensed duopolies. In Europe a system of some 200 separate bilateral agreements between 22 countries has emerged, in which designated carriers provide services whose cost, capacity and conditions are either directly or indirectly regulated. Rights by a Community carrier to offer services between two other Member States, so-called fifth freedom rights, are effectively prohibited: of some 400 routes operated within the Community only 44 tolerate the fifth freedom, of which only one has been granted to a Community airline. In 1987 only 5 % of European routes had multiple designation, i.e. more than one airline per State per route. In a number of cases the revenues on city pair routes are pooled and split 50:50 between both carriers. Price competition is limited, despite various possibilities for discount fares. The large scale ban on new entrants in Europe, except for transatlantic services and charter flights, has meant that even the 'contestable markets' model of oligopoly has not prevailed in the sector.

The White Paper envisages that the Community should move to a more liberalized regime, notably with respect to tariffs, capacity controls and access to the market. After lengthy negotiations, the Council agreed in December 1987 to an initial 3-year package covering air fares, capacity access to the market and the application of the competition rules of the Treaty to civil aviation. As regards bilateral capacity control, the ranges accepted by the Council move from the initial 50:50 rules to a 45:55 range in the first two years, followed by 40:60 in the third year. On fares, the package ensures that regulatory authorities at one end of a route will no longer be able to reject arbitrarily lower fares put forward by innovative airlines; a range of new discount and cheap discount fares and conditions are to be introduced. On market access, greater competition will be achieved by allowing a greater number of airlines to compete especially on dense traffic routes; links between hubs and regions will be expanded considerably, and certain fifth freedom rights will be exercised by airlines within the Community.

Within the context of a single internal market for services, it is regrettable that intra-Community tariffs should be based on outdated IATA exchange rates, whereas periodically adjusted exchange rates based on the ECU would reduce many existing distortions in demand patterns.

Within the context of the 1992 objective of completing the internal market, the next stage would achieve greater competition by limiting significantly the interventions by governments on fare approvals, capacity constraints, and route licensing. In addition, the development of a Community air transport market will require a common approach to negotiations with third countries on air transport issues, including traffic rights.

Costs of market restrictions. The main result of the regulatory regime prevailing so far has been inefficiences in resource utilization and a loss for consumers. While the nationalized European firms have recorded profit levels far below those of private industry, costs were far higher than for US airlines during the early 1980s. Almost half of available seats have been flown empty, except over the North Atlantic, and relatively small aircraft (though this situation may be changing in the late 1980s) offering lower-scale economies, widely employed. A study by R. Pryke (1987) provided many instances of the unproductive use of staff and equipment by European airlines compared to US companies, even after corrections have been made for such objective differences as fuel costs, size of aircraft and length of haul. Continued high costs are attributed to a lack of pressure on scheduled airlines to cut costs because of a lack of competition. During the period 1978-82, the costs of international services in Europe were, on average, 60 % higher than international services in North America. Data also show that corrected costs for European carriers per available tonne/kilometre were over 50 % higher than for US carriers' domestic services. Unadjusted maintenance costs were 119 % higher, administrative overheads 365 % higher and ground and passenger service costs 315 % greater. Five leading US carriers flew their narrow-bodied aircraft 8,33 hours per day, compared to 6,7 for five top European carriers. Salaries of cabin crew in regulated European airlines were also relatively higher than in the US. European civil aviation is characterized more by inefficiencies on the cost side than high profitability. In 1985, a relatively good year financially for the airlines, the average operating profitability ratio of operating revenue to expenditure excluding interest for 17 leading European airlines was only 5,1 %.

A report on air transport in Europe by *The Economist* (1986) estimated the variable costs of flying a similar route length to be 20 % higher in Europe than in North America, while ticket costs were, on average in 1986, 35 to 40 % higher. The conclusion was that an increase in competition in Europe would allow a reduction in tariffs by 15 to 20 %.

The calculations assembled in Part E assume a 10 % reduction in civil aviation costs and prices in the hypothesis of a competitive civil aviation market in Europe — a substantial figure, but still a conservative one in the light of the foregoing studies.

Lower prices would help increase load factors in the industry. The often unquestioned argument that demand for business travel is inelastic seems quite questionable, especially for smaller businesses whose trading activities beyond national frontiers should be particularly stimulated by the completion of the internal market (see inset as an example).

Liberalization in practice: a regional example

In May 1986, the Irish Department of Tourism and Transport designated a new private airline to offer service on the Dublin/London route. A substantial reduction in the fare to just below IRL 100 return, which was matched by the main carrier, had the effect of an increase in traffic on the route by some 29 %, or 200 000 extra passengers between May and December 1986, a considerable number of these being small businessmen. A survey conducted in autumn 1986 showed that some 30 % of passengers on this route indicated they were travelling entirely as a result of the lower fare.

5.5. Telecommunications services

The telecommunications services sector plays an increasing role in determining the competitiveness of marketable services and manufacturing industry in a modern society. Community PTT revenue from the service sector totalled over four times that for equipment in 1985, at 63 billion ECU. By comparison in the US the sector is twice as big as in the Community. Voice telephony accounted for 85 to 90 % of total PTT telecommunications revenue in 1985, with up to 10 % deriving from facsimile and up to 5 % from telex.

With the arrival of the new digital signalling and switching systems, telecommunications are increasingly converging with the digital technology of electronic data processing. The process will be greatly enhanced with the imminent introduction of the integrated services digital networks (ISDNs), sometimes called the 'global digital highway'. As von Weizsäcker (1987) observes, digital telecommunications are now doing for the computer what the railway network did for the steam engine: they likewise do for information transfer what transport infrastructure does for trade in physical goods. Telecommunications will thus play a major role in promoting the integration of the Community economy by 1992.

The change over to digital forms of traffic will not only allow the interlinkage of a wide range of monitors, computers and high-speed printers, but will have a major effect on the structure of the telecommunications system itself. In the opinion of many sectoral experts, growth of data, text and image transmissions should continue to grow at a multiple of that for voice transmissions so that it should bypass the value of the former within 20 years.

The traditional market structure that was suitable for voice telephony is not the most suitable for newly emergent network services known as 'value-added services' or VANs, such as data banks, electronic mail and electronic data interchange. International voice telephone services are provided jointly by national administrations. Except for transit traffic, there has been little effective international trade of a competitive nature in these services. However, the new value-added services now open up the way to international trade and specialization based on cost advantage, efficiency, innovation and, to a lesser extent, economies of scale in the national network.

As noted in Section 4.6 on equipment, the typical structure of the operating authority is one based on the 'natural monopoly' model due to high fixed investment in the network. Recently in the UK, USA and Japan a degree of competition, deregulation on long-distance services, and privatization has been introduced. But generally in Europe, national PTTs maintain their monopoly on access to the network, determining what range of services is provided and forbidding large subscribers who rent 'leased lines' from arbitraging any spare capacity to another user. For example, in one Member State the national broadcasting and railway authorities have substantial spare capacity on their leased lines but are contractually prevented from selling this to other firms.

In exchange for a legal monopoly on service traffic the PTTs shoulder social obligations, such as the provision of universal services. The cost of linking outlying rural regions to the network is traditionally subsidized by profits on heavy routes and on long-distance calls. But there are a number of developments which now makes the traditional market structure less suitable. New technology has considerably reduced the cost of long-distance traffic and the introduction of new value-added services is being severely handicapped by current restrictions on network use. The new range of sophisticated equipment and service possibilities may only be achieved under less restricted market structures. Finally, competitor economies, especially the USA, are liberalizing their service sectors to stimulate greater international competitiveness and innovation.

Telecommunications are similar to computers in that they constitute a classic case of a learning industry where competitive structures unburdened by taxes are most conducive to market growth. Von Weizsäcker argues (1987) 'such distortions in tariff structures act as an indirect tariff on inter-State trade within the common market ... and are incompatible with the goals of the common European market'. The introduction of a more rational tariff-based policy, (i.e. cost-based) would also reduce the likelihood of 'cream skimming' of the most profitable traffic by new entrants in case of liberalization, a possibility frequently advanced as an argument against network liberalization.

If the telecommunications services sector is to maximize its contribution to the integration and competitiveness of Community industry, it is becoming increasingly apparent that a more appropriate institutional structure is needed. Existing restrictions on network-user and service-producer freedom must be reduced to a minimum, and the current policy of cross-subsidization at the expense of long-distance traffic revised. A comparison of long-distance rates shows that in many instances, intra-Community cross-border traffic can cost more than longer distance calls within a country. In any community charges should be related to duration and distance and treated as if part of the domestic system.

Community proposals. The main objective of Community policy as set out in the Green Paper (CEC, 1987) is to ensure that Community industry derives the maximum benefit in terms of cost, quality and variety from the full development of the sector. To this end, a number of actions have been initiated, in particular, the RACE advanced communication research programme which has now been adopted; the proposals for introduction of common ISDN standards within the Community; the STAR programme for helping less-favoured regions by improving access to advanced telecommunications services; directives on mutual recognition of type approval and on the first phase of opening up access to public contracts; a European Telecommunications Standards Institute and, finally, conditions for open network provision.

The Green Paper accepts that the role of national administrations in the provision of basic network infrastructure, especially voice telephony, should be maintained. But a distinction is drawn between such 'reserved services' as voice telephony and 'competitive services', especially value-added services. Unrestricted provision of such competitive services between Member States is proposed, as well as requirements for interoperability and access to transfrontier service providers. Liberalization should be introduced in such a fashion as to minimize the risk of 'cream skimming' referred to above. The Commission believes that the general principle that tariffs should be cost-related can be achieved by 1992.

Estimating the costs of non-Europe. An attempt to quantify the costs of non-Europe in telecommunications services has been made in the study of J. Müller. In order to place current policy options in perspective Müller has analysed three scenarios: firstly, a status quo scenario, where it is assumed the recommendations of the Green Paper were not made but other developments still take place; secondly, one based on current provisions of the Green Paper; and, thirdly, a scenario of full network competition in long-distance and international transmission, but excluding competition in the local loop (e.g. that for local calls). A number of telecommunication costs are considered:

(i)   Open competition for equipment procurement (as discussed above in Section 4.6) could lead on its own to a reduction in tariff levels of between 2 and 8 % depending on current national procurement policies. If, on average, tariffs were reduced by 5 %, the effect of extra network demand could lead to increasing economies of scale and fill (i.e. using available network to a higher capacity) which could yield savings of 0,75 billion ECU per annum.

(ii) More competitive conditions for the 'non-reserved services' would offer several kinds of benefit. Harmonization of standards for terminal equipment and networks should reduce barriers to entry, increase market growth, stimulating learning and scale effects. A liberalized equipment certification programme, with mutual recognition of standards, could also increase network use. Resource savings of 0,5 to 0,7 billion ECU would be possible. Further liberalization of the value-added services market, as proposed in the Green Paper, would stimulate additional service offerings and further network use. It would also reduce the importance of geographic space as a barrier to the spreading of the new service industries in the Community. Benefits resulting from extra network use are estimated to be between 0,3 and 0,5 billion ECU by 1990. The availability of open network provision could further encourage the growth of VANs and increase the above benefits by 0,2 billion ECU by 1990.

(iii) Moving tariff structures closer to costs would cause users to make more allocatively efficient decisions and increased network utilization. The static welfare losses of the current tariff structure are estimated at up to 10 % of call revenue or 4 billion ECU.[1] These estimates do not allow for the effects of current tariff restrictions on user and producer freedom regarding arbitrage and 'cream skimming' which Müller estimates to be considerable.

Alternative analyses rely upon comparisons between some EC Member States, and between the EC and Canada, and these confirm that there are big differences between levels and rates of growth of productivity not explained by scale. If increased network competition or improved regulatory policies could reduce such 'X-inefficiencies', Müller estimates that productivity growth rates,

---

[1]   This compares to the estimate of DM 2 billion, or almost 10 % of the value of the domestic German voice market in 1979 by K.H. Neumann, U. Schweizer and C.C. Von Weizsäcker, published in 'Welfare analysis of telecommunications tariffs in Germany', edited by J. Finsinger, *Public sector economies*, MacMillan Press, London 1983. Meanwhile von Weizsäcker (op. cit.) estimated the welfare loss of non-cost pricing of the expected market for value-added services to build up to some DM 10 billion by the year 2007.

currently of the order of some 2 % per annum, could accelerate by a further 0,5 to 1 percentage points per annum, which could imply cumulating gains of 0,6 billion ECU per year.

The conclusions of the detailed estimates contained in the Müller paper are briefly summarized in Table 5.5.1. These indicate that the potential economic gains of the Green Paper scenario could be of up to 2 billion ECU. Extending the estimates to cover a more ambitious, but technically feasible, degree of network competition for long-distance and international traffic, a further 4 billion ECU of economic gains might be achieved.

Table 5.5.1.

Effects of regulatory reforms for European telecommunications services

Measures	Minimum Green Paper effect	'Full network competition' effect[1]
1. Lower equipment costs (as described in Section 4.6) lead to lower tariffs and thereby economies of scale and fill in the network use	0,75 billion ECU per annum savings[2]	Slightly larger
2. More competitive 'Non-reserved services'		
a. Easier CPE certification, increased product variety, lower CPE prices, larger network use	0,5 to 0,7 billion ECU savings	Not estimated
b. Liberalization of VANs	0,3 to 0,4 billion ECU savings by 1990	Larger, because fewer network restrictions
c. Open network provision	0,2 billion ECU savings by 1990	Not estimated
3. Tariff reforms (closer to cost)	Not estimated	4 billion ECU p.a.

[1] For long-distance and international traffic.
[2] These gains exclude the direct savings on equipment purchases, which are accounted for in Section 4.6.
Source: Study by J. Müller.

Part D

The effects of market integration

The analytical framework used for studying the cost of non-Europe has clearly shown how important are the assumed indirect effects and how difficult it is to quantify them. Completion of the internal market will induce a series of integration effects which will promote the efficiency and competitiveness of Community firms through two channels — market size and increased competition.

This chapter seeks to analyse these effects in more detail, in each case explaining, on the basis of a number of horizontal studies, the potential gain and the economic mechanisms which can lead to part of that potential being realized. To illustrate the various mechanisms at work, Figure 6.1 below shows the interconnections between the principal effects.

The removal of non-tariff barriers results directly in the reduction of initial costs, as was analysed and explained in Part C with regard to certain barriers and industries particularly concerned. Lower initial costs have an impact on prices and margins and spread through the whole economy via a corresponding reduction in the cost of intermediate consumption in the various fields of economic activity. But additional mechanisms are set in motion by the barriers being removed: the constraints imposed on economic activities by the small size of markets are removed and, at the same time, the spur from competition is increased. The sequence of effects thus becomes more complex, since it unfolds simultaneously through two channels — size and competition — whose mechanisms may mesh or clash depending on the circumstances.

Thus the initial reduction of costs and prices is translated into an increase in domestic and external demand and, hence, in the volume of goods and services produced. At the same time, removing barriers and opening up all markets increases the possibility of arbitrage and so reinforces the pressure — both effective and potential — of competition. Faced with the prospect of increased demand and greater competition, firms will have to allow in their strategies for both the opportunities and risks arising and will have to influence what variables they can. The expected economic effects can be divided primarily into three groups:

(i)   lower costs resulting from economies of scale and learning, made possible by the larger volume of output and by restructuring processes;

(ii) the pressure of competition on prices should lead (mainly in the formerly protected sectors) to a reduction in price cost margins and to incentives for firms to increase their technical efficiency by minimizing their costs (X-inefficiency) so as to maintain their margins;

(iii) increased competition should also have non-price effects, firms being encouraged to improve their organization, the quality and range of their products and, in particular, to engage in process and product innovation.

In short, after a process of adjustment to the new circumstances, the various economic linkages described have productivity and competitiveness effects which can considerably improve the welfare of both consumers and producers and, hence, the general macroeconomic situation. It is nevertheless very difficult to provide a single, exact assessment, despite the fact that the main economic effects of completing the internal market stem from this integration process.

The assessment is complicated partly because size and competition effects are closely linked and reinforce each other to such an extent that one ought to investigate a situation in which they arise simultaneously. However, to facilitate presentation, the two types of effect are discussed separately. The first chapter examines size phenomena, its first section describing the potential for cost reductions as a result of economies of scale (through larger markets and units of production) and economies of learning, while the second section discusses the relationship between the development of trade and economies of scale. The gains in technical efficiency resulting from market integration can thus be assessed. The second chapter discusses the effects of competition. These show up first in prices. Price levels vary considerably between the Member States. Firms are therefore encouraged to reduce their margins to the levels imposed by competition and do something about their costs. The available theoretical and empirical evidence is discussed. The following section analyses the relationship between competition and innovation. It is shown, in particular, that opening up frontiers should, through increased competition, have strong dynamic effects on innovation and technological progress. However, whether these various effects do in fact materialize depends to a large degree on the behaviour of firms. The third chapter discusses how firms see the opportunities provided by the internal market and then analyses their possible response strategies.

At each stage, the mechanisms at work and, where possible, the potential economic effects are highlighted. However, the numerous interrelationships make it difficult to perceive the totality of effects. Finally, by way of illustration and for perspective, a partial equilibrium economic model describing the effects of European integration is proposed. Since it incorporates all the mechanisms described above and makes it possible to measure their relative importance, this provides a very useful basis for the overall evaluation attempted in Part E.

FIGURE 6.1: **Integration and the effects of size of markets: schematic presentation**

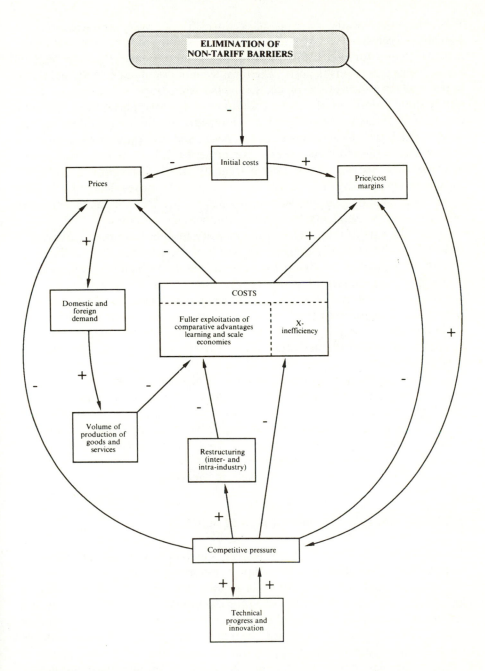

Note: The sign '+' indicates an increase.
The sign '−' indicates a reduction.

6. Integration and the effects of market size

The completion of the internal market which will bring an expansion — sometimes considerable — of the market in which enterprises do business, provides scope for increasing the size of operations, and this can lead to considerable reductions in costs. The term 'economies of scale', used generally to describe the effects of size on costs, covers a wide range of phenomena, from purely static economies of a technical nature to dynamic phenomena linked to experience. Today's technological developments are continually altering the way in which size influences production costs, and economic analysis of scale phenomena is therefore very tricky. Nevertheless, it is clear from the studies available that, because of the present fragmentation of economic activities in the Community, many of these activities — especially those affected by various forms of protection, e.g. public procurement — are still too small and their productivity is consequently less than in competing economies.

In the first part of this chapter a number of activities have been surveyed to show what is a technically efficient size and how costs increase below that size. A fairly large number of industries have been identified which have considerable potential for economies of scale. To the extent that this potential has not yet been fully exploited, European integration could produce significant cost reductions in these industries. In services, on the other hand, there seems generally to be less potential. In several sectors dynamic savings can also be identified. These are activities where learning or experience can increase productivity in line with aggregate output.

After the existence of potential economies of scale has been established in part one, part two seeks to analyse how far the integration of national economies in a large market is accompanied by an increase in the size of activities as a result of restructuring phenomena in which access to new markets and the growth of trade play a considerable part. This analysis thus provides material with which to evaluate the economies of scale and, hence, reductions in cost which completion of the internal market may generate.

6.1. Size phenomena: economies of scale

Main features of the situation. Many sectors of activity have scope for economies of scale. These arise if an increase in inputs results in a more than proportionate increase in output, and hence in a fall in unit costs. Economies of scale of a technical origin which can be achieved for a product, plant or multi-plant firm are discussed initially. In principle, these are purely static economies although it is not always possible to isolate them from the gains associated with the learning curve and technological progress. These are discussed subsequently.

The economies of scale possible in a given sector are appraised empirically using the concepts of minimum efficient technical scale (METS) and cost gradient. The latter represents the increase in unit output costs where the firm is of less than the optimum size (i.e. it is either half or one third of the optimum size). Both concepts are measured on the basis of surveys carried out among engineers, but additional sources have been used to corroborate engineering estimates (i.e. census data, econometric estimates, cost and price data, etc.). Because of the paucity of data available, estimates relating to these two concepts concentrate on the economies that can be made in production and development and disregard distribution, marketing and transport costs.

Most of the estimates compiled relate to the United Kingdom or the United States and some to Germany. The fact that few countries are covered should be without consequence for determining optimum size, which varies very little from one country to another (see Scherer 1975). However, this does not in any way mean that economies of scale are exploited to a similar degree in different countries. On the contrary, it is fair to assume that firms with access to a larger market are closer to minimum efficient size than those which operate in more restricted markets. The cost gradient will differ from country to country in accordance with factor prices, but this aspect should only affect countries whose factor costs diverge sharply.

Since most of the data relate to the 1960s, it is fair to ask whether they still reflect production conditions in the 1980s. Minimum efficient size observed in the 1960s was therefore compared with estimates for the early 1980s in 11 industries.[1] The comparison indicates that, if anything, minimum efficient size has increased since the 1960s. Minimum efficient size appears, therefore, to vary over time with technological change, which would seem to exert pressure to create ever-larger production units. In the long run the curve for aggregate minimum efficient size would slope downwards. Yet certain industries now see the reappearance of small firms, which are adapting faster to technological change by using new production processes (flexible manufacturing systems, laser cutting, etc.).

Technical economies of scale in industry. An inventory of recent studies concerning economies of scale was made (see Pratten) so as to collect quantitative and qualitative information on each branch of industry in the NACE three-digit classification. This proved a very difficult task, since the definitions used in the various studies are not necessarily the same and the data do not therefore relate to the same concepts. The aim of the inventory was to determine the sectors where economies of scale play an important part and which might therefore benefit from the creation of a large internal Community market to the extent that their products can be traded and that the full potential for cost reductions has not yet been exploited.

---

[1]   Motor vehicles, electrical household appliances, tyres, oil refineries, steel, cement, beer, cigarettes, bricks, glass and footwear.

To provide a coherent overall picture, Table 6.1.1 lists branches of industry according to the importance of the economies of scale which can be achieved, irrespective of the level at which they can be made (i.e. product, plant or firm). The third column in the table describes the variation in costs as size departs from the minimum efficient size. The values are simply indicative, since it is difficult to describe the cost gradient for branches which are so aggregated. In some branches, the importance of economies of scale varies considerably within subsectors, and the range of variation in costs is therefore relatively large. For instance, in branch 36, other means of transport, the additional cost burden for a size 50 % smaller than the minimum efficient size is 8 % for shipbuilding and 20 % for aircraft. For such branches it is recommended, therefore, to refer to the table in the Pratten study describing the economies of scale at the NACE three-digit classification level. But even at this level of disaggregation, considerable differences can arise depending on the products concerned. Thus, in branch 251, manufacture of basic industrial chemicals, extra costs range from 1 % (sulphuric acid) to 17 % (dyestuffs).

An overall assessment of the significance of potential economies of scale in manufacturing industry can nevertheless be attempted. Table 6.1.1 suggests that extra unit costs for a size that is 50 % of the minimum efficient size range from 1 % to 36 %. In five of the 20 branches the addition may be higher than 10 %.

Overall, it can be seen that economies of scale are larger in transport equipment, chemicals, machinery and instrument manufacture (office machines, agricultural and industrial machinery, electrical and electronic equipment) and paper and printing. These sectors account for about 55 % of industrial production in the Community of Twelve and about 65 % of industrial employment in the Community of Ten.[1] They are often sectors where demand is growing strongly and products have a high technological content (office machinery, electrical and electronic equipment, precision instruments, chemicals, pharmaceuticals and aerospace). Overall, as was pointed out in Part B, it is in these sectors that the Community's competitive position is currently most under threat. The creation of a large internal Community market could therefore have particularly positive effects here. Other sectors are typically using manufacturing processes (robotization in the means of transport sector; rolling in metal processing, paper and printing) which also provide scope for significant economies of scale.

By contrast, economies of scale are smaller in food, drink and tobacco, textiles, clothing, leather goods and timber. These sectors with small economies of scale are characterized by relatively stagnant demand and low technological content of products. In certain cases, e.g. food, drink and tobacco, economies of scale can be achieved, at the level of the firm in the areas of distribution and

---

[1] Excluding Spain and Portugal.

Table 6.1.1.

Branches of manufacturing industry ranked by size of economies of scale

NACE Code	Branch	Cost gradient at half METS[1]	Remarks
35	Motor vehicles	6-9%	Very substantial EOS[2] in production and in development costs.
36	Other means of transport	8-20%	Variable EOS: small for cycles and shipbuilding (although economies are possible through series production level), very substantial in aircraft (development costs).
25	Chemical industry	2,5-15%	Substantial EOS in production processes. In some segments of the industry (pharmaceutical products), R&D is an important source of EOS.
26	Man-made fibres	5-10%	Substantial EOS in general.
22	Metals	> 6%	Substantial EOS in general for production processes. Also possible in production and series production.
33	Office machinery	3-6%	Substantial EOS at product level.
32	Mechanical engineering	3-10%	Limited EOS at firm level but substantial production.
34	Electrical engineering	5-15%	Substantial EOS at product level and for development costs.
37	Instrument engineering	5-15%	Substantial EOS at product level, via development costs.
47	Paper, printing and publishing	8-36%	Substantial EOS in paper mills and, in particular, printing (books).
24	Non-metallic mineral products	> 6%	Substantial EOS in cement and flat glass production processes. In other branches, optimum plant size is small compared with the optimum size for the industry.
31	Metal articles	5-10% (castings)	EOS are lower at plant level but possible at production and series production level.
48	Rubber and plastics	3-6%	Moderate EOS in tyre manufacture. Small EOS in factories making rubber and moulded plastic articles but potential for EOS at product and series production level.
41-42	Drink and tobacco	1-6%	Moderate EOS in breweries. Small EOS in cigarette factories. In marketing, EOS are considerable.
41-42	Food	3,5-21%	Principal source of EOS is the individual plant. EOS at marketing and distribution level.

Table 6.1.1 (*continued*).

Branches of manufacturing industry ranked by size of economies of scale

NACE Code	Branch	Cost gradient at half METS[1]	Remarks
49	Other manufacturing	n.a.	Plant size is small in these branches. Possible EOS from specialization and the length of production runs.
43	Textile industry	10% (carpets)	EOS are more limited than in the other sectors, but possible economies from specialization and the length of production runs.
46	Timber and wood	n.a.	No EOS for plants in these sectors. Possible EOS from specialization and longer production runs.
45	Footwear and clothing	1% (footwear)	Small EOS at plant level but possible EOS from specialization and longer production runs.
44	Leather and leather goods	n.a.	Small EOS.

[1] Minimum efficient technical scale.
[2] Economies of scale.

Source: Pratten (1987).

marketing. It has not been possible to quantify these, but their significance in the context of the internal Community market will be analysed in what follows.

The potential for economies of scale has also been investigated using a sample of 68 plants in different sectors of industry. The minimum efficient size of plant was compared to that for the Community market and — where information was available — the extra cost for a size 50 % smaller than the minimum efficient size was given. The data are summarized in Tables 6.1.2 and 6.1.3. Table 6.1.2 shows, that, for the samples studied, the minimum efficient size accounts for less than 2.5 % of the Community market in 54 % of the plants

Table 6.1.2.

Comparison of the minimum efficient technical size (METS) of plant with the size of the Community market

METS as % of Community production total	Distribution of sample[1]
0-1	29
1-2,5	25
2,5-5	19
5-10	16
10-20	7
20-50	3
50-100	1
100 and over	—

[1] Percentage of plants in the sample (68 altogether) falling within each category.
Source: Pratten (1987).

Table 6.1.3.

Supplementary costs borne for a plant size below 50% of the minimum efficient technical size (METS)

Extra costs (as %)	Distribution of sample[1]
0-2	4
2-5	36
5-10	29
10-15	25
15-20	2
20-25	2
25 and over	2

[1] Percentage by category of plants in the sample for which a cost gradient was available (45 plants).
Source: Pratten (1987).

surveyed and less than 5 % in 73 %. The results show that in most of the industries in question, the Community market can accommodate 20 plants of minimum efficient size, whereas the national market of the four large economies in the Community (Germany, France, Italy and the United Kingdom) could accommodate only four. According to Table 6.1.3, the extra cost for a plant whose size is half the minimum efficient size can be as much as 25 % or more, but is over 10 % only in 31 % of the plants in the sample. The extra costs most frequently observed are 2-5 % (36 % of plants), 5-10 % (29 %) and 10-15 % (25 %).

Within each industrial branch certain subsectors are likely to be particularly affected by the completion of the internal market. These are activities where the minimum efficient size accounts for at least 20 % of the national market (in the United Kingdom) and where the cost increase at 50 % optimum size is 10 % or more. Tables 6.1.4 and 6.1.5 show the industries which present one or other of these characteristics and where economies of scale — whether at product, plant or firm level — could be exploited to a significant degree.

Eight industrial activities satisfy both criteria: aircraft, chemicals (dyestuffs, titanium oxide, synthetic rubber, petrochemicals), electric motors and, possibly, paper (kraft paper) and printing (books). If the threshold is reduced to a 5 % cost increase at 50 % optimum size, the following sectors can be added: cars and trucks, iron and steel, non-ferrous metals (rolled aluminium), office machinery (computers and electric typewriters), tractors, ball-bearings, electrical machinery (turbo-generators), telecommunications equipment (television sets), shipbuilding (marine diesel engines) and synthetic fibres (rayon).

Lastly, in sectors such as building materials (bricks), foundries and carpets the cost gradient is admittedly steep, but the minimum efficient size is small compared with the national market (less than 3 %). In these sectors, the national market is therefore large enough to allow production units to attain their optimum size. But, if this is the case, the increase in competition induced by the removal of trade barriers could still result in a substantial fall in costs.

The results suggest that the gains to be expected from European integration are far from negligible, since possible cost reductions range from 1 to 36 % for plants which, by doubling their size, attain the optimum level. The internal Community market makes it possible to combine the advantages of a market in which production units can reach a technically efficient size and real competition continues to operate (20 efficient plants can co-exist in such a market). Such a finding constitutes a weighty argument in favour of creating a Community internal market, since only a market of such size can give European firms the benefits of technical and economic efficiency simultaneously. It would, however, be unrealistic to expect European integration to lead immediately to full exploitation of economies of scale. The orders of magnitude expressed here are maximum potential effects in the long run. The effective achievement of economies of scale will take time and require adjustments in the allocation of resources. The costs of adjustment and the imperfections of competition could, therefore, obstruct the exploitation of economies of scale.

Table 6.1.4.

Products for which the minimum efficient technical size (METS) is superior or equal to 20% of the production of the United Kingdom

NACE Code	Product	METS as % of production		Cost gradient at ½ METS
		UK	EC	
351	Cars	200	20	6-9
26	Cellulose fibres	125	16	3
224	Rolled aluminium	114	15	8
351	Trucks	104	21	7,5
33	Computers	> 100	n.a.	5
33	Electric typewriters	n.a.	33	3-6
364	Aircraft	> 100	n.a.	20
251	Dyes	> 100	n.a.	17-22
321	Tractors	98	19	6
346	Refrigerators	85	11	4
221	Steel	72	10	6
251	Titanium oxide	63	50	8-16
342	Electric motors	60	6	15
346	Washing machines	57	10	4,5
342	Large turbine-generators	50	10	5
344	Telephone exchanges	50	10	3-6
345	TV sets	40	9	9
26	Rayon	40	23	5
361	Marine diesel engines	30	5	8
429	Cigarettes	24	6	1,4
251	Synthetic rubber	24	3,5	15
251	Petrochemicals	23[1]	3[1]	12
256	Fertilizers	23	4	n.a.
223	Wire netting	20	4	n.a.
326	Ball-bearings	20	2	8-6

[1] Probable underestimate.

Source: Pratten (1987).

Technical economies of scale in services. The services which appear to be particularly affected by completion of the internal market belong principally to the insurance, banking and distribution sectors. They are services which can be traded internationally. Theoretically economies of scale in these sectors can be estimated using a similar method to that adopted for industry. There are, however, considerable difficulties of empirical measurement (e.g. determining the output of a bank).

Consequently, only the conclusions of some recent analyses are given here without any claim to deal exhaustively with this very complex subject.

In the area of banking services, Gilligan, Smirlock and Marshall (1984) stress that the majority of empirical studies have tended to underestimate the economies of scale which can be achieved by banks because these studies treat different activities individually. In so doing they consider that production costs of the different types of banking servics are independent and so intermix economies of scale and product range. The authors therefore suggest a method-ology which can take account of the characteristics of banks as multiproduct firms. Their study, covering 714 American banks, concludes that economies of scale can only be achieved in small banks (deposits under USD 25 million). On the other hand, these economies of scale will disappear when the size of banks increases and diseconomies will even appear for large banks (deposits over USD 100 million). These results are not confirmed by Murray and White (1983) who, on the basis of a similar methodology to that of Gilligan *et al.*, find increasing returns to scale in the majority of 61 Canadian savings banks (credit unions) studied. However, the two studies stress the existence of economies of product range: the first on the level of borrowing and lending activities, the second between mortgages and other categories of loans. Finally, Berger *et al.* (1987) arrive at the same conclusions as Gilligan *et al.* in so far as economies of scale are concerned but they refute, at the same time, the finding of the existence of economies of product range in banking services.

In the area of life assurance, a study by Kellner and Mathewson (cited by Baumol (1986)) also rejects the hypothesis of the existence of economies of scale but not economies of product range. Finally in the transport services sector studies have been carried out for road and rail transport (see Baumol (1986)). Here also the conclusions are divided. However, it appears that if economies of scale exist they are generally small. On the other hand, in these sectors economies of product range could play a more important role.

Therefore the very question of the existence of economies of scale in services is far from being resolved empirically let alone their magnitude. Consequently, no estimate of the technical economies of scale that can be achieved in the service sector is given here.

Non-technical economies of scale. Firms can achieve economies of scale of a different sort to the technical ones described in the preceding paragraphs, which relate principally to production units. Here we are concerned in particular with economies at the level of the firm associated with control of a number of plants and achievable in common functions such as sales promotion, R&D, management and financing, and at the level of transport costs (see Scherer 1987). The minimum efficient size of a plant can vary according to the function in question (production, marketing, R&D, finance). Thus a plant may be of minimum efficient size as regards production, but not as regards R&D or marketing. In general, where non-technical functions are concerned, there is a minimum threshold of expenditure which, if not reached, may constitute a source of inefficiency. Non-technical economies of scale are often regarded as less significant than those which are possible at production level (see Owen, 1983, and Pratten, 1987). To what extent can the completion of the internal

Table 6.1.5.

Products for which the cost slope at $\frac{1}{2}$ minimum efficient technical size (METS) is superior or equal to 10%

NACE Code	Product	METS as % of production		Cost gradient at $\frac{1}{2}$ METS
		UK	EC	
473	Books	n.a.	n.a.	20-36
241	Bricks	1	0,2	25
251	Dyes	> 100	n.a.	17-22
364	Aircraft	> 100	n.a.	20
251	Titanium oxide	63	50	8-16
242	Cement	10	1	6-16
251	Synthetic rubber	24	3,5	15
342	Electric motors	60	6	15
471	Kraft paper	11[1]	1,4[1]	13
251	Petrochemicals	23[1]	3[1]	12
26	Nylon	4[1]	1[1]	12
311	Cylinder block castings	3	0,3	10
311	Small cast-iron castings	0,7	0,1	10
438	Carpets	0,3	0,04	10
328	Diesel engines	> 100	n.a.	10

[1] Probable underestimate.
Source: Pratten (1987).

Community market affect such economies of scale? The likely answer is that a wider geographical market tends to encourage the creation of multi-plant firms in industries where transport costs are high or in industries which will undergo significant restructuring (mergers, joint ventures, etc.).

As regards advertising expenditure, the fruits of European integration will probably be more limited on account of differences in language and in consumers' tastes. The introduction of Community trade marks, however, represents a source of gain, since it would make it possible to spread the cost of advertising over a wider audience. This seems to be confirmed by the appearance of new forms of European advertising (e.g. by satellite broadcast), where the message is manifestly aimed at a European market. Higher gains are expected where development costs are concerned (market research for new products, preparation of catalogues, etc), since these can be spread over a larger volume of sales and since technical barriers will be abolished.

Turning to the cost of financing, large firms will also have a certain advantage. They can limit their risks by diversifying the projects they develop, thus making it possible to reduce their financing costs. Evidence was found of a 4 % difference in interest rates paid by small businesses and the largest firms (see Pratten), which is a considerable margin.

As regards economies of scale in R&D, two separate questions arise. The first is whether there are increasing returns to scale when research inputs are transformed into innovation outputs. The second, closely linked to the first, concerns the relationship between size of firm, R&D activities and innovation effort.

Many empirical studies conclude that there are no economies of scale in the innovation process. The function of transforming research inputs into innovation outputs seems to be characterized by constant or even decreasing returns to scale (see Scherer (1980) and the survey carried out by Kamien and Schwartz (1982)).

Moreover, while it is clear that expenditure on R&D increases with the size of firm, this by no means implies that large firms carry out proportionally more research or that they are relatively more efficient in their use of research funds, as measured by the number of innovations produced. The advantage of large firms is that they can spread their R&D costs over a larger sales volume and, hence, employ a greater number of more specialized researchers and undertake more ambitious research programmes (R&D indivisibles). However, according to Ergas (1984), industries where these aspects play a significant part are exceptional (e.g. chemicals and aerospace). According to empirical studies, the elasticity of R&D activities with respect to size of firm is less than unity (see Jacquemin (1975) and Kamien and Schwartz (1982)). It seems that research activities increase proportionally more than size, up to a certain threshold (which varies with the industry), but that large firms spend relatively less on research than small and medium-sized enterprises.

The above two results (constant or decreasing returns to scale and elasticity of R&D with respect to size less than unity) mean that the efficiency with which research inputs are transformed into innovation outputs does not increase with size of firm (see box). Most of the empirical studies confirm this finding and show that, apart from the chemical industry, large size does not favour innovation (see Jacquemin (1979) and Kamien and Schwartz (1982)). This is also the conclusion in a recent study by P. Geroski, who found that, in the United Kingdom, firms with fewer than 10 000 employees generated 56,1 % of innovation in the period 1945-83, with 33,2 % attributable to firms with fewer than 1 000 employees, and 17 % to firms with fewer than 200 (see Geroski). Moreover, small firms seem to be playing a growing role in the innovation process: 43,2 % of innovations came from firms with fewer than 1 000 employees in 1983, as against 29,6 % in 1945. Small firms also contribute more in terms of innovation than large firms in the most innovative sectors, i.e. machinery, mechanical and electronic equipment, chemicals, electrical equipment and instruments.

These results, which appear to show that large firms are less efficient innovators, must be examined cautiously. The measures given of a firm's innovative activity — innovations expressed in terms of the number of patents, and research input in terms of R&D staff or expenditure — are not perfect. For instance, not all R&D staff have the same professional experience, and some employees in production or marketing may also produce innovation. Similarly, R&D expenditure may vary depending on firms' accounting practices and patents do not all have the same value — some are never turned into marketable products, and some innovations are never patented. Also, this indicator takes no account of how each patent is exploited. Large firms are very probably better equipped to make commercial use of innovation. Thus it would seem that there is some complementarity between small and large firms: the small firms being more dynamic in the process of innovation while the large firms are content to take second place in the innovation race and concentrate on commercializing new products and processes rapidly and on a large scale. It is still true, however, that firms must be sufficiently large in order to undertake the riskier R&D projects. This conclusion tallies with the findings of a recent study of 4 000 innovations registered in the United Kingdom. In this study (Pavitt, 1983, cited in Walsh, 1987), based on a more precise measure of the results of innovation, the contribution of small as well as very large firms is more significant than that found in previous work.

It must also be emphasized in this respect that in the field of R&D, cooperation between European firms is economically justified and desirable, the disadvantages of reduced competition being offset by the social benefit resulting from the increase in innovations and the speed of their dissemination (see Jacquemin 1987). Cooperation makes it possible to avoid duplication of effort in R&D and can improve and accelerate the transfer of information from one firm to another, which is very beneficial where there is great technical complementarity between firms. Cooperation could also increase the speed of innovation at less risk: more projects can be undertaken simultaneously and a project's costs can be shared by a greater number of firms. Lastly, cooperation increases the resources devoted to R&D, thereby promoting the implementation of more ambitious programmes. Cooperation between firms would appear to play a particularly favourable role in sectors experiencing high growth and technological development. Large firms — which are less efficient as regards R&D — occupy an important place in such sectors, and the financial needs are substantial. On this subject, it should be pointed out that high technology projects are already the subject of European cooperation (Esprit, Eureka, etc.).

Altogether, European integration should both stimulate cooperation among European firms in the field of research and development and, as will be seen in Section 7.2, increase each firm's innovative effort through increased competition. It is principally in these two ways that the efficient use of R&D expenditure should be increased.

The effects of experience and learning. So far, only static economies of scale have been analysed. We have measured for one unit of production the cost advantage which technically efficient size confers at a particular moment in time. In addition to these static economies of scale, there is the phenomenon of experience or learning, however, which reflects the unit cost advantage to a firm resulting from the experience it acquires through the cumulative production of goods and services. Studied in an aerospace context and subsequently investigated by the Boston Consulting Group for numerous industrial activities, the learning effect consists of a fall in the total unit cost of a product at constant prices when the cumulative production of that product is doubled. The actual fall in cost will depend on the type of product observed (see Table 6.1.6). Learning effects arise through the capacity of workers to improve their performance over time and the technological improvement of production processes and organizational structures. All firms manufacturing the same type of product do not, therefore, benefit equally from the cost advantages of learning effects. The more dynamic, creative ones will realize productivity gains faster than the others. Nevertheless, the average cost reductions observed for various industrial activities (see Table 6.1.6) are representative of most of the firms in the same sector of activity. The effects, although very important to certain sectors, are nevertheless not quantified in the overall economic assessment due to the empirical difficulty of such a quantification.

Table 6.1.6.

Examples of total unit cost reductions observed for various activities as a result of doubling cumulative production

%

Industry or service sector	Fall in unit costs as a result of cumulative production being doubled
Electric components	30
Microcomputing	30
Ball-bearings	27
Industrial plastics	25
Equipment maintenance	24
Life insurance	23
Aerospace	20
Electricity	20
Starters for motor vehicles	15
Oil refining	10

Source: Boston Consulting Group (1971) and (1981), Hirschman (1964).

As regards the characteristics of activities where learning effects are relevant and the implications of these effects in an integrated internal market, it has been found that:

(i)   industrial activities which rely heavily on skilled labour should benefit most from such effects. According to Hirschman (1964) and Yelle (1979), in an activity where total labour costs represent about 75 % of total production costs (including capital costs), learning effects are twice as great as those observed in activities where labour costs account for only 50 % of total production cost (see Table 6.1.7);

Table 6.1.7.

Cost structure and learning effects

%

Cost structure		Fall in unit costs as a result of cumulative production being doubled	Example
Labour costs	Machinery costs		
75	25	20	Aerospace
50	50	15	Vehicles
25	75	10	Refining

Source: Hirschman (1964).

(ii) the learning effect is the stronger the higher the rate of market growth. In the case of activities at the start of their life-cycle, where growth rates can be spectacular (higher than 25 % a year), less than three years may be needed to double cumulative production. It is very much in the interest of firms, therefore, to increase their production as fast as they can in growth markets, and it is in this type of market that it is generally easiest, initially, to increase market share (competitors misjudging effective growth rates). In mature markets, gains in market share will be substantially at the expense of competitors. It is noteworthy in this respect that the strategy of Japanese firms with regard to products for which demand is growing strongly (video tape-recorders and cameras, etc.) has been to acquire rapidly the largest cumulative production feasible so as to establish as low a unit output cost as possible *vis-à-vis* their competitors;

(iii) in sectors where learning effects are particularly marked, demand and supply are closely linked. Here, the cumulative value of previous consumption represents the experience built up by the industry and, hence, the importance of the learning effect. The larger this effect, the greater the quantity, attractiveness and availability of that industry's products and, hence, the demand for them. A strong learning effect, therefore, sets up a virtuous circle of increased supply and expanding demand (see the illustration in Figure 6.2).

From this point of view, it has been established that the volume of output of several European industries which show such learning effects is artificially constrained by various barriers and national policies, whether these be differentiated standards, pricing systems which do not reflect costs, or discriminatory public purchasing (the telecommunications industry is a typical case in point).

139

Particularly harmful dynamic consequences result from this, since the learning process is checked and technological dependence on the rest of the world may develop. Completion of the internal market is, by contrast, likely to give a fresh boost to these new advanced technology industries and, through a cumulative process, revive European competitiveness. By providing the opportunity to serve a large market without constraint, the White Paper programme is therefore conferring a considerable potential advantage on firms operating in markets with strong demand.

6.2. Trade expansion and gains in technical efficiency

Analysis of the potential for economies of scale, whether technical or other, static or dynamic, had identified prospects for considerable cost reductions. An explanation must now be provided of the economic mechanisms through which market integration will make it possible to achieve some of this potential. Much of the reasoning on the subject is based on empirical observation of productivity levels and the size of European and American firms. In particular, the work done by Scherer and his team (1975) has shown that:

(i) the size of the domestic market has a significant effect on the size of production units (which would explain in particular why American establishments are larger than their European counterparts);

FIGURE 6.2: **Consumer's surplus and learning effects**

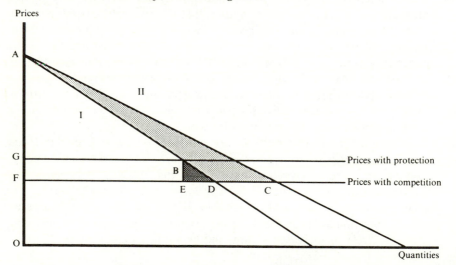

Note: Assume that the competitive price is F. Demand at time t = 1 is expressed by the straight line I, corresponding to a total consumer's surplus equal to AFD. As a result of the total volume demanded at t = 1, the learning effect ensures, at time t = 2, increased demand as represented by the straight line II so that the consumer's surplus now equals AFC, after an increase of ACD. Suppose that, at time t = 1, a set of non-tariff barriers applies to the industry putting the price at G. The static loss of consumer's welfare is usually taken to be the triangle BED, but the level of previous cumulative production caused by the higher price has a negative effect on the level of total demand at t = 2, which instead of running at line II stays at I. The total loss of consumer's surplus is, therefore, much greater, i.e. BED + ADC.

Source: von Weizsäcker (1987).

(ii) the expansion of an industry's market through foreign trade is generally accompanied by a significant increase in the average size of production units.

The fact that in most industrial sectors, establishments of very different size exist side-by-side — and have very different unit costs — shows, to a certain extent, the limits to the working of competition. This applies in particular to the limits within which producers who enjoy a cost advantage on account of their larger size are ready, in order to expand their market and thus reach the technically efficient size, to lower their prices temporarily and eliminate their smaller, high-cost competitors. This is the approach, developed by Owen (1983) and taken up in Müller and Owen (1985), according to which international trade accelerates structural change by giving the more competitive (i.e. the larger) firms more opportunity to replace high-price producers both on the domestic market and abroad. It provides a clear illustration of the role played by competition in causing firms to move towards a scale of operations which is more efficient both technically and economically.

However, it should be recalled that in the present economic situation, there exists, in a certain number of sectors, unutilized production capacity. As a result, the growth of final and intermediate demand resulting from a removal of barriers should, equally, lead to a considerable rise in the rate of utilization of the available resources.

The opening-up of frontiers and the parallel development of external trade, in particular intra-Community trade, should lead to a number of moves towards rationalization via:

(i) a better employment of existing capacity and resources leading to a reduction in unit cost (see Figure 6.3);

(ii) a reallocation of resources within each industry: the smallest and least efficient production plants would be replaced by larger and more efficient ones which, by means of exports, would find a way to increase the size of their market and thus reduce their costs by exploiting consequent scale economies;

(iii) a reallocation of resources between countries in favour of those enjoying a comparative advantage.

Far from being a course open to all industries, such restructuring looks possible only in sectors where the minimum technically efficient scale is large in relation to the domestic market. Thus Eastman and Stykolt (1976) suggested that, where the domestic market was more than 15 times minimum efficient size, external trade was very unlikely to influence the structure of the industry.

To test this approach, a number of empirical studies have been carried out. These seek to explain, in respect to a given product, the gap between the average size of units of production (or of the largest establishment whose aggregate production accounts for 50 % of the total output of the product in question) and the minimum efficient technical scale (METS) in the light of the magnitude of external trade and the potential of economies of scale.

FIGURE 6.3: **Market dimension and exploitation of economies of scale**

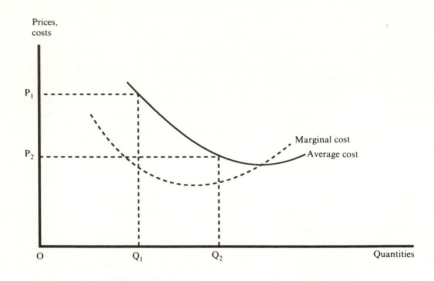

Note: The declining average cost reflects the existence of economies of scale. In the case of a small market, with a low demand, we assume a given firm constrained to produce Q_1. Assuming that it sets its prices equal to average cost (allowing for normal profits) it will sell this quantity at price P_1. Free access to a European internal market, making possible full exploitation of scale economies even for a specialized product, allow the producers to sell the quantity Q_2 at a much lower unit cost, and the consumers to buy this product at price P_2. Note that the consumers' benefit is not obtained at the producers' expense, but rather, thanks to the economies of scale, the latter can sell at a lower price without reducing their profits.

The estimates based on these data provide a set of fairly convergent results which confirm the role played by external trade in the expansion of the size of units of production. Thus Müller and Owen (1985) show that in the case of Germany:

(i)   the growth of trade between 1963 and 1978 resulted in a doubling of the average size of production units in the industrial sectors studied;

(ii) this doubling was itself accompanied by an increase in technical efficiency — as a result of economies of scale — equivalent to a reduction of 8 % in unit costs;

(iii) measured in terms of the volume of trade recorded in 1978, the gain in efficiency represents 20 % of the growth in trade.

Studies have been carried out with a view to updating these results, and broadening both the geographical coverage (D, I, UK) and the number of products studied. Using models akin to those tested by Müller and Owen, these analyses broadly confirm the results obtained by those two authors (see the studies by J. Schwalbach and P. Ranci). In particular, the role played by external trade, as a means of market expansion that makes it possible to bring the effective size of units of production closer to the optimum and thus achieve gains in technical efficiency, has been established. However, a number of qualifications should be mentioned concerning the nature of the results obtained. First, it should be noted that the explanatory power of exports is, in general, systematically greater and more significant than that of imports. It is clear in this respect that the explanatory role attributed to imports needs to be clarified. The fact that imports have a positive effect on the development of the size of production units can be interpreted as meaning that, faced with the greater competition resulting from imports, domestic firms seek to invest to have larger, and consequently more efficient, production units, while units that are too small are eliminated. Imports also have the direct effect of making the smallest units disappear and thus helping to increase mechanically the average size of the surviving units of production.

Analysis using intra-Community exports and imports, rather than total external trade as explanatory variables proved in some cases to be more significant. This is particularly interesting in that much of intra-Community trade is intra-branch trade, one of the more frequent justifications for which in the existence in the branches concerned, of considerable economies of scale.

Thus, the growth in (essentially) intra-Community trade resulting from completion of the internal market, gives rise to improved technical efficiency — through the influence of competition and attendant restructuring — which translates into a significant fall in production costs.

The gain in productivity corresponding to this fall is not, obviously, limited only to the share of production involved in international trade. In effect, the scale economies which can be gained by enlargement of market size are converted into a reduction of costs affecting the sum of production (in Figure 6.3 reduction in costs affects the sum of production OQ_2 and not just quantity Q_1Q_2).

In this regard the data assembled in the studies of J. Schwalbach and P. Ranci show that, for those industrial sectors included in their analyses (20 in the case of Germany, 19 in the UK and 14 in Italy) the average size of production units is markedly smaller than the minimum efficient size. This results, on average for these sectors, in higher production costs of the order of 15 % in Germany, 23 % in Italy and 25 % in the UK. Of course, most of these cases refer to sectors for which potential scale economies are reasonably large, either because the minimum efficient size is high in relation to the size of the domestic market, or else because the additional cost of the shortfall from optimal scale is large.

As an illustration of the way in which the growth of trade, resulting from achievement of the internal market, is transformed into a closing of the gap between the average size of production units and minimum efficient scale, the regression analyses carried out in the German case have been cited. Thus, under a hypothetical simultaneous doubling of both exports and imports and presuming, for reasons of simplification, that total domestic consumption remains unchanged, the average size of units would grow, in the sectors under consideration, by the order of 110 % and the excess costs of a suboptimal size be reduced to just below 7 %, i.e. a reduction of such excess costs by over one half. This shows clearly the orders of magnitude of changes in cost which may be associated with the relationship between foreign trade and size of production units. In Chapter 10, which provides an overall analysis of the internal market, similar relationships have been employed, on a more hypothetically restricted basis, in relation to the growth of trade (in the order of 25 %).[1] Taken together these have provided evidence of reductions in unit costs slightly above 1,5 % of production for industrial and energy sectors (i.e. in total 0,7 % of the total production of the Community).

[1] By way of comparison, the volume of external trade increased, for the Community of Twelve, by 120 % between 1960 and 1973, whereas intra-Community trade rose during the same period by about 200 %.

7. Integration and competition effects

The other way in which the effects of removing barriers within the Community make themselves felt is through the enhancement of competition. One must bear in mind here the relative nature of market conditions and structures. Thus, the expression 'competition effect' as used in this context means, of course, the effect produced by the strengthening of competition or the weakening of monopoly power, and not the bringing about of a — purely theoretical — state of perfect competition.

Increased competition is an obvious consequence of removing barriers, but it can take many forms and, depending on the sector, have an enormous potential for improving economic efficiency.

The first section below assesses the impact of increased competition on costs and prices. To start with, a statistical survey shows the degree of price disparity for a given product between Community countries. The removal of barriers and the freedom of supply which businesses will enjoy as a result, should lead, through increased competitive pressure, to some downward convergence of prices of benefit to the customer. From the point of view of producers, the competitive pressure will be exerted first and foremost on price-cost margins, particularly in those sectors in which they held a certain monopoly power or position. Producers will also be induced — urged on by the pressure on their margins — to become more efficient and thus cut their production and distribution costs. The increased pressure which will be brought to bear in this way on costs and price-cost margins will be a powerful means of causing prices to converge on levels more consistent with economic and technical efficiency. The second section deals with the non-price effects of competition and, in particular, the impact of competition on the spread of technological progress through innovation. Analysing the part played by competition is far from easy. The studies presented in this section show that the degree of competition has, if anything, a positive impact on the flow of innovation; by liberalizing trade and intensifying competition, European integration should therefore have particularly favourable dynamic effects on the development of competitiveness.

The various indicators that are provided of the potential gain from increased competition hold out the prospect of a particularly significant overall economic impact; however, as with all the indirect effects of eliminating barriers, this impact is very difficult to quantify, and its achievement depends on numerous conditions.

7.1. Effects of competition on costs and prices

The price gap between Community countries. The existence of barriers which fragment the Community market is an obstacle to the working of competition which reduces considerably the economic efficiency of the Community as a whole. Differences in the price of a given product from one country to another are a particularly useful indicator in this respect. But comparing price levels in different countries has always been an extremely difficult exercise. To be meaningful, such a comparison has to be between products which are not only available in all the countries surveyed but representative of each of the national consumption patterns. The more the countries constitute a homogeneous whole in terms of tastes, habits and cultural traditions, the easier it is to find a large number of products which satisfy the above two conditions. Because of its size and historical origins, however, the Community is far from being a homogeneous entity and there is a great variety of consumption patterns, not only at national level but at regional level as well. It is not easy, therefore, to select a large number of products whose price can, with certainty, be compared as between all Member States.

A comprehensive set of price data for the Community is painstakingly put together by Eurostat in the form of the price review it conducts every five years with the help of the national statistical offices. This survey, which covers all final products (goods and services), forms the basis for calculating purchasing power parities. Eurostat has devised a method of ensuring the highest possible degree of comparability between 'basic headings'.[1] These (320 or so) headings are based on a classification of final consumption of households by function. In the case of equipment goods, the classification is based on type of product. For the purposes of the present study, account has been taken only of 93 basic headings (67 for goods and 26 for services) as far as final consumption by households is concerned, and 20 categories of equipment goods. These goods and services are broadly representative of final demand for tradable goods. Eurostat has compiled data on consumer prices inclusive of tax, and on prices net of deductible VAT in the case of equipment goods. In the case of consumer goods, VAT and excise duty were deducted *ex post* so as to produce a set of prices net of tax (this is impossible in the case of services). Altogether, a matrix of price level indices by country for nine Member States (EUR 9) concerning 113 groups of products for the years 1975, 1980 and 1985 has been put together.

As can be seen from Table 7.1.1, price levels differ appreciably from one Member State to another. In 1985 the price dispersion (all taxes included), measured by the standard deviation, came to about 22 % of the average price in the Community in the case of final consumption (goods and services) by households. It was 19,4 % for consumer goods alone (excluding services and energy). It should be noted that this composite calculation method (standard deviation related to the Community average) reduces the size of the gap considerably: the absolute price differences between countries and by product (between minimum and maximum prices) are obviously much bigger.

---

[1] For a description of the methods employed by the Statistical Office of the European Communities, see *Comparison in real values of the aggregates of ESA,* Eurostat (1983).

Table 7.1.1.

Price dispersion in the EC (EUR 9) by product group[1]

Products	Without taxes			All taxes included		
	1975	1980	1985	1975	1980	1985
1. Total consumer goods	—	—	—	22,7	23,9	22,2
A. Consumer goods, excluding energy and services	16,5	17,1	15,1	20,4	20,9	19,4
1.1. Food	16,3	15,2	14,3	19,2	18.0	17,3
Rice	17,9	17,9	9,8	20,3	20,4	11,6
Flour, other cereals	20,7	7,3	15,7	22,9	12,5	17,8
Bread, cakes and biscuits	12,8	12,9	11,5	15,8	17,1	15,1
Noodles, macaroni, spaghetti	12,4	11,9	8,8	13,7	14,3	11,0
Beef	21,2	17,5	11,3	23,9	19,9	14,3
Veal	10,5	23,2	16,4	13,6	21,9	15,9
Pork	10,9	9,4	14,9	14,2	13,3	20,5
Mutton, lamb or goat meat	23,8	18,2	10,2	26,4	20,0	12,3
Poultry	11,6	9,27	10,4	14,8	9,7	14,5
Delicatessen	17,4	12,3	21,0	20,7	16,0	23,5
Meat preparations, other meat products	15,1	18,0	11,1	15,5	22,6	14,4
Fish and other seafood	13,7	13,2	13,5	16,5	16,5	15,4
Fresh milk	12,2	13,1	15,5	14,0	12,9	16,9
Milk, preserved	18,3	19,8	24,6	19,0	16,9	22,2
Cheese	11,7	12,4	11,3	14,0	18,6	13,7
Eggs	8,8	7,2	15,6	11,5	10,6	17,6
Butter, animal and vegetable fats	18,6	15,4	5,3	20,8	13,8	10,0
Edible oils	23,2	22,1	22,3	25,4	24,1	23,2
Fresh fruits	24,3	16,7	16,0	28,4	18,2	19,0
Fruits dried, frozen, preserved, and as juice	15,8	10,9	14,5	18,0	13,6	19,0
Fresh vegetables	19,2	25,4	24,9	23,5	30,3	27,5
Vegetables dried, frozen, preserved, soups	14,1	16,4	12,0	16,6	20,3	20,0
Potatoes	27,5	27,7	28,4	31,7	31,7	29,1
1.2. Food products subject to excise duty	18,9	21,1	17,0	31,3	38,3	32,6
Sugar	14,4	26,2	17,9	10,5	33,1	19,1
Coffee and cocoa	20,3	17,8	10,8	28,9	27,3	14,1
Tea	41,9	30,8	26,9	46,0	37,2	23,0
Chocolate and confectionery	26,6	22,2	19,2	33,9	25,9	16,5
Jams, honey, syrups, ice-cream	16,5	10,6	16,8	16,9	12,4	19,8
Mineral water and other soft drinks	17,1	25,9	24,8	21,6	31,6	33,1
Liqueurs and spirits	14,8	11,5	18,2	33,4	47,0	37,2
Wine and cider	15,9	33,3	15,8	22,6	58,8	41,5
Beer	24,2	25,7	20,9	26,5	34,3	41,4
Cigarettes	10,3	19,6	15,8	49,6	51,7	42,1
Other tobacco products	35,3	35,4	23,0	28,3	34,4	43,5

Table 7.1.1 *Continued).*

Price dispersion in the EC (EUR 9) by product group[1]

Products	Without taxes			All taxes included		
	1975	1980	1985	1975	1980	1985
1.3. Textiles, clothing and footwear	13,6	16,3	12,8	15,8	17,7	13,5
Outergarments, sportswear, industrial clothing	12,5	15,9	10,7	15,0	17,6	10,5
Underwear and knitwear for children	12,4	16,2	13,4	17,2	19,6	18,2
Underwear and knitwear for women	10,2	29,2	30,7	10,6	28,9	31,8
Materials and drapery	14,6	23,1	23,0	14,6	25,3	23,6
Men's and children's footwear	12,3	15,4	15,0	15,7	16,7	15,7
Women's footwear	20,4	22,0	16,4	21,3	24,4	19,5
Household textiles	17,9	12,1	13,4	16,9	10,1	12,8
1.4. Durable goods	12,4	13,9	12,2	17,6	17,6	17,4
Furniture and furnishing accessories	17,5	16,8	8,1	18,3	16,1	9,3
Refrigerators, freezers, washing machines	13,2	12,6	9,8	14,2	13,5	11,7
Cookers, heating appliances	15,6	21,5	10,6	15,8	23,1	11,8
Cleaning equipment, sewing machines	6,7	8,6	8,3	8,7	10,4	12,2
Glassware and tableware	7,3	27,7	21,4	8,1	24,9	19,9
Other domestic utensils	9,5	11,3	15,7	10,3	10,7	17,5
Motor-cars, motorcycles, bicycles	9,7	13,6	13,6	26,6	26,6	26,8
Radio sets, tape and cassette recorders	7,7	15,8	15,5	13,3	17,0	18,9
Photographic equipment, musical instruments, boats	12,5	5,6	10,1	11,1	6,7	12,5
Gramophone records, tapes, cassettes, flowers	14,6	9,9	12,0	14,7	9,0	11,5
1.5. Other manufactures	21,3	21,3	19,3	21,7	19,9	20,0
Floor coverings	19,8	11,1	15,7	18,7	11,2	16,1
Non-durable household articles	18,7	13,6	9,7	18,2	12,7	11,0
Medical and pharmaceutical products	30,0	28,8	32,6	33,9	31,9	33,3
Therapeutic appliances and equipment	16,3	19,8	21,1	17,2	22,4	22,6
Tyres, inner tubes, parts and accessories	19,1	18,9	17,8	19,0	17,9	17,0
Petrol, lubricants	19,5	12,8	5,4	19,0	9,6	11,7
Books	18,9	82,5	48,6	21,0	79,7	57,0
Magazines, newspapers, other printed matter	23,9	19,8	15,8	24,4	19,3	15,8
Toiletries, perfumes	21,3	12,1	15,6	22,7	15,1	18,0
Jewellery, watches, alarm clocks	15,8	23,5	22,0	17,7	24,2	24,6
Lighters and travel goods	11,6	7,1	11,6	10,9	7,7	13,9
Writing and drawing equipment and supplies	23,3	24,0	14,6	22,6	25,4	16,8

Table 7.1.1 *(continued)*.

Price dispersion in the EC (EUR 9) by product group[1]

Products	Without taxes			All taxes included		
	1975	1980	1985	1975	1980	1985
B. Energy	—	—	10,4	20,4	21,9	15,4
Electricity	—	—	9,0	23,0	25,3	13,4
Town gas	—	—	14,3	26,3	31,2	18,8
Fuel oil, other heating products	—	—	6,7	6,9	9,2	14,2
Coal, coke, fuels	—	—	12,5	21,3	22,3	15,8
C. Services	—	—	—	27,3	29,1	27,2
Repairs to clothing	—	—	—	28,0	29,3	26,9
Repairs to footwear	—	—	—	31,4	27,5	19,7
Expenses for repairs and maintenance	—	—	—	21,3	17,6	10,8
Water charges	—	—	—	71,2	54,7	49,3
Repairs to textiles	—	—	—	30,0	42,2	9,6
Repairs to electrical appliances	—	—	—	22,4	22,0	41,8
Repairs to other appliances	—	—	—	16,2	58,7	33,8
Laundry and dry cleaning	—	—	—	27,8	25,7	38,8
Domestic services	—	—	—	31,3	28,2	19,6
Local transport	—	—	—	36,0	26,0	22,2
Rail transport, road transport and other	—	—	—	21,4	23,7	27,9
Postage	—	—	—	38,4	22,9	20,1
Telephone and telegraph services	—	—	—	33,0	38,6	50,0
Repairs to recreational goods	—	—	—	29,3	17,6	32,0
Hairdressing services	—	—	—	20,4	31,8	21,1
Expenditure in restaurants, cafes	—	—	—	26,2	18,9	16,6
Expenditure in hotels	—	—	—	6,9	18,7	30,8
Other lodging services	—	—	—	25,7	25,9	44,8
Financial services n.e.c.	—	—	—	—	—	28,5[2]
2. Equipment goods[3]	13,6	13,7	12,4			
Structural metal products	9,2	13,3	8,0			
Products of boilermaking	15,5	25,9	22,1			
Tools and metal goods	14,1	14,7	10,4			
Agricultural machinery and tractors	7,6	13,0	8,3			
Machine tools for metal working	19,3	12,5	10,7			
Textile machinery and sewing machines	11,8	6,8	10,9			
Machinery for food, chemicals, rubber, plastics	12,9	11,5	12,2			
Mining equipment	10,1	9,3	18,0			
Machinery for working wood, paper, leather	16,3	11,7	12,9			
Other machines and mechanical equipment	8,0	11,1	8,9			

Table 7.1.1 *(continued)*.

Price dispersion in the EC (EUR 9) by product group[1]

Products	Without taxes			All taxes included		
	1975	1980	1985	1975	1980	1985
Office and data-processing machines	8,5	9,4	8,0			
Electrical equipment, wires and cables	9,7	15,6	8,8			
Telecommunications equipment, meters	21,0	15,6	8,8			
Electronic equipment, radio and television	43,6	12,9	7,1			
Optical instruments, photographic equipment	12,9	17,5	13,7			
Motor vehicles and engines	19,7	13,9	17,0			
Ships, warships	24,4	32,8	12,2			
Locomotives, vans and wagons	17,5	24,3	21,7			
Other transport equipment (cycles, etc.)	22,0	21,8	15,2			
Aircraft, helicopters, aeronautical equipment	17,4	25,0	17,1			

[1]   Coefficient of variation of prices for EUR 9.
[2]   Consultant's estimate.
[3]   Prices net of deductible VAT.
Source: Eurostat.

For example, for cars, cycles and motorcycles the dispersion of prices net of tax is 14 %, but the absolute difference between the countries at either end of the spectrum (DK-UK) is 55 %; for refrigerators and washing machines the dispersion is 10 % and the absolute difference (I-F) 39 %.

Indirect taxes (VAT and excise duty), which vary considerably from one country to another for the same categories of product, are responsible for a significant part of these price differences: the coefficient of dispersion of consumer goods prices thus falls from 19,4 % for prices inclusive of tax to 15,2 % for prices net of tax. Nevertheless, these tax differences account for only a quarter or thereabouts of the price dispersion: the remaining three quarters stem from differences in prices net of tax. This is particularly interesting from the point of view of the abolition of tax frontiers: because the differences in prices, and hence in competitiveness, stem mainly from sources other than indirect taxation, the abolition of tax frontiers (after closer alignment of the rates and structures of indirect taxation) should not, by itself, upset to any large degree relative competitive strengths.

The dispersion of prices net of tax (15,2 % for consumer goods and 12,4 % for equipment goods) is particularly marked in some sectors (see Table 7.1.1):
(i)   in the case of consumer goods, the products concerned (mainly food) are those normally subject to excise duties (although they are deducted here),

pharmaceutical products, therapeutic apparatus, books, certain articles of clothing, jewellery, tableware, etc.;

(ii) in the case of equipment goods, the products in question are boilers, certain types of machine, railway rolling stock, motor cars, cycles, aircraft, etc.

If price differences appreciably greater than the average are taken to be indicators of the existence of barriers to trade which prevent or reduce effective choice and hence competition, a number of useful conclusions can be drawn. Firstly, since the price dispersion is smaller in the case of equipment goods, it can be deduced that the obstacles to trade are also smaller for these categories of goods and that the degree of competition from abroad is higher than in the case of consumer goods. However, it is clear that, in the case of a number of equipment goods (boilers, railway rolling stock and transport equipment), there are substantial price differences which bear witness to high barriers. It is interesting to note that these goods belong to the categories of product which are mainly purchased by the public sector and/or for which there are sizeable differences in technical regulations or standards. In this respect it will be noted that the price surveys bear out the trends reported in the study on public procurement (see Section 3.4).

It is not all that easy to draw definite conclusions from the trend in the dispersion of prices over the period 1975-85. Between 1975 and 1980 the dispersion increased in the case of consumer goods and was unchanged in that of equipment goods (see Table 7.1.1). Foodstuffs (not subject to excise duties) were alone in registering a reduction in disparities. By contrast, the dispersion narrowed between 1980 and 1985, more than cancelling out the increase previously recorded, with the result that the coefficients of variation for all categories of product were in 1985 lower than in 1975. Generally speaking, therefore, there was a certain alignment in price levels between 1975 and 1985, but this was the net result more of movements in the opposite direction than of a linear movement of price convergence between Member States.

An attempt has been made to link the change in price dispersion to the relative size of non-tariff barriers. This is a highly instructive exercise. In those sectors where there are non-tariff barriers, price dispersion has tended to increase very slightly over the last 10 years (+ 5 %), whereas it narrowed appreciably in the sectors more open to Community competition (− 24 % over 10 years). It is therefore reasonable to assume that the removal of non-tariff barriers will have a direct impact on the dispersion of prices and that the effect will be most marked in those sectors in which barriers to trade currently exist.

It is clear, however, that even after the opening-up of public procurement, the removal of technical barriers (by harmonization or mutual recognition), the closer alignment of indirect taxes and the abolition of physical frontiers, numerous factors will continue to justify price differences between countries as, indeed, within each country. This is the case, for example, with transport costs, differences in distribution networks and for quality, regional and cultural differences or different competitive pressures. The point to note, therefore, is that there is a limit to how closely prices will converge at more competitive levels, so that ultimately — in the very long term, say — the dispersion of prices in the Community might resemble the 'natural' dispersion found in a given country. To illustrate this, a comparison has been made between the price dispersion existing, for a clearly identified sample of durable goods, between Germany (prices observed at different outlets in different cities in the Federal Republic) and the average for the Member States (Eurostat survey plus the findings of a survey by the European Bureau of Consumers' Associations). It will be seen (see Table 7.1.2) that on average the price dispersion in Germany is half that in the Community. Such a comparison shows the considerable potential for a reduction in the price differentials existing within the Community. The price-levelling role of competition highlighted here is a particularly strong argument in favour of abolishing frontiers. Moreover, bearing in mind that prices are to a large extent (input) costs borne by producers in their manufacturing operations, the potential for improving the costs and competitiveness of the Community economies is considerable.

Table 7.1.2.

Comparison of price dispersion: national and intra-Community (coefficients of variation as %)

	D[1]	Community[2]
Compact-disc players	10,6	14,9
Radio recorders	7,3	16,2
Turntables	9,6	10,8
Video recorders	5,7	13,2
Camera recorders	6,8	11,3
Video cassettes	5,7	13,3
Washing machines	3,3	13,4
Colour TVs	6,4	13,5

[1] *Source:* IFAV. The coefficient of variation was calculated on the basis of the average prices in the largest German cities.
[2] *Source:* BEUC and Eurostat (for the last two products). The number of Member States covered varies according to the number of products.

By way of illustration, a few calculations have been carried out to assess the effects of a convergence of price levels in the Community. These purely mechanical calculations are based on the findings of the Eurostat price survey and combined with the structure of expenditure on private consumption and equipment goods. The estimates concern the prices net of tax of 83 categories of product (63 consumer goods and 20 equipment goods) which account for approximately 43 % of the Community's GDP. Given the difficulties associated with obtaining tax-exclusive prices for certain services, the results for services are presented separately (see Table 7.1.3). If added to the results for goods, the

Table 7.1.3.

Evolution of potential gains from price convergence under different hypotheses (prices without taxes, 1985)

Hypotheses	Billion ECU			% of GDP	
	Goods	Civil engineering and services[1]	Total	Goods	Total goods and services
H1: convergence on the minimum price	192	58	250	6,5	8,3
H2: convergence on average EUR 9	51	13	64	1,7	2,1
H3: convergence on average EUR 9 less a standard deviation	150	54	204	5,1	6,7
H4: convergence on average EUR 9 less half a standard deviation	93	29	122	3,2	4,0

[1] Including the following services: communications, civil aviation, railways, financial services and postal services. The calculations are based on pre-tax prices except in the case of the last three categories, where post-tax prices were used. The results are, therefore, not totally comparable with those for goods alone.

estimates of price convergence cover a range of products which represents about 50 % of Community GDP.

Various hypotheses are possible as to the minimum reference price towards which the mechanical convergence should move. In order to furnish several illustrations of the scale of the potential gain, the results of the calculations are presented for four hypotheses which, although highly theoretical, may constitute the limits (mini-maxi) of the expected effects. These hypotheses are as follows:

H1 assumes that the single price law applies: competitive arbitrage operates fully so as to eliminate price differences and causes prices to converge on the lowest level attained in the Community. Under this extreme hypothesis, there is no room for any price differences, be they due to transport costs or whatever.

H2 is a conservative hypothesis under which only prices above the Community average converge on the current level of that average, the other prices remaining unchanged.

H3 and H4 are intermediate hypotheses used to illustrate the sensitivity of the results to different price dispersion hypotheses. In the first case (H3) the highest prices are assumed to converge on the Community average minus one standard deviation, and in the second (H4) those same prices converge on the Community average less half a standard deviation (see Figure 7.1).

Table 7.1.3 sets out the results of the application of these various hypotheses. The 'gains' have been evaluated by multiplying the price variations by the amount of expenditure on each category of product in each country, the overall effect being the result of aggregation for the Community of Nine (EUR9). The

FIGURE 7.1: **Hypothetical schematic representation of price differences for a given product**

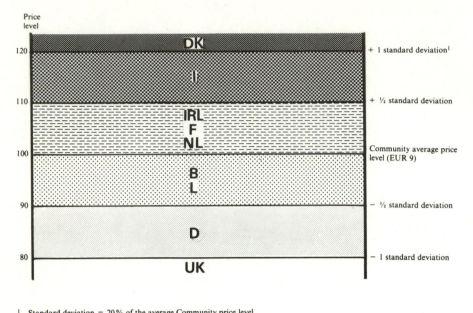

---

[1] Standard deviation = 20 % of the average Community price level.
½ standard deviation = 10 % of the average Community price level.

potential gains thus calculated range from 250 billion ECU, or 8,3 % of 1985 GDP, of which 192 billion ECU, 6,5 % of GDP in respect of goods alone, under hypothesis H1 to 64 billion ECU, or 1,7 % of GDP, of which goods represent 51 billion ECU, 1,7 % of GDP, under hypothesis H2. The other two hypotheses give, by definition, intermediate values.

It must be stressed that these calculations are purely mechanical and illustrative, being intended only to give some idea of the potential that price differences in the Community represent. Recognition of that potential is but the first step; one must now define the means by which competitive pressure can help achieve effective gains by exercising an influence both on prices (via price-cost margins) and on costs themselves (notably via an increase in the technical and economic efficiency of firms).

Competition and price-cost margins. As a direct result of the removal of barriers, competition will be accentuated — or in some extreme cases introduced — in markets which so far have enjoyed various forms of protection and in which businesses therefore have a certain monopoly power. This should squeeze price-cost margins in those sectors or strengthen price competition. It is interesting to note in this connection that the price differences recorded are fairly closely bound up with the degree of concentration in the corresponding sectors. A simple correlation exercise between price disparities and degrees of concentration at Community level has produced a correlation coefficient of + 0,82. It is therefore reasonable to expect increased competition to have an appreciable impact on prices, especially in the sectors most affected by completion of the internal market. A series of theoretical and empirical studies (see, in particular, Scherer (1980) and, for a more up-to-date analysis, Cubbin (1987)) have shown, moreover, in a closed economy context, that there is a positive relationship between various structural measures of monopoly power (degree of concentration, market share, height of barriers to entry, degree of product differentiation) and the size of price cost margins. These studies have sparked off a controversy over the transitional nature of the phenomena analysed in instant cross-section and the part played by efficiency in the achievement of high profits in concentrated industries. The most plausible conclusion is, however, that more competitive market structures tend to reduce the gap between price and unit cost.

But it is possible to go even further and show that potential competition, represented in particular by freedom of market entry, plays at least as important a role as market structures themselves. In this respect, certain studies, looking at an open economy situation, have tried to establish a relationship between margin size and a number of variables expressing the impact of competition from abroad. The clearest findings are those relating to the disciplining effect of imports on the relative gap between price and unit cost (see Zimmermann (1987)). This effect is illustrated in Figure 7.2. Under the oligopoly models of

FIGURE 7.2: **Effects of import competition on prices and costs**

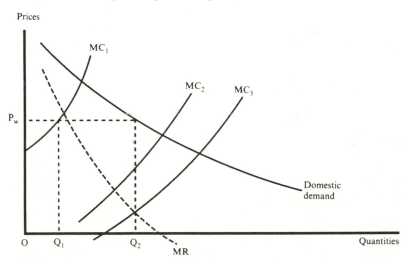

Note: In the chart, industry is faced with perfectly elastic import supply. This supply is going to discipline domestic producers assumed to have at the outset a monopoly power. The competition effect will vary in intensity, however, depending on the level of domestic marginal costs, which reflect the degree of efficiency of domestic producers. For a marginal cost MC_1, and a world price (incorporating the cost of tariff and non-tariff barriers) P_w, the monopolist will produce a quantity Q_1, for which P_w is equal to his marginal cost. The quantity imported is $Q_1 - Q_2$. If his marginal cost is MC_2 reflecting greater efficiency, the monopolist will receive a price higher than his marginal cost, but he will be unable to exploit his position to the full. It is only with marginal cost MC_3 that the domestic market is entirely protected.

Similarly, the lower the tariff and non-tariff barriers, the lower the level of the price P_w and the smaller the difference between the price and the domestic marginal cost. On the basis of this chart, the expected effect of completion of the internal market is twofold: firstly, a fall in prices and, secondly, a possible reduction in the level of domestic marginal costs, reflecting the desire of domestic firms not to lose their market.

Source: Jacquemin (1982).

the Cournot-Nash type, it is shown that, in equilibrium, there is in fact a negative relationship between the import ratio and the relative gap between price and marginal cost. Moreover, the impact of the import ratio interacts with the degree of concentration of domestic industry: the higher the degree of concentration, the greater the impact (Jacquemin, 1982).

The empirical studies confirm the disciplining effect of imports. Whether in the United States, the United Kingdom, Germany or France, there is a negative and significant relationship between the mark-up ratio and the import ratio.

A recent study (de Gehellinck, Geroski and Jacquemin, 1987) shows that, in the case of Belgian industries, external trade has a competitive disciplining effect on the performance of those industries in about 70 % of the sectors examined.

However, although a whole series of analyses agree on the nature of the impact of increased competition on price-cost margins, a direct quantitative assessment of the possible price effect of a fully integrated internal market cannot be carried out on the basis of those analyses. What is more, competitition does not only have the effect of increasing the pressure on margins; faced with stronger price competition, businesses will try to compress their costs and, in particular, increase their internal efficiency.

Competition and internal economic efficiency. How much influence monopoly power exerts on production costs is a particularly difficult question to answer, especially from the empirical point of view (see Siegfried and Wheeler, 1981). Even if the scope of the enquiry is limited to examining how far the opening-up of markets at Community level might act as a 'cold shower'[1] by submitting economies which are sheltered in various ways to the pressure of competition and the need to minimize costs, the empirical evidence is very thin on the ground. Neither the analyses employing the theory of international trade nor those devoted to various aspects of customs union are able to explain how and, above all, to what extent the 'cold shower' of competition may increase internal technical efficiency (see Pelkmans, 1982). It is therefore by turning to the analyses of internal behaviour of the firm that certain evaluations can be found, in particular in the literature on what is commonly called X-inefficiency (see Leibenstein (1966) and Comanor and Leibenstein (1969)).

The basic idea is that, in the absence of sufficient competitive pressures, there would be, for a given level of inputs, a poor exploitation of production facilities, an inefficient internal allocation of human, physical or financial resources, an under-employment of certain factors and duplications and redundancies that reflect excess 'organizational fat'. Such phenomena are particularly important in the area of managerial and executive duties. These excessive overhead costs are generally brought to light by internal or external audits. Consultants thus frequently succeed in identifying ways of reducing overhead costs by between 10 and 25 % through internal reorganization alone. On the basis of his analyses of American firms, Porter (1985) identifies the key areas where cost control is

---

[1] The 'cold shower' notion was used especially in the discussions on UK accession to the Community — see in particular J. Pelkmans (1982).

most often lacking: exclusive focus on production costs at the expense of the purchasing conditions for inputs, non-exploitation of the interdependencies between cost-affecting operations, effort to improve costs in a particular value chain and not for a globally restructured chain.

Through econometric studies, several authors have sought to identify the extra cost due to an environment protected from competition. They generally find a negative relationship between various measures of internal efficiency and various indicators of restriction of competition (concentration, cartelization, customs tariffs, etc.) (Scherer, 1980, Chapter 17).

A particularly meticulous study is that carried out by Primeaux (1977). It compares the costs of electricity generating companies, some faced with competition and others in a monopoly position. The study shows that the average cost is reduced on average by 10,75 % as a result of competition. This order of magnitude was confirmed by similar research into Belgian electricity distribution companies (De Bondt, 1981).

In the light of these studies, the new competitive pressures brought about by completion of the internal market can be expected to lead to rationalization within European enterprises and thus produce appreciable gains in internal efficiency. It is clear that the mechanisms referred to here, which correspond more often than not to changes in firms' decision-making practices in response to competition (see Nelson and Winter (1980) and Pelkmans (1982)), constitute much of what can be called the dynamic effects of the internal market. They amount, in effect, to changes in the behaviour of firms, which, inasmuch as they view the completion of the internal market as an opportunity (but also as a risk calling for a strategic response), experiment more and look around for new production processes or new products. This relationship with the non-price effects of competition should be clearly understood since it may be an additional source of dynamic gain for the internal market.

7.2. Non-price effects: competition and innovation

The analysis of the effects on costs and prices of removing barriers focuses mainly on studying the improvements in technical and economic efficiency which could result from the intensification of competition. However, competition has an impact not only on prices and costs; it can also have other favourable effects, *inter alia* through encouraging firms to improve their organizational structure, improve the quality and broaden the range of the products they offer to consumers and also through the promotion of technical progress and the diffusion of innovation. It is obvious that if the analysis is extended to cover this latter type of dynamic effect, the quantitative magnitude of the benefits to be anticipated from completing the internal market can go well beyond the direct gain that results from removing existing barriers (see in this regard Scherer (1987)).

The question arises as to whether European integration could also have beneficial effects on innovation and to reply to this question it is necessary to examine the link between the degree of competition and the rate of innovation. There are arguments which support two opposing views, namely that monopoly power increases the capacity for innovation and that it decreases the incentive to innovate. This section considers the theoretical grounds that underpin them and the empirical studies done on them.

It is possible to cite two main reasons for the greater innovative capacity of monopolists. In the first place, the profits to be anticipated from an innovation are greater for a firm that enjoys monopoly power on the end-user market than for a firm in a more competitive situation. By its very nature, a firm in a monopoly situation is in a position to make excess profits from the new product or process which its innovation enables it to manufacture or apply. However, it can, in addition, delay or even prevent imitations of the innovation which it has placed on the market, either by registering a patent or trade mark which affords it exclusive manufacturing rights or by erecting market-entry barriers (e.g. controlling distribution channels, advertising campaigns, economies of scale, etc.).

The second reason capable of attesting to monopolists' greater innovative capacity is bound up with the material advantages conferred by monopoly power. Such material advantages make it easier for firms to bear the costs and risks inherent in any innovation. For example, such advantages include the possibility of using an innovation to produce an adjunct to an existing product which only the monopolist manufactures. Likewise, the accumulation of monopoly profits makes it easier to finance research and development. Innovation can be financed internally and this confers on monopolists greater freedom of action.

Conversely, arguments can also be put forward to account for the fact that, in the absence of competitive pressure, the innovative urge withers away. The monopoly position gives rise to a feeling of security which, by encouraging conservative thinking and paralysing creativity, reduces innovative activity. Thus, a firm which makes monopoly profits has less incentive to endeavour to secure further profits through innovation than a firm in a more competitive situation which does not make excess profits on its routine business. Lastly, by preventing or delaying imitations, the firm which enjoys monopoly power can delay the diffusion of innovation.

In fact, three separate questions arise here. Firstly, there is the question of the direct effect of monopoly power on innovative activity. Secondly, it is necessary to examine the indirect relationship between market structure and innovations, i.e. the relationship which operates via the anticipated return from innovations. Lastly, an analysis is made of the rebound effect of innovation on market structure (see Figure 7.3). There is general agreement that the indirect effect is positive: monopoly power enables the anticipated return from innovations to be increased and it has, accordingly, a favourable influence on innovative activity. However, opinions differ as far as the direct effect is concerned. Supporters of the view that increased competition favours innovation argue the view that not only is the direct effect negative (the lack of

FIGURE 7.3: **Competition and innovation**

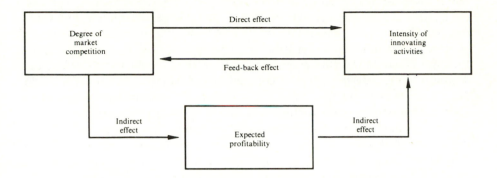

incentive to innovate which results from the absence of competitive pressures has a greater influence than the material advantages which the monopolist enjoys) but the adverse direct effect outweighs, moreover, the indirect effect.

In principle, the controversy regarding the part played by competition in regard to innovation could be settled on the basis of the findings of empirical studies. However, empirical verification of the link between competition and innovation raises a number of problems: defining and measuring innovative activity and the degree of competition, the uncertain direction of causality between these two variables (while the degree of competition can influence the rate of innovation, the converse is equally possible, in particular because the exploitation of an innovation makes it possible to erect market-entry barriers), the difficulty of isolating the impact of the degree of competition from other factors such as the potential for technological development and market growth. These questions are gone into in the empirical studies described below.

Empirical verification. Numerous empirical studies have considered the link between competition and innovation. These studies indicate that the concentration ratio — the variable generally used to measure the degree of competition[1] — is not the main factor explaining innovation. Thus, in Jacquemin (1979), it is found that research effort is accounted for more by a firm's belonging to a technological group than by the concentration ratio. The survey carried out by Kamien and Schwartz (1982) makes similar findings but those two writers demonstrate that additional factors can account for innovation, in particular ease of market entry and the potential for growth.

---

[1]   The degree of competition is generally measured by indices of concentration such as the Herfindahl index (sum of the squares of total market shares) and the market share held by the largest firms. In this connection, it should be noted that the degree of concentration — even if corrected for imports and exports — is not always a satisfactory indicator of monopoly power. The latter also depends on other factors such as barriers to market entry or the degree of differentiation of products. From this standpoint, the Lerner index, defined as (price-marginal cost)/price, is a better indicator of monopoly power. It is less frequently used in empirical studies because the available data do not always enable it to be calculated.

P. Geroski recently produced a study on the relationship between competition and innovation, covering the United Kingdom. The advantage of this study is that it distinguishes between the direct effect of competition on innovation and the indirect relationship between those two variables, i.e. the relationship which operates via the anticipated return from innovation. It also enables the rebound effect of innovation on market structure to be measured.

Another feature of this empirical study is that it endeavours to isolate relatively accurately the effect of competition on innovation. In order to do this, it identifies, in the first place, the influence on innovation of other factors such as technological development and market growth prospects so as not to distort the part played by competition.[2] Secondly, it takes account of six indicators of the degree of competition so as to include various differing aspects of competitive pressures. The indicators in question are the degree of concentration, barriers to market entry and exit and access for foreign products.

The findings would appear to support the proposition that a low level of competition is unfavourable to innovation since five of the six indicators used show an adverse direct effect of monopoly on innovation. Only the rate of penetration variable is not significant. However, it is quite clear that innovations are more numerous in industries which are less concentrated and where the barriers to market entry are low and there are relatively few withdrawals from the market.

The positive influence exerted by ease of market access is confirmed by Ergas (1984), who takes the view that the absence of barriers to market entry encourages the setting-up of new firms and therefore plays a particularly important part in the innovative process. New firms often have a greater incentive to experiment with new products or processes than well-established firms which have sometimes invested heavily in existing technology. Ergas also supports the view that the establishment of firms and, accordingly, innovation are assisted by ease of withdrawal from a market i.e. the ease with which companies can be wound up. This proposition is at variance with the findings made by Geroski.

Geroski's findings also indicate that there is a positive correlation between innovation and growth of production. This supports the view that expanding sectors are more innovative than stagnant sectors. This finding is in line with a recent study by Zimmermann (1987) covering Germany; here an attempt is made to identify the factors which account for innovation by distinguishing between product and process innovation in exporting and non-exporting firms. The study shows that the prospects for market growth constitute the main factor which determines innovation in industry — whether product or process

---

[2] Since the sectors characterized by high technological content of products and rapid growth of demand are generally more innovative and also more concentrated, there is a danger of overestimating the influence on innovation of the degree of concentration — and hence of competition — if the part played by each of those two factors is not identified separately.

innovation — but in the case of exporting firms, the part played by external demand outweighs that played by domestic demand. The study also finds that trade liberalization should have a favourable impact on innovation due, however, to competition on export markets rather than to import competition. Thus, the favourable effect which European integration would have on innovation through the medium of competition could be enhanced if such integration also improved the Community's openness to international trade and its growth potential. On the other hand, Geroski's study finds that market size does not, as such, have a significant effect on innovation. This supports the view set out above in point 6.1 that the beneficial effects of European integration on innovation derive more from the intensification of competition than from phenomena linked to size.

This empirical analysis also confirms the favourable impact of technological development on innovation. It would even appear that differences in the innovative effort of industries are due more to the degree of technological advance than to the degree of competition or the potential for growth. This study also shows that those sectors which are the most advanced technologically are the most concentrated, the most profitable and the largest. This explains why in numerous studies in which the influence of technological development is not isolated, there is a tendency to overestimate the impact on innovation of the degree of concentration, profitability and market size. It should be noted that *a priori*, technological development should likewise benefit from European integration by virtue of the greater mobility of scientists and the more rapid diffusion of technical progress between European firms.

It is more difficult to ascertain the indirect effect of competition on innovation. Although there is a clear positive relationship between monopoly and profitability, the influence of profits on innovation is not significant. In other words, it is not because monopolists can make more profits from innovation that they are encouraged to innovate more. Profits would not therefore appear to be an engine of innovation. This finding is in line with those of other empirical studies (see Kamien and Schwartz (1982)) which indicate that R&D activities require a certain level of profitability but that there is no positive correlation between innovative effort and the profits from that effort.

Lastly, this empirical study attempts to measure the rebound effect of innovation on market structure. It finds that innovation clearly has an adverse impact on the degree of concentration of markets. According to this finding, the long-term dynamic effects of completing the European internal market should be larger than those felt in the medium term. Intensification of competition could initially stimulate innovation which in its turn would intensify competition. This latter result is, however, not certain. It should be emphasized that the analysis of the reciprocal relationship between innovation and market structure in the Geroski study is relatively perfunctory. This extremely complex question has given rise to a wealth of recent writings and has been investigated using more sophisticated models in which economic agents are presumed to take successive decisions, taking full account of the potential reactions of their competitors in the innovation race and of the consequences of their actions on their market shares (see, notably, Kamien and Schwartz (1982)). This work shows that findings regarding the impact of innovation on market structures are far from being definitive.

In conclusion it would seem that the completion of the European internal market should have a positive overall effect on innovation through a set of interrelated mechanisms: increased competition, more openness to international trade, increased growth potential, intensification of technological development by virtue of increased mobility of researchers, etc. This favourable effect will be most evident in high technology sectors and those in which the outlook for growth is favourable. These are precisely the sectors in which Europe suffered the sharpest loss of market share between 1979 and 1985 (see Part B). It is possible that by increasing the effort to innovate in these sectors the completion of the European internal market could check the contraction of market share.

European integration would thus assist the emergence of a virtuous circle of innovation and competition — competition stimulating innovation which in turn would increase competition. This is not to say that the desired form of competition corresponds to the theoretical and simplified model of perfect competition. The relationship between competition and innovation is not linear and indeed there exists an optimal level of competition beyond which competition has an adverse effect on innovation because of the difficulty of allocating gains and the greater risks which obtain in highly competitive markets. The optimum market structure from the standpoint of innovation ought rather to promote strategic rivalry between a limited number of firms.

8. Business perceptions, strategies and accompanying policies

Analysis of the phenomena of scale and of the mechanisms associated with intensified competition has revealed considerable potential for an improvement in economic efficiency. It has also very clearly demonstrated the essential role played by the firm in responding to the challenge and the opportunities offered by the large internal market and the removal of non-tariff barriers which it implies. To realize this potential to the full, firms will have to launch themselves into a far-reaching process of adjustment to the new circumstances of the European economy. Furthermore, accompanying microeconomic policies are required to facilitate the adaptation of both private and public agents to the new market conditions.

The first section of this chapter looks at how firms view the opportunities and constraints and how they perceive the workings of the economic mechanisms involved in the integration process.

The second section looks at the strategies adopted by European firms in response, particularly restructuring and cross-border cooperation.

The last section describes concisely the anticipated role of Community competition policy, common external policy and also redistributive policy.

8.1. Business perceptions

This analysis of European business perceptions of the prospects opened up by completion of the internal market is based on the results of a wide-ranging survey of Community firms organized by the Commission departments (see the Nerb study, and Chapter 3.1, for perceptions of the relative importance of barriers). This has made it possible to highlight particularly interesting points of information and replies.

The perception of the effects on costs (see Table 8.1.1). In general, firms surveyed feel that the removal of barriers will result in lower costs (62 % of respondants for EUR 12 of which 25 % believe that the reduction will be very substantial), but a large minority (36 %) does not expect any effect while very few (2 %) expect their costs to increase. The most significant divergences are between Belgium and Italy at one extreme (about 85 % of firms expect lower costs) and at the other extreme Spain (reduction 49 %, no effect 34 %, slight increase 2 %), Germany (reduction 52 %, no effect 47 %, slight increase 1 %), and France (reduction 53 %, no effect 40 %, slight increase 7 %).

As regards the size of this cost effect (see Table 8.1.1), the answers given by firms show a very large measure of convergence, with an expected average fall of around 2 % in total unit costs for the firms main product line. The wording of the question suggests that the effect reported is a static effect, or more precisely what has been defined as the direct effect of the removal of barriers. The indirect consequences resulting from greater exploitation of economies of scale and of economies of product range, and even more of the restructuring of firms, are not being taken fully into account in this estimate.

It should be noted, too, that this fall in costs is expressed as a proportion of total costs; if the estimate is related to total value-added, the net economic effect is about $3\frac{1}{4}$ % of value-added, which is a very appreciable figure.

An analysis of the causes reported by industrialists for this reduction in costs is also very informative (see Table 8.1.1). Lower distribution costs are cited first (in first place in nine countries out of 12, which is very significant), followed by lower costs of imported material and then higher productivity in the production process. However, while the direct cost reduction effects resulting from the removal of barriers (distribution, imported inputs) are certainly put first, it is interesting to note that reduced production costs are also seen as an important factor in the fall in costs in a sizeable number of countries (B, DK, D and UK, where this cause is cited in second place).

By contrast, banking costs and the costs of insurance and of marketing, although significant, generally rank lower. But it should be noted that in certain countries (E, I, L) banking costs are cited in second or third place; in Greece they are in first place. These results confirm those obtained in the Price Waterhouse study on the cost of non-Europe in financial services.

Perception of the impact on sales volume. Firms' expectations as to the effects of the removal of barriers on the volume of their sales were the subject of questions which tried to distinguish between effects according to the geographical destination of sales (Table 8.1.2).

In general, firms expected very little change in their home sales (no change 62 % for EUR 12), and expectations of increases (20 %) and decreases (18 %) are remarkably evenly balanced overall. But in some countries the proportion of respondents fearing a fall in sales on the home market was far from negligible, and in the case of Greece and France, taken together with very modest expectations of increased sales, the net result is an expectation of reduced sales on the home market.

A negative impact is also expected, though by far fewer respondents, in Belgium, Denmark, Ireland and Portugal. It should be noted, though, that businessmen anticipate the overall volume of the market to grow, as we shall see, so that even in countries where the net result is stable home sales would in reality mean a loss of market share.

On the other hand, the expected impact on exports to other Community countries is particularly clear-cut, and illustrates very well the role which in businessmen's opinion is played by the Community market. A total of 67 % of respondents expect an increase in their sales to other Community countries (between 55 % in Greece and 89 % in the Netherlands), while very few expect a reduction (a total of 3 %). This expectation in part reflects optimism among businessmen as regards their capacity to win market share in the Community, but it has very positive implications in terms of the expansion of the overall

Table 8.1.1.

Business opinions on the effects on costs of removing barriers (replies in %)

Industry as a whole	B	DK	D	GR	E	F	IRL	I	L	NL	P	UK	EUR 12
Cost reduction													
— very significant	27	1		10	8	8	6	26	20	11	32	8	25
— slightly significant	58	52	52	61	41	45	61	57	60	44	36	50	37
No effect/no answer	15	46	47	23	34	40	30	17	10	45	30	37	36
Cost increase													
— very significant	0	0		1	0	0	0	0	0	0	1	0	2
— slightly significant	0	1	1	5	2	7	3	0	10	0	1	0	0
Net effect 1(a)	−85	−52	−51	−65	−47	−46	−64	−83	−70	−55	−66	−58	−60
Net effect 2(a)	−56	−26		−35	−27	−27	−34	−55	−40	−33	−49	−33	−43
Total effect (%)			−2	−3	−3	−2	−2	−2	−2	−2	−2	−2	−2
Source of cost reduction (classification (b))													
Production process	2	2/3	2	5	4	3	5	4	3	3	2	2	3
Banking costs	4	5/6	4/5	1	2/3	4	3/4	2/3	2	4	4	5	4
Distribution costs	1	1	1	3/4	2/3	1	1	1	1	1	3	1	1
Marketing costs	5	2/3	4/5	6	5	6	6	6	6	5/6	6	4	5
Costs of imported material	3	4	3	2	1	2	3/4	2/3	4/5	2	1	3	2
Insurance costs	6	5/6	6	3/4	6	5	2	5	4/5	5/6	5	6	6

(a) Net effect 1 = percentage difference between firms expecting a reduction in costs (−) and firms expecting an increase (+).
Net effect 2 = weighted difference (%) between firms expecting a reduction in costs ('very significant' −1, 'slightly significant' −0.5) and firms expecting an increase ('slightly significant' +0.5, 'very significant' +1).
(b) Classified on a scale of 1 to 6 in order of importance of the various sources of the reduction in costs (1 being the most important).

165

Table 8.1.2.

Business opinions on the expected effects on sales volumes of completing the internal market

Industry as a whole	B	DK	D	GR	E	F	IRL	I	L	NL	P	UK	EUR 12
Home sales													
Increase substantially	0	0	2	1	11	0	2	6	0	12	5	0	3
Increase somewhat	15	8	15	10	26	8	12	21	10	25	20	6	15
Remain unchanged/don't know	63	81	75	54	46	64	68	64	90	54	48	81	58
Decrease somewhat	20	10	7	6	11	27	14	1	0	4	23	12	11
Decrease substantially	2	1	1	29	6	1	4	8	0	5	4	1	3
Net effect (a)	−7	−3	+9	−24	+20	−20	−4	+18	+10	+28	−2	−7	+4
Net effect (b)	−5	−2	+5	−26	+13	−11	−3	+8	+5	+18	−1	−4	+2
Exports to EEC countries													
Increase substantially	13	11	14	4	35	7	16	25	10	37	17	9	17
Increase somewhat	74	49	50	51	22	50	55	43	70	52	48	69	50
Remain unchanged/don't know	13	39	35	43	40	34	28	30	20	11	35	22	30
Decrease somewhat	0	1	1	0	2	9	1	0	0	0	0	0	2
Decrease substantially	0	0	0	2	1	0	0	2	0	0	0	0	1
Net effect (a)	+87	+59	+63	+53	+54	+48	+70	+66	+80	+89	+65	+78	+64
Net effect (b)	+50	+35	+39	+28	+44	+28	+43	+45	+45	+65	+41	+44	+40
Exports to non-EEC countries													
Increase substantially	3	0	6	5	17	1	1	9	10	8	3	0	6
Increase somewhat	30	12	22	18	23	16	8	27	30	15	22	13	20
Remain unchanged/don't know	67	86	71	75	57	76	82	62	60	74	71	86	72
Decrease somewhat	0	2	1	0	2	7	9	1	0	3	4	1	2
Decrease substantially	0	0	0	2	1	0	0	1	0	0	0	0	0
Net effect (a)	+33	+10	+27	+21	+37	+10	0	+34	+40	+20	+21	+12	+24
Net effect (b)	+18	+5	+17	+12	+27	+6	+1	+21	+25	+14	+12	+6	+15

Total sales to all markets

Increase substantially	5	6	4	3	22	1	7	13	0	11	12	3	7
Increase somewhat	76	44	54	37	19	42	57	59	70	39	49	68	52
Remain unchanged/don't know	19	47	38	45	52	47	27	24	30	50	29	26	36
Decrease somewhat	0	2	3	4	3	40	8	1	0	0	8	3	4
Decrease substantially	0	1	1	11	4	0	1	3		9	2	0	1
Net effect (a)	+81	+47	+54	+25	+34	+33	+55	+68	+70	+40	+51	+68	+54
Net effect (b)	+43	+26	+29	+9	+26	+17	+31	+39	+35	+31	+31	+36	+30
Total effect	+7	+6	+5	+1	+9	+3	+7	+7	+5	+7	+7	+5	+5

Net effect (a) = Percentage difference between firms expecting an increase in sales (+) and firms expecting a reduction (−).
Net effect (b) = Percentage weighted difference between firms expecting an increase in sales ('substantially' + 1, 'somewhat' + 0.5) and firms expecting a reduction ('substantially' − 1, 'somewhat' − 0.5).

market which it assumes and the importance of the effects of product range and the diversification of products.

Exports to non-Community countries are also fairly generally cited as a source of growth in sales, but to a far smaller extent than exports within the Community (increase 26 %, no change 72 %, decrease 2 %).

Taken overall, the feeling prevails that there will be general growth in sales. Nevertheless, in some countries (particularly Greece and France) the net increase in sales expected is relatively modest, and a majority of businessmen expect sales to remain static. When it comes to estimating the size of the total increase in sales, the net effect is very high (+ 5 % on average); this clearly illustrates businessmen's belief that the overall market will expand very significantly. A particularly interesting comparison can be made here with the average estimate of the fall in costs (2 %). It should be noted at the outset that the question concerning sales expectations was worded so as to take account not only of the immediate direct effects of the removal of barriers but also of the more long-term dynamic effects resulting from the whole process of adjustment. In addition, while producers expect their share of home markets to contract in general, as a result of increased competition, export sales, particularly in the Community market, are expected to grow quite appreciably. A parallel can be drawn with previous studies devoted to the link between the growth of trade (within the EEC in particular) and technical and economic efficiency (scale and production costs). The role played by the scale/competition mechanism in the achievement of particularly appreciable economic gains has been demonstrated, and can certainly be seen as an important factor in the dynamic economic process that causes the total market to expand.

To check the coherence of the replies concerning reduced costs and increased sales, an analysis of the basic micro-economic information was carried out. The relationship found between movements in costs and movements in sales is much as expected: the more a firm believes it would be able to reduce its costs, the more it expects a big increase in sales. But clearly there are a great many additional factors which guide firms' strategy for the development of sales (product quality, capacity for innovation, market situation, buoyancy of final demand, link with product cycle — see Figure 6.1 for experience effects), so that the expected movement in costs can provide only part of the explanation.

As regards the main reasons cited for the expected positive effect on sales volume (Table 8.1.3), it is particularly interesting to see that the answers given are generally in line with the overall economic logic. The reason reported in first place is ability to enter new regional markets, which is another illustration of the part played by 'external' markets in enlarging the sphere of activity. Two reasons are cited in equal second place. One is an improvement in non-price competitiveness, with particular reference to a widening of the product range; this is indeed an important variable, though difficult to quantify, in the list of gains expected from the internal market. The second of the two reasons given is the reduction in product price in existing markets, which may indicate that in addition to a fall in costs, industrialists expect that with intensified compe-

Table 8.1.3.

Principal reasons invoked for positive effects on sales (rank ordering)

Industry as a whole	B	DK	D	GR	E	F	IRL	I	L	NL	P	UK	EUR 12
Reduction of product prices in existing markets	1	4	1	4	1	3	2	3	3	5	4	3	2/3
Ability to enter new (regional) markets	4	2	2	3	2	1	3	2	1	1	2	1	1
Improvement in non-price competitiveness (e.g. changes in the product range)	2	1	3	1	3	2	1	1	3	2	2	2	2/3
Withdrawal of competitors	5	5	5	5	4	5	4	4	3	3	5	5	5
Generally faster-growing markets thanks to completion of the internal market	3	3	4	2	5	4	5	5	2	4	1	4	4

Classified on a scale of 1 to 5 in order of importance of the reasons cited (1 being the most important).

169

tition (on existing markets) they will have to reduce their price-cost margins (see Section 7.1).

To sum up, European firms on the whole see the completion of the internal market as an opportunity for themselves (56 %) and for the economy of their country (49 %) far more than as a threat (7 % for themselves, 14 % for their country, see Table 8.1.4). It does therefore represent a challenge in response to which European firms seem to want to seize the opportunity to improve their competitiveness and consequently their market share.

8.2. Business strategies

The survey presented in the preceding section also provides some information regarding the strategies envisaged by firms to prepare for 1992.[1] Two main responses emerge: measures to improve productivity, and increases in the number of international cooperation agreements. It should be noted that the intention to increase the number of agreements is by far the dominant one, with partners located in other Community countries being preferred to partners in non-member countries. Firms of all sizes display a similar desire for cooperation.

The investment envisaged is mainly in R&D and in enlarging the firm's product range. The need for investment of this kind is felt particularly strongly by small and medium-sized enterprises. Its location would mainly be the home market in the case of such enterprises, while large firms would aim rather more at the markets of the other Member States.

This information is useful, but fragmentary; it could usefully be supplemented by a more general view of the problems and challenges now confronting European firms. That is the purpose of this section. It should be pointed out right away, however, that firms' ability effectively to meet these challenges depends on their managerial capacity, and raises the whole question of the training of European managers and of the internal system of organization adopted (see De Woot, 1987, European Management Forum, 1985).

Over the last few years the economic environment of European business has changed substantially. Given slower economic growth and competition which has the world as its setting, the priority is no longer to make fine optimization calculations or establish a system of corporate planning for given demand and cost conditions; the task is more to build dominant positions by combining flexibility and strategic investment.[1]

---

[1]   This was an optional question. The firms which replied were those from Greece, Spain, Luxembourg, Ireland, the Netherlands and the United Kingdom.

[1]   A typical example is that of 'platforms' in motor vehicle manufacture. These platforms combine features of the production line and of flexible production systems, allowing mass production to be combined with the making of differentiated products aimed at different market segments.

Table 8.1.4.

Opportunities and risks in the completion of the internal market (replies in %)

Industry as a whole	B	DK	D	GR	E	F	IRL	I	L	NL	P	UK	EUR 12
For your company													
Opportunities much greater	35	12	15	15	26	9	33	26	20	26	35	21	19
Opportunities somewhat greater	38	42	37	40	33	36	33	38	40	25	25	45	37
About the same/don't know	25	42	41	19	30	49	28	30	40	44	30	29	37
Risks somewhat greater	2	3	6	21	6	5	3	5	0	2	11	4	5
Risks much greater	0	1	1	5	5	1	3	1		3	7	1	2
Net effect (a)	+71	+50	+45	+29	+48	+39	+60	+58	+60	+46	+42	+61	+49
Net effect (b)	+53	+31	+30	+20	+35	+24	+45	+42	+40	+35	+35	+41	+33
For the economy of your country													
Opportunities much greater	35	15	17	14	25	7	23	21	40	30	31	18	18
Opportunities somewhat greater	45	44	33	19	24	29	43	28	20	32	23	38	31
About the same/don't know	18	33	43	19	37	40	17	36	40	31	22	33	38
Risks somewhat greater	2	7	6	29	6	20	14	10	0	5	16	10	10
Risks much greater	0	1	1	19	8	4	3	5	0	2	8	1	3
Net effect (a)	+78	+51	+43	-15	+35	+12	+49	+34	+60	+55	+30	+45	+36
Net effect (b)	+57	+33	+30	-10	+26	+8	+35	+25	+50	+42	+27	+31	+26

Net effect (a) = Percentage difference between firms saying opportunities were greater (+) and firms saying risks were greater (−).
Net effect (b) = Weighted difference (%) between firms saying opportunities were much greater (+1) or somewhat greater (+0.5) and firms saying risks were much greater (−1) or somewhat greater (−0.5).

In this context competition is no longer a set of interactions between passive agents but rather a dynamic interplay where the application of new forms of organization, the opening-up of new markets, the introduction of new products and new production methods constantly threaten any possible equilibrium, manipulate the rules of the game and shift the terms of the contest in favour of certain participants (see Jacquemin, 1985).

But the strategic interplay between firms cannot be studied as a whole, because it depends to a great extent on the structural characteristics of the field of activity in which it takes place. In each of the broad types of structural environment the impact of the achievement of the internal market will be different. Three cases can be distinguished (see Porter, 1985).

In a structural environment of the fragmented type small firms dominate and few firms hold a market share sufficient to enable them to exercise a powerful influence in the industry. The costs of market entry and withdrawal are low, and diseconomies of scale outweigh economies of scale. Product and customer differentiation comes in many guises and changes over time, so that many small firms co-exist, with varying and unstable margins which often depend on the quality of their management. In these industries ('creative' activities, wood, furs, retail trade, see Table 8.2.1), the achievement of the internal market should

Table 8.2.1.

Sectors for which the share of small enterprises (less than 20 persons) is superior to 25% of the total turnover of the sector

NACE		Average[1]
456	Manufacture of furs and of fur goods	60,4
419	Bread and flour confectionery	46,8
231	Extraction of building materials and refractory clays	43,0
491	Manufacture of articles of jewellery and goldsmiths' and silver-smiths' wares; cutting or otherwise working of precious and semi-precious stones	39,1
465	Other wood manufactures (except furniture)	38,5
461	Sawing and processing of wood	36,3
504	Building completion work	34,4
372	Manufacture of medical and surgical equipment and orthopaedic appliances (except orthopaedic footwear)	34,3
464	Manufacture of wooden containers	34,0
245	Working of stone and of non-metallic mineral products	31,4
442	Manufacture of products from leather and leather substitutes	29,7
492	Manufacture of musical instruments	29,3
416	Working of grain	26,4
463	Manufacture of carpentry and joinery components and of parquet flooring	26,1

[1] Average of figures available for large Member States.

Source: Eurostat industry survey (1983).

have a limited impact, except in so far as it might change the rules of the competitive game and encourage a changeover to mass production of standardized products. Non-tariff barriers play a marginal role as compared with factors such as local or regional differences in consumer tastes.

In a structural environment of the specialized type, small and large firms divide the market between them. Product differentiation is frequent, and it is exploited. There is a large number of niches for quite specific products, but each niche market is generally fairly small, which goes some way towards explaining the large number of small firms in these areas. Within each niche, however, the competitor with the largest market share is generally more profitable than the others. It is worth pointing out that the emerging industries are often of the specialized type, and include a high proportion of newly-formed firms (lasers, aquaculture, micro-computers, medical and surgical equipment etc.). Several technologies may co-exist, and there is no dominant standard. Technological development can substantially change the boundaries and nature of the activity. The fundamental choices for firms in these industries are the breadth of the range and the geographical area to be served. Achievement of the internal market will have a considerable effect on these specialized industries. The product/market niche will grow substantially with the geographical area served, since non-tariff barriers (standards, various approval procedures) have slowed down trade within the Community.

In mass production environments, market share has a high value and the potential for differentiation is low. Here profitability is clearly linked to market share, and large firms predominate. Firms with more than 500 employees generally account for more than 80 % of total turnover in the industry (see Table 8.2.2): office machines, data-processing equipment, telecommunications equipment, basic chemicals. These industries are also those in which demand is currently expanding rapidly, and where the minimum level of R&D spending is high. Concentration and cooperation at European level are thus often necessary (but not sufficient) conditions for the recovery of lost market share, particularly as European productivity is lagging far behind in these areas. These industries also depend to a great extent on public contracts.

Completion of the internal market thus provides an opportunity for European firms to achieve better control of these various types of structural environment in the Community context and in the world. Certain aspects of the appropriate strategies can be explained in more detail.

Let us look first at restructuring and at cooperation with other firms. Restructuring can be internal or external. Internally, it will often be necessary to rationalize and to concentrate on particular products. Many firms will have to concentrate on their main product line, and to withdraw from other activities. Geographical coverage will also need to be extended within the internal market. Externally, mergers and takeovers will permit strategies aimed at better exploitation of returns to scale, wider geographical diversification, and greater international division of labour within the European market. These operations may create truly European companies which have no special links to a particular country and are thus able to escape from the 'national champion' mentality.

In 1985/86 we do observe an increase in the number of Community and international mergers, and a decline in purely national amalgamations, even though in 1986 almost two-thirds of mergers and acquisitions of majority holdings were still inside the national borders of one or other Member State. At international level, merger transactions within the Community were on average about twice as numerous as international transactions involving non-Community countries.[1] If we look at the breakdown of the acquisitions of majority holdings by size of company (combined turnover of the participants), we see that this type of transaction continues to be dominated by large firms. About 50 % of the transactions involve companies which belong to the upper group of the sample studied by the Commission, meaning that they have a combined turnover of over a billion ECU. Achievement of the internal market could encourage mergers between smaller firms currently specialized in similar products or markets inside a Member State (see Table 8.2.7). Mergers could enable them both to preserve their flexibility and to acquire access to larger markets, which would allow scale and learning economies to be made. However, in view of the frequent failure of horizontal mergers, the even more frequent abortive attempts at conglomerate diversification, we should mistrust amalgamations based exclusively on financial or personal links which do not lead to any genuine integration reflected in an overall strategy. Some mergers ultimately produce groups with no internal coherence, and can represent a desperate attempt at survival on the part of ailing companies unable to make any new investment.[2]

Cooperation arrangements, with or without the setting-up of a joint venture, can also in certain circumstances facilitate the exploitation of the new opportunities opened up by an open internal market. Hitherto there have been many obstacles in the way of cooperative agreements, and the failure rate has been high. In addition to the difficulties of finding a partner able to make balanced contribution, setting up a management structure to minimize the running costs of cooperation, and ensuring full and fair use of the proceeds, there is also a set of regulatory and political obstacles to cooperation in Europe. According to a recent survey there are seven barriers which play a role of this kind[3]: discrimination in national industrial policy; differences in company law and taxation systems; disparities in the regulatory framework governing goods and production; obstacles to trade within the Community; certain purely national

---

[1] See Commission of the European Communities (1987), *Sixteenth Report on Competition Policy*, Part Four; and Tables 8.2.3 to 8.2.6 of this report.

[2] For a systematic analysis of the negative effects of many mergers where the management problem is central, see Scherer (1984).

[3] Study by European Research Associates and Prognos, based on interviews with about 70 companies located in four countries (Germany, France, Italy and the United Kingdom) and having subsidiaries or parent companies in most Member States.

Table 8.2.2.

The importance of larger enterprises in European countries in certain sectors (share of firms employing more than 500 people in total turnover of the industry)

NACE Code	Branches	B	DK	D	F	I	NL	UK
	High-demand, high-technology industries							
33	Office machinery and data-processing machinery	79,2	—	89,4	93,5	92,8	—	74,9
344	Telecommunications equipment	—	50,7	84,3	71,5	79,9	—	72,2
251	Basic chemicals	70,8	—	95,0	81,8	75,7	—	74,2
	Low-demand traditional industries							
43	Textiles	20,9	—	40,2	43,3	24,1	23,1	—
41/42	Food, drink and tobacco	48,2	—	46,7	44,4	—	43,1	—

Source: Eurostat.

arrangements concerning capital markets; and differences in social policy, particularly pension and social security schemes. The biggest of these barriers, both in terms of launching a cross-border activity and in terms of the administration and location of that activity, is believed to be differences in company law and tax systems. This raises the problem of Community-level consolidation for tax purposes and intra-group transfers. Barriers to the mobility of human resources arising out of social legislation, particularly as regards pensions and education, are also important. Finally, adaptation to different national standards seems in some cases to absorb a large proportion of the budget which firms devote to R&D.

The paradox which emerges is that cooperation with Community partners has so far been less frequent than cooperation with partners in non-member countries. The total number of joint ventures set up has remained very stable; in 1985/86 Community operations still lagged behind (24,7 % of the total) by comparison with domestic operations (42 %) and international operations (33,3 %). The situation is much the same in the case of acquisitions of minority holdings. But European cooperation could grow substantially as a result of the removal of some of these barriers. Let us note here that cooperation arrangements with non-Community partners are an effective way of using the internal market as a springboard for penetrating the world market. One example is a European firm acquiring a high level of competitiveness thanks to cost savings and learning economies achieved on the internal market, building up a strategic capacity by means of its resources in R&D, qualified staff and marketing, and

Table 8.2.3.

Breakdown of mergers/take-overs and majority shareholding acquisitions by nature of the operation

Year	National		Community		International		Total	
1982/83	59	(50,5)	38	(32,5)	20	(17,0)	117	(100)
1983/84	101	(65,2)	29	(18,7)	25	(16,1)	155	(100)
1984/85	146	(70,2)	44	(21,2)	18	(8,7)	208	(100)
1985/86	144	(63,7)	52	(23,0)	30	(13,3)	226	(100)

Figures in brackets indicate percentage of total.

Source: Commission, *Sixteenth Report on Competition Policy,* 1987.

Table 8.2.4.

Breakdown of minority shareholding acquisitions by nature of the operation

Year	National	Community	International	Total
1982/83	20	9	4	33
1983/84	37	8	9	54
1984/85	45	10	12	67
1985/86	88	20	22	130

Source: Commission, *Sixteenth Report on Competition Policy,* 1987.

Table 8.2.5.

Breakdown of the creation of subsidiaries by nature of the operation

Year	National	Community	International	Total
1982/83	23	8	15	46
1983/84	32	11	26	69
1984/85	40	15	27	82
1985/86	34	20	27	81

Source: Commission, *Sixteenth Report on Competition Policy,* 1987.

deciding to win foreign market share through an alliance with a local firm or a firm in a non-member country.

This brings us to the problems of entry of new firms on to markets. One of the sources of American dynamism has always been the scale of the constant renewal and rejuvenation of the population of firms, as firms enter and leave markets all the time. This is especially so in the field of advanced technology (Ergas, 1984), where new arrivals on the market have brought more than their proportionate share of new processes and new products. In Europe, on the other hand, the large established firms have more often than not monopolized the scene, taking advantage in particular of the special relationship they have with their domestic public authorities.

But with the intensification of trade caused by the removal of non-tariff barriers, opportunities for entry, whether by setting up a new firm or diversifying an existing one, are going to grow more frequent, and will permit a rejuvenation of the industrial base. Cooperation between small and medium-sized European firms will facilitate market entry and allow them to move on from the Community market to the world market.

Table 8.2.6.

Evolution of concentration in manufacturing industry

Year	Share of largest firms in total turnover (%)				
	25	50	100	200	400
1975	13,0	18,7	24,0	29,0	33,8
1978	13,6	18,7	23,9	29,0	33,6
1981	14,4	20,0	26,3	32,2	37,6
1982	14,4	20,2	26,2	32,0	37,4

Source: Commission, *Fourteenth Report on Competition Policy,* 1985.

Table 8.2.7.

The place of small enterprises (less than 20 persons) in industrial production, 1983

Share of small firms	DK	D	F	UK	JAP
In total number of firms (%)	74,6	83,3	88,1	74,1	78,2
In total employment (%)	12,3	9,7	11,1	9,4	25,8
In total turnover (%)	11,0	6,8	7,8	8,0	11,7

Source: Eurostat.

177

On the other hand the question needs to be asked as to whether European firms have the capacity to resist market entrants from non-member countries who will try to be the first to take advantage of the large market. That capacity depends on the existence of strategic barriers to entry. The main tools for creating such barriers are the exploitation of the position of innovator and first firm on a market ('first mover advantage'); the use of more rapid learning processes, which amplify the first mover advantage; special relationships with customers and suppliers, which create durable links by increasing the cost of changing partner; control of a range of products, including substitutes, etc. Thus a distinctive European character can be affirmed in different ways, reflecting a 'Community preference'. This makes European standards (information, compatibility, quality etc.) an essential weapon in the great industrial battles of today; they are keys opening up and controlling markets through technological alliances. The same is true of joint European research programmes which stimulate cooperation across borders between Community firms and research centres.

Ultimately the competitiveness of Europe in a completed internal market will be the competitiveness of its firms.

8.3. Accompanying microeconomic policies

Completion of the internal market and abolition of the large number of non-tariff barriers are expected to exert downward pressure on costs and prices. After a time lag, the increased dynamism of the competitive process will also promote new investment, prompt the restructuring and multinationalization of companies, lead to relocation, disengagement and 'creative destruction' and, finally, encourage technological progress through an increased flow of innovative processes and products. Although these effects are generally favourable, they are likely to create a climate of increased uncertainty for those involved in the economic process. Firstly, there is the question of the competition rules which will govern the new dynamism. These rules and their implementation must ensure that any private or public abuse likely to distort this interplay of competitive forces to the advantage of certain participants is prevented. Secondly, expectations concerning the distribution of benefits between factors of production, sectors and regions are a further cause for concern among certain groups in the economy. Community measures will therefore need to meet some of the adjustment costs, such as those relating to the retraining of workers and the adaptation of local infrastructure to the requirements of a larger market. Finally, completion of the large internal market requires choices to be made on the external policy front.

Let us briefly examine these three aspects.

If the favourable effects of completion of the internal market are to materialize, the competitive process must be maintained. That process enables firms to exploit new opportunities; productivity gains and cost reductions lead to lower prices, improved quality and a wider choice of products; and finally, the general level of welfare improves.

Yet it is by no means certain that, in this new context, economic agents will accept the operation of free competition. As experience following the lowering of tariff barriers has shown, the Community authorities may well be confronted with more and more private and public strategies that seek to diminish or distort competition. There is a particular danger of:

(i) private or public concentration operations which are designed to create dominant positions and which may lead to such forms of abuse as the setting up of barriers to the entry of new firms, market sharing discrimination and predatory pricing;

(ii) an intensification of direct and indirect government intervention to safeguard a policy of 'national champions' or to prevent the opening up of certain national markets and activity sectors.

In all of these cases, the Community authorities must ensure implementation of credible rules which are directly applicable to all, including third country companies which may seek to exploit the integrated market unfairly to their own advantage. The competition rules of the Treaty of Rome are already applicable to both public and private restrictions of competition. At both levels, however, selective tightening up is to be expected.

Firstly, in a situation in which takeovers and acquisitions of holdings move large sums on the stock markets Community legislation enabling the Commission to authorize operations which are in the Community's interest would be beneficial to those companies which wish to develop their activities throughout the integrated market. In addition, the 1992 deadline necessitates adoption of the Commission's proposed system of prior and rapid control of mergers that are likely to reduce competition substantially in the Community. In the meantime, the European Court of Justice has confirmed the Commission's right to apply both Article 85 and Article 86 of the Treaty of Rome to share acquisitions between competing companies (Philip Morris case).

Secondly, monitoring of state aids which may affect trade between Member States has been stepped up at both regional and sectoral levels. The Commission is pursuing a policy of requiring repayment of aid granted unlawfully by Member States and judged to be incompatible with the common market; it has also decided to apply this principle where Member States have failed to comply with the obligation to notify the Commission in advance of proposed aid schemes (see *Sixteenth Report on Competition Policy, 1987*).

Competition must also play an increasing role in distribution and services. In the case of distribution, the Commission and the European Court of Justice have adopted a series of decisions and judgments ensuring that distribution systems do not prevent parallel imports and that no category of purchaser is discriminated against and excluded from supplies.

As to services, their gradual deregulation requires the dimension of the large internal market for effective operation. National markets in the Community are generally too small to leave real scope for competition following deregulation, as each market tends to constitute a natural monopoly. Such is the case in telecommunications and air transport. The Community area is becoming the appropriate dimension for competition in all those fields in which national markets are too small for effective competition. It was with this in mind that the Commission and the Court of Justice have clearly stated that the rules of competition are applicable to banking and air services as well as to other sectors of the economy.

A general principle applicable to the various types of services (transport, financial services, telecommunications) is therefore that there should be the greatest possible scope for competition, within the limits set by important aspects of the public interest, such as the safety of users and continuity of supply of services. Thus, in the financial services field the Commission is working for harmonization of the basic rules so as to ensure minimum prudential supervision and for freedom to supply services throughout the Community for any company established in a member country.

The redistributive effects of completion of the internal market concern both the incomes of factors of production and the income of regions. The basic assumption is that, in the absence of government action, certain factors of production and certain regions will be adversely affected.

According to traditional theory of international trade, a country should specialize in those sectors in which it has the greatest relative (or comparative) advantage. Completion of the internal market should therefore accentuate specialization by sector. Each country will experience a contraction of some of its sectors or industries (for example, textiles) and an expansion of other sectors or industries (for example, cars). The implication is that the redistributive effects will be considerable. The firms and the factors of production principally used in the contracting sectors will experience sharp reductions in profit and remuneration in the short term. In the long term, activities will disappear or will be relocated and certain regions will undergo a cumulative decline. At the same time, the expanding sectors will permit the setting-up of new firms and the commitment of factors of production and resources, and the corresponding regions will enter a virtuous circle of expansion. In this way, the rich would become richer and the poor poorer.

Recent theories concerning international trade cast considerable doubt on this kind of reasoning and suggest that there is no general argument to support this pessimistic view (see in particular Krugman, 1981, and Helpman, 1987).

A basic theme is that the nature of international and regional specialization is much less radical than the traditional approach suggests. Firstly, the existence of economies of scale in many sectors, coupled with the differentiated nature of many products, promotes narrow specialization in certain fields of activity, which usually entails only reallocation within the same industry or even within the product range of the same firm.

Secondly, the competitive advantages of a region or firm are less determined by what happens to be their 'natural endowment' and are to a large extent the result of deliberate strategies reflected in investment in productivity, people and R&D (for an empirical approach, see Abd-El-Rahman, 1987).

More specifically, the new theories relating to international trade suggest that there is no general basis for identifying in advance the Community regions and countries which will experience particularly serious and lasting redistributive problems.

Firstly, the redistributive effects empirically observed in the past (notably following the abolition of tariff barriers within the EEC) have been relatively slight (Hufbauer and Chilas, 1974; Baldwin, 1984).

Secondly, the theoretical arguments suggest that the new Member States and the smaller countries should benefit considerably from the opening-up of markets, both in geographical terms and in terms of the range of products, owing to the exploitation of economies of scale and learning (Markusen, 1985).

Thirdly, intra-industrial trade, in which similar but different products are traded (e.g. France and Germany sell to and buy from each other cars) has few reallocative and redistributive effects. It accounts for the bulk of intra-Community trade and is rapidly growing in the new Member States (Jacquemin and Sapir, 1987).

Also, transitional measures should cushion the negative redistributive effects which certain factors of production, activities and regions will experience. On the one hand, the new member countries and the developing regions must be assured that they will have the means of overcoming their current structural handicaps of a lack (in some cases critical) of basic infrastructures (primarily of the technological kind) and of inadequate vocational training. On the other, the completion of the internal market will help the declining regions by ensuring a freer circulation of information, technologies and services beyond national frontiers. The economic and socio-cultural reintegration of these regions into the overall Community framework could thus be facilitated in such a way that the current dichotomy between dynamic centres and lethargic peripheral areas is gradually replaced by a more even pattern of trade and activity. Here again, credible policies which minimize the adjustment costs and promote reintegration are vital if essential Community solidarity is to be safeguarded. Special attention has been paid in the Single European Act to the means of achieving this objective. It provides both for the structural Funds to be reinforced and for national economic policies to be conducted in a way which serves the Community aim of strengthening economic and social cohesion.

Finally, with the internal market completed, firms from non-member countries will also be much freer to pursue their activities throughout Europe and will no longer be confronted by national non-tariff barriers. This opening-up process requires choices to be made regarding the common external policy. Two extreme positions are conceivable: it might be argued that the situation and treatment of all operators should be wholly identical, irrespective of whether they come from the Community or third countries: it might be countered that existing non-tariff barriers should be transferred from national to Community level.

A more realistic approach, however, is to recognize both the existence of differentiation in certain limited fields and also the desire to keep the Community open to the rest of the world under stable and equitable arrangements. Let us explain these two aspects of the problem.

The expression 'European dimension' is not merely a geographical term. The Commission has explained the specific nature of the common market. 'It can only be defined', it writes, 'by differentiating between Community members and countries that are not part of the Community. A differentiation of this type is inherent in any customs union and any economic union. The very term "internal market" presupposes that the identity of the unit involved differs from that which lies outside. The rules governing international economic relations comprise the principles set out within the GATT framework which allow the Community to reserve for its members the advantages resulting from an intensification of their mutual ties as long as this does not involve a deterioration in the treatment of non-Community countries by comparison with the earlier situation.

However, differentiation does not mean isolation, particularly since economic activity takes place in an increasingly interdependent world. The consensus which allowed the negotiation of the Treaty instituting the EEC — as well as the economic interests of the Community dictated by its nature as a processing region — mean that it must remain open to dialogue and negotiation with its trading partners. Thus the Community, the largest trading power in the world, has a clear responsibility to maintain a stable and equitable framework for international economic relations.'[1]

This provides the framework for implementation of the common commercial policy provided for in Title II, Chapter 3 of the Treaty of Rome, a policy based on uniform principles, particularly in regard to the conclusion of tariff and trade agreements, the achievement of uniformity in measures of liberalization, export policy and measures to protect trade against unfair commercial practices such as dumping or subsidies (Article 113 of the Treaty).

This is also the spirit in which negotiations with non-member countries on a number of special situations (ranging from the establishment of banks on Community territory to the opening-up of public procurement) must lead to reciprocal agreements.

In this way, completion of the internal market can contribute to rolling back protectionism in the world and at the same time promote increased European competitiveness.

[1] Commission of the European Communities, 'Assessment of the function of the internal market', Commission report to the Council, COM(83) 80 final of 18 February 1983.

9. Illustration of gains from market integration

This chapter illustrates the gains from completing the internal market, using a partial equilibrium model (see study by Venables and Smith) that reflects the latest developments of the theory of international trade and takes account of economies of scale and the effects of product differentiation in situations of imperfect competition. This model, which captures size effects and competition effects, is a very useful instrument for describing the consequences of European integration. In particular, it simulates certain effects to be expected from the removal of non-tariff barriers and greater integration of European markets in 10 industrial sectors and five Community countries (Germany, France, Italy, United Kingdom, rest of the EC). The effects are:

(i)   welfare gains associated with an increase in the range of products offered to consumers (due not only to trade growth but also to the extension in the range offered by domestic producers);

(ii)   technical efficiency gains due to the exploitation of economies of scale generated in the short term by increased output and in the long term by restructuring;

(iii) the fall in prices and costs resulting from greater competition.

The main point of this exercise is not to put precise figures on the overall gains to be expected from European integration. The figures produced depend on a whole series of assumptions about economic behaviour and the values of the main parameters of the model. But it is rather the illustration of the importance of indirect gains, linked to scale and competition effects, relative to direct gains, from the removal of barriers, which is of interest. However, the indirect effects described in previous sections, such as the dynamic effects due to the impact on innovation of stronger competition, are not all described in this model, its approach being rather a comparative static one. Moreover, this analysis also attempts to determine how far the benefits of completing the European internal market can vary from one industry to another, and it tries to highlight the causes of these variations.

The scenarios and their variants. To describe the effects of European integration, two scenarios have been adopted; a first scenario of segmented markets and then a second scenario of an integrated market.

In the first scenario, the tariff equivalent of barriers to intra-Community trade[1] is calculated, and it is assumed that trade barriers are lowered so as to reduce the cost of intra-Community trade by 2,5 %. This seems a fairly modest assumption, in that the costs of customs formalities are already put at 1,5 % of intra-Community trade (see Chapter 3.2).

---

[1]   This tariff equivalent corresponds to the extra cost that explains the difference between firms' shares of the home market and their share of the export market. It should be noted that the difference in market shares is not just attributable to barriers to trade, but also to transport costs and consumer preference. This indicator therefore includes factors other than non-tariff barriers.

In the second scenario, as well as this assumption of a decline in the cost of intra-Community trade, it is further supposed that firms operate on a totally integrated Community market, with no room left for price discrimination between the domestic market and external markets (the only surviving cost differences are those due to trade costs). Eight variants of these two scenarios have been considered for each industry (see Table 9.1) thus combining the possibilities stemming from the following hypotheses:

(i)   hypotheses concerning market structure:
       either a fixed number of firms,
       or free access to and exit from the market;
(ii) hypotheses concerning the range of products manufactured by firms:
       either a fixed number of models,
       or a variable number determined endogenously;
(iii) hypotheses concerning the competitive behaviour of firms:
       either competition on quantities produced (Cournot type),
       or competition on prices (Bertrand type).

In the simulations the impact of these different hypotheses on the results depend on the main characteristics of the industries in question, in particular the relationship between intra-EC trade and consumption, the potential for

Table 9.1.

Simulations of segmented or integrated market scenarios: Definition of variants for each scenario

Cournot competition (competition on quantity)[1]

Number of firms	Constant	Variable
Number of models		
Constant	1	2
Variable	3	4

Bertrand competition (competition on price)[2]

Number of firms	Constant	Variable
Number of models		
Constant	5	6
Variable	7	8

In the 'integrated market' scenario, variants 3, 4, 7 and 8 are not modelled.
[1]   Each firm considers that the output of other firms will be unchanged when it varies its own output.
[2]   Each firm considers that other firms will not modify their prices when it changes its own price.

economies of scale and scope, the level of concentration and product differentiation (see Table 9.2 for the empirical indicators). The results of these different variants are not all presented here, but are described in the study by Venables and Smith.

Analysis of findings. In the first scenario of segmented markets, the lowering of non-tariff barriers generally improves welfare in the Community: the increase ranges from 0,3 to 2,6 %, depending on sectors and the variants considered (see Table 9.3).[1] The improvement in welfare is always accompanied by an expansion in trade and output in the Community, and by a decline in average production costs of between 0,1 and 2,5 %. The growth of intra-Community trade is particularly strong; in most industries, it amounts to between 15 and 55 %. It is only partially offset by a decline in imports from outside the Community, ranging from 2 to 25 %. It would seem therefore that integrating the European internal market is more likely to result in trade creation rather than trade diversion. Moreover, the decline in costs and prices leads to an improvement in the competitiveness of European industries, so that exports to non-Community markets improve.

The decline in average production costs is associated with the increased output and the resulting greater intensity of exploitation of economies of scale. This decline in production costs leads, together with the reduction in non-tariff barriers, to a fall in prices, to the benefit of consumers, whose surplus improves. However, producers' profits decline, at least when the number of firms on the market remains constant. This is because price declines squeeze the profits of the least competitive firms which manage neither to reduce costs nor to increase output.

When the number of firms is constant, i.e. in a short-term equilibrium situation, welfare improves most and production costs decline furthest in sectors where both economies of scale and intra-Community trade are high. This is the case in man-made fibres, office machinery and motor vehicles, sectors where welfare increases by about 1 % and production costs decline by 0,5 to 1 % (variant 1 of Table 9.3).

On the assumption of free access to and exit from the market (variant 2 of Table 9.3), greater welfare gains and cost reductions are observed in most industries. This variant corresponds more closely to long-term equilibrium after the elimination of the least efficient firms and the restructuring of markets. In this case, there are large declines in production costs due to the greater increase in the output of those firms remaining on the market. But the fall in the number of firms increases the concentration of markets, which tends to raise prices and push up producer profits. Nevertheless, thanks to the faster reduction in costs,

---

[1] A single exception: the cement industry, where welfare declines when the number of firms is constant. This is because the main impact of a reduction in non-tariff barriers is to boost trade for which transport costs are very high.

Table 9.2.

Simulations of segmented or integrated market scenarios: Main features of industries studied

NACE Code	Branches	Share of intra-EC trade in EC consumption	Economies of scale[1]	Economies of scope[2]	Indexes of concentration[3]	Indicator of product differentiation[4]
242	Cement, lime, plaster	1,6	20	0	0,066	35,54
257	Pharmaceutical products	10,0	22	5	0,050	5,80
260	Man-made fibres	36,4	10	3	0,050	21,54
332	Machine tools	22,4	7	1	0,004	13,55
330	Office machinery	23,6	10	5	0,120	32,77
342	Electrical machinery	8,8	15	5	0,022	7,35
346	Domestic-type electric appliances	19,6	10	5	0,110	10,77
350	Motor vehicles	24,8	16	8	0,199	13,32
438	Carpets	18,8	6	3	0,031	21,40
451	Footwear	27,0	2	2	0,010	53,29

[1] % increase in average cost at $\frac{1}{2}$ output per model.
[2] % increase in average cost at $\frac{1}{2}$ number of models.
[3] Herfindahl index.
[4] Elasticity of demand for a variety of model with Cournot competition.

Source: Venables and Smith, 1987.

Table 9.3.

Simulations of segmented or integrated market scenarios: Effects of a reduction in non-tariff barriers in the segmented market scenario

NACE Code	Branches	Change in welfare[1]			Change in average production costs		
		Variant 1[2]	Variant 2	Variant 4[3]	Variant 1	Variant 2	Variant 4[3]
242	Cement, lime, plaster	−0,1	0,64	—	−0,03	−0,93	—
257	Pharmaceutical products	0,29	0,30	0,44	−0,08	−0,15	−0,15
260	Man-made fibres	0,99	1,84	—	−0,51	−2,45	—
332	Machine tools	0,84	0,82	—	−0,12	−0,05	—
330	Office machinery	0,88	1,45	1,65	−0,98	−2,48	−1,95
342	Electrical machinery	0,29	0,29	0,39	−0,05	−0,09	−0,09
346	Domestic-type electric appliances	0,64	0,81	1,37	−0,32	−0,93	−0,85
350	Motor vehicles	0,83	1,34	2,56	−0,56	−1,51	−1,83
438	Carpets	0,67	0,76	—	−0,17	−0,49	—
451	Footwear[4]	0,35	0,40	—	−0,03	−0,03	—

[1] Change in consumer surplus and in profits expressed as % of consumption in base year.
[2] For definition of variants, see Table 9.1.
[3] This variant has been simulated only in the industries where products are highly differentiated and economies of scope are high.
[4] For branch 451, barriers are reduced by 1 %, not by 2,5 %.

Source: Venables and Smith, 1987.

the average price in the Community falls more than in the short term since product variety decreases with the disappearance of a number of firms.

In some branches, the impact of stronger competition (whether real or potential, when the number of firms present on the market declines) and consequent restructuring is particularly marked. This is the case for office machinery, motor vehicles and man-made fibres, where welfare increases by 1,3 to 1,8 %, and production costs decline by 1,5 to 2,5 %; the same happens, though to a lesser extent, in domestic electric appliances and carpets. However, in other branches, such as machine tools, electrical machinery and footwear, there is virtually no effect. This is because these sectors are already very competitive: their Herfindahl index (see Table 9.2) is less than 0,025.

In the long term, welfare improves even more when firms can choose the number of models produced (variant 4 of Table 9.3). The improvement in welfare is more marked in industries where products are highly differentiated (the price elasticity of demand for a variety of models is low) and where economies of scope are high (see Table 9.2). This is the case in domestic electrical appliances, and especially in motor vehicles where the increase in welfare is twice as high, at 2,6 %. This improvement in welfare is due to an increase in consumers' surplus induced by the extension of the product range on offer. However the decline in costs is lower than or equal to that obtained in the case where the number of models is constant. Firms shorten their production runs as they expand their model range; the economies of scope are usually smaller than the returns to scale in production of a particular model.

Only one branch, motor vehicles, is an exception to this rule. Here, economies of scope are substantial and the fall in costs is larger than that obtained when the number of products is constant. Assuming a reduction in trade barriers, the first scenario whose results have just been analysed merely describes the effects transmitted through the expansion of intra-Community trade: first, increased export sales bring economies of scale that enable firms to improve their technical efficiency, and secondly, stronger competition from imports induces them to bring prices down and eliminates the least efficient firms. However, in this scenario, the various domestic markets remain segmented, and the firms with a degree of monopoly power on their domestic market can continue to enjoy a higher mark-up than that obtained on outside markets. A recent study of Italy (Zimmermann and Pupillo, 1987) confirms that the present segmentation of European markets does indeed produce such an outcome. That study even indicates that the more the sector is concentrated, the greater is the scope for price discrimination between domestic and external markets.

However, the second scenario assuming a perfectly integrated Community market goes further in the analysis of the effects of competition. In this scenario, European firms can no longer practise price discrimination between domestic and foreign markets. Even in industries that are highly concentrated nationally, the share of the Community market held by one firm is no longer sufficient to confer monopoly power. Consequently, in those industries, margins and prices should decline.

The increase in potential competition and the consequent fall in prices on domestic markets lead to a contraction in producers' profits. On the other hand, thanks to the price reduction, the consumer surplus improves, so that, overall, welfare improves by between 1 and 4 %, and by as much as 12 % in the motor vehicle industry (see Table 9.4). The improvement in welfare is much more marked than in the first scenario in the more concentrated industries, where the price-cost margin is higher. This applies to pharmaceuticals, man-made fibres, office machinery, domestic electrical appliances and motor vehicles. In those sectors, the improvement in welfare is from twice to four times as large in the 'integrated market' scenario as in the 'segmented markets' scenario.

Before closing this section on the presentation of results, two points should be made. The first concerns the sensitivity of the results to the competitive strategy adopted by firms. The results presented so far are based on the assumption that firms are competing on quantity (Cournot), so that their price-cost margin is a direct function of their market share. It is worth asking what happens when the price-cost margin depends only on the degree of product differentiation, that is when firms adopt more competitive behaviour of the Bertrand type. In this case, the effects transmitted through stronger competition will logically be less marked.

Table 9.4.

Simulations of segmented or integrated market scenarios: Comparison of results in the two scenarios

NACE Code	Branches	Change in welfare[1] (as %)				Change in average production costs (as %)			
		Variant 1[2]		Variant 2		Variant 1		Variant 2	
		SM	IM[3]	SM	IM	SM	IM	SM	IM
242	Cement, lime, plaster	−0,1	0,22	0,64	−0,1	−0,03	−0,12	−0,93	0,09
257	Pharmaceutical products	0,29	1,11	0,30	1,45	−0,08	−0,73	−0,15	−3,43
260	Man-made fibres	0,99	4,14	1,84	2,91	−0,51	−1,77	−2,45	−1,04
332	Machine tools	0,84	0,86	0,82	0,83	−0,12	−0,16	−0,05	−0,10
330	Office machinery	0,88	3,88	1,45	3,43	−0,98	−2,71	−2,48	−2,59
342	Electrical machinery	0,29	0,52	0,29	0,53	−0,05	−0,26	−0,09	−1,30
346	Domestic-type electric appliances	0,64	1,79	0,81	3,85	−0,32	−1,15	−0,93	−9,04
350	Motor vehicles	0,83	4,09	1,34	12,1	−0,56	−1,72	−1,51	−16,9
438	Carpets	0,67	0,75	0,76	0,97	−0,17	−0,30	−0,49	−2,79
451	Footwear	0,35	0,46	0,40	0,64	−0,03	−0,26	−0,03	−1,36

[1] Change in consumer surplus and in profits expressed as % of consumption in base year.
[2] For a definition of variants, see Table 9.1.
[3] IM = integrated markets; SM = segmented markets.
Source: Venables and Smith, 1987.

The fall in costs and the improvement in welfare are smaller in the variants where the model assumes Bertrand behaviour (see Table 9.5). In the first scenario, welfare improvements are, at worst, halved (in the man-made fibres sector), but in the second scenario, the welfare is considerably lower in several sectors: a third or a fourth in pharmaceuticals, man-made fibres, office machinery and domestic electrical appliances, and a twelfth in motor vehicles. These results are consistent with the conclusions described by the general equilibrium models with increasing returns to scale that have been used to measure the effects of trade liberalization between the United States and Canada (the Harris and Cox model, 1984). In those studies, the welfare gain varies from one to four depending on the assumptions adopted for the strategy of firms: 4,3 % on the assumption that firms fix their prices in a competitive manner, over 16 % if they fix them by collusion and 8,9 % when the modelled behaviour of the firms corresponds to a combination of those two strategies (see Harris, 1984). Thus the results described in Table 9.5 supply a range within which welfare gains ought to be situated according to the European integration scenario considered.

The second point relates to the definition of the relative size of direct and indirect effects. Direct effects measure gains from the fall in the cost of intra-Community trade, while indirect effects incorporate the benefits of scale economies and stronger competition. In the 'segmented markets' scenario, direct gains in the short term account for between 67 and 92 % of total benefits (see variant 1 of Table 9.6). In the long term, the proportion is between 41 and 83 % when the number of models produced is fixed (variant 2), but only 24 to 57 % when the number can vary (variant 4). This result shows what major restructuring effects can be expected from completing the European internal market. It tallies with the conclusions of certain sectoral studies, such as those on public procurement. Lastly, in the 'integrated market' scenario, the share of direct effects in total gains is even lower in the most concentrated sectors: between 15 and 30 %, but as low as 5 % in motor vehicles. This confirms that gains induced by greater competition and by restructuring are greater than those generated by the lowering of non-tariff barriers. This conclusion highlights the need for intensified competition within the Community to ensure that all the favourable effects of completing the internal market do in fact materialize.

Assessment. Illustrating the main scale effects and competition effects through this model as described in foregoing sections is a worthwhile exercise as long as the limits to the approach are borne in mind. It is important to remember that results of this type of model depend on assumptions about the behaviour modelled (e.g. the competitive strategy adopted by the firms) and on the values for the parameters in the model. In this type of approach (what P. Krugman calls 'industrial policy exercises calibrated to actual cases', or Ipecac — see Venables and Smith, 1986), the values of the parameters are obtained from econometric estimates and techniques found in the literature or fixed so as to reproduce reality observed in a given year. Thus, to verify the robustness of the orders of magnitude obtained, it would be useful to test the sensitivity of

Table 9.5.

Simulations of segmented or integrated market scenarios: Comparison of results depending on firms' competitive strategy

NACE Code	Branches	Change in welfare (as %)[1]			
		Segmented market scenario		Integrated market scenario	
		Variant 2[2] (Cournot)	Variant 6 (Bertrand)	Variant 2 (Cournot)	Variant 6 (Bertrand)
242	Cement, lime, plaster	0,64	0,04	− 0,1	0,04
257	Pharmaceutical products	0,30	0,34	1,45	0,34
260	Man-made fibres	1,84	0,97	2,91	0,97
332	Machine tools	0,82	0,83	0,83	0,83
330	Office machinery	1,45	0,98	3,43	0,98
342	Electrical machinery	0,29	0,31	0,53	0,31
346	Domestic-type electric appliances	1,34	0,71	3,85	0,72
350	Motor vehicles	1,34	0,89	12,10	0,90
438	Carpets	0,76	0,74	0,97	0,74
451	Footwear	0,40	0,38	0,64	0,38

[1] Change in consumer surplus and in profits expressed as % of consumption in base year.
[2] For a definition of variants, see Table 9.1.
Source: Venables and Smith, 1987.

Table 9.6.

Simulations of segmented or integrated market scenarios: Direct gains as percentage of total gains

NACE Code	Branches	Change in welfare (as %)[1]				
		Segmented market scenario			Integrated market scenario	
		Variant 1[1]	Variant 2	Variant 4	Variant 1	Variant 2
242	Cement, lime, plaster	—	6	—	18	—
257	Pharmaceutical products	86	83	57	22	17
260	Man-made fibres	92	49	—	22	31
332	Machine tools	67	68	—	65	67
330	Office machinery	67	41	36	15	17
342	Electrical machinery	76	76	56	42	41
346	Domestic-type electric appliances	77	60	36	27	13
350	Motor vehicles	75	46	24	15	5
438	Carpets	70	62	—	62	48
451	Footwear	77	67	—	59	42

[1] For a definition of variants, see Table 9.1.
Source: Venables and Smith, 1987.

the results to the values of certain parameters, as has been done for the competitive behaviour of firms.

What is more, it should not be forgotten that this is a partial equilibrium model. Such models examine changes in one industrial sector at a time, ignoring the consequences of those changes for the rest of the economy. This implies in particular that effects associated with interactions between industries, intersectoral resource reallocation or income redistribution, are not taken into consideration. Their impact is difficult to determine *a priori*: for example, cost reductions may be amplified if goods produced in one sector serve as inputs in other sectors; on the other hand, the growth of output should push up factor costs.

These various additional effects can be taken into account in a general equilibrium model. Models of this type have been widely used to measure the effects of reducing tariff and non-tariff barriers (see the surveys by Shoven and Whalley (1984) and by Baldwin (1984)). There are two lessons to be learned from that work.

First, in the present context of trade between industrialized countries, the gains from removing non-tariff barriers seem higher than those from removing tariff barriers. For example, Brown and Whalley (1980) calculate that the elimination of non-tariff barriers can lead to gains twice as high as simple multilateral abolition of tariffs.[1] Similarly, Deardorff and Stern (quoted by Baldwin (1984)) find that the reduction in non-tariff barriers under the Tokyo Round could have more effect on welfare than the cut in tariffs: the gains from the first are equivalent to 0,11 % of GDP, those from the second to 0,06 %. These results suggest that the current integration process and the removal of obstacles such as frontier formalities, public procurement closed to foreign suppliers and differing standards are at least as important a step as the establishment of customs union.

Next, while traditional general equilibrium models show only small gains in world welfare from liberalizing trade — less than 1 % of GDP — this is not the case for models incorporating economies of scale and imperfect competition. Thus, in the work mentioned above by Harris and Cox (1984), the liberalization of trade between the United States and Canada leads to welfare gains that can be in excess of 16 % for Canada. Although this effect varies with the competitive strategy adopted by firms, it is nevertheless true that the effects induced by increased competition and by the exploitation of economies of scale are greater than those revealed by traditional analysis of comparative advantage. And they are precisely the effects expected from European integration.

Consequently, the analysis of work carried out with the help of general equilibrium models tends to confirm the main conclusions of the simulations by Venables and Smith. The figures, despite their shortcomings, do describe the consequences of removing non-tariff barriers, and show the extent of scale effects and competition effects resulting from completing the internal market.

---

[1] These simulations are based on a simplified theoretical hypothesis, i.e. the total abolition of all tariff and non-tariff barriers, enumerated by the two authors.

On the basis of two separate scenarios for completion of the internal market, the Venables and Smith simulations produce a range for welfare gains, as a function of the degree of European integration achieved. The first scenario corresponds to a minimalist hypothesis, measuring only the consequences of a fairly modest lowering of trade barriers. The second scenario describes a maximalist hypothesis, with European firms operating on a totally integrated Community market.

Under the two scenarios, long-term welfare gains vary according to the sector — from 0,5 to 2 % in the first scenario, and from 0,5 to 4 % in the second. But that conclusion needs to be qualified for the second scenario, in which most of the effects come from the intensification of competition. In the sectors where prices on segmented national markets were already determined in a fairly competitive way, gains are only 0,5 to 1 %.

Next, the study shows that reducing non-tariff barriers leads, at Community level, to very fast expansion of trade, an improvement in welfare and a fall in average production costs in the 10 manufacturing sectors considered. The gains are a lot more marked in the sectors with the largest exports and the highest economies of scale (office machinery, domestic electrical appliances and motor vehicles). This analysis also confirms that free market entry contributes to restructuring by eliminating the least competitive producers and enabling the output of the survivors to expand. Restructuring leads to greater welfare gains and sharper reductions in costs, particularly in the most concentrated sectors (pharmaceuticals, man-made fibres, office machinery, domestic electrical appliances and motor vehicles).

Lastly, the gains from increased competition on a totally integrated Community market should be higher than those from lower barriers to trade, i.e. obtained exclusively through the expansion of intra-Community trade. The results obtained also illustrate the share of the indirect effects of economies of scale and increased competition in total benefits from an open internal market: indirect effects represent 50 to 85 %, depending on the industrial branch, of total gains in the 'integrated market' scenario.

Part E

Overall quantitative assessment

10. Microeconomic and macroeconomic approaches

For the purpose of summarizing the benefits which are to be expected from completion of the large Community market, two types of methodology have been used: microeconomic (Section 10.1) and macroeconomic (Section 10.2).

The consequences of completing the internal market will originate at the most disaggregated microeconomic level. The agents will be firms: the removal of many different non-tariff barriers will compel them to rethink their development strategies, to adapt to a new situation of increased competition and to exploit the opportunities thus created. The beneficiaries will be individual households: the elimination of the unproductive costs of non-Europe and the pressure of competition will bring prices down; the expansion of trade will increase both the quantity, quality and choice of the goods and services at their disposal. The opening-up of public procurement will enable government purchasing agencies to cut the cost of their spending. The mobility of capital and labour will lead to a more efficient allocation of the factors of production.

The assessment of the consequences of the large internal market must therefore begin at the microeconomic level.

The approach adopted is based on the normal principles of microeconomic theory, such as those applied in particular to the analysis of international trade or industrial policy. The reference framework is that of partial equilibrium analysis; it enables an estimate to be made of the way in which costs, prices, supply and demand will be affected in each individual sector when non-tariff barriers are removed or competition intensifies. The effects are expressed using microeconomic concepts: in terms of changes in consumer's surplus, producer's surplus and general welfare. These concepts broadly correspond to the changes in the net incomes of consumers, producers and the economy as a whole (see Chapter 3).

All the available sources of information have been drawn upon for each sector or branch; reasoned hypotheses were made where important sectors were not covered by those sources. Although not all the information is perfectly consistent with the theoretical framework, it has been possible to make an overall assessment; the margins of uncertainty are, however, relatively wide.

For a variety of reasons which will soon become clear, a macroeconomic assessment also proved to be necessary.

Firstly, the completion of the large internal market is likely to affect most parts of the economic system. The reductions in costs, and therefore in prices, which the large internal market should produce have important macroeconomic counterparts: improvement in the purchasing power of incomes; changes in the competitive positions of the Member States or the Community in relation to the outside world; the possibility of substitution between factors of production; increased growth potential, etc.

In addition, the completion of the internal market is likely to lead to an easing of the major macroeconomic constraints which currently affect the Community's economic situation: budget deficits, but also external deficits and inflationary dangers. Thus, the consequences of the internal market — static and dynamic — could well be further magnified by accompanying economic policies which make use of the room for manoeuvre created in this way.

Finally, macroeconomic analysis can throw light on the time scale of adjustment processes, such as those set in train by changes in the conditions of supply. This is particularly important in the case of the labour market.

The difficulty of the task is made all too apparent by the many different facets of the problem and the very complex mechanisms which will be set in motion. Can we be sure of the outcome? Can we assert that the completion of the internal market will lead the Community towards a uniform economic situation? Certainly not. To avoid the illusion of a single, unequivocal assessment, estimates will therefore be given in terms of ranges. To ensure that they are not too wide, however, these ranges assume effective implementation of the programme set out in the White Paper and a positive attitude by firms in their strategic response to the new environment.

Another source of imprecision arises from the problem relating to the geographic cover of the analyses. Although the large Member States are always included, coverage of the basic studies has been, in general, incomplete and differs according to the individual theme studied. The extrapolation of the result to a Community of 12 has proved to be a delicate task. It has been treated in a cautious way, by means of a simple linear extrapolation; however, this entails the risk of underestimating the potentialities of the achievement of the internal market (see box 'Geographic cover and extrapolation to EUR 12').

Geographic cover and extrapolation to EUR 12

The basic studies from which the majority of evaluations contained in this report are drawn are geographically incomplete, and vary according to the area analysed. The four large Member States (Germany, France, Italy and the UK) are always included; in some cases Belgium, Luxembourg and the Netherlands also, but the peripheral Member States (Denmark, Spain, Greece, Ireland and Portugal) are seldom included. Only the business opinion survey of European industry provides complete coverage of the Community of Twelve. The comparison of the effects anticipated by firms in each country, or group of countries, contains much instructive material.

	EUR 7[1]	DK	E	GR	IRL	P	Average[1]	EUR 12[1]
		\multicolumn{5}{c}{Rest of the Community}		
Reduction in production costs (%)	−2	:	−3	:	−2	:	−2,9	−2
Increase in sales	4,7	6	9	1	7	7	7,3	5,0

[1] Aggregated according to the relative level of GDP in 1985.
Source: Business survey (Nerb).

Nevertheless, to be consistent and in order to avoid the risk of overestimating the results, we have preferred to suppose that the effects on the peripheral Member States will be proportionate to those analysed for the other countries. In other words, when, for example, a gain equal of 1 billion ECU 85 for EUR 7 has been calculated, this is considered equivalent to 1,13 billion ECU 85 for EUR 12.[1] In comparison to this linear extrapolation, an extrapolation adjusted according to the business survey would result in a figure of 1,2 billion ECU 85 for EUR 12.

For this reason, the linear extrapolation used for all the calculations presented in this report may well underestimate the results by the order of 5 % for the Community aggregate or 50 % for the countries in question. But only studies specifically undertaken for these countries and, in particular, for those whose industrial structure is the least developed, can confirm this diagnosis.

[1] $1,13 = 1 \times \dfrac{\text{GDP EUR 12}}{\text{GDP EUR 7}} = \dfrac{3\,314 \text{ billion ECU 85}}{2\,927 \text{ billion ECU 85}}$

10.1. Microeconomic evaluation

10.1.1. The schema for aggregation of cost and price reductions

The aggregation of microeconomic evidence on the costs of barriers and the benefits of integrating markets has been fitted into the following schema:

	Sectors, branches of the economy 1 2 3 .... N	Total economy
Barrier removal effects		
Stage 1: Cost of barriers affecting trade directly		
Stage 2: Cost of barriers affecting all production		
Market integration effects		
Stage 3: Economies of scale from restructuring and increased production		
Stage 4: Competition effect on X-inefficiency and monopoly rents		
Total effects		

Some further comments may clarify the significance of each stage.

Barrier removal effects

Stage 1: Barriers affecting trade directly are typically border delays at customs posts and related administrative costs. In the first instance only trade is affected, even though there will ultimately be indirect effects on the domestic economy as a result of greater competition. As these barriers are lifted the costs to exporters and importers are reduced, purchasers of consumption and investment goods gain from lower prices, and as a result either expenditure on these goods is increased, or resources are released for alternative production.

Stage 2: Barriers affecting all production are typically those that limit market entry or competition. Government procurement restrictions keep domestic prices above competitive levels, as well as excluding cheaper imports. National technical regulations may have similar effects. In the service sectors regulatory policies may operate also in a protective way, raising the level of domestic costs and prices. When these barriers are removed costs and prices are reduced.

These first two types of effect are essentially short-term in nature.

Market integration effects

Stage 3: As competition leads to the restructuring of industries, with inefficient plants closing and investment made in new plants, gains in terms of economies of scale are achieved. The structure of individual branches of the economy moves closer towards an optimal one. Some other types of economy of scale of relatively small importance are also introduced here (see Annex A).

Stage 4: It is well established, however, that there are important sources of inefficiency other than those resulting from a sub-optimal structure of production units. These are grouped here under the term 'X-inefficiency', and cover overmanning, excess inventories and excess overheads costs. Increased competition will also tend to eliminate excess profit margins that are protected by monopolistic or oligopolistic market structures (sometimes called 'monopoly rents').

These market integration effects will often take several years to materialize. The categories listed in the schema do not cover certain types of dynamic effect which could not be quantified, for example those concerning innovation (as discussed above in Section 7.2).

The preceding elements add up to the main factors that will explain the downward convergence of product prices to competitive equilibrium levels, as a result of removing the various types of barrier to the full integration of markets.

Conceptually, the four stages all represent different phenomena. However, in practice, as will be seen below, it is not always possible to distinguish between some of the sources of price reductions. For example, the effects of some barriers, such as technical regulations, may be difficult to place clearly as between stages 1 and 2. Again, some of the market integration effects may be difficult to distinguish, especially as between X-inefficiency and monopoly rents in stage 4.

Given these practical difficulties in delimiting different types of effect, the important requirement is at least to keep a careful check in the assembly of overall totals to avoid both double-counting and gaps in the coverage of the different branches of the economy. Care has also to be taken to respect input-output consistency, as the following example shows. The total gross output or sales of all branches of the Community economy amounts to about 6 000 billion ECU, whereas total value-added (or gross domestic product) amounts to only a little over half as much — about 3 300 billion ECU. Thus, half of all sales are intermediate, not final sales. This means, for example, that if every branch of the economy reduced its costs sufficiently to reduce its sales price by 1 %, the total gain for the economy would amount to nearly 2 % of gross domestic product.

10.1.2. Use of empirical data sources for aggregation

The compilation of an aggregate estimate in accordance with the above schema is, in practice, something of a jigsaw puzzle, where not all of the pieces fit so well, some are missing, and some are overlapping pieces. None the less, these problems can partly be compensated for by comparing the results from several methods or sources, which permits a cross-checking of the findings. The procedure at least uses all available sources of information, and provides a consistent framework into which they can be inserted.

Many information sources have thus been used in practice to build up a very approximate but rather comprehensive picture in the form of a matrix detailed by type of effect and economic branch. These sources are as follows:

(a) An opinion survey of all manufacturing industry was conducted in all Community countries, in which enterprises gave estimates of the margin of total cost reduction that might be expected from removal of all the main barriers listed in the White Paper. The average result was a cost reduction of 1,7 %, which, taking into account the input-output structure of industry, could imply a cost reduction for industry in the aggregate of about 40 billion ECU for the Community as a whole. This estimate may be interpreted as corresponding to the main barrier removal effects (stages 1 and 2), but does not represent the market integration effects resulting from enhanced competition. They represent the producer's view of barriers that impose extra costs, and not the consumer's view of how increased competition would ultimately affect the structure of industry and price levels. These results are available by country and by branch of industry, on the basis of a harmonized questionnaire. This source has therefore the merit of being comprehensive and comparable, even if the economic concepts that are estimated here are limited, as mentioned.

(b) A set of more detailed studies was undertaken for certain types of barriers affecting all or many industries: notably customs delays, public procurement restrictions and technical standards and regulations. This enabled some estimates to be made of the cost of these individual classes of barrier, notably as regards customs procedures and public procurement. In the case of customs procedures, it was estimated that a cost saving of the order of 8 to 9 billion ECU could be obtained as a result of eliminating frontier delays and associated administration costs, which contribute to filling in stage 1 of the schema. In the case of public purchases it was estimated that savings of 20 billion ECU could be made as a result of competitive public purchasing. (These latter savings contribute partly to filling in stage 2 in the schema, but also include economies of scale from restructuring, as in stage 3.)

(c) A further set of detailed studies were made of cost savings to be expected in six goods-producing industries (foodstuffs, pharmaceuticals, automobiles, textiles and clothing, building materials, and telecommunications equipment). These studies were addressed to all observable barriers affecting the industries in question, and as a result offer in some degree a check against the sources just mentioned. The results were frequently in the range of 1 to 2 % cost savings, sometimes rising, however, to 5 % or more. They generally corroborate the findings from other sources quite well. They show in particular that the cost-increasing barriers such as technical standards and customs delays result in relatively modest extra costs, but where the barriers operate as severe restrictions on market entry, the costs become much higher. The total for these industries was about 10 billion ECU. (These data thus offer additional or alternative information for stages 1 or 2, and to some extent stage 3 also.)

(d) Similarly, detailed studies were also made for several service industries, including financial and business services, part of the transport sector and telecommunications services. These point to relatively large cost or price reductions, averaging over 10 % for financial services, and totalling nearby 40 billion ECU for all the services covered. These high percentages further underline the point just made as regards industry: market-entry restrictions result in particularly heavy costs. The failure to separate regulatory functions for the service sectors from the issue of openness to external competition is at the source of these costs. (The potential savings concern the whole of production, not just trade, and so enter into stage 2: however, to a substantial degree, they also represent market integration effects as well, and to this extent could have been entered under stages 3 and 4 had the data permitted those different effects to be separated.)

(e) There is considerable overlapping between these four preceding sources of information, albeit with relatively concordant results where there are two or more sources. However, there were also problems of gaps in this sectoral information, for example with respect to some important sectors concerned by the internal market programme or particular market adjustment policies, such as agriculture, steel and energy. To ignore these sectors would risk substantial underestimations. To make it possible to consider the sensitivity of the overall results to these omissions, simplified hypotheses for these sectors, drawing on analyses already available, were adopted in a variant to the aggregate result. (The variant hypotheses relate mainly to stage 2.)

(f) As regards economies of scale (stage 3), a considerable number of earlier sectoral studies have been brought together, together with additional economic analyses of industry structure and concentration. This offers an independent source of estimates on potential gains from exploiting economies of scale more fully in industry and energy. The extent of unexploited economies of scale in the Community varies greatly between sectors. They are very slight for clothing and footwear but could be considerable for metal products (boilers for example) or some types of transport equipment (railway equipment, for example).

On the basis of detailed sectoral analysis (NACE 3-digit classification) about one-third of industry appears capable of moving closer towards the minimum efficient scales through a restructuring of production units. These presently unexploited economies of scale are significant and could represent reductions in total costs of production of the order 1 to 6 % for the sectors concerned, or, on average 1,5 % of the total cost of production of the industry and energy sectors as a whole. The transmission of these cost reductions through the production situation (through the input and output of intermediate goods) leads to a total reduction in the cost of final goods of all kinds (agriculture, energy, industry and services) of the order of 60 billion ECU.

(g) As regards X-inefficiency and monopoly rents, these are difficult to estimate independently of the other sources of cost or price reduction so far mentioned. However, it is known from various consultants' case studies of industries undergoing restructuring, that X-inefficiency often emerges as a substantial source of cost reduction. Some new microeconomic modelling analyses have begun to take into account such phenomena as economies of scale, product differentiation and the imperfectly competitive behaviour of enterprises which have a power to determine their prices. A work of this type has been used in the present study to illustrate the possible gains from integration of the European market (see Venables and Smith study). This model can describe the indirect gains resulting from a reinforcement of competition and restructuring in a completely integrated European market, and makes it possible to compare these indirect gains with the direct gains due to the removal of barriers. The simulations performed with this model indicate that, in the sectors that are most concentrated and have the greatest unexploited economies of scale, these indirect gains can be several times higher than the direct gains. On the basis of the model's simulations, and through classifying industries according to these criteria, it was possible to evaluate the orders of magnitude of the indirect gains due to restructuring and competition effects together (stages 3 and 4), as well as those due only to competition effects (stage 4). In the first case a total of about 62 billion ECU is obtained (stages 3 and 4), and in the second case a total of 46 billion ECU (stage 4). These results, while only illustrative, confirm that indirect gains that accumulate over the long run through the effects of competition and restructuring are likely to be high compared to those due to the removal of the most concrete trade barriers.

(h) Actual differences in prices between Member States can also be used as a source for estimating the possible gains from the removal of barriers and market integration (see Section 7.1). It is particularly striking that these price differences are most wide in sectors where trade barriers have reduced competition below what it could be. This is the case, for example, for public markets (boilers, railway equipment, other transport equipment). For the Community, calculations have been made to estimate the amount of potential savings in relation to ranging hypotheses for the downward convergence of prices in an integrated market (see Annex A). The total of 142 billion ECU savings for consumers is substantial, but relates only to sectors for which data was available. The equivalent amount obtained for the same sectors by the partial equilibrium method (variant 1B) is 162 billion ECU. These totals are therefore comparable, although there are significant differences at the sectoral level. These are explained by several reasons. For example, in certain sectors even the companies actually practising the lowest prices could see their production costs fall further (restructuring, mergers in electrical and electronic industries).

10.1.3. The aggregate results from partial equilibrium calculations

The summary presentation of the estimated economic gains from the partial equilibrium calculations are presented in Table 10.1.1. The gains in question, as already indicated in Chapter 2 (including the box inset), are often called 'welfare gains' in the economic literature. These welfare gains amount to the sum of the gains for consumers and producers, and approximate to the increase in real income in the economy (the expression 'economic gains' may alternatively be used, as long as the precise concept is clear).

The diverse sources of information and assumptions may be grouped in four different totals, ranging from 127 to 187 billion ECU, with an average of 157 billion ECU. This gives a range of 4,3 to 6,4 % of GDP, with 5,3 % as the average. The barrier removal effects turn out to be somewhat less than half the total. The market integration effects, which would rely heavily on the effectiveness of competition policy to be fully achieved are, therefore, a little over half the total.

A number of considerations need to be borne in mind as regards the relative probability of over- or underestimation in these figures.

First, the amounts in ECU just quoted relate to seven Member States (Germany, France, Italy, the United Kingdom and the Benelux) and to economic values of 1985, since most of the studies were done on this basis. The seven countries account for 88 % of the GDP of the EC total for the 12 Member States. If the foregoing amounts in ECU are proportionally scaled up to be equal percentages of EUR 12's GDP in 1988, then the range becomes 173 to 257 billion ECU, with an average of 215 billion ECU. As pointed out above (box in Section 10), this linear extrapolation is more likely to be an underestimate than an overestimate.

Secondly, a possible source of overestimation is the policy hypothesis about 'completing' the internal market. This may turn out to be stronger than the actual outcome, if some barriers were in effect to escape effective elimination. However, it is not for the present study to offer alternative scenarios on this point. On the contrary, the study aims to supply information on the potential gains.

Thirdly, on the other hand, a source of underestimation is that not all types of dynamic effect could be estimated, notably those relating to the likely favourable impact of competition on innovation and technological progress, and on the strategic behaviour of European enterprises in relation to European and world markets.

Fourthly, there is the issue of whether the 'equilibrium' postulate, that all resources released in rationalization would be re-employed, is realistic. Undoubtedly it is only a matter of time before such resources are effectively re-employed. For economies of scale from restructuring and dynamic effects generally, the adjustment period between the policy change and the new equilibrium situation may take quite a few years: five years would probably see the larger part of adjustments completed, 10 years probably almost all. However, a wider variety of outcomes is surely possible over a short- to medium-term period, when the impact of the internal market action on both the labour market and other key macroeconomic variables needs to be taken into account. Full evaluation of this question requires, however, different models of economic analysis, as well as discussion of macroeconomic policy options that would arise. This is the subject of the next section. As will be seen, this further analysis does not require that a pessimistic view be taken on the question raised at the beginning of this paragraph.

Fifthly, in order to arrive at a measure of economic gain defined in terms of 'net welfare', it is necessary to exclude reductions in economic rents. This has been done where there was information available (e.g. for agriculture). In general, however, there was insufficient information to identify the impact of competition on economic rents separately from the impact of X-inefficiency. For some sectors this could be a significant source of overestimation, notably for the financial services, although in this case there were other, offsetting sources of welfare gains that could not be estimated. On the whole, therefore, this measurement problem may not be of major importance to the overall result.

Sixthly, there is the possibility of bias due to the summation of 'partial' rather than 'general' equilibrium estimates. The results are 'partial' in the sense that they add up estimates made independently for many individual sectors, and do not work through the 'general equilibrium' result that would take into account second-order effects due to changes in relative prices between sectors. While this distinction between the partial and general is of fundamental importance in economic theory, it is an open matter empirically, depending upon the circumstances of the case, whether the partial equilibrium results risk being seriously biased by comparison with the likely general equilibrium results. To resolve this question thoroughly would have required a large research effort to construct a complex general equilibrium model, which, while theoretically possible, could not be achieved within the time-constraints of the present project. However, there are reasons to suppose that this possible source of measurement error is not so important, compared to many other primary issues which the present study has had to face.

Therefore, all things considered, it is suggested that the aggregate estimates presented here according to the partial equilibrium method do not have any obvious net bias in terms of over- or underestimation. However, there is surely a wide margin of error surrounding the figures, and this is suggested in the range of results offered in Table 10.1.1.

Table 10.1.1.

Estimates of the total economic gains from completing the internal market, according to partial equilibrium estimation methods (EUR 7, based on bench-mark data for 1985, at 1985 prices)

| | billion ECU | | % GDP | |
| | Variants | | Variants | |
	A	B	A	B
Stage 1: Cost of barriers affecting trade only	8	9	0,2	0,3
Stage 2: Cost of barriers affecting all production	57	71	2,0	2,4
Total direct costs of barriers(a)	65	80	2,2	2,7
Stage 3: Economies of scale from restructuring and increased production	60	61	2,0	2,1
Stage 4: Competition effects on X-inefficiency and monopoly rents	46	46	1,6	1,6
Total market integration effects				
Variant I (sum of stages 3 and 4 above) (b)	106	107	3,6	3,7
Variant II (alternative measure for stages 3 and 4) (c)	62	62	2,1	2,1
Total of costs of barriers and market integration effects				
Variant I = (a) + (b)	171	187	5,8	6,4
Variant II = (a) + (c)	127	142	4,3	4,8

Notes: Variants A and B relate to the use of alternative primary sources of information introduced in the calculations in stage 1 and 2.
Variants I and II relate to different approaches to evaluating competitivity effects.
Details of these procedures are given in Annex A.
When the total figures, ranging above from 127 to 187 billion ECU for seven Member States in 1985 prices are scaled up to represent the same GDP share for the 12 Member States in 1988 prices, the range becomes 173 to 257 billion ECU.

10.2. Macroeconomic evaluation

A macroeconomic assessment of completing the internal market has been made to accompany the microeconomic estimates presented in the previous chapter.

This chapter is entirely devoted to this subject and aims to provide an overall and summary assessment of the effects of the internal market. The methodology used is first described (Section 10.2.1) and then a quantitative assessment given by major fields (Catinat, 1988): abolition of frontier controls, opening up of public procurement, liberalization of financial services and the strategic reactions of firms faced with a new competitive environment which we have called 'supply effects' (Section 10.2.2 to 10.2.5). Finally, the analysis of the potential created by the easing of macroeconomic constraints leads on to an attempt to quantify a series of effects to be anticipated — pure effects not accompanied by economic policy measures and maximum effects where the room for manoeuvre created is exploited by measures to support activity (Section 10.2.6).

10.2.1. Methodology

Macroeconomic assessment of the large internal market is based on simulations made or scenarios worked out with the help of macroeconometric models (see Annex B).

They have been used under rather special circumstances, since, because of the way in which they are constructed, these models cannot describe in an endogenous manner the consequences of measures such as those covered by the White Paper programme. It was therefore decided to proceed in two stages: firstly, the studies made by various external consultants were used to assess quantitatively the primary effects of completion of the large internal market on the partial fields covered by each of those studies; secondly, those effects assessed 'upstream' of the models were fed into the latter, thereby compelling them, as it were, to incorporate changes in mechanisms or behaviour.[1] In that way, the inability of the econometric models to describe the primary effects was circumvented; on the other hand, full use was made of their ability to simulate secondary effects, i.e. all the normal macroeconomic mechanisms (multiplier and accelerator effects, income-sharing effects, price competitiveness effects, inflation mechanisms, capital accumulation, growth potential, etc.).

The macroeconomic simulations made are scenarios; the consequences described are totally conditioned by the primary 'shocks' quantified 'upstream' of the models. Only the macroeconomic feedback effects are simulated, and in particular the easing of various macroeconomic constraints (improvement in budgetary and external deficits, reduction in inflationary dangers).

---

[1] Technical details of the simulations are given in Annex B. For a full description, see Catinat-Italianer (1988).

Despite the methodology used and the precautions taken, the results provided by the models are likely to err on the side of conservatism: because of the design, the behaviour estimated by reference to the past is assumed to continue[2] and structural phenomena are poorly represented. The simulated consequences should therefore be regarded as covering the medium/long term (5 to 10 years). Beyond that time horizon, structural changes cannot be ignored.

Two econometric models were used: the Commission's Hermes model and the OECD's Interlink model.[3] The Hermes model is a macrosectoral model (nine branches) covering the principal Community countries;[4] the other countries or areas are formalized more simply. The national economies are interlinked through bilateral trade in goods (five products). Its sectoral detail therefore enables it to tackle structural problems. The Interlink model complements it very closely: a macroeconomic model, it describes all the Community countries and in addition other non-Community countries or areas; it provides a disaggregated description of monetary and financial mechanisms. The national economies are also interlinked through bilateral trade in goods and services (five goods, one service) but also through flows of capital and factor incomes.

10.2.2. Abolition of frontier controls

The primary effects of the abolition of frontier controls were analysed and quantified by Ernst and Whinney. They are of two kinds:
(i)   a contraction of the price of intra-Community trade through abolition of the extra costs stemming from the existence of frontiers (customs delays, administrative formalities);
(ii)   job losses either in the public sector (customs officers) or in the private sector (forwarding agents, staff of exporting companies handling the administrative work connected with customs clearance).

The shocks incorporated into the Hermes model simulate these two primary effects; they are equivalent to 0,26 % of Community GDP (see Annex B).

The macroeconomic consequences would stem for a large part from the reduction in the price of intra-Community imports. This would give rise to two types of substitution for each Member State: firstly, substitution between national production and imports from the Community in favour of the latter; secondly, substitution between extra-Community and intra-Community imports in favour of the latter.

Each Member State would benefit from improved terms of trade brought about by the fall in import prices; the Community as a whole would increase

---

[2]   Except, of course, for behaviour modified by calculations 'upstream' of the models.
[3]   See Annex B or documents Interlink (P. Richardson 1987) and Hermes (Valette and Zagamé, 1988) respectively for a full description of these econometric models. The Interlink simulations were conducted within the Commission services and the OECD is in no way responsible.
[4]   Belgium, France, Italy and the United Kingdom; as Germany and the Netherlands are not yet complete, the corresponding national blocks of the Comet model have been used and linked up to the rest of the Hermes model.

its trade balance in volume terms in relation to the rest of the world (second substitution effect). External trade would therefore have a positive effect on Community GDP. According to the Hermes model simulations, Community GDP could rise in the medium term by almost 0,4 % and produce an external surplus of 0,16 of a percentage point of GDP (see Table B.1 in Annex B).

Compared with the initial shock (0,26 of a percentage point of GDP), the multiplier effect is relatively slight in the medium term. This is primarily due to the initial job losses and the consequent reduction in personal disposable incomes, which in the short term counteract the favourable impact of trade with the outside world. In the short term, these job losses, if they all occur over a short time-span, could even bring about a relative fall in Community GDP. Once the initial static effect has passed, however, the favourable dynamic effect of external trade will persist: for the Community as a whole 200 000 jobs could well be created in the medium term (see Table 10.2.1).

The general government balance should improve in the short and medium term although for different reasons: in the short term, this would result mainly from the budgetary savings made through the abolition of jobs in the customs service; in the medium term, it would stem largely from the upturn in economic activity and the consequent increase in tax revenue. In the medium term, the net budget position would improve by some 0,2 of a percentage point of GDP on average for the Community.

Finally, the abolition of frontier controls could dampen inflation; disinflation-ary pressures (reduced production costs of exporting companies and improved terms of trade for each Member State) would largely outweigh the inflationary strains which might be induced by the upturn in economic activity: the rate of inflation could fall by some 1,0 of a percentage point in the medium term.

With an upturn in activity (almost 0,4 % of GDP in the medium term), job creation (200 000 jobs in the medium term), disinflation (-1 % of consumer price inflation in the medium term) and an easing of budgetary and external constraints (respective improvements of about 0,2 of a percentage point of GDP in the medium term), the abolition of frontier controls has the exceptional characteristic of being beneficial whatever aggregate is considered. Even though its effects may seem tiny and even microscopic compared with the level of unemployment in the Community, the abolition of frontier controls nevertheless remains psychologically and strategically essential: it will be the intangible mark of the irreversibility of the political process of completing the internal market. Its indirect effects may therefore be considerable because of the expec-tations it will generate. This will be a major factor in the credibility of the internal market.

10.2.3. Opening-up of public procurement

Atkins-Planning, the consultancy firm asked to produce a study of public contracts, distinguishes three types of effect which may be generated by the opening up of such markets:

(i)   a static effect; savings would be achieved as a result of the wider use of foreign suppliers whose prices are lower;

(ii) a competition effect; the pressure of competition would compel national suppliers to adjust their prices downwards;

(iii) a restructuring effect; supplier branches would have to restructure and achieve productivity gains to withstand the pressure of competition.

Each of these three effects was incorporated into the Hermes model; the size of the shocks corresponds to the median values of the ranges provided by Atkins-Planning (0,35-0,70 % of Community GDP). For the simulated scenario, the shocks incorporated into the Hermes model therefore represent 0,50 % of Community GDP. The central simulation was carried out assuming that the opening-up of public procurement was limited to the Community area and therefore benefited only Community suppliers.[1]

The macroeconomic consequences of the opening-up of public procurement will spread throughout the economy through three channels, which will be dealt with separately in the interests of clarity: public enterprises, public administration and public contract suppliers.

In the case of public enterprises (principally enterprises in the energy, transport services and telecommunications sectors), the opening-up of public procurement would primarily entail reductions in the average cost of investment spending and therefore a steady fall in their production costs. Starting in these public services, such reductions would spread to all the productive branches which are normally large-scale users of public services. The overall effect could therefore well be a slowdown in the general rate of price inflation and an improvement in the Community's competitive position in relation to the outside world, all other things being equal (in particular unchanged currency parities). Both macroeconomic phenomena promote growth.

In the case of public administration, the opening-up of public procurement would entail budgetary savings and would therefore help to cut public deficits. The upturn in activity initiated by public enterprises would also increase tax revenue and would further reinforce the budget deficit reduction process.

Whether and to what extent the economy as a whole would benefit would depend on the approach adopted by the public authorities. Benefiting from an easing of the budgetary constraint, those authorities could choose between three different types of reaction: accelerating the debt-cutting process, reducing the tax burden or directly bolstering demand. In the last two cases, the budgetary savings would have the effect of giving direct support to growth and employment.

Finally, in the case of public contract suppliers, the pressure of competition would trigger necessary restructuring and contraction — in some cases sharp

---

[1] Another case is that of an opening-up of Community public procurement negotiated on the basis of reciprocity with the rest of the world (Catinat, 1988). Such a scenario could be similar to the central scenario (opening up limited to the Community area) but with quantitative increases in the macroeconomic consequences.

Table 10.2.1.

Macroeconomic consequences of completion of the internal market: Community as a whole in the medium term

	Frontier controls	Public procurement	Financial services	Supply effects[1]	Total Average	Total Range
Relative change						
As % of GDP	0,4	0,5	1,5	2,1	4,5	(3,2 to 5,7)
Consumer prices	−1,0	−1,4	−1,4	−2,3	−6,1	(−4,5 to −7,7)
Absolute change						
Employment (× 1 000)	200	350	400	850	1 800	(1 300 to 2 300)
General government borrowing requirement as a % of GDP	0,2	0,3	1,1	0,6	2,2	(1,5 to 3,0)
External balance as a % of GDP	0,2	0,1	0,3	0,4	1,0	(0,7 to 1,3)

[1] Scenario including the supply effects estimated by the consultants, the economies of scale phenomena (industry) and the competition effects (monopoly rents, X-inefficiency).

Source: Hermes and Interlink models. The Interlink simulations were conducted within the Commission services and the OECD is in no way responsible for them.

— of their production costs. The direct beneficiaries of this would of course be governments and public enterprises. It is probable, however, that this restructuring would also affect products not exclusively intended for public agencies. In that case, beneficial effects could appear directly on private markets and reinforce the macroeconomic consequences described above.

The simulations made with the help of the Hermes model corroborate this view (see Table B.2 in Annex B). If the opening-up of public procurement were limited to the Community area, that would lead in the medium term to an increase of approximately 0,55 % in Community GDP and to the creation of almost 400 000 additional jobs. These simulations implicitly describe a situation where the public administrations adopt a policy of reducing their debt; the favourable impact on growth would therefore largely stem from the dissemination of the price reductions made by public enterprises.

The macroeconomic consequences show — once again — the exceptional combination of an increase in Community GDP and an improvement in the other aggregates: a fall in consumer prices (almost 1,5 % in the medium term), a reduction in budget deficits (0,3 % of GDP in the medium term) and an improvement in external balances (0,10 % of GDP in the medium term) on average for the Community as a whole.

However, they would be less favourable if it were assumed that there would be an opening up on a world-wide basis (and so not limited to the Community) without reciprocity by the rest of the world . In that case, a proportion of public purchasing would be met by imports from outside the Community and the impact on Community GDP, employment and budgetary and external balances would be reduced. The credibility of the process of achievement of the internal market will depend largely on the degree to which public authorities execute their role. Thus it goes without saying that the consequences of the opening-up of public procurement extend beyond the restricted macroeconomic effects quantified above.

Even in the most favourable outcome these consequences would remain limited, though they should be considerably larger than those resulting from the lifting of customs barriers. As is the case with the latter, the opening-up of public procurement would have a symbolic value. This would be politically symbolic since it would be the public authorities themselves who, as a result of their own behaviour, would apply the rules of competition, and ensure the Community interest rather than the strictly national interest.

10.2.4. Liberalization of financial services[1]

The liberalization of financial services and the removal of existing barriers (limitations on the right of establishment, regulatory constraints) would promote free competition and limit the monopoly rents which the segmentation of

---

[1] Banking, insurance and stock market activities.

the Community market into so many national markets currently provides. Under pressure of competition, the prices of financial services in each of the Member States should therefore steadily converge towards those of the most efficient suppliers.

Price-Waterhouse's estimates of the reductions in the prices of financial services were incorporated into the Interlink model. They cover both cuts in the cost of credit and actual price reductions (in the insurance field in particular).

The shocks incorporated into the Interlink model represent some 0,70 % of Community GDP (middle of the 0,4-1,0 % range supplied by Price- Water-house).

The reduction in the price of financial services would spread widely and the final macroeconomic consequences would exceed by far the primary effects estimated by Price-Waterhouse (see Table 10.2.1 and Table B.3 in Annex B).

The multiplier effect would stem very largely from the fall in the cost of credit. This would promote productive investment and so boost growth potential. It would facilitate not only the necessary modernization of the Community's productive system — thereby guaranteeing competitiveness — but would also reinforce the expansion of productive capacity — thereby ensuring growth. Viewed from this angle, the liberalization of financial services would play a crucial supporting role in the completion of the internal market: it would ensure that its potentially favourable impact on Community growth was not thwarted by a shortage of capital. Together with the free movement of capital, it would also lead to a better allocation of financial resources; in other words, it would ensure that the most worthwhile investment projects could be financed smoothly. At the same time, the fall in the cost of credit would bolster the. upturn in residential construction, thereby providing a boost to the job-creating building sector.

These effects, which would stem primarily from the banking sub-sector (lending activity), would be supplemented by the consequences of the reduction in the price of other financial services (other banking activities, insurance, stock market activity). Firms would serve as a relay, passing on the reductions in their production costs (fall in the price of their intermediate consumption of financial services) to their selling prices. A disinflationary trend would therefore emerge, which would stimulate both internal demand through gains in purchasing power and external demand through increased competitiveness. Households would therefore benefit not only from the direct reduction in the price of financial services but also from the general fall in prices spreading to all goods and services.

It is not surprising, therefore, that the macroeconomic consequences quantified by the Interlink model are substantial: an increase in Community GDP of almost 1,5 %, a less rapid rate of price increase of some 1,4 % and an improvement in the net budget position of 1,1 % of GDP (all these beneficial effects are the Community average in the medium term). The external balance could only improve slightly in the medium term: 0,3 % of GDP for the Community; the gains in competitiveness would be strongly counteracted by the growth in imports brought about by the additional growth and in particular the upturn in investment. Despite a substitution process which would be detrimental to employment (fall in the user cost of capital), a major job-creating effect would emerge in the medium term: as a result, some 400 000 jobs could well be created in the Community as a whole.

10.2.5. Supply effects: strategic reactions of firms faced with a new competitive environment

Quantification of the strategic reactions of firms faced with a new competitive environment is quite difficult, so complex and interconnected are the phenomena which give rise to them. A definite forecast is not possible since the subject concerns the expectations and choices of businesses.

In view of these difficulties different scenarios were envisaged (see Annex B) which should be considered as illustrative; they represent both optimistic as well as pessimistic hypotheses. They are said to be illustrative since they describe phenomena which could happen but which are not completely foreseeable; they are said to be optimistic, since they presuppose a reasonably high degree of success of firms in the light of newly created opportunities; finally, they are said to be pessimistic since they do not include all sectors nor take account of all the supply effects. The effects analysed correspond to the direct costs of technical barriers, of economies of scale and the pure effects of competition (a reduction of monopoly rents and of X-inefficiencies) but do not take account of the effects of competition on innovation nor take account of instances of transnational cooperation.

Supply effects — essentially microeconomic — are transmitted to the macroeconomic sphere by means of two principal channels. On the one hand, this occurs through a price reduction. These reductions come about hand-in-hand with reductions in the cost of production; the causal relationship between them is especially complex. In particular, an intensification of competition will bring about a change in the normal order of causality: price reductions occasioned by competitive pressures will force firms to look actively for reductions in costs through the elimination of areas of low productivity or by a greater exploitation of scale economies. Throughout the system of industrial interrelationships reductions in cost of upstream will reinforce further reductions downstream.

On the other hand these (supply) effects are transmitted via the improvement of the productivity of factors of production. These result from a better allocation of human, technological and financial resources (the exploitation of comparative advantage, for example), or via a revitalization of industrial organization (economies of scale) or via an improvement in the internal organization of firms.

All the macroeconomic consequences result from these two phenomena. The beneficial effects of the first, in the medium term, are contrasted to unfavourable effects of the second. In effect, the reduction in the price level implies a gain in the level of internal demand as a result of an improvement in real income (that of households, in particular) and an increase in foreign demand through improvements in competitiveness. But these gains in productivity imply a more economic use of the factors of production — both labour and capital. Moreover, all other things being equal, such economies are synonymous with a fall in the level of demand (less investment, less income from the labour force). There is a risk of a loss of employment in the short term (see Figure 10.2) as a result of both of these dynamic factors, while these effects are felt over different time periods. These will combine progressively as the beneficial effects linked to advances in efficiency and flexibility on the supply side become apparent. In the medium term, a substantial amount of employment creation may be expected (about 0,9 million in the Community according to calculations made here). The costs of adjustments, in the short term, even though they may appear large or undesirable, are closely linked with this process; they sometimes constitute a *sine qua non* of success. They will be proportionately weaker and short-lasting to the extent that they efficiently and rapidly provoke a restructuring of the processes of production.

In the case of a successful outcome for the strategy of firms an especially positive macroeconomic balance sheet can be envisaged: an increase in Community GDP by over 2 % in the medium term, and a relaxation on the number of macroeconomic constraints — a significant reduction in the price level (over 2 % according to calculations made here), and an improvement in the public and trade balances (0,5 % percentage points of GDP). Even more favourable consequences could result over a longer time-scale.

Thus, supply effects should prove quite large both from the point of view of their magnitude and their dynamic effects. They should prove proportionately greater if they occur in a competitive environment, since improvements in supply conditions will have a knock-on effect, via the price level, on the level of demand, thus ensuring a harmonious and parallel development of both constituent parts of the overall market.

10.2.6. Actual and potential consequences of the large internal market

These simulations paint a highly favourable overall picture. According to the econometric models, whatever aspects are analysed — removal of frontier controls, opening-up of public procurement, liberalization of financial services or 'supply effects' (technical and regulatory obstacles, economies of scale, competition) — the macroeconomic consequences would be favourable for the Community in the medium term (see Table 10.2.1).

According to the simulations, completion of the internal market would combine activity-bolstering effects (increase in Community GDP of between 3,2 and 5,7 % in the medium term) with reduced inflationary strains (fall in consumer prices of between 4,5 and 7,7 % in the medium term) and an easing of budgetary and external constraints (improvements of between 1,5 and 3,0 %

of GDP and between 0,7 and 1,3 % of GDP respectively in the medium term). The labour market situation would also improve (creation of between 1,3 and 2,3 million jobs in the Community as a whole in the medium term). However, that improvement would not be sufficient to bring about any significant reduction in the current unemployment figure, since the unemployment rate would fall by only 1 to 2 percentage points in the medium term.

All these effects can be depicted in a diagram (see Figure 10.1).

The abolition of non-tariff barriers is synonymous with a reduction in production costs which, under the impact of greater competition, would largely be passed on in prices. Everything would then flow from that: the improved purchasing power of incomes would stimulate economic activity, increased competitiveness would reinforce that upturn and at the same time improve the Community's balance on current account, the initial price reductions would prevent the upturn in activity from degenerating into inflationary pressure — there would even be disinflationary tendencies — and, finally, public deficits could be alleviated through the twin effect of the opening-up of public procurement and the upturn in activity. A virtuous circle could even be established which would prolong those beneficial effects into the medium term or even beyond: under the impact of increased competition and the enlargement of markets to cover the whole of the Community area, firms would continue to seek to cut their production costs (greater use of economies of scale, stimulus to innovation, reduction in X-inefficiency). The beneficial effects due to the productivity- induced reduction in production costs could thus be self-sustaining.

All in all, even on unchanged macroeconomic policy, completion of the large internal market would boost activity, improve the labour market situation and, at the same time, ease three constraints on the Community's macroeconomic situation: first of all, budget deficits and then external imbalances and inflationary risks.

However, in the short term, the costs of adjustment risk obscuring the benefits which may be expected in the medium term. On the labour market, in particular, a reduction in employment may be feared in the initial stages of the process. On the one hand, the suppression of intra-European frontiers would be accompanied by a reduction in employment both private and public (transit agents, customs and excise agents). On the other hand, and most importantly, the liberalization of financial services and the effects on supply imply, in the short term, reductions in employment as a result of the substitution of capital-labour in the first case and by means of productivity gains in the second. Although undesirable, they represent an inevitable stage in the improvement of supply conditions as outlined in the White Paper. This is shown in Figure 10.2 which traces the growth path of the labour market. It may be noted that it is in construction that adjustment costs are concentrated in the first year. In this graph and in the absence of accompanying policies the negative trend of the order of 250 000 persons annually (the negative area of the schedule) has as its counterpart a positive trend representing more than 1 million persons

FIGURE 10.1: **Principal macroeconomic mechanisms activated in the course of completion of the internal market**

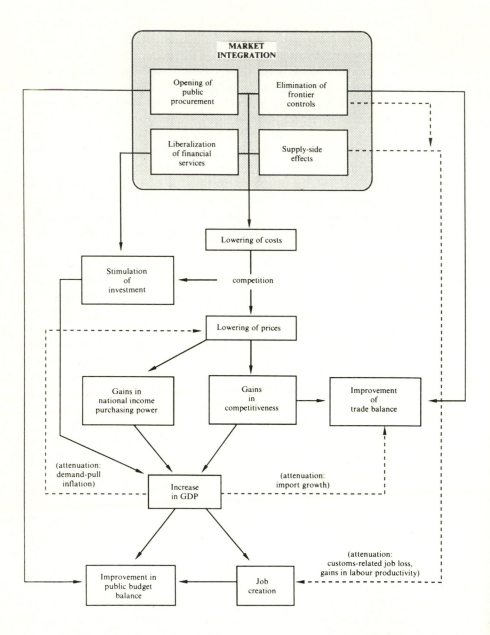

annually (positive area of the schedule): this represents, on average, over a period of six years, the creation of some 700 000 jobs annually which the completion of the internal market could imply for the Community as a whole.

The easing of the macroeconomic constraints, which form part of the process of achieving the internal market, must be seen as additional growth potential. Such potential could perhaps only be realized in the medium or long term. The reduction in public deficits, for example, may lead to a political resolve on the part of the public authorities to reduce the level of their indebtedness, and this would speed up the process of restoring balance to public finances. Exploitation of the room for manoeuvre so created, even if deferred to the future (following the return to balanced public finances referred to in our example), will none the less take place. But it is also possible that this room for manoeuvre will be used in the short term in the form of an easing of the tax burden or of participation in large-scale European infrastructure projects. In that case, the easing of the budgetary constraint would immediately translate into a spur to activity. Similarly, any improvement in the external balance or any fall in the rate of inflation is equivalent in the short, medium or long term to an upturn in activity achieved through the application of expansionary economic policies which properly exploit the room for manoeuvre created.

The relationship between additional activity and the easing of inflationary, public finance or external balance constraints, depends directly on the economic policy measures taken. For the purposes of this report, we have used the average relationship corresponding to customary economic policy action.[1]

If the large internal market were backed up by economic policy measures, this would clearly reinforce the impact on activity and employment (see Table 10.2.2).

Given the current level of public deficits in the Community, the easing of this constraint (i.e. the improvement in public finances brought about spontaneously by completion of the internal market) should play a central role. In the event of all the room for manoeuvre available in respect of the public deficit being used (second line in Table 10.2.2), Community GDP could be increased in the medium term by 7,5 % and employment by 5,7 million without any attendant increase in inflation (consumer price levels down by 4,3 % in the medium term). However, a deterioration in the Community's external balance would have to be accepted (−0,5 % of GDP); this would be possible only if the Community's external balance on completion of the large internal market were initially in surplus by an equivalent amount. Historically, such a surplus

---

[1] According to the estimates (simulations on Hermes and a comparative study by Brookings (Bryant *et al.*, 1988)), the relationships are as follows (in the medium term):
  (i) an improvement in the public finance position of one percentage point of GDP is equivalent to a potential increase in GDP of 1,4 %;
  (ii) an improvement in the external balance of one percentage point of GDP is equivalent to a potential increase in GDP of 2,0 %;
  (iii) a contraction in nominal GDP of 1 % is equivalent to a potential increase in GDP in volume terms of 0,5 %; or, put another way, an increase in GDP in volume terms of 0,5 % costs 0,5 % in increased price inflation.

Table 10.2.2.

Macroeconomic consequences of completion of the internal market accompanied by economic policy measures (medium-term estimates for EUR 12)

Nature of economic policy	Room for manoeuvre used	Economic consequences				
		GDP as %	Consumer prices as %	Employment (in millions)	Public deficit as % point of GDP	External balance as % point of GDP
Without accompanying economic policy measures (from Table 10.2.1.)		4,5	− 6,1	1,8	2,2	1,0
With accompanying economic policy measures[1]	Public finance	7,5	− 4,3	5,7	0	− 0,5
	External position	6,5	− 4,9	4,4	0,7	0
	Disinflation[2]	7,0	− 4,5	5,0	0,4	− 0,2

Margin of error: ± 30%

[1] The accompanying economic policy (public investment and reduction in direct taxation) is such that the room for manoeuvre created by completion of the internal market in respect of the public finance position (or in respect of the external balance or prices) is fully exploited.

[2] It has been assumed, in this case, that the accompanying economic policy is so arranged as to exploit 30% of the room for manoeuvre created by the fall in consumer prices. Full use of that room for manoeuvre would give unrealistic results (sharp deterioration in the external balance in particular).

Source: Hermes and Interlink models. The Interlink simulations were conducted within the Commission services and the OECD is in no way responsible for them.

is high (on average 0,2 % of GDP since the beginning of the 1980s). If the dollar remains at the level obtaining at the beginning of 1988, or if it continues to fall, there is unlikely to be a Community external surplus of that size. In that event, the accompanying economic policy would have to be less expansionary. Maintenance of the external balance at its initial level would then be consistent only with GDP growth of some 6,5 % (third line in Table 10.2.2) and the creation of some 4,4 million new jobs in the Community.

The third case shown in Table 10.2.2 — half way between the two previous cases — might thus be the most plausible: partial exploitation of the room for manoeuvre created by the fall in prices and the reduction in the public deficit; by contrast, the room for manoeuvre for the external balance is fully or even slightly more than fully utilized.

Thus, the macroeconomic simulations and this third scenario (last line in Table 10.2.2) indicate that completion of the internal market, if accompanied by economic policy measures which exploited the room for manoeuvre created (public deficit, external balance and disinflation), could increase Community GDP by 7 % and create about 5 million new jobs in the medium term. Within that range, it would be accompanied by disinflationary pressure and would entail no deterioration in the average public finance situation in the Community. In the short term the accompanying measures would assist in reducing adjustment costs, especially in the case of the labour market (see Figure 10.2).

FIGURE 10.2: **Illustrative profile of evolution of employment**

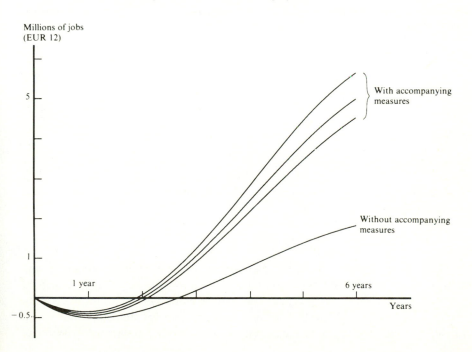

10.3. Synthesis and conditions for success

In the previous chapters, two methods of assessing the gains that can be expected from completion of the large internal market were described: a microeconomic and a macroeconomic method. Being complementary, they are mutually reinforcing.

Their theoretical bases are of course different. The first approach probably errs on the side of excessive flexibility: price flexibility, absence of adjustment cost, perfect adaptability of behaviour, etc. The second probably errs on the side of excessive conservatism: rigidity of markets, persistence of behaviour and of macroeconomic mechanisms, etc. Is it going too far to suggest that reality lies somewhere between these two extremes and that the probable consequences of the large internal market should thus be within the range established by these two approaches?

The first approach expresses the gains to be expected in terms of collective welfare; the second translates them into aggregates: growth in GDP, job creation, reduced price inflation and improvements in public or external balances.

Condensed into a few figures, the estimates derived from the two approaches are convergent (see Table 10.3.1).

Table 10.3.1.

Potential consequences of completion of the internal market for the Community in the medium/long term

Microeconomic approach	Welfare gains as % of GDP $4\frac{1}{4}$-$6\frac{1}{2}$				
Macroeconomic approach	GDP as %	Prices as %	Employment in millions	Public balance as percentage point(s) of GDP	External balance as percentage point(s) of GDP
Without accompanying economic measures[1]	$4\frac{1}{2}$	-6	$1\frac{3}{4}$	$2\frac{1}{4}$	1
With accompanying economic measures[1]	7	$-4\frac{1}{2}$	5	$\frac{1}{2}$	$-\frac{1}{4}$

[1] Margin of error ≅ 30 %.

While these estimates must be treated with all due caution in view of the many difficulties involved, the consequences are shown to be not only beneficial but also of considerable magnitude. The welfare gains could amount to between $4\frac{1}{4}$ % and $6\frac{1}{2}$ % of GDP in the medium to long term for the Community as a whole. The increase in economic activity would be of a similar order. Without accompanying economic measures, the additional GDP could amount to $4\frac{1}{2}$ % and the number of jobs created to 1,75 million. A further possible scenario, however, is where the easing of macroeconomic constraints — improved public or external balances, reduced inflationary pressure — is used to boost activity by means of expansionary economic policy measures. The GDP gain would then be 7 % in the medium term over the Community as a whole and 5 million additional jobs would be created — and this without inflationary risks or any deterioration in public finances.

Among the various indicators of success, the most crucial today is that relating to employment. Whereas in recent years stress has sometimes been laid on the role of demand-stimulating policies, our analysis has shown that an improvement in Community supply conditions — in terms of efficiency, flexibility and competitiveness — is a pre-condition of any improvement in the labour market (see Danthine, 1987).

It must be stressed, however, that it is difficult to predict precisely when these micro- and macroeconomic effects will materialize: that depends on both the type of effect in question and the behavioural changes expected.

Firstly, there are at least two types of effect to be considered. The first takes the form of a shock which occurs once only and which raises the level of Community GDP and other macroeconomic aggregates. Such is the case, for example, with the removal of certain customs barriers. The second type of effect (for example, that caused by product or process innovation) improves the potential rate of growth of the economy and lays the foundations for a more rapid rate of increase in collective welfare well beyond 1992. In addition, the first type of effect is restricted to the short term, whereas the effects brought about by industrial restructuring or the dynamic impact of innovation may be felt only in the long term. Similarly, while increasingly large numbers of jobs are bound to be created in the medium term, some slight reduction may occur in the short term.

Secondly, for these effects to materialize at micro and macroeconomic level, it must be assumed that economic agents (including the social partners) change their behaviour. Adjustment to the new conditions gives rise to major costs. Whether it is a matter of reducing the rigidities in product or factor prices or of modifying the Member States' macroeconomic policies, there is a high degree of inertia which is partially linked to the questioning of protected situations at company, sectoral, regional or national levels. The restructuring of the productive system, the shift of employment to other areas, the mobility and retraining of labour and the regional redistributive effects are all aspects which make the adjustments to the new market conditions costly in social and political terms. They are all potential constraints. In order to ease those constraints, it is necessary to introduce a series of accompanying microeconomic and macroeconomic policies and to ensure that there is a credible programme for implementing them. To conclude this report, mention should again be made of some of the principal factors on which the full success of the programme of achieving the internal market is likely to depend.

With regard to the protagonists involved, the success of the internal market will clearly depend first and foremost on European firms. As we have seen in Chapter 8.2, everything will hinge on their strategic reactions, on their capacity to exploit the new competitive conditions in the market and on their ability to seize the opportunities offered to them. Equally essential will be the capacity of managements to use this new context to reduce conflict in industrial relations, to promote worker participation processes which place less stress on hierarchical structures and more on information and dialogue and, finally, to share with workers the productivity gains resulting from the adjustment efforts jointly made.

With regard to accompanying policies, stress has already been laid on the importance of maintaining the competitive process through a firm and credible Community competition policy. Maintenance of that process will ensure that the reduction in production costs feeds through to prices, i.e. that the improvement in supply conditions shows up in increased demand as a result of additional internal purchasing power and external competitiveness gains. The maintenance of that process will also play a central part in boosting the dynamism of the system and ultimately in promoting the emergence of new technologies and innovation and their dissemination, improvements in product quality, encouragement for new activities and new methods of organization.

The need for continued solidarity, particularly between regions, and the role of distributive policies have also been highlighted in Chapter 8.3. In addition, there is the whole question of consensus between the social partners. As early as 1985, they expressed their support for the planned completion of the internal market and have since regularly confirmed that support. The scale of the potential economic gains identified by the report should reinforce the consensus which has emerged. The dynamic growth process which should result in Europe, together with its corollary of new job creation, open up new prospects for a reduction in unemployment. The need to promote social awareness of the changes in prospect has led the Commission to draft a report on the social dimension of the internal market. That report continues the economic analysis of the sectoral and regional impact of abolishing non-tariff barriers and sets out the accompanying social measures which can reduce the adjustment costs: vocational training and mobility, labour market adaptability and the role of the Community's reformed structural Funds. It also shows that the economic and social cohesion associated with the internal market plan is an essential factor in its success. Such success will come neither from general harmonization nor from decentralized regulation but rather from measures to ensure complementarity between the Community and national levels on the one hand, and between a legislative approach and one based on agreement on the other.

With regard to macroeconomic accompanying policies, Chapter 10.2 has demonstrated that expansionary measures are useful in supporting demand. They could be deployed without risking increased inflation or worsening budgetary or external balances by exploiting the room for manoeuvre created by completion of the internal market. As in the case of the microeconomic policies, the European dimension is essential. In the absence of common policies, however, there is a need here to reinforce coordination. Completion of the internal market produces increased interdependence between Member States, since it is based on an expansion of intra-Community trade and free movement of people and capital. The perverse effects which may arise between countries which are highly interdependent but which fail to coordinate their economic policies are well-known. Observation of economic facts shows that any inconsistency in macroeconomic objectives between countries or any external disequilibrium in one of them is frequently resolved by downward adjustment, the correction being made through recessionary rather than expansionary measures. Thus, any disinflationary policy is in part a burden on trading partners suffering a loss of competitiveness and a contraction of their export markets, whereas, conversely, any expansionary policy benefits the others. While in one case the costs of adjustment are exported, in the other it is benefits which are exported. In order to prevent such effects, greater coordination of economic policies between Member States is inevitable. In the monetary field, completion of the internal market may well increase the current fluctuations in exchange rates. The growth in intra-Community trade and the liberalization of capital movements, while playing an essential part in achieving integration and the benefits expected, nevertheless constitute a potential cause of instability. The Community must therefore reinforce the European Monetary System and provide itself with the institutional means to safeguard the stability of intra-Community foreign exchange markets.

This brings us to the more general expectations concerning policy implementation. This will certainly have to play its part if the potential benefits are to materialize. The key words will have to be 'credibility' and 'determination'. While the collective advantages of the internal market are great, the individual risks are equally great. Firms will not venture into the unknown. They will seize the opportunities offered and exploit the new market conditions if the programme for implementing the White Paper is a credible one. The irreversibility of the process and the clarity of the decisions taken will be fundamental determinants which will shape the expectations of the private and public interests involved and will serve as a basis for their development strategies. Excessive slippage in the timetable, obscure compromises and inconsistent decision-making may all undermine the process. Determination will be needed to ensure that we stay on course for 1992!

Annex A — Microeconomic methodology

1. *Cost savings according to primary studies and surveys.* A first approach to assessing the overall cost of technical and administrative barriers to trade is to take the results of the sectoral and horizontal studies undertaken for the Commission (discussed in Chapters 4 and 5) and simply aggregate the estimates of the costs for each type of barrier (see Table A.1). While this procedure is intuitively reasonable, and offers a total in the region of 70 billion ECU (avoiding double counting), there are some serious defects in such an approach.

First, a large number of sectors is not covered. This can be made up very roughly by exploiting results of an opinion survey of industrialists (see below) and making informed working hypotheses for some other sectors such as agriculture and energy.

Table A.1.

Estimates of costs of barriers based on sectoral studies or working hypotheses, EUR 12 (1985)

billion ECU

I. *Costs of specific types of barriers*	
1. Customs formalities 1,7-1,9 % of intra-Community trade flows	8-9
2. Public procurement	21
Total	29-30
II. *Costs of barriers in specific industries*	
1. Food $\frac{2}{3}$-1$\frac{1}{2}$% turnover	0,5-1,0
2. Pharmaceuticals 1-2% turnover	0,3-0,6
3. Automobiles 5% turnover	2,6
4. Textiles and clothing $\frac{1}{2}$-1 % turnover	0,7-1,3
5. Building materials 1$\frac{2}{3}$% turnover	2,8
6. Telecommunications (equipment) 10-20% turnover	3-4,8
Total	9,9-13,1
III. *Costs of barriers in specific service sectors*	
1. Financial services 10% average prices	22
2. Business services 3% turnover	3,3
3. Road transport 5% turnover	5
4. Air transport 10% turnover	3
5. Telecommunications (services)	6
Total	39,3

Note: The table records the results of special studies undertaken by consultants, except the transport cases which rely on earlier published sources. Working hypotheses have also been adopted, for the purpose of the partial equilibrium calculations below, for cost or price reductions for agriculture (0 to 5%), steel (0 to 5%) and energy (2%), following assumptions described in the text.

Categories I and II should not simply be added, since this would imply some double counting, some but not all the costs of customs formalities and government procurement being covered under branches in II.

Secondly, no attempt is made to separate intermediate from final goods. Building materials, for example, although intermediate goods, are counted as part of the total, but reductions in the costs of other production may include some allowance for the reduced cost of inputs. On the other hand, some of the studies do not incorporate comprehensive estimates of reductions in the costs of intermediate goods, and where these goods are not specifically included in the table, there will be some underestimation of the overall effects.

Thirdly, the costs are typically estimated on the basis of unchanged output. The consumer gains from eliminating the barriers will initially come, through price reductions on final goods, as increased real incomes. This will generally imply an increase in demand and output and associated producer gains (increases in factor incomes), which will in turn lead to further increases in demand output. These output changes have been ignored.

Finally, the treatment of the market integration effects is clearly inadequate. In general, estimates were rarely included in the studies for the impacts of more intense competition on eliminating inefficiencies or monopoly rents.[1] The estimates for potential economies of scale tend to be minimal, in that output was assumed unchanged and economies of scale as a result of the restructuring of productive capacity were considered only in a few cases.

Another approach to quantifying the costs of barriers is through an opinion survey of industrialists. Table A.2 summarizes the responses to the questions asking for estimates of cost reductions. The question was only used in five of the countries included, Germany, Ireland, the Netherlands, Spain and the United Kingdom. The estimated cost reduction was on average 1,7 %, which, if applied to manufacturing output, would imply a cost saving of 37.6 billion ECU (1985 prices) for the Community. From the response to the other questions, it is clear that this is mainly made up of distribution costs (which include the administrative costs and delays associated with customs barriers), the cost of imported products and costs of production (notably the costs of satisfying national standards in partner countries).

The surveys pick up essentially the direct costs of barriers. The respondents were not invited to consider the impacts of a major restructuring of output among firms and countries or the effects of keener competition. Some consideration of opportunities for economies of scale was invited by the questions on likely changes in domestic and foreign sales, but it is not possible to determine the extent to which expected cost reductions were attributable to economies of scale. Nevertheless, the overall average cost reduction from the survey does provide some approximate check on the results of other partial equilibrium estimates of the static effects.

---

[1] The welfare effects are not equivalent. Both imply a reduction in prices with positive impacts on demand. The reduction in X-inefficiency means that resources are being used more efficiently at no extra cost, while the elimination of monopoly rents implies a redistribution of real income from producers (including proprietors, management and labour) to consumers.

Table A.2.

Cost effects of barriers: findings from business surveys

Sector	Results for EUR 4[1] % of turnover	Reason most often cited
1. Food, drink and tobacco	2,3	Distribution costs
2. Textiles	1,3	Distribution costs
3. Footware and clothing	1,4	Distribution costs
4. Timber and wood furniture	1,5	Distribution costs
5. Manufacture of paper, paper products, printing and publishing	1,5	Distribution costs
6. Leather and leather goods	1,3	Lower costs and greater availability of imported material
7. Processing of plastics	1,6	Distribution costs
8. Mineral oil refining	0,6	Distribution costs
9. Production and preliminary processing of metals	3,5	Distribution costs
10. Manufacture of non-metallic mineral products	1,4	Distribution costs
11. Chemicals	1,3	Distribution costs
12. Man-made fibres	3,3	Distribution costs
13. Manufacture of metal articles	1,6	Distribution costs
14. Mechanical engineering	2,0	Distribution costs
15. Manufacture of office machinery and data-processing machinery	0,4	Distribution costs
16. Electrical engineering	2,1	Production process
17. Manufacture of motor vehicles, vehicle parts and accessories	2,2	Distribution costs
18. Manufacture of other means of transport	1,3	Production process
19. Manufacture of rubber products	0,5	Distribution costs
20. Precision engineering, optics and the like	1,9	Distribution costs
Weighted average	1,7	

[1] Ireland, Germany, the Netherlands and the United Kingdom.

2. *The use of partial equilibrium analysis*. One approach to assessing the economic costs in terms of trade flows and real income foregone of the various forms of physical and technical barriers to intra-Community trade is through standard partial equilibrium analysis. This sets out to be both more precise and consistent about the various effects being measured, to be comprehensive with respect to the sectoral coverage and to be systematic in the distinction between intermediate and final goods.

Partial equilibrium analysis of the effects of trade barriers was originally developed to quantify the effects of the reduction or abolition of tariffs. It has been used extensively both to assess the impacts of the establishment of the common market in traded goods of the original Community and its later extension, and to quantify the impacts of successive multilateral tariff reductions in the Kennedy and Tokyo Rounds (e.g. Cline *et al.*, 1978).

The basic methodology usually consists of estimating for each product (or service) the amount of additional trade that will be created by a tariff reduction, since the reduction in prices of imported goods will induce their substitution for domestically-produced goods. The net gain to the importing country will consist of the increase in the welfare of consumers, less the sum of the loss in welfare of the producers and the loss in tariff revenue. The loss in producer welfare may be borne by all or any of factor incomes, profits, wages or return to land. The net gain, however, must be positive, or, in exceptional circumstances, zero.

For the analysis of customs union formation not only will there be trade creation, as trade is induced by the elimination of tariffs between members of the union, but there will be trade diversion as a member country changes its source of supply from countries outside the union to countries within. From a global viewpoint, trade creation is mutually beneficial if that production is reallocated to countries where the costs of production are lower. Trade diversion, on the other hand, reduces global welfare, because, in this case, differential tariff reduction leads to production being reallocated from lower cost producers outside the union to higher cost producers within.

The elimination of non-tariff barriers leads to analogous trade-creating and trade-diverting effects. As regards an individual member country, the gains from removing such barriers will be greater than when a tariff is eliminated, in that there is no loss in tariff revenue on imports from other Member States. From the Community point of view there will be net gains from the concentration of production in the low-cost countries. Against the gains from trade creation must be offset the losses from any relocation of production from lower-cost producers outside the Community, (who continue to face the common external tariff), to producers within the Community. These losses are equivalent to the loss in tariff revenue on non-Community imports.

There are further effects resulting from the integration of markets, which stem from the rationalization of production and the exploitation of economies of scale, and from the positive impact of more intense competition on X-inefficiency and monopolistic or oligopolistic power. These effects can in principle be analysed using the same partial equilibrium models. However, problems arise from the difficulties of assessing the impact on unit costs, first, of economies of scale, engendered by both increased output and output concentrated more among the lowest cost Community producers, and, secondly, of reduced X-inefficiency and monopoly rents. However these effects may be of greater welfare significance than the direct cost effects of barriers and so it is important to attempt to assess them quantitatively, if only in terms of rough orders of magnitude.

The international trade model on which the partial equilibrium analysis is based strictly requires the assumption of perfect competition. Clearly this assumption is not valid for all sectors in the Community economy. The result of using this model for sectors in which the market is in reality characterized by a monopolistic or oligopolistic structure is likely to be some overestimation of welfare gains. This will derive from an upward bias in the estimate of increased output, but this will be slight. Secondly, there will be a different distribution of gains, more being taken in the form of producer welfare than of consumer welfare. This will not, however, affect the calculation of net welfare gains.

In the analysis of the impact of increased competition, additional gains accrue from structural economies of scale and the elimination of technical inefficiency. Oligopolistic or monopolistic rents are also likely to be reduced, leading to a redistribution of gains from producers to consumers. The amount of this redistribution is not quantified, except in the case of agriculture, where the initial inputs were price reductions rather than cost reductions. The details are explained in Section 4 below.

The approach followed here examines the costs of a trade barrier in a partial equilibrium method by considering the production, consumption and trade flows of single commodity groups before and after that barrier is eliminated. A general equilibrium approach would consider the impact of the removal of any trade barrier not only on the product concerned, but also the effect on other goods, which may be substitutes or complements (the relative price effect), and the effect on all goods via changes in factor incomes (the income or output effect). Despite major developments in the use of general equilibrium models for trade analysis, they are themselves subject to a number of problems, not least of which is the difficulty of deriving estimates for the large number of model parameters.

3. *The methodology: effects of removing market barriers*. This section will briefly, and in a non-technical way, discuss the way in which the sectoral impacts of eliminating physical and technical barriers have been estimated, and then aggregated, using the partial equilibrium approach. More detailed explanations are provided in 'Partial equilibrium calculations of the impact of internal market barriers in the European Community' (Davenport, Cawley).

The calculations are carried out in several stages:

A. *Effects of removing barriers*:

1. of removing barriers affecting goods traded between countries within the Community;
2. of removing barriers affecting goods produced in the Community, whether traded or not;
B. *Effects of market integration*:
3. of economies of scale associated with increased output using existing plant as well as with the restructuring of output among plants, firms and Member States;
4. of increased competition through the elimination of X-inefficiencies and monopoly rents.

Stage 1: trade and income effects of direct cost reductions. These reductions stem from the removal of barriers which raise the price in one Community country of goods imported from another Member State to a level above that paid in the producing State. They create a wedge between the cost to the producer of goods destined for his home market and those destined for other Community countries. The most obvious of these are the costs associated with border controls and with technical norms and administrative regulations in the importing country. Intermediate goods categories are excluded at this stage, in order to avoid double counting. Demand for intermediate goods derives from the demand for the final goods into which they are inputs, and to the extent that the location of the production of final goods will change with the elimination of barriers, variations in the trade flows of intermediate goods cannot be treated independently.

Changes in trade flows between each Member State, the rest of the Community and the rest of the world are calculated for each category, as well as the welfare or income effects, which derive from both the consumer gain from lower prices in the importing country, less the producer loss from reduced production in that country, and the producer gains from the reallocation of production towards the rest of the Community. For each category the potential overall welfare gain for the Community is calculated (see box). Since 1985 data are used, this gain can be expressed in ECUs at 1985 prices or as a percentage of actual 1985 trade flows. It is important to note that the analysis generally predicts that a country will import more of a particular category of goods, while, at the same time, if it is a significant Community producer, it will probably also export more of the same good to the rest of the Community. Even for a commodity as precisely defined as, say, automobiles, the removal of barriers is likely to stimulate both imports and exports between any one Member State and the rest of the Community. Indeed, the completion of the internal market is likely to stimulate intra-industry trade to a greater extent than inter-industry trade, implying a reinforcement of the trend in the pattern of trade witnessed in recent decades.

To some extent the elimination of barriers will benefit exporters from outside the Community as well as those within. This is most clearly the case where technical norms currently prevent the same good being sold throughout the Community. The harmonization of such norms will mean that the extra costs of meeting individual country specifications will be saved by external as well as internal producers. Other barriers, for example Community border controls, are less important to external producers. It has been assumed that a given percentage of direct cost reductions would also apply to the exports of non-Community producers. In the light of the sectoral studies findings on the cost savings from the abolition of technical barriers, this percentage was set at 10 %.

Stage 2: direct and indirect production cost reductions. This is designed to capture the direct cost reductions which can be best treated horizontally across the Community. The first stage can be thought of as quantifying the impact of the elimination of barriers specifically affecting the cost of producing for export to another Member State. Once the barriers are eliminated, the Community can be treated as a single economic entity, producing and trading with the outside world. Any horizontal cost savings will now reduce the costs of Community production, reduce imports from and, perhaps, raise exports to the rest of the world. To the extent that trade ´vis-à-vis the outside world expands because the Community is now producing at lower cost than the rest of the world, trade creation will have taken place and world welfare will have increased. However, trade diversion will have taken place where Community production displaces imports from the rest of the world, which still enjoys lower production costs, as a result of the Common External Tariff.

The cost reductions that are treated in the second stage cover sections covered by consultants' studies including financial, business, transport and telecommunications services and the business survey. Working hypotheses for agriculture, steel and energy are also introduced. At this stage, also, estimates of the gains from economies of scale as they affect intermediate goods are incorporated. It should be noted, however, that these effects are reported together with other economies of scale results in Table A.7.

Since stage 2 evaluates cost reductions of intermediate goods and services as well as those for certain final goods — financial services clearly falls under both classes — the input-output table of the Community economy is used to calculate the implied cost reductions for final consumption and investment goods. The partial equilibrium analysis is then used to quantify trade and welfare impacts for the Community and for the rest of the world.

4. *Data sources for estimation of barrier removal effects*. The full details of the sources of the estimates of cost reductions, elasticities and trade and production data are given in Davenport, Cawley (1988). Here only a brief outline of the derivation of the cost reduction estimates is given. All the input data for both the calculation of the effects of removing barriers and of market integration are summarized in Table A.3.

Table A.3.

Input parameters for barrier removal and integration effects

	Effects of removing barriers					Effects of market integration		
	Cost reduction Stage 1 (%)		Cost reduction Stage 2 (%)		EOS parameter	EOS restructuring parameter	Scaling coefficient Variant I	Scaling coefficient Variant II
	A (i)	B (ii)	A (iii)	B (iv)	Stage 3 (v)	(vi)	(vii)	(viii)
Agriculture	1,9	1,5	0,8	5,9	0	0	0	0
Solid fuels	—	—	1,1	1,3	0	0	0	0
Coke	—	—	1,4	1,6	0	0	0	0
Oil, gas, petrol	0,7	2,2	1,3	1,3	0,12	0,6	0	0
Electricity, gas, water	—	—	5,8	5,9	0	0	0	0
Nuclear fuels	—	—	1,6	1,7	0	0	0	0
Ores, metals	—	—	1,9	6,9	0,11	1,0	0	0
Non-metallic minerals	—	—	1,6	1,8	0,05	2,3	1,5	2,5
Chemicals	0,8	1,1	1,9	2,1	0,12	2,6	2,5	3,5
Metal articles	1,5	1,4	1,4	2,4	0,06	2,2	0,5	1,5
Mechanical engineering	2,5	2,3	1,4	1,9	0,1	2,0	2,5	3,5
Office machinery	1,6	0,9	1,7	2,0	0,11	2,5	2,5	3,5
Electrical goods	1,6	2,0	1,4	1,8	0,08	3,0	5,0	6,0
Motor vehicles	0,5	1,6	1,5	2,1	0,14	2,2	5,0	6,0
Other transport	0,5	0,9	1,5	1,9	0,12	5,8	2,5	3,5
Meats, preserves	1,0	2,2	0,9	4,0	0,04	1,6	0,5	1,0
Dairy products	1,0	2,2	1,1	4,3	0,04	1,6	1,5	2,0
Other food products	1,0	2,2	1,1	2,6	0,04	1,6	1,5	2,0
Beverages	1,0	2,2	1,3	1,7	0,04	1,6	1,5	2,5
Tobacco products	1,0	2,1	0,5	0,7	0,03	1,6	5,0	5,5
Textiles, clothing	2,3	1,1	1,3	1,5	0,03	0,4	0,5	1,0
Leather	2,3	1,1	1,4	1,7	0,03	0	0,5	1,0
Timber, furniture	3,2	2,2	1,3	1,8	0,04	0	0,5	1,0
Paper and products	1,6	1,4	1,5	1,6	0,07	1,8	2,5	3,5
Rubber, plastics	1,6	2,1	1,6	1,8	0,04	1,7	1,5	2,5
Other manufacturing	1,6	1,6	1,5	2,1	0,04	0	0,5	1,0
Building, civil engineering	—	—	1,3	1,5	0	0	0	0
Wholesale, retail trade			1,1	1,1				
Lodging, catering			1,1	1,7				
Inland transport			4,4	4,4				
Sea, air transport			6,2	6,3				
Auxiliary transport			1,1	1,2				
Communications			5,7	5,8				
Credit and insurance			11,5	11,6				
Rent			0,7	0,7				

Table A.3 *(continued)*.

Input parameters for barrier removal and integration effects

	Effects of removing barriers				Effects of market integration		
	Cost reduction Stage 1 (%)		Cost reduction Stage 2 (%)		EOS parameter Stage 3	EOS restructuring parameter	Scaling coefficient Variant I	Scaling coefficient Variant II
	A (i)	B (ii)	A (iii)	B (iv)	(v)	(vi)	(vii)	(viii)
Other market services			3,8	3,9				
Non-market services			0,9	1,0				
Average	1,6	1,9	2,4	3,0				

(i)   Final goods only; average for EUR 7. Based on aggregation of NACE(3) breakdown of border costs estimated from sectoral studies and study on costs of border formalities. See text.
(ii)   As (i) but incorporates results of business survey on costs of barriers. See text.
(iii)   Incorporates estimates of cost savings from barriers and potential economies of scale (of increased output) on intermediate goods and cost savings in financial services, business services, telecommunications, air transport, road transport and electricity production. See text.
(iv)   As (iii), plus cost savings in agriculture and steel.
(v)   Estimates by Pratten (1987) of percentage reductions in average cost for a 1 % increase in output given existing plants.
(vi)   Estimates of percentage reduction in average costs associated with restructuring.
(vii)   Ratio of indirect gains (due to reinforced effects of competition) to barrier removal gains, based on the Venables and Smith study (1987). See text.
(viii) Ratio of indirect gains (due to economies of scale and reinforced competition) to barrier removal gains, based on the Venables and Smith study. See text.

FIGURE A.1 : **Removal of trade barriers between country I and the Community: Comparative static representation**

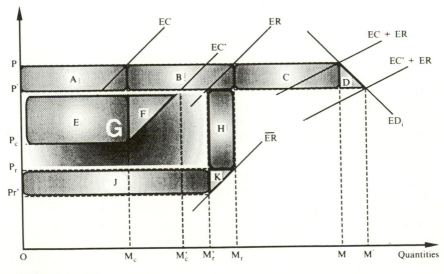

Notes: OM$_c$ + OM$_r$ = OM
         OM$_c$' + OM$_r$' = OM'

Explanation of Figure A.1.

Following traditional trade theory, the welfare effects can be shown by a diagram based on the concept of supply of exports and demand for imports curves, alternatively known as excess supply and demand curves. (Under perfect competition, these can simply be derived as the horizontal difference between domestic demand and supply curves.) Figure A.1 represents the situation where one Community country I is importing from both the rest of the Community C and the rest of the world R. It is assumed that non-tariff barriers between I and C disappear while the tariff (inclusive of any non-tariff barrier effects) against the rest of the world remains constant.

The excess demand curve for a Community country I is represented by ED_i. ER and EC represent excess supply curves for the rest of the world and the rest of the Community respectively. The combined excess supply curves are shown as (EC + ER). After barrier removal, EC shifts downwards by an amount corresponding to the cost of the barrier for the sector concerned. Initially, I imports M_c from the Community and M_r from the rest of the world, a total of M.

When internal barriers are removed, I's total imports rise from M to M', with imports from C rising from M_c to M_c' and from R falling from M_r to M_r'.

The effects for country I are:
(a) a consumer surplus gain (net of producer surplus loss) of $(A + B + C + D)$;
(b) a loss of tariff revenue of $(A + B + G + H) - (G + J)$.

Therefore the net gain to I is given by areas $(C + D - H + J)$. These areas may be interpreted as gains or losses from terms of trade changes. Area C equals the terms of trade gain on existing imports from C, while D gives the gains on additional imports from C. Area H represents the terms of trade loss on imports diverted from the lower cost producer R to C, while area J is the terms of trade gain from the reduced price paid on remaining imports from R.

The welfare effect on the rest of the Community C consists of the producer surplus gain (net of consumer surplus loss) of areas $(E + F)$. E equals the terms of trade gain on existing exports to I while F is the producer surplus gain on additional exports. The rest of the world is characterized by a loss of producer surplus (or terms of trade loss) equal to $(J + K)$.

Stage 1: The calculations in the first stage cover the 65 predominantly final goods sectors selected from the NACE 3-digit classification of 166 sectors. The calculations of the trade, price and welfare effects of the internal barriers are made for those Community countries for which the necessary data are available: France, Germany, Italy, the United Kingdom and the Benelux countries. The base year for the calculations is 1985, in which year these countries contributed almost 90 % of total Community GDP.

The two principal sources of data on the cost reductions which would ensue from the elimination of barriers are the study on the costs of border formalities (Ernst and Whinney, 1987) and the survey of firms' estimates of the costs of barriers, undertaken by the Commission. Two sets of estimates of the cost reductions are used, each based primarily on one of these sources. However, in each case sectoral cost reduction estimates have been checked for consistency with information from consultant studies where this exists.

The Ernst and Whinney study is used to derive the first set of input data (column (i) of Table A.3). The costs of border formalities include the internal administrative costs (staff, computers, overheads etc.) and agents' fees borne by exporting and importing firms, respectively. The study provides estimates of these costs both per consignment and in relation to intra-Community trade value for exporters and importers, within 13 sectors, based on surveys of firm samples in Belgium, France, Germany, Italy, the Netherlands and the United Kingdom. These estimates have been converted (using an import share matrix) into an average cost figure (as a percentage of intra-Community imports) for each Member State and each sector.

No adjustment is made to these figures for the additional costs of satisfying national product norms. Thus, in general, the percentages in column (i) may be considered as a low estimate of the costs of internal barriers affecting intra-Community trade.

The cost data used in column (ii) are derived by first transforming the survey data on firms' estimates on the costs of barriers (by an import share matrix), to give a cost reduction figure for each sector and each Member State as an importing country. On the basis of input-output coefficients, these figures have been adjusted downwards to account for the fact that the survey results included the indirect effects of anticipated price reductions of inputs of intermediate goods and services. They have then been adjusted upwards to take account of the cost of border formalities met by the importers, data derived from the Ernst and Whinney study. In general, the resulting cost reduction estimates used in column (ii) are greater than those used in column (i).

It should be stressed that stage 1 has been calculated using each of the Community countries in turn as an importing country. The input numbers listed in Table A.3 show a weighted average for the seven countries. Column (i) is based on overall average cost reductions amounting to 1,6 % of trade flows, while column (ii) is based on 1,9 %.

Stage 2: In the second stage the calculations are based on aggregated Community data (covering the same Member States as in the first stage — see Table A.4). These calculations cover 44 sectors (classified by NACE-CLIO headings as used in the Community input-output tables). Again two different sets of input data are used to give column (iii) and column (iv).

This input data broadly includes three sources of cost reduction, from the reduced cost of intermediate inputs imported from other countries, from economies of scale on intermediate goods and from specific sectoral cost reductions due to deregulation.

To cover traded intermediate goods, cost reductions are derived from the survey and scaled down by the share of intra-Community trade in Community output. The effects of economies of scale in intermediate goods are incorporated using the parameters derived for stage three and the output increases which emerge from iterative calculations. The cost reductions in financial and business services and telecommunications are based on the commissioned studies for these sectors (Price Waterhouse, 1987; Peat Marwick McLintock, 1987; Muller, 1987). Estimates for air and road transport and energy have been added for the sake of completeness. These data form the basis for column (iii). For column (iv), price reductions are also assumed for agriculture and steel.

In the case of the agricultural and financial services sectors, estimated price reductions are used in Stage 2. To some extent, these price reductions are likely to result from reductions in economic rents and, to that extent, reflect a transfer of economic welfare from producers to consumers rather than a net welfare gain. It is appropriate to use the full price reductions in the input-output exercise, but thereafter the amount of welfare represented by the transfer needs to be subtracted to derive the net gain. The proportion of price reductions due to the compression of rent was taken to be three fifths in the case of agriculture (see K.J. Thomson, 1985). For financial services there was no adequate basis for estimating the likely reduction in economic rents, although this overstatement would be compensated by other categories of economic gain to be derived from financial integration (as indicated in Section 5.1).

Similar considerations arise for energy. Deregulation would lead to cost reductions for the electricity sector and for the production of refined petroleum products. However, in the case of coal, the effects are the ones of price rather than cost. The reduction of internal subsidies allows the importation of coal at world prices, i.e. an external trade barrier is essentially being removed.

The result of this transformation is that the overall cost reductions in the calculations are 2,4 % and 3,0 % respectively of total final output.

5. *Incorporating savings from opening public procurement markets.* The extension of public purchases from one Community country to the rest of the Community is rather different as a source of savings and welfare gains than that of a non-tariff barrier, in that it involves eliminating a self-imposed constraint on the normal pattern of buying where the (identical) goods are cheapest. In principle the widening of public procurement could be treated as an increase in demand for Community-traded goods and incorporated into the first stage.

In practice, there are inadequate disaggregated data on public expenditure, and, moreover, no comprehensive data exist on the extent to which public purchasing bodies currently buy, directly or indirectly, from abroad. Thus the direct trade effects of opening up public procurement have been taken from the consultants' report and simply added, in 1985 prices, to the other trade effects calculated in the first stage of the analysis (Atkins, 1987). There is no problem of double counting here. To the extent that public procurement already involves purchases from abroad, there may be gains from the removal of

Table A.4.

Initial values, trade and output EUR 7 (1985)

billion ECU

	Stage 1			Production	Extra-EC imports	Stage 2		
	Initial intra-EC imports (i)	Initial extra-EC imports (ii)		(iii)	(iv)	Extra-EC exports (v)	Apparent consumption (vi)	Final production (vii)
Agriculture	11,15	6,81	Agriculture	173,28	101,33	17,54	257,07	35,77
Oil, natural gas	5,12	6,59	Solid fuels	30,44	5,23	0,21	35,46	3,85
Mineral oil refining	9,47	5,66	Coke	4,09	0,18	0,44	3,82	0,92
			Oil, gas, petrol	238,73	95,34	16,38	317,69	69,64
Pharmaceuticals	3,57	5,73	Electr., gas, water	170,64	0,58	0,51	170,71	55,78
Soap, detergents	1,94	2,24	Nuclear fuels	3,47	1,67	1,35	3,79	1,86
Household chemicals	4,01	6,53						
Metal products	1,32	1,63	Ores, metals	158,30	29,30	24,90	162,70	16,16
Boilermaking	0,67	0,81	Non-met. minerals	79,20	4,31	7,52	75,99	14,55
Tools, metal goods	5,35	7,90	Chemicals	235,08	23,30	42,61	215,77	69,69
			Metal articles	134,81	4,44	13,11	126,14	48,71
Agric. machinery	2,45	2,98	Mechanical engineering	158,52	17,51	54,59	121,44	103,05
Machine tools	2,75	5,12	Office machinery	48,49	19,47	14,97	52,98	31,60
Textile machinery	1,24	2,23	Electrical goods	154,85	26,81	32,46	149,20	85,00
Food, chemical mach.	3,44	5,02	Motor vehicles	146,19	14,09	36,73	123,55	107,06
Mining equipment etc.	4,40	6,55	Other transport	45,61	6,50	10,70	41,41	25,94
Transmission equip.	2,19	3,56						
Other mach. industry	2,17	3,39	Meats, preserves	48,32	3,78	1,88	50,22	38,91
Other mach. equip.	10,44	17,72	Dairy products	58,67	0,67	3,08	56,27	43,80
			Other food products	158,94	8,60	7,55	159,99	89,57
Office machinery	13,51	26,70	Beverages	54,93	0,69	4,14	51,48	27,85
			Tobacco products	39,62	0,10	0,66	39,06	33,96
Electrical machinery	4,48	7,99						

Table A.4 (*continued*).

Initial values, trade and output EUR 7 (1985)

billion ECU

	Stage 1	
	Initial intra-EC imports (i)	Initial extra-EC imports (ii)
Telecom. equipment	9,42	20,09
Radio, television	6,18	13,87
Dom. electrical equip.	3,19	4,49
Vehicles, engines	27,83	39,90
Vehicle bodies	0,57	0,67
Shipbuilding	0,42	1,20
Rail rolling stock	0,18	0,29
Cycles, motorcycles	0,61	1,34
Aerospace	9,07	13,94
Optical, photographic	2,41	5,43
Clocks, watches	0,40	1,73
Vegetable, animal oils	2,87	7,83
Meat preparation	10,27	14,05
Dairy products	6,90	7,57
Fruit, veg. processing	3,28	6,12
Fish processing	0,93	2,30
Grain milling	0,79	1,28
Pasta	0,22	0,25
Starch products	0,62	1,14
Bread, flour	0,90	0,99
Sugar refining	0,58	1,54
Cocoa, choco., sugar	2,34	2,96

		Stage 2			
	Production (iii)	Extra-EC imports (iv)	Extra-EC exports (v)	Apparent consumption (vi)	Final production (vii)
Textiles, clothing	126,01	20,44	17,21	129,24	75,73
Leather	25,48	4,98	5,45	25,02	18,88
Timber, furniture	68,82	7,96	3,99	72,79	32,07
Paper and products	131,11	12,73	6,98	136,86	28,13
Rubber, plastics	69,06	4,15	8,38	64,82	13,60
Other manufacturing	18,95	12,13	15,77	15,30	13,84
Building, civil engin.	327,26	0,00	0,00	327,26	261,27
Wholesale, retail trade	481,01	4,90	19,58	466,34	342,05
Lodging, catering	129,83	1,65	1,16	130,32	103,34
Inland transport	99,38	2,13	3,31	98,20	34,38
Sea, air transport	50,46	9,96	31,09	29,32	34,27
Auxiliary transport	44,90	5,65	5,51	45,04	6,29
Communications	77,97	1,03	0,95	78,05	28,64
Credit and insurance	425,30	11,81	21,19	415,92	90,56
Rent	256,69	0,77	0,46	257,00	220,27
Other market services	213,65	5,22	5,10	213,77	155,28
Non-market services	627,51	0,00	0,00	627,51	627,27
Total/average	5 315,59	469,39	437,47	5 347,51	2 989,55

Animal food	1,25	1,66
Other food products	2,05	3,34
Ethyl, distilling	1,00	1,17
Wine	0,53	0,90
Cider, perry, mead	0,01	0,02
Brewing	0,70	0,82
Soft drinks, water	0,32	0,34
Tobacco products	2,01	2,11
Manufact. of leather	0,69	1,69
Footwear	3,69	6,09
Clothing	5,82	13,19
Household textiles	0,72	1,64
Fur goods	0,44	0,89
Wooden furniture	3,01	4,21
Printing	1,24	1,82
Publishing	1,24	0,22
Rubber products	0,79	0,01
Retread, repair tyres	0,02	0,42
Processed plastics	1,61	0,42
Jewellery	3,60	9,24
Musical instruments	0,17	0,54
Photo. processing	0,12	0,20
Toys, sports goods	1,23	2,88
Miscellaneous	7,49	11,87
Total/average	219,39	341,24

Note: The import figures for stage 1 cover only goods entering final consumption directly. The trade figures for stage 2 cover goods applied to both final and intermediate cases, together with services.

(i)   (ii)   Final goods only.

(iii) (vi)   All goods: apparent consumption equals production plus extra-EC imports minus extra-EC exports.

237

Table A.5.

Results of barrier removal calculations, stage 1

	Change in intra-EC imports (%)		Change in extra-EC imports (%)		Static welfare gains (billion ECU)		Public procurement (billion ECU)	Total gains (billion ECU)	
	A (i)	B (ii)	A (iii)	B (iv)	A (v)	B (vi)	(vii)	A (viii)	B (ix)
Agriculture	6,4	5,0	− 1,8	− 1,4	0,4	0,3	0,0	0,4	0,3
Oil, natural gas	2,7	8,3	− 0,5	− 1,6	0,1	0,2	0,0	0,1	0,2
Mineral oil refining	1,7	5,4	− 1,0	− 2,9	0,1	0,3	0,0	0,1	0,3
Pharmaceuticals	1,8	2,6	− 1,7	− 2,3	0,0	0,0	0,9	1,0	1,0
Soap, detergents	1,1	1,6	− 2,2	− 3,1	0,0	0,0	0,0	0,0	0,0
Household chemicals	1,8	2,5	− 1,5	− 2,1	0,0	0,1	0,0	0,0	0,1
Metal products	2,0	2,5	− 3,3	− 3,9	0,0	0,0	0,0	0,0	0,0
Boilermaking	1,9	2,3	− 3,4	− 3,9	0,0	0,0	0,0	0,0	0,0
Tools, metal goods	2,6	3,2	− 2,7	− 3,4	0,1	0,1	0,0	0,1	0,1
Agricultural machinery	5,7	5,1	− 8,4	− 7,8	0,1	0,1	0,0	0,1	0,1
Machine tools	7,6	7,3	− 4,6	− 4,5	0,1	0,1	0,0	0,1	0,1
Textile machinery	7,6	7,1	− 5,1	− 4,8	0,0	0,0	0,0	0,0	0,0
Food, chemical machinery	6,3	6,0	− 6,2	− 6,0	0,1	0,1	0,0	0,1	0,1
Mining equipment, etc.	6,4	6,2	− 6,2	− 6,0	0,1	0,1	0,0	0,1	0,1
Transmission equipment	7,0	6,7	− 5,5	− 5,4	0,1	0,1	0,0	0,1	0,1
Other machine industry	6,8	6,5	− 5,8	− 5,6	0,1	0,1	0,0	0,1	0,1
Other machine equipment	7,3	7,0	− 5,5	− 5,3	0,3	0,3	0,1	0,4	0,4
Office machinery	4,4	2,9	− 3,1	− 2,1	0,3	0,2	0,2	0,5	0,4
Electrical machinery	4,3	6,1	− 3,0	− 4,1	0,1	0,1	0,0	0,1	0,1
Telecommunications equipment	4,9	6,9	− 2,5	− 3,5	0,2	0,2	0,4	0,5	0,6
Radio, television	4,9	6,9	− 2,3	− 3,2	0,1	0,2	0,0	0,1	0,2
Domestic electrical equipment	3,6	5,0	− 4,0	− 5,6	0,1	0,1	0,0	0,1	0,1
Vehicles, engines	1,1	3,4	− 1,1	− 3,6	0,2	0,5	0,1	0,2	0,6
Vehicle bodies	0,8	2,5	− 1,2	− 4,1	0,0	0,0	0,0	0,0	0,0
Shipbuilding	1,9	5,0	− 0,4	− 1,1	0,0	0,0	0,0	0,0	0,0
Rail rolling stock	1,4	3,3	− 0,6	− 1,6	0,0	0,0	1,1	1,1	1,1
Cycles, motorcycles	1,7	4,6	− 0,6	− 1,5	0,0	0,0	0,0	0,0	0,0
Aerospace	1,5	4,0	− 0,8	− 2,0	0,1	0,2	0,0	0,1	0,2
Optical, photographic	6,3	4,0	− 3,1	− 2,0	0,1	0,0	0,0	0,1	0,0
Clocks, watches	8,0	5,3	− 1,5	− 1,0	0,0	0,0	0,0	0,0	0,0
Vegetable, animal oils	1,0	2,4	0,0	0,0	0,0	0,1	0,0	0,0	0,1
Meat preparation	0,7	1,7	0,0	0,0	0,1	0,3	0,0	0,1	0,3
Dairy products	0,7	1,6	0,0	0,0	0,1	0,2	0,0	0,1	0,2
Fruit, vegetable processing	0,9	2,0	0,0	0,0	0,0	0,1	0,0	0,0	0,1
Fish processing	1,0	2,3	0,0	0,0	0,0	0,0	0,0	0,0	0,0
Grain milling	0,8	1,8	0,0	0,0	0,0	0,0	0,0	0,0	0,0
Pasta	0,6	1,4	0,0	0,0	0,0	0,0	0,0	0,0	0,0
Starch products	0,8	1,9	0,0	0,0	0,0	0,0	0,0	0,0	0,0

Table A.5 *(continued)*.

Results of barrier removal calculations, stage 1

	Change in intra-EC imports (%)		Change in extra-EC imports (%)		Static welfare gains (billion ECU)		Public procurement (billion ECU)	Total gains (billion ECU)	
	A (i)	B (ii)	A (iii)	B (iv)	A (v)	B (vi)	(vii)	A (viii)	B (ix)
Bread, flour	0,6	1,4	0,0	0,0	0,0	0,0	0,0	0,0	0,0
Sugar refining	1,0	2,2	0,0	0,0	0,0	0,0	0,0	0,0	0,0
Cocoa, chocolate, sugar	0,7	1,6	0,0	0,0	0,0	0,1	0,0	0,0	0,1
Animal food	0,8	1,8	0,0	0,0	0,0	0,0	0,0	0,0	0,0
Other food products	0,8	1,8	0,0	0,0	0,0	0,1	0,0	0,0	0,1
Ethyl, distilling	1,3	2,9	− 3,0	− 7,2	0,0	0,0	0,0	0,0	0,0
Wine	2,1	4,9	− 1,8	− 4,3	0,0	0,0	0,0	0,0	0,0
Cider, perry, mead	1,8	4,2	− 2,3	− 5,5	0,0	0,0	0,0	0,0	0,0
Brewing	1,2	2,9	− 2,9	− 7,2	0,0	0,0	0,0	0,0	0,0
Soft drinks, water	1,1	2,4	− 3,5	− 7,2	0,0	0,0	0,0	0,0	0,0
Tobacco products	0,8	2,0	0,0	0,0	0,0	0,0	0,0	0,0	0,0
Manufacture of leather	6,8	3,3	− 3,1	− 1,5	0,0	0,0	0,0	0,0	0,0
Footwear	6,1	2,9	− 3,9	− 1,9	0,1	0,0	0,0	0,1	0,0
Clothing	6,9	3,4	− 2,5	− 1,3	0,1	0,1	0,1	0,3	0,2
Household textiles	6,8	3,4	− 2,6	− 1,3	0,0	0,0	0,0	0,0	0,0
Fur goods	6,2	2,5	− 2,4	− 1,0	0,0	0,0	0,0	0,0	0,0
Wooden furniture	6,2	4,4	− 6,4	− 4,6	0,1	0,1	0,0	0,1	0,1
Printing	3,2	2,8	− 3,2	− 2,8	0,0	0,0	0,0	0,0	0,0
Publishing	3,2	2,8	− 3,2	− 2,8	0,0	0,0	0,0	0,0	0,0
Rubber products	3,6	4,5	− 3,8	− 4,8	0,0	0,0	0,0	0,0	0,0
Retread, repair tyres	3,0	3,6	− 4,0	− 5,2	0,0	0,0	0,0	0,0	0,0
Processed plastics	3,2	4,0	− 4,0	− 5,1	0,0	0,0	0,0	0,0	0,0
Jewellery	3,5	3,9	− 1,2	− 1,3	0,1	0,1	0,0	0,1	0,1
Musical instruments	5,5	6,0	− 1,6	− 1,7	0,0	0,0	0,0	0,0	0,0
Photo processing	4,1	4,4	− 3,0	− 3,3	0,0	0,0	0,0	0,0	0,0
Toys, sports goods	4,8	5,2	− 2,1	− 2,3	0,0	0,0	0,0	0,0	0,0
Miscellaneous	3,6	3,8	− 2,7	− 2,9	0,1	0,2	0,0	0,2	0,2
Total/average	3,7	4,5	− 2,2	− 2,6	3,8	5,1	3,9	7,7	9,0

(i) to (ix)   Except column (vii), derived from partial equilibrium trade model described in the text. A and B based on alternative cost reduction estimates, see Table A.3.

(i)   In the cases of goods subject to, or with primary inputs subject to, CAP regimes, the change in imports from outside the Community was set to zero.

(vii)   From Atkins (1987). These are the static gains. The total of 3,9 billion ECU includes 0,9 billion ECU for the sector NACE 530 (Building and civil engineering works).

(viii) and (ix) Summations of columns (v) and (vii), and (vi) and (vii), respectively.

physical or technical barriers. These will be already incorporated in the first stage. The additional gains included here are those which result from the cost savings currently available to public purchasing agencies if they were permitted to buy on the cheapest Community market. The implicit assumption is that the volume of public sector purchases remains unchanged.

The data on procurement at this stage exclude savings due to economies of scale from restructuring (these are covered in stage 4).

6. *Results: effects of removing barriers*. Tables A.5 and A.6 set out the principal results. The calculated reduction in prices consequent on the elimination of barriers is of the order of 2 to 3 % of GDP. In the case of the stage 2 results, it is estimated that the change in Community output would increase by the same order of magnitude, implying that Community GDP in money terms remains little changed. The relative magnitude of the results from stages 1 and 2 cannot be interpreted as being at all precise. Some of the barriers affecting trade had, for statistical reasons, (notably the difficulty of obtaining trade data for services and the problems caused by intermediate goods), to be treated at the Community level and in stage 2 rather than stage 1. The stage 2 results are significantly affected by the assumed cost reduction for financial, business, transport and telecommunication services, and, in the B simulations, for agriculture and steel. In the case of financial services, the barriers in question to some extent affect trade specifically (and so in principle should be in stage 1), but, more importantly, they limit the establishment of financial institutions from other Members States and, to that extent, are properly within the stage 2 estimates.

As far as the complete results of the barrier removal effects are concerned, a total increase in welfare, or real incomes, of 66 to 82 billion ECU has been estimated. The calculations are in 1985 prices and for a Community of Seven.

7. *Methodology: the market integration effects*. Until now, the methodology has followed the traditional partial equilibrium analysis of tariff reductions or customs union formation. No such methodology is available for quantifying the market integration effects. These will depend critically on the extent to which keener competition leads (i) to a relocation and restructuring of production, stimulated by opportunities for economies of scale, and (ii) to the elimination of the X-inefficiencies and excess factor payments associated with monopolistic or oligopolistic market structures. As such, they are clearly more speculative than the static or barrier removal effects.

The work of Harris and Cox (1984) on the proposed US-Canada customs union shows that the market integration effects may magnify the direct costs of barriers several times over. In a study of the effects of forming the original Community customs union, Balassa (1974) took a ratio between these categories of effect to have been 5:1. However, these studies are hardly comparable to the present, as the effects of tariff reductions in those cases are comparatively much smaller if tariff revenue is subtracted. In order to get some order of magnitude for the market integration effects of eliminating non-tariff barriers in the Community, plausible ratios are derived in the following ways.

Table A.6.

Results of barrier removal calculations, stage 2

	Change in output (%)		Change in extra-EC imports (%)		Barrier removal welfare gains (bn ECU)	
	A (i)	B (ii)	A (iii)	B (iv)	A (v)	B (vi)
Agriculture	0,4	2,9	0,0	0,0	0,4	2,8
Solid fuels	0,0	0,0	2,4	2,9	0,0	0,1
Coke	0,0	0,0	3,9	4,4	0,0	0,0
Oil, gas, petrol	2,7	2,7	−4,3	−4,4	1,1	1,1
Electricity, gas, water	2,7	2,8	−31,5	−32,0	3,3	3,3
Nuclear fuels	0,0	0,0	0,0	0,0	0,0	0,0
Ores, metals	2,3	8,4	−8,6	−31,0	0,5	1,7
Non-metallic minerals	1,1	1,2	−8,3	−9,1	0,3	0,3
Chemicals	1,7	1,8	−9,5	−10,4	1,7	1,9
Metal articles	0,8	1,4	−7,1	−12,4	0,7	1,2
Mechanical engineering	1,4	2,0	−6,0	−8,4	1,6	2,3
Office machinery	3,4	3,9	−5,8	−6,7	1,1	1,3
Electrical goods	1,9	2,6	−5,8	−7,7	1,8	2,3
Motor vehicles	1,4	2,0	−5,4	−7,4	1,8	2,5
Other transport	1,7	2,2	−5,2	−6,7	0,5	0,6
Meats, preserves	0,4	1,5	0,0	0,0	0,4	1,5
Dairy products	0,4	1,5	0,0	0,0	0,5	1,8
Other food products	0,4	1,0	0,0	0,0	1,0	2,2
Beverages	0,5	0,6	−1,9	−2,5	0,3	0,5
Tobacco products	0,2	0,3	−2,2	−3,2	0,2	0,2
Textiles, clothing	1,7	1,8	−5,3	−5,8	1,5	1,7
Leather	1,8	2,2	−5,2	−6,4	0,4	0,5
Timber, furniture	1,6	2,2	−5,4	−7,4	0,6	0,8
Paper and products	1,7	1,8	−6,2	−6,7	0,5	0,6
Rubber, plastics	1,6	1,8	−7,3	−8,1	0,3	0,3
Other manufactures	3,4	4,6	−4,4	−6,0	0,5	0,6
Building, civil engineering	1,0	1,2	−2,0	−2,4	4,2	4,9
Wholesale, retail trade	0,9	0,9	0,0	0,0	3,5	3,8
Lodging, catering	0,9	1,4	0,0	0,0	1,1	1,8
Inland transport	2,8	2,8	−7,6	−7,7	1,5	1,5
Sea and air transport	3,5	3,6	−10,3	−10,4	1,4	1,4
Auxiliary transport	1,1	1,2	−5,3	−5,6	0,1	0,1
Communications	3,0	3,0	−30,7	−30,9	1,7	1,7
Credit and insurance	6,7	6,7	−60,9	−61,3	10,5	10,6
Rent	0,4	0,4	−3,5	−3,7	1,5	1,6
Other market services	0,7	0,7	0,0	0,0	5,9	6,0
Non-market services	0,6	0,7	0,0	0,0	5,8	6,4
Total/average	1,3	1,5	−5,7	−7,7	58,0	71,8

(i) to (vi) Derived from partial equilibrium trade model described in text. A and B based on alternative cost estimates. See Table A.3 and text.

Economies of scale can be induced by an increase in production with an unchanged capital stock, which implies no change in plant size nor a movement to its optimal scale. This type of economy of scale is easier to quantify. None the less the quantification raises certain statistical and conceptual problems. The estimation of these economies of scale is based on the study by C. Pratten (1987) and on discussions with the author. These economies of scale are of small importance, and are included with restructuring economies of scale for simplicity of presentation.

Other larger economies of scale could result from restructuring. These economies of scale are estimated here using a combination of sources of data on the average size of plants for each sector in the Community, the minimum efficient technical size (METS) and estimates of reductions in cost as actual plant size approaches the METS. These restructuring effects were only estimated for the energy and manufacturing data. The method was consistent with the process described by Muller and Owen (1985), whereby increased trade opportunities enable larger firms to expand their market shares, both domestically and in partner countries, by absorbing or putting out of business their smaller rivals. Estimates on changes in plant size or on economies of scale from restructuring, which appear in the sectoral or public procurement studies were given priority. These studies were helpful in the foodstuffs, automobiles, other transport and telecommunications sectors.

Data from Schwalbach (1987) were was used to derive hypotheses of the growth in plant size needed to approach METS. Pratten's data for the economies of scale for that growth in plant size were used. The resulting figures for the percentage change of average costs for each sector are given in Table A.3. In general, it should be noted that these estimates have been made consistent with information on economies of scale and restructuring effects in the consultants' reports. In a similar fashion to stage 2, the set of estimates for scale economies by sector is transformed into a set of cost reductions for final output using the Community input-output table. This implies that the welfare effects of economies of scale appear in Tables A.7 and A.8 in the sector in which the final consumer effect is felt.

The measurement of indirect gains from effects of scale and competition relies on the hypotheses that such gains will be greater in sectors:

(i) where non-tariff barriers permit the survival of firms which are less efficient technically or economically;

(ii) which are highly concentrated, thus favouring the existence of monopoly rents;

(iii) where the potential economies of scale are significant.

The method proposed, therefore, in order to take account of the first hypothesis links the indirect gains to the direct gains resulting from the reduction of non-tariff barriers. Taking the direct gains as a base, the indirect gains are calculated by using coefficients which increase as a function of the degree of concentration and the potential economies of scale.

In applying the method the 20 industrial sectors of the NACE/CLIO classification are split into 9 groups according to their relative degree of concentration (low, medium, high) and their potential for economies of scale. It should be pointed out that the classification of a particular sector in a specific group was sometimes difficult since the degree of concentration and the potential for economies of scale in some sectors could vary widely because of the subsectors comprising them.

The coefficients used to derive the indirect gains from the direct gains are themselves derived from the Smith and Venables model. More precisely, in estimating these coefficients, comparisons were made between the direct gains and total welfare gains in several scenarios and variants.

Therefore the coefficients applied to direct gains to calculate the gains from economies of scale and increased competition were derived from the 'integrated market' scenario where the number of firms can vary. This scenario, which presupposes the end of segmentation in European markets measures both the gains from firms' loss of monopoly power in national markets and those resulting from the disappearance of less efficient firms and the resulting restructuring. The coefficients obtained range from 1 in the case where the degree of concentration and the economies of scale are low (e.g. food products) to 6 where the two indicators are high (e.g. motor vehicles). The coefficients are given in the table below. The welfare gains obtained by the use of these coefficients are presented in column viii of Table A.8 (variant II).

EOS	Concentration ratio:	Low	Medium	High
Low		1,0	2,0	5,5
Medium		1,5	2,5	6,0
High		1,5	3,5	6,0

To isolate the effects of increased competition and to calculate the corresponding coefficients it was necessary to deduct the gains from increased exploitation of economies of scale from the total indirect gains. The economies of scale effects are given by two variants of the 'segmented market' scenario:

(i)   the short-term gains due to increased production, variant in which the number of firms is unchanged;

(ii) the long-term gains due to restructuring, variant in which the number of firms can change.

The multiplier coefficients used to calculate the effects of increased competition are given in the table below. They vary from 0,5 in sectors of low concentration (e.g. clothing) to 5,0 in highly concentrated sectors (e.g. motor vehicles). The welfare gains arising solely from increased competition are given in column v of Table A.8 (Variant I).

243

Table A.7.

Results of economies of scale (EOS) calculations, stage 3

	Welfare gains (billion ECU)				
	EOS from increased output		EOS from restructuring	EOS total	
	A (i)	B (ii)	(iii)	A (iv)	B (v)
Agriculture	0,0	0,0	1,1	1,1	1,1
Solid fuels	0,0	0,0	0,2	0,2	0,2
Coke	0,0	0,0	0,0	0,0	0,0
Oil, gas, petrol	0,4	0,6	1,4	1,8	2,0
Electricity, gas, water	0,0	0,0	0,6	0,6	0,6
Nuclear fuels	0,0	0,0	0,0	0,0	0,0
Ores, metals	0,1	0,4	2,5	2,6	2,8
Non-metallic minerals	0,0	0,0	1,9	1,9	1,9
Chemicals	0,3	0,4	7,3	7,7	7,7
Metal articles	0,1	0,2	3,2	3,3	3,4
Mechanical engineering	0,6	0,7	3,8	4,4	4,6
Office machinery	0,4	0,4	1,3	1,7	1,6
Electrical goods	0,5	0,6	4,9	5,3	5,4
Motor vehicles	0,4	0,7	4,1	4,5	4,7
Other transport	0,1	0,2	2,5	2,6	2,7
Meats, preserves	0,0	0,0	0,9	0,9	0,9
Dairy products	0,0	0,0	1,1	1,1	1,1
Other food products	0,1	0,1	3,0	3,1	3,1
Beverages	0,0	0,0	0,9	0,9	1,0
Tobacco products	0,0	0,0	0,5	0,5	0,5
Textiles, clothing	0,1	0,1	0,5	0,6	0,6
Leather	0,1	0,0	0,2	0,3	0,3
Timber, furniture	0,1	0,1	0,3	0,4	0,4
Paper and products	0,1	0,1	2,8	2,9	2,9
Rubber, plastics	0,0	0,0	1,6	1,6	1,6
Other manufactures	0,1	0,1	0,1	0,2	0,2
Building, civil engineering	0,1	0,1	2,2	2,3	2,3
Wholesale, retail trade	0,1	0,1	1,5	1,5	1,5
Lodging, catering	0,0	0,0	0,9	0,9	0,9
Inland transport	0,0	0,0	0,3	0,4	0,4
Sea and air transport	0,0	0,0	0,3	0,3	0,3
Auxiliary transport	0,0	0,0	0,1	0,1	0,1
Communications	0,0	0,0	0,1	0,2	0,2
Credit and insurance	0,0	0,0	1,1	1,1	1,1

Table A.7 *(continued)*.

Results of economies of scale (EOS) calculations, stage 3

| | Welfare gains (billion ECU) | | | | |
| | EOS from increased output | | EOS from restructuring | EOS total | |
	A (i)	B (ii)	(iii)	A (iv)	B (v)
Rent	0,0	0,0	0,2	0,2	0,2
Other market services	0,0	0,0	0,5	0,5	0,5
Non-market services	0,1	0,1	2,4	2,6	2,6
Total/average	3,9	5,1	56,4	60,3	61,5

(i) and (ii)   Derived from estimates of economies of scale under increased output but with unchanged plants in energy and industrial sectors.
(iii)   Economies of scale from restructuring, see text.
(iv) and (v)   Sum of (i) and (iii), and (ii) and (iii) respectively.

It should be noted that multiplier coefficients are not given for agriculture, energy, steel and services because these sectors are not covered by the Venables and Smith study. But for these sectors, it can be argued that the competition effect is included in Stages 1 and 2.

EOS	Concentration ratio:	Low	Medium	High
Low/Medium		0,5	1,5	5
High		0,5	2,5	5

8. *Results: market integration effects.* The calculations of the integration effects are summarized in Table A.8 where they combined with the barrier effects to produce overall totals. Variant I of the scaling-up process which represents competition effects only results in about 46 billion ECU. When this is added to the calculations of the effects of scale economies (60 to 61 billion ECU) total market integration effects are 106 to 107 billion ECU. The alternative Variant II which represents both restructuring scale effects and competition effects results in 62 billion ECU.

Either of these estimates of the integration effects can be added to barriers effects. The combined totals produce welfare gains ranging from 126 billion ECU to 187 billion ECU. Alternatively, these estimates can be scaled up to give figures for EUR 12 at 1988 prices of between 174 and 258 billion ECU.

Table A.8.

Welfare gains from barrier removal and integration effects (billion ECU)

	Barrier removal effects		Market integration effects					Variant II	Totals			
	Stages 1 + 2		Variant I									
			Stage 3 Economies of scale		Stage 4 X-ineff. econ. rents	Stages 3 + 4 Total		Stages 3 + 4 Total				
	A	B	IA	IB	IA and B	IA	IB	IIA and IIB	IA	IB	IIA	IIB
	(i)	(ii)	(iii)	(iv)	(v)	(vi)	(vii)	(viii)	(ix)	(x)	(xi)	(xii)
Agriculture	0,7	3,0	1,1	1,1	0,0	1,1	1,1	0,0	1,9	4,2	0,7	3,0
Solid fuels	0,0	0,1	0,2	0,2	0,0	0,2	0,2	0,0	0,2	0,2	0,0	0,1
Coke	0,0	0,0	0,0	0,0	0,0	0,0	0,0	0,0	0,0	0,0	0,0	0,0
Oil, gas, petrol	1,2	1,6	1,8	2,0	0,0	1,8	2,0	0,0	3,0	3,7	1,2	1,6
Electricity, gas, water	3,3	3,3	0,6	0,6	0,0	0,6	0,6	0,0	3,8	3,9	3,3	3,3
Nuclear fuels	0,0	0,0	0,0	0,0	0,0	0,0	0,0	0,0	0,0	0,0	0,0	0,0
Ores, metals	0,5	1,7	2,6	2,8	0,0	2,6	2,8	0,0	3,1	4,6	0,5	1,7
Non-metallic minerals	0,3	0,3	1,9	1,9	0,4	2,3	2,3	0,7	2,6	2,6	1,0	1,0
Chemicals	2,8	2,9	7,7	7,7	4,6	12,2	12,3	6,4	15,0	15,2	9,2	9,4
Metal articles	0,8	1,4	3,3	3,4	0,4	3,7	3,8	1,2	4,6	5,2	2,0	2,6
Mechanical engineering	2,6	3,2	4,4	4,6	6,2	10,7	10,8	8,7	13,3	14,0	11,3	11,9
Office machinery	1,6	1,7	1,7	1,6	3,6	5,2	5,2	5,0	6,7	6,9	6,6	6,7
Electrical goods	2,6	3,3	5,3	5,4	11,0	16,3	16,4	13,1	18,8	19,7	15,7	16,4
Motor vehicles	2,1	3,1	4,5	4,7	10,0	14,5	14,7	12,0	16,6	17,8	14,1	15,1
Other transport	1,7	1,9	2,6	2,7	1,4	4,1	4,1	2,0	5,8	6,1	3,7	3,9
Meats, preserves	0,5	1,8	0,9	0,9	0,2	1,1	1,1	0,5	1,6	2,9	1,0	2,3
Dairy products	0,5	2,0	1,1	1,1	0,8	1,9	1,9	1,1	2,4	3,9	1,6	3,0
Other food products	1,2	2,7	3,1	3,1	1,8	4,8	4,9	2,4	6,0	7,6	3,6	5,1
Beverages	0,4	0,5	0,9	1,0	0,5	1,5	1,5	0,9	1,9	2,0	1,3	1,4
Tobacco products	0,2	0,3	0,5	0,5	0,9	1,5	1,5	1,0	1,7	1,8	1,2	1,3

					(iii)+(v)	(iv)+(v)		(i)+(vi)	(ii)+(vii)	(i)+(viii)	(ii)+(viii)
Textiles, clothing	1,6	1,7	0,6	0,6	0,8	1,4	1,4	1,6	3,1	3,2	3,3	3,4
Leather	0,7	0,7	0,3	0,3	0,3	0,6	0,6	0,6	1,3	1,3	1,3	1,3
Timber, furniture	0,7	0,9	0,4	0,4	0,3	0,7	0,7	0,7	1,4	1,6	1,4	1,6
Paper and products	0,6	0,6	2,9	2,9	1,5	4,4	4,4	2,1	5,0	5,0	2,7	2,7
Rubber, plastics	0,3	0,3	1,6	1,6	0,5	2,1	2,1	0,8	2,4	2,4	1,1	1,1
Other manufactures	0,7	0,9	0,2	0,2	0,4	0,6	0,6	0,7	1,3	1,5	1,4	1,6
Building, civil engineering	4,3	4,9	2,3	2,3	0,0	2,3	2,3	0,0	6,6	7,2	4,3	4,9
Wholesale, retail trade	3,5	3,8	1,5	1,5	0,0	1,5	1,5	0,0	5,1	5,3	3,5	3,8
Lodging, catering	1,1	1,8	0,9	0,9	0,0	0,9	0,9	0,0	2,0	2,6	1,1	1,8
Inland transport	1,5	1,5	0,4	0,4	0,0	0,4	0,4	0,0	1,9	1,9	1,5	1,5
Sea and air transport	1,4	1,4	0,3	0,3	0,0	0,3	0,3	0,0	1,7	1,7	1,4	1,4
Auxiliary transport	0,1	0,1	0,1	0,1	0,0	0,1	0,1	0,0	0,2	0,2	0,1	0,1
Communications	1,7	1,7	0,2	0,2	0,0	0,2	0,2	0,0	1,8	1,8	1,7	1,7
Credit and insurance	10,5	10,6	1,1	1,1	0,0	1,1	1,1	0,0	11,6	11,7	10,5	10,6
Rent	1,5	1,6	0,2	0,2	0,0	0,2	0,2	0,0	1,7	1,8	1,5	1,6
Other market services	5,9	6,0	0,5	0,5	0,0	0,5	0,5	0,0	6,4	6,5	5,9	6,0
Non-market services	5,8	6,4	2,6	2,6	0,0	2,6	2,6	0,0	8,4	9,0	5,8	6,4
Total/average	64,8	79,8	60,3	61,5	45,6	106,0	107,2	61,5	170,8	187,0	126,3	141,3
						(iii)+(v)	(iv)+(v)		(i)+(vi)	(ii)+(vii)	(i)+(viii)	(ii)+(viii)

(i) and (ii) Results of Stages 1 and 2, from Table A.5 and A.6.
(iii) and (iv) Results of Stage 3, from Table A.7.
(v) to (viii) See text for explanations.

The totals in columns (ix) to (xii) include the effects of all cost reductions in each sector on the final output of that sector, plus the effects of cost reductions for the intermediate goods used as inputs in that sector. These were calculated using the input-output tables of the Community.

Table A.9.

Comparison of total partial equilibrium results with price convergence exercise

billion ECU

	Barrier removal and integration gains		Price convergence economic gains	
	Variant II.A (i)	Variant I.B (ii)	Hyp. I (iii)	Hyp. II (iv)
Agriculture	0,7	4,2	0,0	0,0
Solid fuels	0	0,2	0,4	0,9
Coke	0	0	0,0	0,0
Oil, gas, petrol	1,2	3,7	2,4	2,4
Electricity, gas, water	3,3	3,9	3,1	4,9
Nuclear fuels	0	0	0,0	0,0
Ores, metals	0,5	14,6	0,0	0,0
Non-metallic minerals	1,0	2,6	2,2	4,4
Chemicals	9,2	15,2	6,6	11,8
Metal articles	2,0	5,1	1,2	1,8
Mechanical engineering	11,3	14,0	5,4	10,8
Office machinery	6,6	6,9	1,8	3,3
Electrical goods	15,7	19,7	3,7	7,4
Motor vehicles	14,1	17,8	5,1	10,2
Other transport	3,7	6,1	1,4	2,8
Meats, preserves	1,0	2,9	2,5	2,5
Dairy products	1,6	3,9	0,7	0,7
Other food products	3,6	7,6	4,4	5,3
Beverages	1,3	2,0	3,2	6,4
Tobacco products	1,2	1,8	1,2	1,2
Textiles, clothing	3,3	3,2	5,6	5,6
Leather	1,3	1,3	0,3	0,3
Timber, furniture	1,4	1,6	1,1	1,1
Paper and products	2,7	5,0	0,9	0,9
Rubber, plastics	1,1	2,4	0,3	0,3
Other manufacturing	1,4	1,5	0,9	1,8
Building, civil engineering	4,3	7,2	12,8	25,5
Wholesale, retail trade	3,5	5,3	0,0	0,0
Lodging, catering	1,1	2,6	0,0	0,0
Inland transport	1,5	1,9	0,0	0,0
Sea, air transport	1,4	1,7	3,4	6,9
Auxiliary transport	0,1	0,2	0,0	0,0
Communications	1,7	1,8	6,8	13,6
Credit and insurance	10,5	11,7	4,6	9,3

Table A.9 *(continued)*.

Comparison of total partial equilibrium results with price convergence exercise

billion ECU

	Barrier removal and integration gains		Price convergence economic gains	
	Variant II.A (i)	Variant I.B (ii)	Hyp. I (iii)	Hyp. II (iv)
Rent	1,5	1,8	0,0	0,0
Other market services	5,9	6,5	0,0	0,0
Non-market services	5,8	9,0	0,0	0,0
Total	126,3	187,0	82,0	142,0

(i) and (ii)   Highest and lowest overall totals from Table A.8.
(iii) and (iv)   Based on price convergence exercises, hypotheses I and II respectively, see text.

Columns (i) and (ii) include the effects of all cost reductions in each sector on the final output of that sector, plus the effects of cost reductions for the intermediate goods used as inputs in that sector. These were calculated using the input-output tables of the Community. On the other hand, columns (iii) and (iv), being based on the prices of final goods, are not based on the systematic treatment of intermediate goods. Where price data in certain service sectors were not available, the gains have been set to zero, ignoring the fact that the prices of inputs into that sector will also converge.

9. *The use of price dispersion data.* As an independent check on the partial equilibrium estimates of the static and dynamic effects, another totally different approach has been followed. This is based on the thesis that prices throughout the Community will converge with the process of market integration, including, firstly, the elimination of barriers *per se* and, secondly, the competitive dynamic that will follow and result in the elimination of inefficiencies and monopoly rents in currently protected markets.

This price convergence cannot be expected to lead to a single price throughout the Community for the same good. Even when taxes are fully harmonized, prices will still reflect differential transport and marketing costs. Certain services, such as housing and haircuts, are by their nature 'non-tradeables' and will be priced in different markets according to different local supply-and-demand conditions. However, it is of interest to consider how different hypotheses about the extent of price convergence within the Community might imply gains from increases in productive efficiency and to compare these with the estimates for welfare gains based on the partial equilibrium analysis. In the partial equilibrium analysis a whole range of effects was estimated, changes in consumer and producer surplus, as well as terms of trade gains and tariff revenue losses *vis-à-vis* the rest of the world. Of these, generally the most important is the gain to consumers that comes from the price reductions induced by the removal of barriers and more intense competition, and the greater part of this gain is simply the price reduction on the prior volume of consumption and investment expenditure.

A rough measure of these gains can be derived by making a hypothesis about the extent to which prices converge, in particular about the extent to which 'excess' prices or prices above a certain norm, say the Community average or the average from the two lowest priced countries, approach that norm. If this is done for a range of goods and the (weighted) average price reduction for each branch and Member State are calculated, these averages multiplied by the sectoral final demand in that country and aggregated over the Community will give such a rough measure of economic gains. The Eurostat price survey data, collected within the framework of the International Comparison Project, of prices of 87 final consumer and investment goods in nine different countries has been supplemented by data on three service sectors, financial services, communications, and air transport. These service data are based on both the consultants' reports for these sectors and on Eurostat. Measures of dispersion of prices within the Community were calculated. These are discussed, as well as how they have evolved since 1975, in Chapter 7.

In order to derive an estimate of consumer gains, manufactured goods were classified into those where intra-Community trade barriers were significant, and those where they were not. In the case of the latter, however, some improved price convergence is still likely as the market is integrated. Production costs will fall as barriers are eliminated, and competition intensifies in the industries on which they depend for their intermediate inputs. In addition, the effects of more intense competition will spill over into all sectors as demand for goods, and ultimately for labour and capital, responds to relative price movements.

Two alternatives hypotheses were adopted:

Hypothesis 1: Manufactured goods without barriers — prices above the Community average were assumed to converge to that average. Other goods and services — prices above the average of those two countries with the lowest prices were assumed to decrease by half their deviation from that average.

Hypothesis 2: Manufactured goods without barriers — as under hypothesis 1. Other goods and services — prices converge to the average of those two countries with the lowest prices. The results of the exercise are shown in Table A.8.

The results of the exercise suggest that the economic gains will amount to some 82 to 142 billion ECU for the nine Member States, depending on how strong is the underlying hypothesis concerning the convergence of prices. This is equivalent to 2,8 to 4,8 % of GDP.

The results for the price convergence exercise do not include gains from a number of important sectors where comparative price data do not exist. These sectors include wholesale and retail trade, lodging, inland transport and non-market services. In practice, the competitive forces which will be released by opening up the European market are likely to have some direct impact on these sectors. More important, perhaps, will be the impact on intermediate inputs, especially of energy products and financial services, which are used in these sectors. Similarly the agricultural sector is omitted from the price convergence exercise. Thus the price convergence exercise considerably underestimates the overall economic gains. If a comparison is made only for those sectors where price data were available, Variant II.A gives an overall welfare effect of 104 billion ECU, and Variant I.B gives 161 billion ECU, compared with the 82 and 142 billion ECU given by hypotheses I and II respectively.

Annex B

Macroeconomic methodology

This Annex is in four sections:

Section B.1.: Method for evaluating macroeconomic effects:
This section describes in detail the method chosen, gives the reasons for this choice and indicates the method's strengths and weaknesses.

Section B.2.: Some characteristics of the Hermes and Interlink models:
This section contains a brief summary of the Hermes and Interlink econometric models.

Section B.3.: Execution of the simulations:
This section describes the numerical hypotheses used in the operation of the models for the four main areas of analysis:
  (i) the removal of frontier controls;
  (ii) the liberalization of public sector procurement;
  (iii) the liberalization of trade in financial services:
  (iv) supply effects (or the consequences of the strategic reactions of enterprises faced with a new competitive environment).

Section B.4.: Principal macroeconomic results:
This section provides the principal macroeconomic results in tabular form for the four main areas of analysis cited above. It also provides a table setting down a synopsis of the consequences of achieving the internal market. The tables are commented upon in the report itself (Chapter 10.2).

B.1. Method for evaluating macroeconomic effects

It is important to be able to express the benefits expected to flow from completion of the internal market in terms of macroeconomic aggregates, namely the impact on GDP, employment or inflation, as well as the effects on the main macroeconomic equilibria such as the budget balance or the current-account balance. With this in mind, the microeconomic partial-equilibrium approach (see Chapter 10.1 and Annex A) has been supplemented by a macro-economic approach.

From a methodological angle, we were faced with the following alternative. The microeconomic partial-equilibrium approach could have been supplemented by a general equilibrium approach in which the interrelationships between economic agents and sectors are taken into account, the advantage of such a methodology being that supply-side behaviour (effect of free market entry, product differentiation, exploitation of economies of scale,[1] etc.) could have been described endogenously. On the other hand, it would not have been possible to describe, in an entirely satisfactory manner, the adjustment costs associated, in particular, with resource reallocation. In other words, the lessons to be learned by general equilibrium models relate primarily to the long term. Furthermore, given the present situation as regards theoretical research, such methodology yields results that are still controversial and dependent on alternative theoretical choices.[2]

Be that as it may, we did not possess any general equilibrium model that could be used directly, and could not contemplate constructing one by the deadline set.

A different methodology was, therefore, developed, based on the use of econometric macrosectoral and macrodynamic models. Since we were aware that this type of model could not describe endogenously the effects of measures such as those advocated in the White Paper, a special operational procedure was followed.

The macroeconomic evaluation of the large internal market took place in two stages:

1. At the initial stage, the studies carried out by the various outside consultants were used to make a quantitative evaluation of the first-round effects on the particular area dealt with by each of the studies. The first-round effects correspond to either direct effects (e.g. the cost of customs delays) or to induced effects (e.g. industrial restructuring in the sectors awarded public procurement contracts). By their very nature, these quantitative evaluations made by the consultants were confined to the particular area under investigation and could not, therefore, take into account intersectoral or macroeconomic interdependencies. Very generally, the information concerned the effects on unit production costs and, in some cases, producer prices and external trade. It is fair to say that the direct effects are satisfactorily captured by the studies; by contrast, the induced effects, which are more difficult to quantify, are often not taken fully into account. For this reason, theme-related and horizontal studies were carried out internally in order to capture the phenomena of economies of scale, industrial restructuring and competition (monopoly rent and X-inefficiency).

2. At the subsequent stage, these effects, which had been evaluated upstream of the models, were incorporated into the latter, forcing them, as it were, to integrate into their mechanism the changes attributable to the large internal market. These changes concern either behaviour (e.g. import demand on the part of public-sector purchasers abandoning their national preference, pricing behaviour on the part of firms having to come to terms with the pressure

---

[1]   However, as far as we are aware, only the general equilibrium model developed by Harris and Cox (1984) to analyse the opening-up of the US-Canada frontier assumes increasing returns to scale.
[2]   In particular, the calibration of the general equilibrium models does not make it possible to test, in the statistical sense of the term, the theoretical choices in the light of observed data.

of competition) or structures (e.g. change in the production functions to reflect exploitation of economies of scale, or increase in labour productivity corresponding to reabsorption of the X-inefficiency).

In this way, the problem posed by the fact that the econometric models are unable to describe what are essentially microeconomic phenomena was circumvented. Since such phenomena are included in the first-round effects, the models were only used to simulate the second-round effects associated with macroeconomic interrelationships (multiplier and accelerator effects, income distribution effects, price competitiveness effects, inflation mechanisms, capital accumulation and growth potential, etc.).

From our point of view, this method displays the following strengths and weaknesses:

Strengths:

(i) The dynamic properties of macroeconomic models, and in particular their multiplier effects, are clearly mapped out. Numerous comparative studies have made it possible to locate them in relation to one another.

(ii) Such models take account of market rigidities (in particular, imperfect price and wage flexibility[1]) and certain adjustment costs (counterpart of productivity gains in terms of employment and demand especially).

Weaknesses:

(i) Since their estimation is based on past developments, they are too conservative. To use them beyond the medium term would be questionable.

(ii) Supply-side behaviour is imperfectly represented. The methodology chosen alleviates this weakness but was unable to endogenize such behaviour altogether.

A further advantage has come to light since: the use of two different microeconomic and macroeconomic methods with differing theoretical bases offered mutual support given that the results turned out to be convergent.

One weakness inherent in any method, whether microeconomic or macroeconomic, whether model-based or not, must be underscored: the difficulty of carrying out a detailed analysis of the evolution of the different phenomena over time. Three aspects can be identified:

(i) the time-frame of the introduction of the measures: this arises from policy decisions and legislative procedures and is particularly difficult to predict. For most of our evaluation exercise, we have assumed that all the measures are put into effect at one and the same time;

(ii) the time-frame of reactions on the part of microeconomic agents: this varies a great deal from one field to another; while it is very rapid where doing away with customs delays is concerned, it is slower in the case of industrial restructuring. It is highly dependent on the flexibility of corporate strategies and on the scale of adjustment costs. For want of detailed

---

[1] From this point of view, they fall mid-way between the general equilibrium models of the Walras type and the disequilibrium models.

information, we have assumed, for the model-based simulations, only two types of lagged reaction on the part of economic agents: immediate (i.e. concentrated in the year of the shock) for customs barriers, for the static effects of the opening-up of public procurement, and for the liberalization of financial services; and spread over five years in the case of the competition and restructuring effects associated with the opening-up of public procurement and for all the supply-side effects (the second type of shock has been spread out evenly in a step-by-step fashion over a five-year period);

(iii) the time-frame of macroeconomic mechanisms (development of the multiplier effects or the price-competitiveness effects, time lag and degree of indexation, etc.). This is the only dynamic element for which the models were able to offer any real, albeit shaky, expertise.

B.2. Some characteristics of the Hermes and Interlink models

The purpose in this section is not to describe the Hermes and Interlink models in detail but rather to summarize their main characteristics. For further details, the reader may refer to P. Valette and P. Zagamé (eds) (1988) and to P. Richardson (1987).

The main characteristics are as follows:

Model	Hermes	Interlink
Constructed by	EEC (DG XII) and national teams	OECD
General characteristics	econometric annual dynamic simultaneous	econometric bi-annual dynamic simultaneous
Horizon	Medium term	Medium term
Geographic coverage	Belgium, France, Italy, United Kingdom + 7 other EC countries[4] + USA + Japan[1] + 5 external areas[1]	24 OECD countries + 6 external areas
Linkage	Bilateral flow covering 5 products	Bilateral flow model covering 4 products + 1 service + capital flows + investment income

[1] National Comet IV models.

254

| Production | Putty-clay with
3 or 4 production
factors | Putty semi-putty
with 3 production
factors (for the main
countries) |
| Size | Large | Large for the main
countries
Average for the
small
countries |

Different methods can be employed in order to analyse the dynamic properties of the two models: i.e. the internal method (calculation of characteristic roots, etc.) or external method (analysis of their multipliers, etc.).

The comparative study of the multipliers of international models undertaken for the March 1985 Brookings Conference (Bryant *et al.*, 1988) has yielded average multiplier values and has produced an area of consensus for conventional economic policy measures (fiscal and monetary policy adjustments in particular).

With reference to the most recent studies on the Hermes and Interlink models (P. Valette and P. Zagamé, (eds) 1988, and P. Richardson, 1987b), it transpires that in the medium term:

(i)   Hermes displays fiscal policy multipliers of average size (assuming fixed interest rates and fixed exchange rates[2]) and fairly small expansionary monetary policy multipliers (assuming fixed exchange rates);

(ii) Interlink displays fairly small fiscal policy multipliers (assuming fixed money supply and fixed exchange rates), fiscal policy multipliers of average size (assuming fixed interest rates and fixed exchange rates), and expansionary monetary policy multipliers of average size (assuming fixed exchange rates).

It goes without saying that the shocks introduced in order to simulate the effects of completing the internal market are intrinsically much more complex (see Section B.3) than straightforward fiscal policy or monetary policy measures. As a result, only simulations similar to those carried out for this report but using other international models would make it possible to better locate our results in relation to an average.

B.3. Execution of the simulations

The execution of the simulations resulted in a document (Catinat-Italianer, 1988) which was used as a reference by the model-builders. This document provided, technically and exhaustively, all the modifications to the models necessary to simulate the macroeconomic characteristics of the internal market.

---

[2] All the simulations carried out to analyse the cost of non-Europe assumed that exchange rates were fixed.

All the simulations, unless otherwise indicated in the text, suppose unchanged budgetary policy in real terms, an accommodating monetary policy, and fixed exchange rates.

The purpose of this annex is to give a broad outline of the nature and amplitude of the shocks introduced.

B.3.1. Removal of frontier controls

The existence of intra-Community frontiers gives rise to two types of additional costs (source Ernst and Whinney):

(i) delays at customs, and especially the administrative formalities of customs, clearance are estimated to cost around 8 billion ECU (around 0,2 % of EC GDP), the administrative costs are partly borne by exporting firms and partly paid to customs agents;

(ii) the employment of customs officials at intra-Community frontiers: the cost to governments is estimated at between 0,5 and 1,0 billion ECU (0,02 to 0,03 % of EC GDP).

The removal of intra-Community frontiers would have as a direct result a reduction in the price of intra-Community trade since the extra costs of delays or administrative formalities are paid either directly or indirectly by importing firms.

According to calculations made by Ernst and Whinney the removal of frontier controls would reduce intra-Community import prices by about 1,7 % on average (between 1,5 % for Belgium and 2 % for Italy).

The bilateral intra-Community import prices[1] of the six countries studied (Belgium, Germany, France, Italy, the Netherlands and the UK) were reduced in accordance with these findings and the resulting substitution between production and imports and between intra- and extra-Community imports was simulated in respect of bilateral trade in goods between countries.

However, these price reductions would be partly offset by a loss of jobs, estimated for the whole Community at about 17 500 in exporting firms (employees dealing with the formalities of customs clearance), and around 40 000 in the case of private sector customs agents. Similarly, the existing costs borne by government represent between 15 000 and 30 000 personnel who would become redundant.

In the absence of detailed information to allow differentiation by country, the job losses fed into the Hermes model were taken as being proportional to the starting levels of employment. In the case of exporting companies, only the agricultural, energy and industrial sectors were taken into account.

The price and employment shocks introduced correspond in all cases to the mid-point of the range and in total are equivalent to 0,3 % of the GDP of the countries studied.

---

[1] The costs borne by exporting firms or carriers are largely passed on to import prices.

B.3.2. Opening-up of public procurement

According to the consultant responsible for the study (Atkins Planning), three types of effect could result from the liberalization of public procurement:

(i) *a static effect* due to increased penetration by foreign products. Through buying from cheaper foreign suppliers, governments and public enterprises would spend less for a given quantity of goods. The static effect presupposes that there will be no price change for either imported goods or those produced within the country. The effect is thus purely structural — substitution between home produced and imported goods.

(ii) *a competition effect,*[2] since, faced with increased competition in previously protected markets, national firms would be forced to lower their prices to compete with the prices of imported goods.

(iii) *a restructuring effect,*[2] under the pressure of competition some supply sectors would be induced to restructure (mergers, exploitation of economies of scale, removal of X-inefficiency, reduction of monopoly rents) and to increase productivity. The reduction in production costs would lead to a parallel reduction in production and import prices.

Many scenarios were envisaged whereby the consultant could scan the range of possibilities and evaluate the sensitivity of the figures to changes in the parameters (level of penetration of public markets, sectoral coverage, competitors' price levels). An average scenario was chosen for those simulations undertaken with the Hermes model. Within the framework of this scenario, the savings in expenditure which public administrations and enterprises could realize were of the following order: static effects 5,5 billion ECU 1984, competition effects 0,8 billion ECU 1984, restructuring effects 6,4 billion ECU 1984, i.e. a total of 12,7 billion ECU 1984 (0,5 % of GDP).

This scenario differs slightly from that chosen and presented in the chapter dealing with public markets. On one hand, it includes those economies which could be gained in the coal sector; on the other hand, it does not take into account supplementary economies in the defence sector.

Compared to the scenario which was chosen for macroeconomic simulations, the other scenarios estimated by Atkins Planning were situated within the following range (− 30 %, + 40 %). In other words, the economies which could be realized by public administrations and enterprises would equal between 0,35 % and 0,7 % of Community GDP.

Technically, the static effects were inserted, in the case of the Hermes model, by altering the level of penetration of public markets (an average increase of some 5,6 %) and thus substituting purchases of lower-priced imported products for those provided by domestic producers. The two other effects of competition

---

[2] These effects correspond in fact, in our classification based on four major areas, to 'supply effects'. Being the direct and identifiable consequence of the opening-up of public procurement, however, they have been classified in that area. To prevent double counting, the sectors in question were removed from the simulations relating to the 'supply effects'.

and restructuring were introduced by changing prices, of production in the first case, of production and of imports in parallel with the reduction of unit cost as a result of restructuring, in the second case. This results in reductions in the purchase price of equipment goods of the order of 0,1 % for governments, of 1,4 % for public enterprises in the energy sector, and of 8,5 % for those in transport and telecommunications.

B.3.3. Liberalization of financial services

The liberalization of financial services and the elimination of existing barriers would allow a greater freedom of competition: with the limiting of monopoly rents the cost of financial services would be reduced. It is on the basis of this competition mechanism that Price Waterhouse has estimated the costs of non-Europe in the financial services sector (banking, insurance, securities). Starting from estimates of price differentials for 16 representative financial products, the consultant calculated the reduction of the cost of financial services which the achievement of the full internal market would allow, country by country. For certain products, the cost equals, in effect, the rate of interest net of the money market rates (differential between two rates). Thus, depending on the representative financial product, the price reductions estimated by Price Waterhouse lead to a reduction in the cost of credit — for households or firms — or the cost of intermediate consumption of financial services by firms or the price of the final consumption of households.

With regard to the cost of medium-term credit for firms (the financing of their investments), the estimates took into account not only the effects of the reduction of the costs of financial services, but also the convergence of interest rates towards the Community average as a result of the integration of Community financial markets.

The estimates of the consultant were transformed, for the requirements of the simulations, and led to the following effects (on average for the Community):

For households:

(i)   Short-term credit (for consumption expenditure), an average reduction of two percentage points on the differential between the rate in the money market and the actual rate paid by households (initially this was at 8 % and was reduced to 6 %).

(ii) Long-term credit (house loans), an average reduction of 0,3 percentage points, and also a reduction in the differential between the monetary market rate and the actual rate of from 2 to 1,7 percentage points.

(iii) Price of financial services (banking other than credit, insurance, etc.), an average reduction of 10 %.

For firms:

(i)   Long-term credit, an average reduction of 0,5 percentage points, thus reducing the differential between the money market rate and actual rate from 2,1 to 1,6 percentage points.

(ii) Cost of intermediate consumption of financial services (other than credit), an average reduction of 12 %.

These reductions correspond to the middle of the ranges supplied by the consultant, with the outlying estimates ranging between 40 % respectively, of the average price reduction.

All of the above price reductions were inserted into the Interlink model. In total, the impact represented 0,7 % of GDP for the countries analysed.

B.3.4. Supply effects or the strategic reactions of firms in the new competitive environment

The simulations which were carried out under the generic term 'supply effects' include an ensemble of phenomena which arise from the strategic reaction of firms to their newly competitive environment: the consequences of eliminating technical barriers and regulations, exploitation of scale economies, the reduction of X-inefficiencies, and the reduction of monopoly rents. The simulations thus describe the macroeconomic consequences which result from the change in behavioural patterns of firms (pricing strategies, for example) and changes in their production conditions (changes in production patterns by reductions of X-inefficiency, for example).

They are based on quantitive information drawn from three sources:

1. *Effects quantified by the external consultants.* Their sectoral coverage is limited: food manufacturing and processing industries (MAC Group); the building materials sector (BIPE), the pharmaceuticals industry (EAG); telecommunications (Insead); the motor vehicle industry, including components (Ludvigsen); textiles and clothing (IFO and Prometeia), and the business services sector (Peat Marwick). These sectors, taken together cover about 25 % of non-agricultural, non-financial market production. The choice of these sectors was dictated by the wish to cover the major part of the relevant cases (different types of non-tariff barriers).

The supply effects quantified by the consultants were either direct or indirect. Taking the direct effects, these should be equivalent to a fall in prices of intermediate consumption.[1] It is in this way that the fall in unit costs of the related sectors have been simulated. However, by their very nature, they do not imply other counterbalancing effects (in terms of a loss of employment for example). Taking the indirect effects they should be capable of analysis as the gains in productivity caused by changing the structure of production or by a better exploitation of economies of scale. In this case the productivity of capital was increased *ex ante* in parallel with the introduction of new vintage investments in the capital stock. It is in this way that the process of restructuring,

---

[1] Reduced cost of ingredients for food-processing industries, cuts in the prices of building materials for the construction sector, reduced price of intermediate consumption of market services for producer branches generally, etc.

or the exploitation of economies of scale, has been incorporated in the models. This supposes implicitly that the latter requires an investment effort (and that they therefore cannot be brought about only by disinvestment or the closures of plants) and that these effects should occur at the same rate as investment. All this is, of course, schematic and formal when compared to economic reality. Less unrealistic, however, is a direct increase in the productivity of the capital being used, because in this latter case no costs (of investment in particular) are taken into account. When the sectoral analyses provided by the consultants gave quantitative information concerning the changes in market share which could be caused by restructuring internal and external markets, these have been integrated. In total, the shock introduced into the system by economies in production costs, whatever their origin, represents 1,1 %. of Community GDP.

2. *Economies of scale effects*. For the industrial sectors not covered by the consultants, quantitative estimations of the existing potentialities in terms of economies of scale have been undertaken, internally, on the basis of work done elsewhere. The hypothesis has been that the average size of the establishments concerned will converge, for each detailed sector (analysed at the 3-digit NACE level) towards the optimum size for which the unit costs of production are minimal. The estimates thus obtained represent, from the range of possibilities, the upper end of that range. However, it was not possible to cover all the detailed sectors of industry because of a lack of statistical and quantitative information. On average, for industry, these economies of scale effects could be less overvalued than might appear at first sight. For the other sectors, services in particular, the quantitative information was too sparse to enable economies of scale effects to be estimated.

Technically, the procedure for putting these effects into the models is identical to that described previously for the indirect effects quantified by the external consultants. The unit costs of production in industry have been reduced by 1,5 % on average for the Community. It is assumed that economies of scale are completely exploited : additional production capacities give rise to an increase in external market share ; that is to say, for the Community taken as a whole, Community market share with the rest of the world increases.

3. *Price competitive effects*. More precisely, these estimates are concerned with the consequences of increased competition on monopoly rents and X-inefficiency. Other consequences which may also be judged important, provoking more dynamic company behaviour (simulation of innovation, putting more active commercial strategies into effect, etc.) have been ignored because they are even more difficult to quantify. The decline in monopoly rents should imply a fall in sales prices, with a decline in profit margins, as a result of increased competition of 0,7 % for industry.

X-inefficiency has equally been simulated by a fall in production prices (0,5 % for industry ; 1,0 % for market services) ; those falls in price result from an elimination of inefficient areas of activity and so of a reduction in unit costs of the same magnitude. The experts have estimated that all these falls in the costs of production taken together may be considered to come from an increase in the productivity of labour (by reorganizing managerial teams). The quantitative estimations upstream, as it were, from the models have been made in a deductive way, by using the differences in prices now observed between Member States as an indicator of future competitive pressures; by using the results of the Smith-Venables model (see Chapter 9); and finally by using the specialist knowledge of the experts (based on an examination of individual company figures). These basic estimates at the company level or at the detailed sector level could have been extrapolated to the macroeconomic level but this would have given rise to unrealistic figures. Consequently these extrapolations have been significantly reduced.

In total the shocks introduced into the Hermes model for simulating supply effects represent about a little more than 3 % of Community GDP of which approximately one third is attributable to each of the two separate phenomena, economies of scale and competitive effects.

B.4. Principal macroeconomic results

This section sets out the principal macroeconomic consequences of the completion of the internal market, first of all by major area (Tables B.1 to B.4) and then for all areas taken together (Table B.5). The comments on these tables are contained in the body of the text (see Section 10.2). The consequences relate to the Community as a whole (by extrapolation of the simulated average effects for the countries analysed — see box 'Geographical cover and extrapolation to EUR 12' in Chapter 10). The reader should not be misled by the precise nature of the figures: there is in fact considerable uncertainty surrounding them, which we have attempted to indicate by the use of ranges.

Table B.1.

Macroeconomic consequences of the abolition of frontier controls in the Community

	Total Community[1]			
	1 year	2 years	Medium term[2]	
			Simulation	Range[3]
Relative changes (as %)				
GDP	− 0,0	0,1	0,4	0,4
Consumer prices	− 0,2	− 0,4	− 1,0	− 1,0
GDP price deflator	− 0,0	− 0,2	− 0,9	− 0,8 to − 0,9
Absolute changes				
Employment (× 1 000)	− 75[4]	− 35	215	205 to 225
Budgetary balance as % of GDP	0,0	0,1	0,2	0,2
External balance as % of GDP	0,2	0,2	0,2	0,2

[1] Extrapolation to EUR 12 of the (weighted) average for the six countries analysed (Belgium, Germany, France, Italy, Netherlands, United Kingdom).
[2] Technically speaking, six years.
[3] Reflects the margin of error estimated by Ernst and Whinney. Where only one figure is given, this margin falls within the rounding of the decimal.
[4] It was assumed that all the job losses (customs officers, forwarding agents, etc.) would occur in the first year. In fact, they will probably be spread over a period of time.
Source: Hermes simulation.

Table B.2.

Macroeconomic consequences for the Community of opening up public procurement[1]

	Opening up limited to Community area[2]			
	1 year	2 years	Medium term[3]	
			Simulation	Range[4]
Relative changes (as %)				
GDP as %	0,2	0,3	0,6	0,4 to 0,8
Consumer prices	− 0,3	− 0,4	− 1,4	− 0,9 to − 1,9
GDP price deflator	− 0,3	− 0,6	− 1,5	− 1,0 to − 2,0
Absolute changes				
Employment (× 1 000)	60	145	360	240 to 480
Budgetary balance as % of GDP	0,1	0,2	0,3	0,2 to 0,5
External balance as % of GDP	0,0	0,1	0,1	0,1 to 0,2

[1] Extrapolation to EUR 12 of the (weighted) average of the five countries analysed (Belgium, Germany, France, Italy and the United Kingdom).
[2] Opening-up limited to the Community area: the opening-up of Community public procurement remains restricted to Community suppliers.
[3] Technically speaking, six years.
[4] Reflects the margin of error estimated by Atkins Planning.
Source: Hermes simulations.

Table B.3.

Macroeconomic consequences of the liberalization of financial services for the Community

	1 year	2 years	Medium term[2]	
			Simulation	Range[3]
Relative changes (as %)				
GDP	0,4	1,1	1,5	0,8 to 2,1
Consumer prices	− 0,5	− 0,8	− 1,4	− 0,8 to − 2,0
GDP price deflator	− 0,5	− 0,8	− 1,4	− 0,8 to − 2,0
Absolute changes				
Employment (× 1 000)	− 225	− 60	400	230 to 570
Budgetary balance as % of GDP	0,0	0,3	1,1	0,6 to 1,5
External balance as % of GDP	− 0,0	− 0,0	0,3	0,2 to 0,5

(Header spanning: Total Community[1])

[1] Extrapolation to EUR 12 of the (weighted) average of the seven countries analysed (Belgium, Germany, Spain, France, Italy, the Netherlands and the United Kingdom).
[2] Technically speaking, six years.
[3] Reflects the margin of error estimated by Price Waterhouse.
Source: Interlink model. The Interlink model simulations were carried out by the Commission's departments; the OECD is in no way responsible for them.

Table B.4.

Macroeconomic consequences of the 'supply effects' for the Community

	1 year	2 years	Medium term[2]	
			Simulation	Range
Relative changes (as %)				
GDP	0,5	0,9	2,1	1,7 to 2,5
Consumer prices	− 0,6	− 0,8	− 2,3	− 1,8 to − 2,7
GDP price deflator	− 0,8	− 1,3	− 2,6	− 2,1 to − 3,1
Absolute changes				
Employment (× 1 000)	− 285	− 85	865	690 to 1 000
Budgetary balance as % of GDP	− 0,0	0,2	0,6	0,5 to 0,8
External balance as % of GDP	0,2	0,2	0,4	0,3 to 0,6

(Header spanning: Total Community[1])

[1] Extrapolation to EUR 12 of the (weighted) average of the four countries analysed (Germany, France, Italy and the United Kingdom).
[2] Technically speaking, six years.
Source: Hermes model.

Table B.5.

Macroeconomic consequences of completion of the internal market

	Total Community[1]			
	1 year	2 years	Medium term[2]	
			Simulation	Range[3]
Relative changes (as %)				
GDP	1,1	2,3	4,5	3,2 to 5,7
Consumer prices	− 1,5	− 2,4	− 6,1	− 4,5 to − 7,7
GDP price deflator	− 1,6	− 2,8	− 6,3	− 4,7 to − 8,0
Absolute changes				
Employment (× 1 000)	− 525	− 35	1 840	1 350 to 2 300
Budgetary balance as % of GDP	0,2	0,7	2,2	1,5 to 3,0
External balance as % of GDP	0,3	0,4	1,0	0,7 to 1,3

[1] Extrapolation to EUR 12 of the (weighted) average of the countries analysed.
[2] Technically speaking, six years.
[3] Reflects the margin of error estimated by the 'upstream' studies carried out by the external consultants.

Source: Hermes and Interlink models (simulations carried out by the Commission's departments. The OECD is in no way responsible for them).

Annex C

Statistical tables

Table C.1.

Dimension and structure of the internal market: production (EUR 12), 1985

NACE Codes	Branches	%	billion ECU
01	**Agricultural, forestry and fishery products**	3,32	200,4
1	**Energy products**	8,43	508,9
—	**Industrial products**	36,60	2 209,5
13	Ferrous and non-ferrous ores and metals, other than radioactive	3,00	181,1
211	Extraction and preparation of iron ore	—	—
212	Extraction and preparation of non-ferrous metal ores	—	—
221	Pig iron, crude steel, hot-rolled and cold-rolled sheets, coated metal sheets (ECSC products)	1,67	100,8
222	Steel tubes	0,26	15,7
223	Extruded and drawn metal, cold-rolled products, cold formed steel parts and sections	0,29	17,5
224	Non-ferrous metals	0,78	47,1
15	Non-metallic mineral products	1,58	95,4
231	Gravel, stone, sand and clay	0,08	4,8
232	Salts of potassium and of natural phosphates	0,05	3,0
233	Rock salt, marine salt	—	—
239	Other minerals, peat	—	—
241	Bricks and pottery products	0,10	6,0
242	Cement, lime, plaster	0,24	14,5
243	Building and construction materials made of concrete, cement or plaster	0,40	24,2
244	Articles made of asbestos (except for articles made of asbestos-cement)	0,02	1,2
245	Stones and other non-metallic mineral products	0,12	7,3
246	Millstones and other abrasive products	0,02	1,2
247	Glass (plate, hollow, technical, fibre glass)	0,32	19,3
248	Ceramic products	0,23	13,9
17	Chemical products	4,12	248,7
251	Manufacture of basic industrial chemicals and manufacture followed by further processing of such products	2,14	129,2
252	Petrochemical and carbochemical products	—	—
253	Other basic chemical products	—	—
255	Paints, varnishes and printing inks	0,33	19,9
256	Other chemical products, mainly for industrial and agricultural purposes	0,37	22,3
257	Pharmaceutical products	0,62	37,4
258	Soaps, synthetic detergents, perfume, cosmetics and toilet preparations	0,37	22,3

Table C.1 *(continued)*.

Dimension and structure of the internal market: production (EUR 12), 1985

NACE Codes	Branches	%	billion ECU
259	Other chemical products mainly for household and office use	0,16	9,7
260	Artificial and synthetic fibres	0,13	7,9
19	Metal products except machinery and transport equipment	2,64	159,4
311	Foundry products	0,33	19,9
312	Metal products which are forged, stamped, embossed or cut	0,18	10,9
313	Products of secondary processing of metals	0,37	22,3
314	Structural metal products	0,41	24,8
315	Products of boilermaking	0,37	22,3
316	Tools and finished metal articles, except electrical equipment	0,96	58,0
319	Other metal workshops nes	0,02	1,2
21	Agricultural and industrial machinery	2,95	178,1
321	Agricultural machinery and tractors	0,28	16,9
322	Machine tools for metal working, tools and equipment for machinery	0,26	15,7
323	Textile machinery and accessories, sewing machines	0,11	6,6
324	Machinery for the food and chemical industries; bottling, packaging, wrapping and related machinery; rubber, artificial plastics working machinery	0,35	21,1
325	Mining equipment, machinery and equipment for metallurgy, for the preparation of building materials, for building and construction, for mechanical handling and lifting	0,58	35,0
326	Gears and other transmission equipment	0,17	10,3
327	Machinery for working wood, paper, leather and footwear, laundering and dry-cleaning equipment	0,17	10,3
328	Other machinery and mechanical equipment	1,03	62,2
23	Office and data-processing machines; precision and optical instruments	0,84	50,7
330	Office and data-processing machines	0,56	33,8
371	Measuring, precision and control instruments	0,11	6,7
372	Medico-surgical equipment, orthopaedic appliances	0,07	4,2
373	Optical instruments and photographic equipment	0,06	3,6
374	Clocks and watches	0,04	2,4
25	Electrical goods	2,78	167,8
341	Insulated wires and cables	0,08	4,8
342	Electric motors, generators, transformers, switches, etc.	0,90	54,4
343	Electrical equipment for industrial use, batteries and accumulators	0,08	4,8

Table C.1 *(continued).*

Dimension and structure of the internal market: production (EUR 12), 1985

NACE Codes	Branches	%	billion ECU
344	Telecommunications equipment, meters and measuring equipment, electro-medical equipment	0,83	50,1
345	Electronic equipment, radio and television receiving sets, sound reproducing and recording equipment, gramophone records and prerecorded tapes	0,50	30,2
346	Electric household appliances	0,27	16,3
347	Electric lamps and other forms of electric lighting	0,08	4,8
348	Assembly and installation of electrical equipment and apparatus (except for work relating to the wiring of buildings)	0,04	2,4
27 + 29	Motor vehicles, other transport equipment	3,34	201,6
351	Motor vehicles and engines	2,09	126,2
352	Bodywork, trailers and caravans	0,07	4,2
353	Spare parts and accessories for motor vehicles	0,44	26,6
361	Boats, steamers, warships, tugs, floating platforms and rigs, materials from the breaking up of boats	0,21	12,7
362	Locomotives, other railway and tramway rolling-stock, vans and wagons	0,07	4,2
363	Cycles, motorcycles, invalid carriages	0,05	3,0
364	Aircraft, helicopters, hovercraft, missiles, space vehicles and other aeronautical equipment	0,40	24,1
365	Perambulators, invalid chairs, carts, etc.	0,01	0,6
31 + 33 + 35 + 37 + 39	Meats, meat preparations and preserves, other products from slaughtered animals, milk and dairy products, other food products, beverages, tobacco products	6,95	419,6
411	Vegetable and animal oils and fats	0,28	16,9
412	Meats, meat preparations and preserves, other products from slaughtered animals	0,99	59,8
413	Milk and dairy products	1,15	69,4
414	Fruit and vegetable preserves and juices	0,22	13,3
415	Fish preserves and other seafood for human consumption	0,18	10,9
416	Cereals, flour and flakes	0,20	12,1
417	Food pastes	0,09	5,4
418	Starch and starch products	0,10	6,0
419	Bread, rusks, biscuits, cakes and pastries	0,31	18,7
420	Sugar	0,28	16,9
421	Cocoa, chocolate, sweets, ice-creams	0,39	23,5
422	Animal and poultry feedingstuffs	0,51	30,8
423	Other food products	0,45	27,2
424	Ethyl alcohol from fermented vegetable products and products based on it	0,30	18,1
425	Champagne, sparkling wines, wine-based aperitifs	0,10	6,0
426	Cider, perry, mead	—	—

Table C.1 *(continued).*

Dimension and structure of the internal market: production (EUR 12), 1985

NACE Codes	Branches	%	billion ECU
427	Malt, beers, brewers' yeast	0,48	29,0
428	Mineral waters, soft drinks	0,18	10,9
429	Tobacco products	0,74	44,7
41 + 43	Textiles and clothing, leathers, leather and skin goods, footwear	2,91	175,7
431	Wool industry	0,29	17,5
432	Cotton industry	0,42	25,4
433	Silk industry	0,14	8,5
434	Preparation, spinning and weaving of flax hemp and ramie	0,03	1,8
435	Jute industry	0,03	1,8
436	Knitting industry	0,34	20,5
437	Textile finishing	0,14	8,5
438	Carpets, carpeting, oilcloth, linoleum and other coated fabrics	0,14	8,5
439	Other textile products	0,13	7,8
441	Leather, skins, hides tanned or otherwise processed	0,10	6,0
442	Leather and skin goods	0,06	3,6
451	Footwear, slippers made wholly or partly of leather	0,29	17,5
452	Production of hand-made footwear (including orthopaedic footwear)	—	—
453	Ready-made clothes and clothing accessories	0,74	44,7
454	Bespoke tailoring, dressmaking and hatmaking	—	—
455	Household linen, bedding, curtains, wall coverings and awnings, sails, flags, bags	0,05	3,0
456	Articles of furs	0,01	0,6
47	Paper and printing products	2,44	147,3
471	Wood pulp, paper, board	0,45	27,2
472	Products of pulp, paper and board	0,63	38,0
473	Products of printing	0,91	54,9
474	Products of publishing	0,45	27,2
49	Rubber and plastic products	1,25	75,5
481	Rubber products	0,44	26,6
482	Re-treaded tyres	—	—
483	Plastic products	0,81	48,9
45 + 51	Other manufacturing products	1,80	108,6
461	Sawn, planed, seasoned, steamed wood	0,13	7,8
462	Veneered and ply wood, fibre board and particle board, improved and preserved wood	0,17	10,3
463	Carpentry, wooden buildings, joinery, parquet flooring	0,26	15,7
464	Wooden containers	0,06	3,6

Table C.1 *(continued)*.

Dimension and structure of the internal market: production (EUR 12), 1985

NACE Codes	Branches	%	billion ECU
465	Wooden articles (other than furniture), sawdust and shavings	0,06	3,6
466	Articles of cork, straw, basketware (other than furniture), brooms, brushes	0,03	1,8
467	Furniture of wood and cane, mattresses	0,71	42,9
491	Precious and costume jewellery, goldsmiths' and silversmiths' products; working of precious and semi-precious stones; diamond cutting and polishing; striking of coins and medals	0,14	8,5
492	Musical instruments	0,02	1,2
493	Products for printing and developing cinematographic and photographic films	0,02	1,2
494	Games, toys, sports goods	0,13	7,8
495	Fountain pens and ballpoint pens, seals, other products n.e.c.	0,07	4,2
53	**Building and construction**	6,19	373,7
	Civil engineering works	1,24	74,9
	Market services	33,53	2 024,2
55 + 57	Recovery and repair services, wholesale and retail trade	8,98	542,1
59	Lodging and catering services	2,46	148,5
61	Inland transport services	2,01	121,4
63	Maritime and air transport services	0,95	57,4
65	Auxiliary transport services	0,92	55,5
67	Communication services	1,45	87,5
69	Services of credit and insurance institutions	5,66	341,7
71 + 73 + 75 + 77 + 79	Other market services	11,10	670,1
81 + 85 + 89 + 93	**Non-market services**	11,93	720,2
	Total	100	6 036,9

Source: Eurostat, *National accounts ESA.* Detailed tables by branch and annual survey of industry structure and activity. Estimates for EUR 12 based on economic structure observed for EUR 7.

Table C.2.

Dimension and structure of the internal market: value-added (EUR 12), 1985

NACE Codes	Branches	%	billion ECU
01	**Agricultural, forestry and fishery products**	2,93	92,7
1	**Energy products**	6,81	215,5
—	**Industrial products**	25,99	822,8
13	Ferrous and non-ferrous ores and metals, other than radioactive	1,11	35,1
211	Extraction and preparation of iron ore	0,00	0,1
212	Extraction and preparation of non-ferrous metal ores	0,01	0,2
221	Pig iron, crude steel, hot-rolled and cold-rolled sheets, coated metal sheets (ECSC products)	0,57	17,9
222	Steel tubes	0,15	4,9
223	Extruded and drawn metal, cold-rolled products, cold formed steel parts and sections	0,11	3,5
224	Non-ferrous metals	0,27	8,5
15	Non-metallic mineral products	1,27	40,2
231	Gravel, stone, sand and clay	0,07	2,4
232	Salts of potassium and of natural phosphates	0,06	1,8
233	Rock salt, marine salt	—	—
239	Other minerals, peat	—	—
241	Bricks and pottery products	0,09	3,0
242	Cement, lime, plaster	0,16	5,1
243	Building and construction materials made of concrete, cement or plaster	0,26	8,1
244	Articles made of asbestos (except for articles made of asbestos-cement)	0,02	0,7
245	Stones and other non-metallic mineral products	0,10	3,1
246	Millstones and other abrasive products	0,02	0,7
247	Glass (plate, hollow, technical, fibre glass)	0,26	8,1
248	Ceramic products	0,23	7,4
17	Chemical products	2,42	76,6
251	Manufacture of basic industrial chemicals and manufacture followed by further processing of such products	1,05	33,2
252	Petrochemical and carbochemical products	—	—
253	Other basic chemical products	—	—
255	Paints, varnishes and printing inks	0,21	6,5
256	Other chemical products, mainly for industrial and agricultural purposes	0,23	7,4
257	Pharmaceutical products	0,51	16,2
258	Soaps, synthetic detergents, perfume, cosmetics and toilet preparations	0,22	7,1

Table C.2 *(continued)*.

Dimension and structure of the internal market: value-added (EUR 12), 1985

NACE Codes	Branches	%	billion ECU
259	Other chemical products mainly for household and office use	0,12	3,9
260	Artificial and synthetic fibres	0,08	2,4
19	Metal products except machinery and transport equipment	2,26	71,6
311	Foundry products	0,33	10,5
312	Metal products which are forged, stamped, embossed or cut	0,18	5,7
313	Products of secondary processing of metals	0,30	9,5
314	Structural metal products	0,29	9,3
315	Products of boilermaking	0,33	10,3
316	Tools and finished metal articles, except electrical equipment	0,82	25,9
319	Other metal workshops nes	0,01	0,4
21	Agricultural and industrial machinery	2,48	78,5
321	Agricultural machinery and tractors	0,19	6,0
322	Machine tools for metal working, tools and equipment for machinery	0,27	8,6
323	Textile machinery and accessories, sewing machines	0,10	3,2
324	Machinery for the food and chemical industries; bottling, packaging, wrapping and related machinery; rubber, artificial plastics working machinery	0,31	9,8
325	Mining equipment, machinery and equipment for metallurgy, for the preparation of building materials, for building and construction, for mechanical handling and lifting	0,44	13,8
326	Gears and other transmission equipment	0,18	5,7
327	Machinery for working wood, paper, leather and footwear, laundering and dry-cleaning equipment	0,17	5,3
328	Other machinery and mechanical equipment	0,82	26,0
23	Office and data-processing machines; precision and optical instruments	0,85	26,9
330	Office and data-processing machines	0,56	17,7
371	Measuring, precision and control instruments	0,12	3,7
372	Medico-surgical equipment, orthopaedic appliances	0,08	2,6
373	Optical instruments and photographic equipment	0,05	1,8
374	Clocks and watches	0,04	1,1
25	Electrical goods	2,57	81,4
341	Insulated wires and cables	0,08	2,6
342	Electric motors, generators, transformers, switches, etc.	0,79	25,1
343	Electrical equipment for industrial use, batteries and accumulators	0,09	2,8

Table C.2 *(continued)*.

Dimension and structure of the internal market: value-added (EUR 12), 1985

NACE Codes	Branches	%	billion ECU
344	Telecommunications equipment, meters and measuring equipment, electromedical equipment	0,94	29,6
345	Electronic equipment, radio and television receiving sets, sound reproducing and recording equipment, gramophone records and prerecorded tapes	0,37	11,6
346	Electric household appliances	0,19	6,1
347	Electric lamps and other forms of electric lighting	0,07	2,3
348	Assembly and installation of electrical equipment and apparatus (except for work relating to the wiring of buildings)	0,04	1,3
27 + 29	Motor vehicles, other transport equipment	2,87	90,8
351	Motor vehicles and engines	1,48	46,8
352	Bodywork, trailers and caravans	0,09	2,9
353	Spare parts and accessories for motor vehicles	0,42	13,5
361	Boats, steamers, warships, tugs, floating platforms and rigs, materials from the breaking up of boats	0,19	6,0
362	Locomotives, other railway and tramway rolling-stock, vans and wagons	0,08	2,5
363	Cycles, motorcycles, invalid carriages	0,05	1,7
364	Aircraft, helicopters, hovercraft, missiles, space vehicles and other aeronautical equipment	0,55	17,3
365	Perambulators, invalid chairs, carts, etc.	0,01	0,2
31 + 33 + 35 + 37 + 39	Meats, meat preparations and preserves, other products from slaughtered animals, milk and dairy products, other food products, beverages, tobacco products	4,12	130,4
411	Vegetable and animal oils and fats	0,48	15,3
412	Meats, meat preparations and preserves, other products from slaughtered animals	0,50	15,6
413	Milk and dairy products	0,17	5,3
414	Fruit and vegetable preserves and juices	—	—
415	Fish preserves and other seafood for human consumption	0,08	2,7
416	Cereals, flour and flakes	0,08	2,7
417	Food pastes	0,05	1,4
418	Starch and starch products	0,09	2,8
419	Bread, rusks, biscuits, cakes and pastries	0,39	12,4
420	Sugar	0,15	4,7
421	Cocoa, chocolate, sweets, ice-creams	0,34	10,9
422	Animal and poultry feedingstuffs	0,21	6,6
423	Other food products	0,37	11,7
424	Ethyl alcohol from fermented vegetables products and products based on it	0,21	6,5
425	Champagne, sparkling wines, wine-based aperitifs	0,10	3,1
426	Cider, perry, mead	—	—

Table C.2 *(continued)*.

Dimension and structure of the internal market: value-added (EUR 12), 1985

NACE Codes	Branches	%	billion ECU
427	Malt, beers, brewers' yeast	0,43	13,7
428	Mineral waters, soft drinks	0,21	6,7
429	Tobacco products	0,26	8,2
41 + 43	Textiles and clothing, leathers, leather and skin goods, footwear	2,05	64,9
431	Wool industry	0,17	5,4
432	Cotton industry	0,25	7,9
433	Silk industry	0,08	2,6
434	Preparation, spinning and weaving of flax hemp and ramie	0,02	0,6
435	Jute industry	0,01	0,3
436	Knitting industry	0,28	8,9
437	Textile finishing	0,11	3,3
438	Carpets, carpeting, oilcloth, linoleum and other co-ated fabrics	0,07	2,1
439	Other textile products	0,10	3,1
441	Leather, skins, hides tanned or otherwise processed	0,05	1,6
442	Leather and skin goods	0,06	1,9
451	Footwear, slippers made wholly or partly of leather	0,23	7,4
452	Production of hand-made footwear (including ortho-paedic footwear)	—	—
453	Ready-made clothes and clothing accessories	0,57	18,1
454	Bespoke tailoring, dressmaking and hatmaking	—	—
455	Household linen, bedding, curtains, wall coverings and awnings, sails, flags, bags	0,04	1,4
456	Articles of furs	0,01	0,3
47	Paper and printing products	1,83	50,7
471	Wood pulp, paper, board	0,26	8,1
472	Products of pulp, paper and board	0,43	13,6
473	Products of printing	0,87	27,7
474	Products of publishing	0,27	8,5
49	Rubber and plastic products	0,98	31,0
481	Rubber products	0,39	12,2
482	Re-treaded tyres	0,00	0,1
483	Plastic products	0,59	18,7
45 + 51	Other manufacturing products	1,18	37,4
461	Sawn, planed, seasoned, steamed wood	0,07	2,2
462	Veneered and ply wood, fibre board and particle board, improved and preserved wood	0,08	2,7
463	Carpentry, wooden buildings, joinery, parquet flooring	0,15	4,8
464	Wooden containers	0,04	1,2

Table C.2 *(continued)*.

Dimension and structure of the internal market: value-added (EUR 12), 1985

NACE Codes	Branches	%	billion ECU
465	Wooden articles (other than furniture), sawdust and shavings	0,05	1,6
466	Articles of cork, straw, basketware (other than furniture), brooms, brushes	0,03	0,9
467	Furniture of wood and cane, mattresses	0,50	15,7
491	Precious and costume jewellery, goldsmiths' and silversmiths' products; working of precious and semi-precious stones; diamond cutting and polishing; striking of coins and medals	0,08	2,5
492	Musical instruments	0,02	0,7
493	Products for printing and developing cinematographic and photographic films	0,02	0,6
494	Games, toys, sports goods	0,09	3,1
495	Fountain pens and ballpoint pens, seals, other products n.e.c.	0,05	1,5
53	**Building and construction and civil engineering works**	5,70	180,2
	Market services	43,97	1 390,4
55 + 57	Recovery and repair services, wholesale and retail trade	11,77	372,2
59	Lodging and catering services	2,04	64,5
61	Inland transport services	2,27	71,8
63	Maritime and air transport services	0,53	16,8
65	Auxiliary transport services	1,12	35,4
67	Communication services	1,96	61,9
69	Services of credit and insurance institutions	7,98	252,4
71 + 73 + 75 + 77 + 79	Other market services	16,30	515,4
81 + 85 + 89 + 93	**Non-market services**	14,49	458,2
	Total	100,00	3 162,0

Source: Eurostat, *National accounts ESA*. Detailed tables by branch and annual survey of industry structure and activity. Estimates for EUR 12 based on economic structure observed for EUR 7.

Table C.3.

Dimension and structure of the internal market: consumption of households by product (EUR 12), 1985

Codes	Branches	%	billion ECU
1.	**Food, beverages and tobacco**	20,82	430,8
11.	Food	16,45	340,4
12.	Non-alcoholic beverages	0,49	10,1
13.	Alcoholic beverages	1,98	41,0
14.	Tobacco	1,90	39,3
2.	**Clothing and footwear**	7,30	151,0
21.	Clothing other than footwear, including repairs	5,90	122,0
22.	Footwear, including repairs	1,40	29,0
3.	**Gross rent, fuel and power**	18,85	390,0
31.	Gross rent and water charges	13,43	277,9
32.	Fuel and power	5,42	112,1
4.	**Furniture, furnishings and household equipment and operation**	7,67	158,7
5.	**Medical care and health expenses**	9,55	197,6
55.	Service charges on accident and health insurance	0,35	7,2
6.	**Transport and communication**	14,27	295,3
61.	Personal transport equipment	3,98	82,3
62.	Operation of personal transport equipment	6,73	139,2
63.	Purchased transport	2,10	43,4
64.	Communication	1,47	30,4
7.	**Recreation, entertainment, education and cultural services**	8,06	166,8
8.	**Miscellaneous goods and services**	13,48	278,9
81.	Personal care and effects	1,82	37,7
82.	Goods n.e.c.	1,65	34,1
Total	**Final consumption of households on the economic territory**	100,00	2 069,1

Source: Eurostat, *National accounts ESA,* Detailed tables by branch.

Table C.4.1.

The Community market: prices of consumer and investment goods by country: price levels and coefficient of variation
Prices with indirect taxes 1985 (EUR 9 = 100)

Products	B	DK	D	F	IRL	I	L	NL	UK	Coefficient of variation %

1. Consumer goods

A. Consumer goods, without energy and services

1.1. Food

Products	B	DK	D	F	IRL	I	L	NL	UK	Coefficient of variation %
Rice	100,9	118,5	112,2	88,2	110,9	90,9	98,4	84,4	100,5	11,6
Flour, other cereals	85,3	118,6	89,4	131,7	79,0	119,2	92,1	97,1	99,2	17,8
Bread, cakes, biscuits	95,1	127,4	105,5	119,7	101,9	98,9	93,0	88,6	78,3	15,1
Noodles, macaroni, spaghetti	100,1	114,4	104,0	106,3	101,0	111,4	101,3	82,7	83,4	11,0
Beef	95,6	129,6	104,4	82,7	93,8	94,6	102,9	115,1	88,6	14,3
Veal	101,3	125,1	94,8	73,1	108,3	93,0	87,2	111,6	115,6	15,9
Pork	84,9	152,7	96,6	89,9	101,5	99,5	92,6	107,9	87,7	20,5
Mutton, lamb or goat meat	119,5	111,7	104,8	96,5	96,7	89,6	106,4	102,8	77,8	12,3
Poultry	96,1	127,7	99,8	121,3	92,8	97,1	100,2	90,4	82,2	14,5
Delicatessen	116,3	118,6	137,6	94,2	73,5	127,6	91,0	91,5	71,3	23,5
Meat preparation, other meat products	100,0	116,5	111,4	99,4	88,5	121,0	106,4	88,0	77,1	14,4
Fish and other seafood	103,5	115,7	97,0	117,8	90,2	125,2	91,8	84,0	83,6	15,4
Fresh milk	89,5	124,1	82,0	96,1	117,1	124,3	86,7	86,4	104,5	16,9
Milk, preserved	117,4	83,4	79,7	122,2	112,3	140,3	83,6	78,6	100,7	22,2
Cheese	104,7	126,9	98,2	88,7	116,7	85,9	91,7	103,1	90,7	13,7
Eggs	91,8	124,4	76,3	116,9	105,5	121,2	99,4	77,5	99,1	17,6
Butter, animal and vegetable fats	104,9	120,8	102,8	104,2	91,3	84,6	98,7	100,0	96,3	10,0
Edible oils	91,4	120,9	110,6	116,9	85,6	142,4	102,5	86,9	64,2	23,2
Fresh fruits	111,5	131,2	118,4	91,6	111,0	68,5	92,9	85,3	104,2	19,0
Fruits dried, frozen, preserved	115,6	138,2	75,3	96,4	90,5	110,8	101,0	105,2	80,6	19,0
Fresh vegetables	114,7	151,1	94,5	81,4	132,9	62,6	79,6	104,0	108,4	27,5

Table C.4.1 *(continued)*.

The Community market: prices of consumer and investment goods by country: price levels and coefficient of variation
Prices with indirect taxes 1985 (EUR 9 = 100)

Products	B	DK	D	F	IRL	I	L	NL	UK	Coefficient of variation %
Vegetables dried, frozen, preserved	105,6	151,6	91,3	99,4	97,8	95,9	97,2	93,8	80,1	20,0
Potatoes	68,1	146,4	125,6	96,8	144,1	90,4	72,6	83,8	103,7	29,1
1.2. Food subject to excise duty										
Sugar	100,5	143,4	90,5	104,8	106,1	74,2	101,2	107,1	85,5	19,1
Coffee and cocoa	86,7	109,1	126,0	105,6	92,3	104,8	111,5	88,9	82,5	14,1
Tea	62,9	104,6	102,1	90,7	115,2	93,8	118,2	87,9	145,4	23,0
Chocolate and confectionery	106,2	111,2	98,4	90,5	90,5	131,8	105,3	105,0	71,8	16,5
Jam, honey, syrup, ice-cream	88,1	133,4	85,6	99,7	105,6	135,9	88,9	86,6	89,9	19,8
Mineral water, non-alcoholic beverages	97,2	157,3	91,7	93,7	156,0	58,9	76,6	95,5	113,0	33,1
Liqueurs and spirits	89,4	175,1	89,3	93,0	147,3	59,0	73,6	93,5	127,9	37,2
Wine and cider	96,4	136,5	69,7	85,5	199,6	79,0	75,8	86,7	122,5	41,5
Beer	81,4	138,3	86,1	120,4	193,9	83,5	66,4	66,9	118,8	41,4
Cigarettes	78,0	178,4	110,2	65,8	157,9	81,1	62,4	89,3	138,3	42,1
Other tobacco products	66,4	128,6	112,8	82,9	186,3	91,3	54,7	84,4	158,7	43,5
1.3. Textiles, clothing, footwear										
Outer garments, sportswear, industrial	116,1	105,0	104,6	103,7	93,7	98,1	110,8	89,1	83,0	10,5
Children's underclothing and knitwear	118,3	140,7	100,1	97,9	78,3	100,0	97,0	90,1	89,2	18,2
Ladies' underclothing and knitwear	131,1	93,6	105,2	128,9	61,2	121,4	153,9	71,1	73,6	31,8
Materials and drapery	94,9	129,5	115,3	143,9	77,4	75,3	107,9	90,7	85,5	23,6
Men's and children's footwear	116,7	125,8	105,3	105,2	90,7	83,5	112,9	83,2	86,1	15,7
Women's footwear	132,8	124,9	92,1	94,3	80,9	96,3	110,5	109,3	73,6	19,5
Household textiles	129,1	99,4	105,9	89,2	85,6	93,8	107,8	95,6	99,4	12,8

1.4. Durable goods

Furniture and furnishing accessories	106,5	100,3	88,6	112,7	111,9	87,5	100,7	91,8	103,2	9,3
Refrigerators, freezers, washing machines	104,5	117,6	99,5	111,6	105,6	79,3	104,6	90,6	91,9	11,7
Cookers, heating appliances	118,9	121,8	92,8	98,7	95,4	96,9	96,0	86,0	98,4	11,8
Cleaning equipment, sewing machines	113,5	122,9	97,3	106,6	101,3	93,3	98,9	84,5	87,1	12,2
Glassware and tableware	94,3	92,0	110,8	112,1	119,1	64,7	94,0	95,0	134,3	19,9
Other household utensils	98,2	138,3	101,7	98,1	105,8	85,5	78,5	90,5	114,3	17,5
Motor vehicles, cycles, motorcycles	78,9	159,1	87,4	96,4	130,0	91,3	74,8	96,6	109,6	26,8
Radio sets, record players	115,6	138,3	88,5	115,8	103,0	84,7	99,5	86,1	81,4	18,9
Photographic equipment, musical instruments	121,2	111,6	83,2	104,8	113,3	91,4	92,2	94,4	93,7	12,5
Records, tapes, cassettes	98,1	108,9	117,3	108,8	108,3	92,7	97,2	78,5	95,3	11,5

1.5. Other manufactures

Floor coverings	95,0	112,3	83,6	101,9	78,6	132,3	104,8	108,2	93,0	16,1
Non-durable household articles	91,6	114,7	104,8	102,8	119,4	94,6	97,1	85,6	93,7	11,0
Medical and pharmaceutical products	83,4	139,7	156,6	65,9	115,6	69,3	83,8	136,2	90,6	33,3
Therapeutic appliances and equipment	100,7	114,8	119,0	112,0	111,9	122,0	96,4	104,6	47,0	22,6
Tyres, inner tubes, parts and accessories	99,3	136,0	97,0	96,5	95,6	82,0	81,5	117,1	105,5	17,0
Petrol and lubricants	93,0	99,7	99,0	116,1	118,1	107,7	82,4	98,7	90,3	11,7
Books	58,2	216,9	101,7	54,6	89,5	112,3	80,9	194,4	90,0	57,0
Newspapers, periodicals, other printed	95,5	130,8	110,4	107,4	102,5	87,5	105,5	96,3	73,8	15,8
Toiletries, perfumes, cosmetics	94,5	139,8	91,2	122,9	100,8	89,9	86,4	91,9	93,5	18,0
Jewellery, watches, alarm clocks	107,8	137,3	132,7	105,7	97,4	51,5	100,5	101,6	93,6	24,6
Cigarette lighters and travel goods	89,4	122,5	99,9	91,6	120,8	102,7	85,5	87,1	107,7	13,9
Writing, drawing equipment and supplies	82,7	129,1	96,1	102,5	118,5	78,2	88,9	101,8	112,8	16,8

B. Energy

Electricity	117,8	99,0	116,4	114,3	90,4	104,3	89,5	95,2	79,9	13,4
Town gas	99,2	137,7	95,1	107,3	122,8	96,4	92,3	85,9	76,1	18,8
Fuel oil, heating products	97,3	111,7	88,4	126,2	104,9	108,9	78,7	102,1	89,4	14,2
Coal, coke, fuels	94,4	108,8	103,2	129,0	108,3	82,9	74,4	104,8	104,1	15,8

Table C.4.1 (continued).

The Community market: prices of consumer and investment goods by country: price levels and coefficient of variation
Prices with indirect taxes 1985 (EUR 9 = 100)

Products	B	DK	D	F	IRL	I	L	NL	UK	Coefficient of variation %
C. Services										
Repairs to clothing	107,2	142,5	68,7	121,2	85,1	59,4	116,0	118,0	113,2	26,9
Repairs to footwear	90,9	142,0	104,4	114,6	78,4	79,5	112,0	97,9	94,4	19,7
Expenses for repairs, maintenance	101,5	116,5	98,9	116,9	100,3	89,9	84,4	102,2	93,7	10,8
Water charges	157,6	174,0	119,3	159,3	104,2	15,9	97,1	144,7	81,9	49,3
Repairs to textile products	108,5	116,0	97,3	108,5	89,9	90,6	106,8	92,6	93,0	9,6
Repairs to electric appliances	99,3	122,5	82,6	86,6	211,0	89,9	76,4	86,8	90,9	41,8
Repairs to other utensils	137,7	116,8	133,6	108,7	76,8	40,2	139,7	123,2	80,3	33,8
Laundry and dry-cleaning	91,8	110,0	108,1	99,8	81,1	201,5	102,6	75,7	72,0	38,8
Domestic services	78,4	109,1	101,9	144,5	84,6	114,3	91,3	95,0	94,1	19,6
Local transport	116,7	136,0	114,5	102,2	110,6	56,4	101,8	99,0	85,2	22,2
Rail transport, road transport, other	102,6	123,9	117,0	101,7	155,4	59,3	80,4	82,6	107,7	27,9
Postage	132,4	102,6	116,2	106,6	113,3	79,0	65,7	93,1	108,0	20,1
Telephone and telegraph services	150,7	90,8	139,1	101,4	139,6	73,9	47,7	52,9	198,0	50,0
Repairs to recreational goods	160,5	118,3	66,7	76,3	75,7	127,5	123,1	115,4	75,1	32,0
Hairdressing services	106,2	152,2	89,0	97,2	80,2	86,0	92,5	106,7	104,7	21,1
Expenditure in restaurants, cafes	99,0	138,9	104,7	97,8	113,2	89,7	85,1	90,9	90,1	16,6
Expenditure in hotels	71,2	119,4	72,7	95,6	94,8	130,8	93,4	86,7	167,6	30,8
Other lodging services	99,2	126,6	94,6	112,1	36,7	205,6	81,8	100,8	120,2	44,8
Financial services nes[1]	156,2	—	88,6	94,9	—	126,3	91,6	92,0	71,3	28,5
2. Equipment goods										
Structural metal products	—	—	—	—	—	—	—	—	—	—
Products of boilermaking	—	—	—	—	—	—	—	—	—	—

Tools and metal goods								
Agricultural machinery and tractors								
Machine tools and metal working								
Textile machinery and sewing machines								
Machinery for food, chemicals, rubber								
Mining equipment								
Machinery for working wood, paper								
Other machinery and mechanical equipment								
Office and data-processing machines								
Wires and cables, electrical equipment								
Telecommunications equipment, meters								
Electronic equipment, radio, televisions								
Optical instruments, photographic equipment								
Motor vehicles and engines								
Ships, warships								
Locomotives, vans and wagons								
Cycles, motorcycles, invalid carriages								
Aircraft, helicopters, aeronautic.								

[1] Consultant's estimate.

Source: Eurostat and calculations of DG II.

Table C.4.2.

The Community market: prices of consumer and investment goods by country: price levels and coefficient of variation
Prices without indirect taxes 1985 (EUR 9 = 100)

Products	B	DK	D	F	IRL	I	L	NL	UK	Coefficient of variation %
1. Consumer goods										
1.1. Food										
Rice	100,7	102,4	111,3	87,7	116,6	94,2	99,3	87,1	104,5	9,8
Flour, other cereals	86,1	102,7	87,5	127,9	83,4	121,8	92,5	100,5	107,1	15,7
Bread, cakes, biscuits	95,4	113,0	107,3	120,2	99,3	102,9	92,7	90,4	84,0	11,5
Noodles, macaroni, spaghetti	100,5	99,5	101,9	107,1	106,1	113,3	101,2	84,3	89,4	8,8
Beef	97,1	114,0	104,9	84,3	101,0	86,2	103,7	118,2	95,8	11,3
Veal	102,7	110,4	95,3	74,6	116,8	85,1	88,5	114,1	123,7	16,4
Pork	86,0	134,5	97,0	91,5	108,7	90,6	93,9	110,4	95,4	14,9
Mutton, lamb or goat meat	117,3	96,2	103,6	97,9	104,4	88,5	109,4	103,4	83,7	10,2
Poultry	96,8	112,2	99,6	122,0	99,6	94,3	99,3	91,9	88,4	10,4
Delicatessen	117,7	99,2	138,9	95,0	77,4	124,7	91,8	93,7	78,1	21,0
Meat preparations, other meat products	101,6	103,6	109,8	99,0	94,1	119,8	105,8	88,5	82,8	11,1
Fish, seafood	101,5	102,2	96,6	115,3	99,2	127,6	90,7	83,1	90,8	13,5
Fresh milk	89,5	105,9	82,5	98,8	118,6	128,7	89,6	88,0	107,7	15,5
Milk, preserved	119,3	71,5	78,2	123,8	120,4	139,1	86,7	77,6	107,5	24,6
Cheese	104,3	110,0	97,7	89,4	123,6	88,0	92,7	104,0	95,2	11,3
Eggs	90,9	109,2	76,6	118,4	112,4	116,1	100,9	78,9	106,8	15,6
Butter, animal and vegetable fats	104,6	104,6	101,6	104,4	96,4	87,7	99,3	100,6	101,7	5,3
Edible oils	91,2	104,9	109,3	117,2	90,6	147,7	102,2	87,6	67,9	22,3
Fresh fruits	111,5	114,3	118,1	92,2	115,5	71,0	94,8	86,5	107,2	16,0
Fruits dried, frozen, preserved, juice	113,1	119,5	74,9	97,0	94,6	115,5	103,3	105,4	85,6	14,5
Fresh vegetables	113,6	129,3	93,0	81,5	141,8	64,1	81,8	104,4	115,7	24,9

Vegetables dried, frozen, preserved	105,1	127,8	90,6	99,9	104,1	99,2	98,9	95,4	84,4	12,0
Potatoes	66,1	128,0	126,6	96,7	152,4	93,0	71,9	85,5	110,8	28,4

1.2. Food subject to excise duty

Sugar	103,1	129,8	90,1	115,5	115,8	68,1	103,6	94,8	92,8	17,9
Coffee and cocoa	89,6	82,9	102,3	110,4	109,4	101,8	117,1	94,9	96,4	10,8
Tea	64,0	89,0	95,4	92,8	124,4	92,9	120,4	90,4	156,9	26,9
Chocolate and confectionery	111,5	102,5	103,3	93,7	80,8	133,7	109,9	112,2	67,8	19,2
Jam, honey, syrup, ice-cream	92,8	116,5	90,0	105,3	98,3	138,3	94,2	86,4	88,3	16,8
Mineral water, non-alcoholic beverages	98,7	126,3	99,2	101,8	148,8	66,3	82,9	84,0	115,7	24,8
Liqueurs and spirits	88,6	78,0	110,2	125,1	129,1	91,1	101,7	107,8	81,4	18,2
Wine and cider	94,8	97,0	81,9	103,1	128,8	95,1	96,1	87,5	125,1	15,8
Beer	96,1	107,7	111,1	142,2	95,5	119,4	90,9	75,4	78,2	20,9
Cigarettes	108,3	85,6	100,8	83,3	132,9	112,6	85,2	100,1	100,9	15,8
Other tobacco products	89,5	123,1	130,1	67,6	128,6	89,8	78,2	116,7	97,6	23,0

1.3. Textiles, clothing, footwear

Outer garments, sportswear, industrial	112,9	99,4	105,9	100,9	98,3	103,4	114,9	86,3	82,8	10,7
Children's underclothing and knitwear	111,7	129,6	98,6	92,7	88,0	103,1	97,3	85,0	100,2	13,4
Ladies' underclothing and knitwear	127,2	90,8	106,5	122,6	65,4	117,0	158,7	68,4	79,8	30,7
Materials and drapery	91,8	126,3	115,9	144,3	80,7	78,5	109,4	89,2	83,6	23,0
Men's and children's footwear	116,3	118,8	106,3	103,1	96,7	82,7	117,2	80,6	87,4	15,0
Women's footwear	127,6	118,7	93,2	90,7	94,6	93,3	112,1	106,4	74,2	16,4
Household textiles	126,7	95,5	108,4	88,2	82,6	95,2	112,2	95,4	102,8	13,4

1.4. Durable goods

Furniture and furnishing accessories	103,2	99,7	92,3	109,1	107,1	86,5	107,4	91,9	105,6	8,1
Refrigerators, freezers, washing machines	100,2	97,3	105,3	112,5	105,4	81,2	111,8	92,4	98,0	9,8
Cookers, heating appliances	114,2	115,3	100,2	97,2	91,0	95,1	106,4	82,2	103,0	10,6
Cleaning equipment, sewing machines	112,3	102,3	102,6	107,5	98,5	95,8	106,6	86,1	91,2	8,3
Glassware and tableware	93,0	89,6	114,5	110,6	113,2	63,5	98,5	94,7	141,3	21,4
Other household utensils	96,7	133,0	104,2	97,1	100,5	87,1	82,4	90,9	117,2	15,7
Motor vehicles, cycles, motorcycles	87,6	78,9	105,8	102,4	116,5	105,9	93,1	95,2	122,0	13,6
Radio sets, record players	109,1	127,9	96,6	108,6	101,3	73,8	111,6	91,1	90,0	15,5

Table C.4.2 *(continued)*.

The Community market: prices of consumer and investment goods by country: price levels and coefficient of variation
Prices without indirect taxes 1985 (EUR 9 = 100)

Products	B	DK	D	F	IRL	I	L	NL	UK	Coefficient of variation %
Photographic equipment, musical instruments	119,1	107,8	87,4	102,4	108,9	90,1	98,1	94,1	96,1	10,1
Records, tapes, cassettes, flowers	93,7	101,7	124,3	98,7	105,0	101,3	103,3	77,7	100,1	12,0
1.5. Other manufactures										
Floor coverings	93,8	111,1	84,8	99,6	75,9	129,6	110,0	106,8	98,3	15,7
Non-durable household articles	88,9	111,3	108,7	102,7	113,5	94,0	101,1	85,5	98,1	9,7
Medical and pharmaceutical products	83,8	136,8	155,7	66,1	116,2	69,3	84,1	136,3	91,9	32,6
Therapeutic appliances and equipment	103,3	107,1	116,2	103,7	125,5	115,9	103,2	97,3	51,3	21,1
Tyres, inner tubes, parts and accessories	96,7	137,3	99,6	95,6	93,0	81,2	81,5	117,8	108,9	17,8
Petrol and lubricants	91,5	103,4	103,4	105,9	108,4	97,9	96,1	98,9	95,7	5,4
Books	57,7	185,3	104,4	53,3	95,9	121,5	80,7	186,7	95,9	48,6
Newspapers, periodicals, other printed	98,3	135,0	107,8	106,1	96,0	90,4	103,2	96,7	76,1	15,8
Toiletries, perfumes and cosmetics	90,9	132,7	94,4	123,3	96,6	90,8	92,1	92,4	95,5	15,6
Jewellery, watches, alarm clocks	99,6	125,5	135,7	109,4	97,0	56,7	99,4	104,3	94,4	22,0
Cigarette lighters and travel goods	89,0	118,8	104,7	91,9	112,7	101,2	90,8	86,3	110,0	11,6
Writing and drawing equipment	81,0	121,6	99,1	104,0	114,6	79,1	94,1	101,5	113,9	14,6
2. Equipment goods[1]										
Structural metal products	89,9	114,0	94,7	105,6	91,9	98,8	—	105,2	101,7	8,0
Products of boilermaking	85,5	118,8	93,8	88,4	137,3	98,2	—	122,7	71,6	22,1
Tools and metal goods	87,6	116,8	101,0	113,4	103,6	91,3	—	97,5	92,2	10,4
Agricultural machinery and tractors	94,0	106,9	100,1	95,0	102,2	85,8	—	108,2	110,1	8,3
Machine tools for metal working	87,7	106,4	98,0	105,0	94,1	106,4	—	87,4	118,7	10,7
Textile machinery, sewing machines	94,9	122,8	103,2	104,2	103,6	96,7	—	86,7	91,6	10,9
Machinery for food, chemicals, rubber	101,5	101,8	96,3	122,0	89,2	109,0	—	103,6	81,5	12,2

Mining equipment	137,4	86,4	89,7	93,2	99,9	88,7	—	94,5	120,	18,0
Machinery for working wood, paper	82,4	103,3	111,6	119,3	91,2	86,3	—	103,3	108,2	12,9
Other machinery and mechanical equipment	93,6	98,5	112,0	107,4	105,0	84,3	—	96,2	105,5	8,9
Office and data-processing machines	95,1	105,2	86,9	108,4	107,3	97,4	—	93,7	107,9	8,0
Wires and cables, electrical equipment	96,8	113,0	93,9	110,2	94,4	109,2	—	93,5	91,3	8,8
Telecommunications equipment, meters	96,8	113,0	93,9	110,2	94,4	109,2	—	93,5	91,3	8,8
Electronic equipment, radio, television	97,0	115,2	101,4	98,0	91,8	104,8	—	96,7	96,4	7,1
Optical instruments, photographic equipment	101,5	83,1	123,5	113,2	91,2	96,7	—	109,0	87,9	13,7
Motor vehicles and engines	79,7	132,5	88,6	91,3	118,0	96,7	—	96,4	106,1	17,0
Ships, warships	100,2	123,7	85,9	95,5	94,1	109,7	—	89,6	105,9	12,2
Locomotives, vans and wagons	93,1	132,5	96,4	117,4	68,7	99,7	—	83,0	125,6	21,7
Cycles, motorcycles, invalid carriages	100,7	133,4	84,7	93,7	100,9	99,8	—	86,6	107,1	15,2
Aircraft, helicopters, aeronautical equipment	112,2	116,7	77,7	80,1	117,4	118,8	—	95,6	91,6	17,1

1 Prices net of deductible VAT.

Source: Eurostat and calculations of DG II.

References

Abd-el-Rahman, K. 'Hypothèses concernant le rôle des avantages comparatifs des pays et des avantages spécifiques des firmes', *Revue d'économie politique*, 97, 1987, pp. 165-192.

Adriaenssens, G. and G. Sermeus. *Who pays what? Drug prices and drug reimbursement in the EEC*, Brussels, Bureau européen des unions de consommateurs, 1987.

Albert, M. *Un pari pour l'Europe*, Seuil, Paris, 1983.

Albert, M. and R. Ball. *Vers le redressement de l'économie européenne dans les années 80*. Report presented to the European Parliament, July 1983.

Atkan, O. 'The second enlargement of the European Communities', *European economic review*, 28, 1983, pp. 279-308.

Balassa, B. 'Tariff reductions and trade in manufactures among the industrial countries', *American economic review*, 56, 1966, pp. 466-473.

Balassa, B. 'Trade creation and trade diversion in the Common Market', *Manchester School of Economic and Social Studies*, 42, 1974, pp. 93-135.

Balassa, B. *The changing international division of labour in manufactured goods*. The World Bank, Washington DC, 1979.

Baldwin, R. A. 'Trade policies in developed countries', in R. W. Jones and P. B. Kenen, eds, *Handbook of international economics*, Vol. I, Amsterdam, North-Holland, 1984.

Baltensberger, E., and J. Dermine. 'Banking deregulation in Europe', *Economic policy*, April, 1987.

Borges, A. 'Applied general equilibrium models: an assessment of their usefulness for policy analysis', *OECD Economic Studies*, No 7, Paris, 1986.

Boston Consulting Group. *Perspectives on experience*, Boston, 1971.

Boston Consulting Group. *Les mécanismes fondamentaux de la compétitivité*. Hommes et Techniques, Paris, 1981.

Brown, F. and J. Whalley. 'General equilibrium valuations of tariff cutting proposals in the Tokyo Round and comparison with more extensive liberalization of world trade', *Economic journal*, 90, 1980, pp. 838-866.

Bryant, R., D. Henderson, G. Holtham, P. Hooper and S. Symansky. *Empirical macroeconomics for interdependent economics*. Brookings Institution, Washington DC, 1988.

Buigues, P. A. *Prospective et compétitivité*, Paris, MacGraw-Hill, 1985.

Buigues, P. and Ph. Goybet. 'La compétitivité de l'industrie européenne: un bilan', *European economy*, 25, 1985a, pp. 9-33.

Buigues, P. and Ph. Goybet. 'Les déterminantes de l'offre industrielle communautaire', *European economy*, 25, 1985b, pp. 35-70.

Catinat, M. 'Radioscopie du grand marché intérieur européen', *Economie prospective internationale*, 33, 1988, pp. 5-28, Documentation française.

Catinat, M. and A. Italianer. 'Achèvement du marché intérieur — Effets primaires microéconomiques et mise en œuvre dans les modèles macroéconométriques', EC Commission, Directorate-General for Economic and Financial Affairs, forthcoming, 1988.

Cho, C., C. Eun and L. Senbet. 'International arbitrage pricing theory: an empirical investigation', *Journal of Finance,* 41, 1986, pp. 313-329.

Cline, W., N. Kawanabe, T. Kronsjo and T. Williams. 'Multilateral effects of tariff negotiations in the Tokyo Round' in W. G. Devald, ed., *The impact of international trade and investment on employment.* US Department of Labor, Washington DC, 1978.

Comanor, W. and H. Leibenstein. 'Allocative efficiency, X-efficiency and the measurement of welfare losses', *Economica,* 36, 1969, pp. 304-309.

Commissariat Général au Plan. *Rapport du groupe de stratégie industrielle — Travaux publics,* Paris, 1987.

Cooper, J., M. Browne and D. Gretton. *Freight transport in the European Community: making the most of UK opportunities.* Transport Study Group. Polytechnic of Central London, London, 1987.

Corden, M. 'The normative theory of international trade' in R. W. Jones and P. B. Kenen, eds, *Handbook of International Economics,* Vol. I, Amsterdam, North-Holland, 1984.

Cubbin, J. 'Market structure and market performance: the empirical research', mimeo., 1987.

Danthine, J. P. 'Restoring Europe's prosperity: a review essay', *Journal of monetary economics,* 20, 1987, pp. 521-526.

Davidson, R., M. Dewatripont, V. Ginsburgh and M. Labbé. 'On the welfare effects of anti-discrimination regulations in the EEC car market', mimeo., 1987.

De Bondt, R. and G. Van Herk. 'De controversie 'zuiver versus gemengde intercommunales'', *Tijdschrift voor Economie en Management,* 26, 1981, pp. 117-151.

De Ghellinck, E., P. A. Geroski, and A. Jacquemin. 'Inter-industry and inter-temporal variations in the effect of trade on industry performance', forthcoming in *The Journal of Industrial Economics,* 1988.

De Woot, Ph. 'Capacité stratégique et performance économique à long terme des entreprises européennes dans les secteurs à haute technologie', *Projet Pénélope,* Brussels, 1987.

Deardorff, A. 'Testing trade theories and predicting trade flows', in R. W. Jones and P. B. Kenen, eds., *Handbook of International Economics,* Vol. I, Amsterdam, North-Holland, 1984.

Debonneuil, M. and M. Delattre. 'La 'compétitivité-prix' n'explique pas les pertes tendancielles de parts de marché', *Economie et statistique,* 203, 1987, pp. 5-14.

Delaney, R. V. 'The disunited States: a country in search of an efficient transport policy', mimeo. CATO Institute, Washington, 1987.

Dixit, A. and V. Norman. *Theory of international trade.* Cambridge, Cambridge University Press, 1984.

DRI Europe. *European road freight deregulation — intentions and proposals,* London, MacGraw-Hill, 1986.

EC Commission. 'Completing the internal market'. White Paper from the Commission to the European Council, Brussels, 1985.

EC Commission. 'Improving competitiveness and industrial structures in the Community', COM(86) 40 final, Brussels, 1986a.

EC Commission. 'The Single European Act', *Supplement to the Bulletin of the EC,* No 2/86, Brussels, 1986b.

EC Commission. Green Paper on the development of the common market for telecommunications services and equipment, COM(87) 290 final, Brussels, 1987a.

EC Commission. *16th Report of the Commission of the EC on European Competition Policy,* Part 4, Brussels, 1987b.

EC Commission. 'Annual economic report 1987-88 — Using the Community dimension to reinforce internal growth', *European economy,* No 34 (November), 1987c.

EC Commission. 'The Single Act: a new frontier', *Supplement to the Bulletin of the EC,* No 1/87, Brussels, 1987d.

EC Statistical Office. *EC external trade in services,* Luxembourg, ECSO, 1984.

Eastman, H. C. *The tariff and competition in Canada,* Toronto, MacMillan, 1967.

Ergas, H. *Why do some countries innovate more than others?* Brussels Centre for European Policy Studies, 1984.

European management forum. *Report on international competitiveness,* Geneva, 1985.

Geroski, P. A. *Competition and innovation,* Report prepared for the EC Commission, Brussels, 1987.

Geroski, P. A. and A. Jacquemin. 'Industrial change, barriers to mobility and European industrial policy', *Economic policy,* 1, 1985, pp. 170-217.

Graner, R. and N. Hakansson. 'Gains from international diversification: 1968-85 returns on portfolios of stocks and bonds', *Journal of Finance,* 42, 1987, pp. 721-741.

Greenaway, D. and B. Hindley. 'What Britain pays for voluntary export restraints'. *Thames Essay* No 43, London, Trade Policy Research Centre, 1985.

Gual, J. 'An econometric analysis of price differentials in the EEC automobile market', mimeo., 1987.

Guinchard, P. 'Productivité et compétitivité comparées des grands pays industriels', *Economie et statistique,* 162, 1984, pp. 3-13.

Harris, R. 'Applied general equilibrium analysis of small open economies with scale economies and imperfect competition', *American Economic Review,* 74, 1984, pp. 1016-1032.

Harris, R. G. and D. Cox. *Trade and industrial policy and Canadian manufacturing,* Toronto, Ontario Economic Council, 1984.

Helpman, E. 'Imperfect competition and international trade: evidence from fourteen industrial countries', *Journal of the Japanese and International Economics,* 1, 1987, pp. 62-81.

Hirschman, W. B., 'Profits from the learning curve', *Harvard Business Review*, 42, 1964, pp. 125-139.

Hufbauer, J. and J. Chilas. 'Specialisation by industrial countries: extent and consequences', in H. Giersch, ed., *The international division of labour: problems and perspectives*, Tübingen, Mohr, 1974.

Jacquemin, A. *Economie industrielle européenne. Structures de marché et stratégies d'entreprises*, Paris, Dunod, 1979.

Jacquemin, A. 'Imperfect market structure and international trade — some recent research', *Kyklos*, 35, 1982, pp. 75-93.

Jacquemin, A. 'Sélection et pouvoir dans la nouvelle économie industrielle', *Economica*, Paris, 1985.

Jacquemin, A. 'Collusive behaviour, R&D and European policy', *Economic papers*, Brussels, EC Commission, 1987.

Jacquemin, A. and A. Sapir. 'International Trade an Integration of the European Community: An Econometric Analysis', *European Economic Review*, 1988.

Kamien, M. I. and N. L. Schwartz. *Market structure and innovations*, Cambridge, Cambridge University Press, 1982.

Krugman, P. 'Increasing returns, monopolistic competition and international trade', *Journal of International Economics*, 9, 1979, pp. 469-479.

Krugman, P. 'Intra-industry specification and the gains from trade', *Journal of Political Economy*, 89, 1981, pp. 959-973.

Krugman, P. 'L'intégration économique en Europe — problèmes conceptuels' in 'Efficiency, stability and equity. A strategy for the evolution of the economic system of the European Community' (Report of a study group appointed by the EC Commission and presided by T. Padoa-Schioppa), mimeo. Brussels, EC Commission, 1987.

Laskar, D. 'La contrainte extérieure dans un cadre multinational', mimeo. Paris, Cepremap, 1985.

Laussel, D., C. Montet and A. Peguin-Feissole. 'Optimal trade policy under oligopoly: a calibrated model of the Europe-Japan rivalry in the EEC car market', presented at the conference 'Commerce international en concurrence imparfaite', Aix-en-Provence, 18 and 19 June 1987.

Leibenstein, H. 'Allocative efficiency versus X-efficiency', *American Economic Review*, 56, 1966, pp. 392-415.

Levy, H., and M. Sarnat. 'International diversification of investment portfolios', *American Economic Review*, 60, 1970, pp. 668-675.

Markusen, J. 'Canadian gains from trade in the presence of scale economies and imperfect competition', in J. Whalley, ed., *Canada-United States free trade*, Toronto, University of Toronto Press, 1985.

Mathis, J. and J. Mazier. *Niveau des coûts de production et performances extérieures des grands pays industrialisés*, Paris, IRES, 1987.

Mertens, Y. and V. Ginsburgh. 'Product differentiation and price discrimination in the European Community. The case of automobiles', *The Journal of Industrial Economics*, 34, 1985, pp. 151-166.

References

Müller, J. and N. Owen. 'The effect of trade on plant size', in J. Schwalbach, ed., *Industry structure and performance*, Berlin, Sigma, 1985.

Nelson, R. and S. Winter. 'Firm and industry response to changed market conditions: an evolutionary approach', *Economic enquiry*, 18, 1980, pp. 179-202.

OECD. *Spécialisation et compétitivité des industries manufacturières en haute, moyenne et faible intensité en R&D*, Paris, OECD, 1984.

OECD. *National policies and agricultural trade*, Paris, 1987.

Office of Technology Assessment. *International competitivity in services*, Washington DC, 1987.

Owen, N. *Economies of scale, competitiveness and trade patterns within the European Community*, Oxford, Clarendon Press, 1983.

Padoa-Shioppa, T. *et al.* 'Efficiency, stability and equity. A strategy for the evolution of the economic system of the European Community' (Report of a study group appointed by the EC Commission and presided by T. Padoa-Schioppa), Oxford University Press, Oxford, 1987.

Pelkmans, J. 'Customs union and technical efficiency', *De Economist*, 130, 1982, pp. 536-559.

Pelkmans, J. *Market integration in the European Community*, The Hague, Martinus Nijhoff, 1984.

Porter, M. *Competitive advantage*, New York, Free Press, 1985.

Pratten C. *A survey of the economies of scale*, Report prepared for the EC Commission, Brussels, 1987.

Primeaux, W. 'An assessment of X-efficiency gained through competition', *Review of Economics and Statistics*, 59, 1977, pp. 105-108.

Pryke, R. *The competition among international airlines*, London, Trade Policy Research Centre, 1986.

Ranci, P. and R. Helg. *Economies of scale and the integration of the European economy: the case of Italy*, Report prepared for the EC Commission, Brussels, 1987.

Revell. *Costs and margins in banking. An international survey*, Paris, OECD, 1980.

Richardson, P. 'Recent developments in OECD's international macroeconomic model', *OECD Working Papers*, No 46, Paris, 1987a.

Richardson, P. 'A review of the simulation properties of OECD's interlink model', *OECD Working Papers*, Paris, 1987b.

Roy, A. D. 'Labour productivity in 1980: an international comparison', *National Institute Economic Review*, 101, 1982, pp. 26-37.

Scherer, F. *Industrial market structure and economic performance*, Chicago, Rand McNalley, 1980.

Scherer, F. *Mergers, sell-offs and managerial behaviour*, Berlin, International Institute of Management, 1986.

Scherer, F. 'Antitrust, efficiency and progress', mimeo. 1987.

Scherer, F., A. Beckenstein, E. Kaufer and R. Murphy. *The economics of multi-plant operation: an international comparison study*, Cambridge, USA, 1975.

Shoven, J. and J. Whalley. 'Applied general-equilibrium models of taxation and international trade: an introduction and survey', *Journal of Economic Literature*, XXII, 1984, pp. 1007-1051.

Siegfried, J. and E. Wheeler. 'Cost efficiency and monopoly power: a survey', *Quarterly Review of Economics and Business*, 21, 1981, pp. 25-46.

Silberston, Z. *The Multi-Fibre Arrangement and the UK economy*, London, HMSO, 1984.

The Economist. 'Europe's air cartel', *The Economist*, 11 November 1986, pp. 19-23.

Thomson, K. J. 'A model of the common agricultural policy', *Journal of Agricultural Economics*, May, 1985, pp. 193-210.

Valette, P. et P. Zagamé. (ed.) 'Hermes: a European system of econometric models', EC Commission, forthcoming, 1988.

Venables, A. J. 'Trade and industrial policy under imperfect competition; some simulations for EC manufacturing', presented at the conference 'Commerce international en concurrence imparfaite', Aix-en-Provence, 18 and 19 June 1987.

Venables, A. J. and A. Smith. 'Trade and industrial policy under imperfect competition', *Economic policy*, 2, 1986, pp. 622-671.

Vignon, J. 'Sept ans pour construire le vrai marché commun', *Economie prospective internationale*, 25, 1986, pp. 5-24, Documentation française.

Von Weizsäcker, C. 'The economics of value-added networks', mimeo. 1987.

Vredeling, H. *Report of a group of independent experts presided by H. Vredeling*, Brussels, NATO, 1987.

Waterson, M. *Economic theory of the industry*, Cambridge, Cambridge University Press, 1984.

Wheatcroft, S. and G. Lipman. *Air transport in a competitive European market*, London, Economist Intelligence Unit, 1986.

Winters, A. *The economic consequences of agricultural support: a survey*, OECD Economic Studies, No 8, Paris, 1987.

Yelle, L. E. 'The learning curve: historical review and comprehensive survey', *Decision Science*, 10, 1979, pp. 302-328.

Zimmermann, K. F. 'Trade and dynamic efficiency', *Kyklos*, 40, 1987, pp. 73-87.

Zimmermann, K. F. and L. Pupillo. 'Relative export prices and firm size imperfect markets', mimeo., 1987.

Economie prospective internationale, 25, 1986, pp. 5-24, Documentation française.

Von Weizsäcker, C. 'The economics of value-added networks', mimeo. 1987.

Vredeling, H. *Report of a group of independent experts presided by H. Vredeling*, Brussels, NATO, 1987.

Waterson, M. *Economic theory of the industry*, Cambridge, Cambridge University Press, 1984.

Wheatcroft, S. and G. Lipman. *Air transport in a competitive European market*, London, Economist Intelligence Unit, 1986.

Winters, A. *The economic consequences of agricultural support: a survey,* OECD Economic Studies, No 8, Paris, 1987.

Yelle, L. E. 'The learning curve: historical review and comprehensive survey', *Decision Science,* 10, 1979, pp. 302-328.

Zimmermann, K. F. 'Trade and dynamic efficiency', *Kyklos,* 40, 1987, pp. 73-87.

Zimmermann, K. F. and L. Pupillo. 'Relative export prices and firm size imperfect markets', mimeo., 1987.

List of studies

The following studies were undertaken for the 'Costs of non-Europe' project. The volume of publication appears in brackets. See below for further details.

Studies concerning specific types of barrier

1. 'The cost of non-Europe: Border related controls and Administrative Formalities', (volume 4)
   Ernst & Whinney
2. 'Technical Barriers in the EC: an illustration by six industries', (volume 6)
   Group MAC
3. 'The cost of non-Europe: Some case-studies on technical barriers', (volume 6)
   Gewiplan
4. 'The cost of non-Europe in public sector procurement', (volume 5)
   W.S. Atkins Management Consultants
5. 'The cost of non-Europe: Obstacles to trans-border business activity', (volume 7)
   European Research Associates

Studies concerning specific industries

6. 'The cost of non-Europe in the foodstuffs industry', (volume 12)
   Group MAC
7. 'The cost of non-Europe: The pharmaceutical industry', (volume 15)
   Economists Advisory Group
8. 'The EC 92 Automobile sector', (volume 11)
   Ludwigsen Associates Limited
9. 'The cost of non-Europe in the textile-clothing industry', (volume 14)
   IFO-Institut für Wirtschaftsforschung, and Prometeia Calcolo Srl
10. 'Le coût de la non-Europe des produits de construction', (volume 13)
    BIPE — Bureau d'informations et de prévisions économiques
11. 'The benefits of completing the internal market for telecommunications equipment in the Community', (volume 10)
    J. Müller, Insead

Studies concerning specific service sectors

12. 'The cost of non-Europe in financial services', (volume 9)
    Price Waterhouse Economic and Management Consultants
13. 'The cost of non-Europe for business services', (volume 5)
    Peat, Marwick, McLintock

14. 'The cost of non-Europe: An illustration in the Road Haulage sector', (volume 4)
Ernst & Whinney

15. 'The benefits of completing the internal market for telecommunications, services in the Community' (volume 10)
J. Müller, Insead

Studies based on particular analytical approaches

16. 'The completion of the internal market: A survey of European industry's perception of the likely effects', (volume 3)
G. Nerb, Directorate-General for Economic and Financial Affairs, Commission of the European Communities

17. 'A survey of the economies of scale', (volume 2)
C. Pratten, Department of Applied Economics, University of Cambridge

18. 'Economies of scale and intra-Community trade', (volume 2)
J. Schwalbach, International Institute for Management

19. 'Economies of scale and the integration of the European economy: The case of Italy', (volume 2)
R. Helg, P. Ranci, Istituto per la Ricerca Sociale

20. 'Competition and innovation', (volume 2)
P. Geroski, University of Southampton and Centre for Business Strategy, London Business School

21. 'The costs of non-Europe: An assessment based on a formal model of imperfect competition and economies of scale', (volume 2)
A. Smith, University of Southampton, and A. Venables, University of Sussex

22. 'Partial equilibrium calculations of the impact of internal market barriers in the European Community', (volume 2)
M. Davenport, R. Cawley

23. 'Conséquences macroéconomiques de l'achèvement du marché intérieur — l'enseignement des modèles', (volume 2)
M. Catinat, E. Donni and A. Italianer, Commission of the European Communities

24. 'The North American internal market', (volume 16)
J. Pelkmans, European Institute of Public Administration

These studies have been published in the course of 1988 by the
Office for Official Publications
of the European Communities
L-2985 Luxembourg
in its series 'Documents'
The series includes three compendium volumes:

— Volume One 'Basic studies: Executive summaries'
Documents series CB-52-88-485-EN-C
ISBN 92-825-7946-8
(this volume includes summaries of studies 1 to 15 and 24)

— Volume Two 'Studies on the economics of integration'
Documents series CB-52-88-493-EN-C
ISBN 92-825-7947-6
(this volume includes studies 17 to 23)
— Volume Three 'The completion of the internal market:
A survey of European industry's perception of the likely effects'
Documents series CB-52-88-502-EN-C
ISBN 92-825-7948-4
(this volume includes study 16)

Index

Index

Index

DRI Europe 114
durable household goods *see* electrical
dynamic effects of barrier removal 27, 29–30, 126–40, 157–70

EAG *see* Economists Advisory Group
Eastman, H. C. 141
economic concepts for internal market program 28–30
Economic Intelligence Unit 115
economies of scale 13, 123, 126–40
  case studies of industries 66, 77, 79, 81, 86–7
  learning effect 137–40
  macroeconomic evaluation 260
  microeconomic evaluation 196–7, 199, 201–3
  non-technical 134–7
  technical 127–34
  trade expansion and efficiency gains 140–4
Economists Advisory Group 72, 73, 259
ECSC (European Coal and Steel Community) 91, 94
efficiency
  gains and market integration 140–4
  internal economic 156–7
  size *see* economies of scale
EFTA *see* European Free Trade Association
electrical/electronic/durable household goods industries 267, 271–2, 277–8, 280, 282–4
  internal market 11–18
  market barriers 42, 44–5, 50, 60
  market integration 128, 130, 133, 138, 139
    competition effects 148, 150, 152
    gains from 186–90, 192
  microeconomic evaluation 236
electricity *see* energy
empirical
  data sources for microeconomic evaluation 197–200
  estimates 3–7
employment *see* labour
energy/fuel/power 3, 12, 138, 200, 265, 270, 278
  market barriers 35, 43, 50, 52, 60–1
    case study of 67, 93–7
  market integration, competition effects 149, 157
  microeconomic evaluation 225, 230, 234, 235, 239, 241
engineering industries 129
  market barriers 32, 35, 42–3, 45, 48
  microeconomic evaluation 225, 230, 235, 239, 241, 245, 247, 249
environment issues 39, 42, 44
EOS *see* economies of scale
equilibrium 24–7, 30, 201–3
  see also microeconomic evaluation

equipment goods and market integration, competition effects 146, 149–50, 151
Ergas, H. 136, 160, 177
Ernst and Whinney 37–9, 114, 205, 233, 256, 262, 292
Eun, C. 109
European Bureau of Consumers' Associations 152
European Coal and Steel Community 91, 94
European Court of Justice 40, 68, 100–1, 114, 179–80
European Free Trade Association 41, 66, 75
European Management Forum 170
European Monetary System 98, 110
European Research Associates 174*n*
European Telecommunications Standards Institute 87, 119
Eurostat (statistics) 20, 246, 265–84
  market barriers 49, 72, 83, 97, 99
  market integration 146–50, 152, 172
evaluation methods *see* market barriers
exchange rates 101–2, 109–10, 116
excise duty market barriers 21, 22, 33–5, 57, 58, 61, 65, 67
  market integration, competition effects 146, 150
experience *see* learning effect
exports *see* trade

feedback *see* rebound
Fiat/Alfa 76
fibres *see* textiles
Finance Ministers: Nyborg meeting (1987) 110
financial services 3, 269, 274
  internal market 11–12, 19–20
  macroeconomic evaluation 208, 209–11, 214, 258–9, 263
  market barriers 50, 53
    case study of 98, 100–10
  market integration 134, 138, 180
    competition effects 149
  microeconomic evaluation 199, 223, 231, 234, 236, 238, 241, 246, 248, 250
financing economies of scale 134, 135
firms *see* business
fiscal *see* taxation
fisheries *see* agriculture
food processing/beverages/tobacco industries 3, 267–8, 272, 275–7, 281–2
  internal market 11–18
  macroeconomic evaluation 259
  market barriers 35, 40, 43, 44, 45, 60–1
    case study of 66, 67–71
  market integration 128–9, 133, 172, 175
    competition effects 147, 150, 151
  microeconomic evaluation 198–9, 223, 225, 230, 235–41, 245, 247, 249
footwear *see* textiles

Index

Index